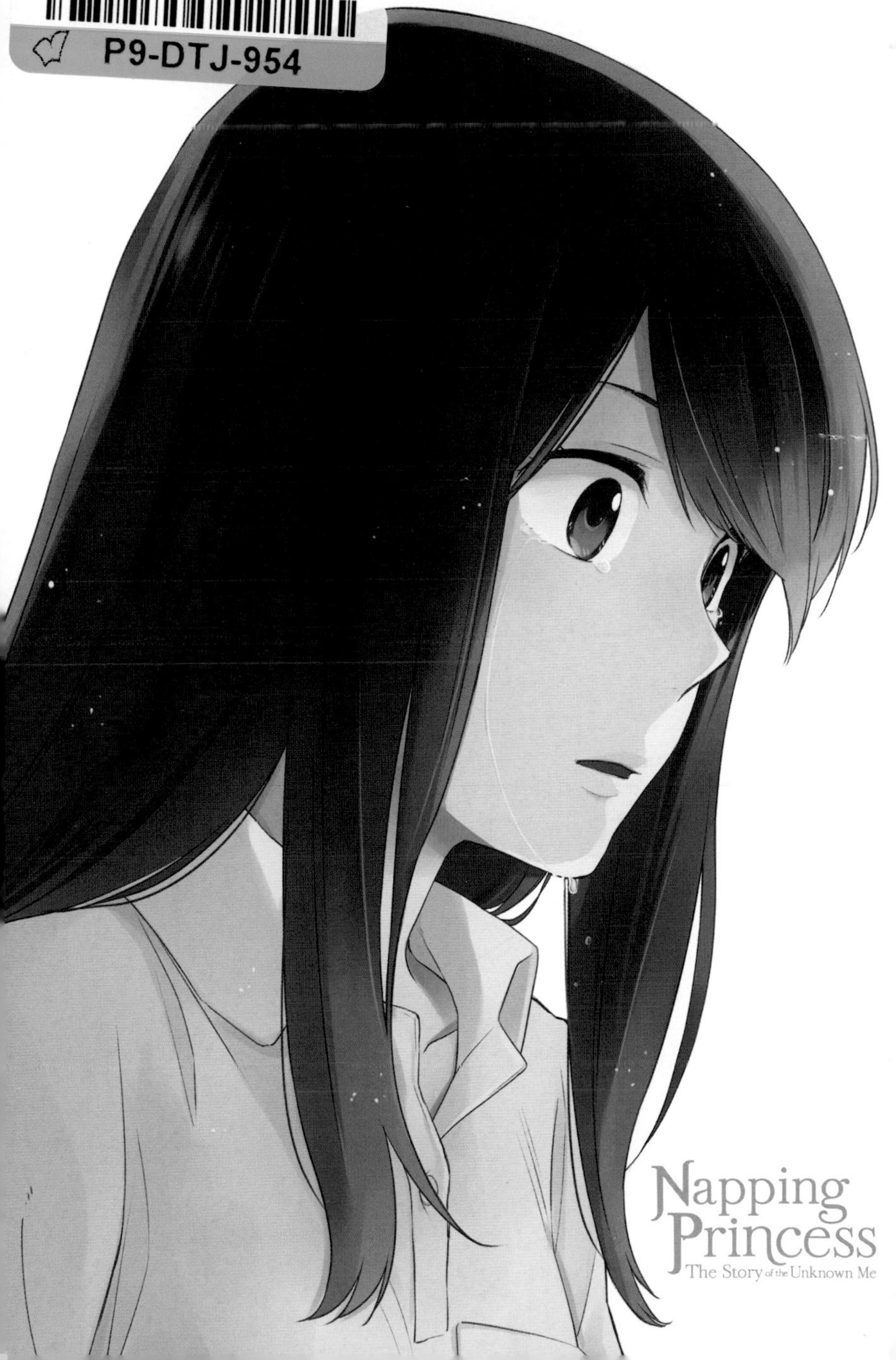
Napping
Princess
The Story of the Unknown Me

Contents

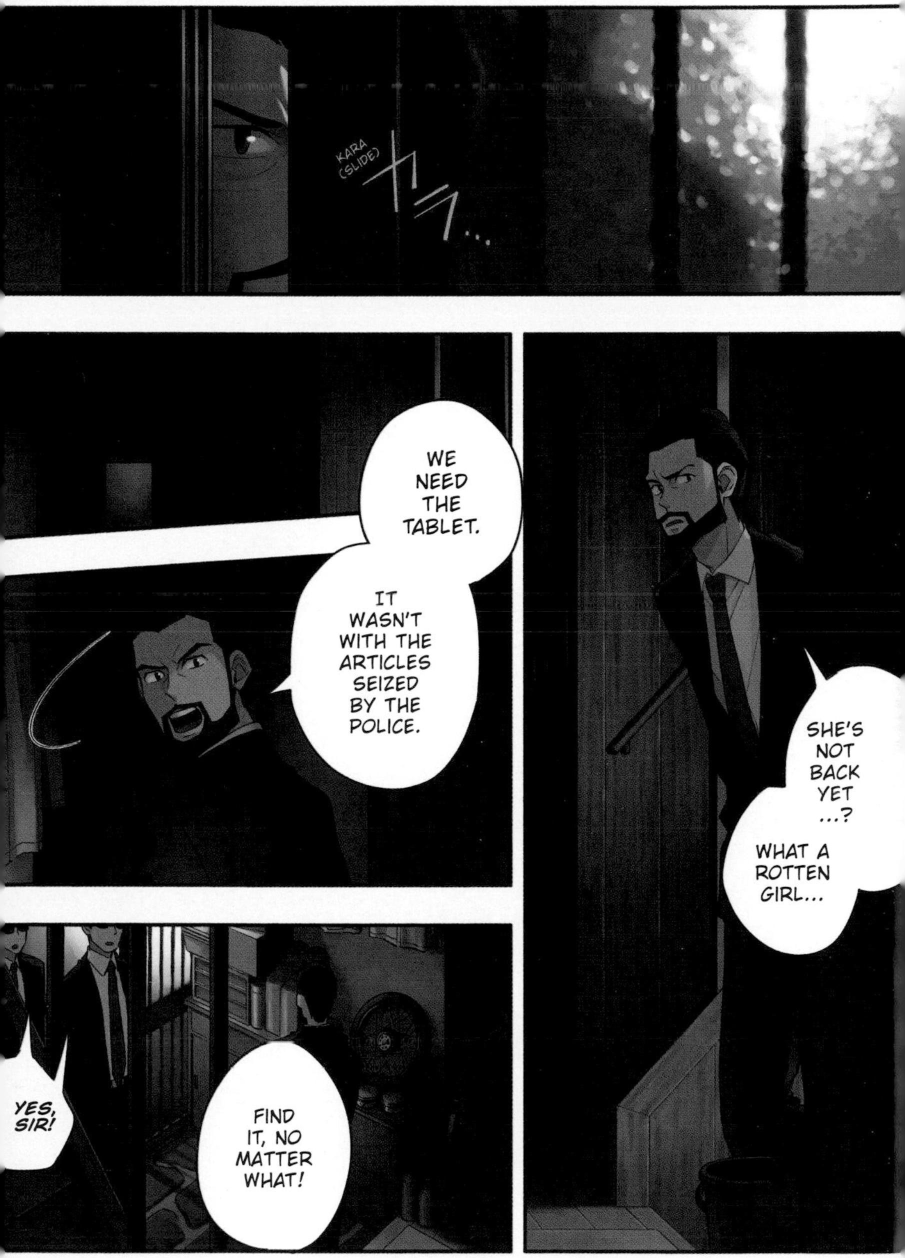
KARA (SLIDE)
SHE'S NOT BACK YET ...?
WHAT A ROTTEN GIRL...
WE NEED THE TABLET.
IT WASN'T WITH THE ARTICLES SEIZED BY THE POLICE.
FIND IT, NO MATTER WHAT!
YES, SIR!

Scene IV

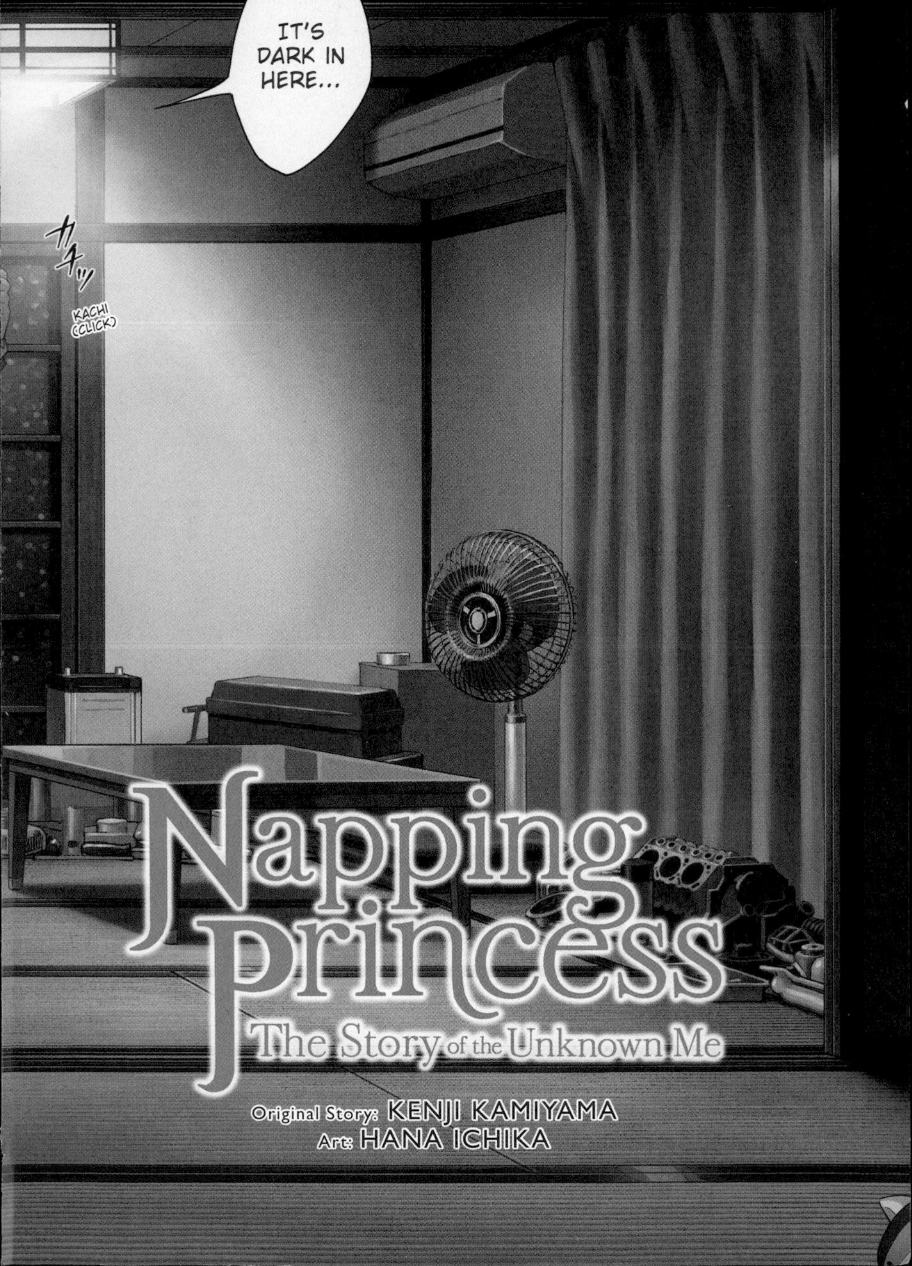
IT'S DARK IN HERE...
カチッ
KACHI (CLICK)
Napping Princess
The Story of the Unknown Me
Original Story: KENJI KAMIYAMA
Art: HANA ICHIKA

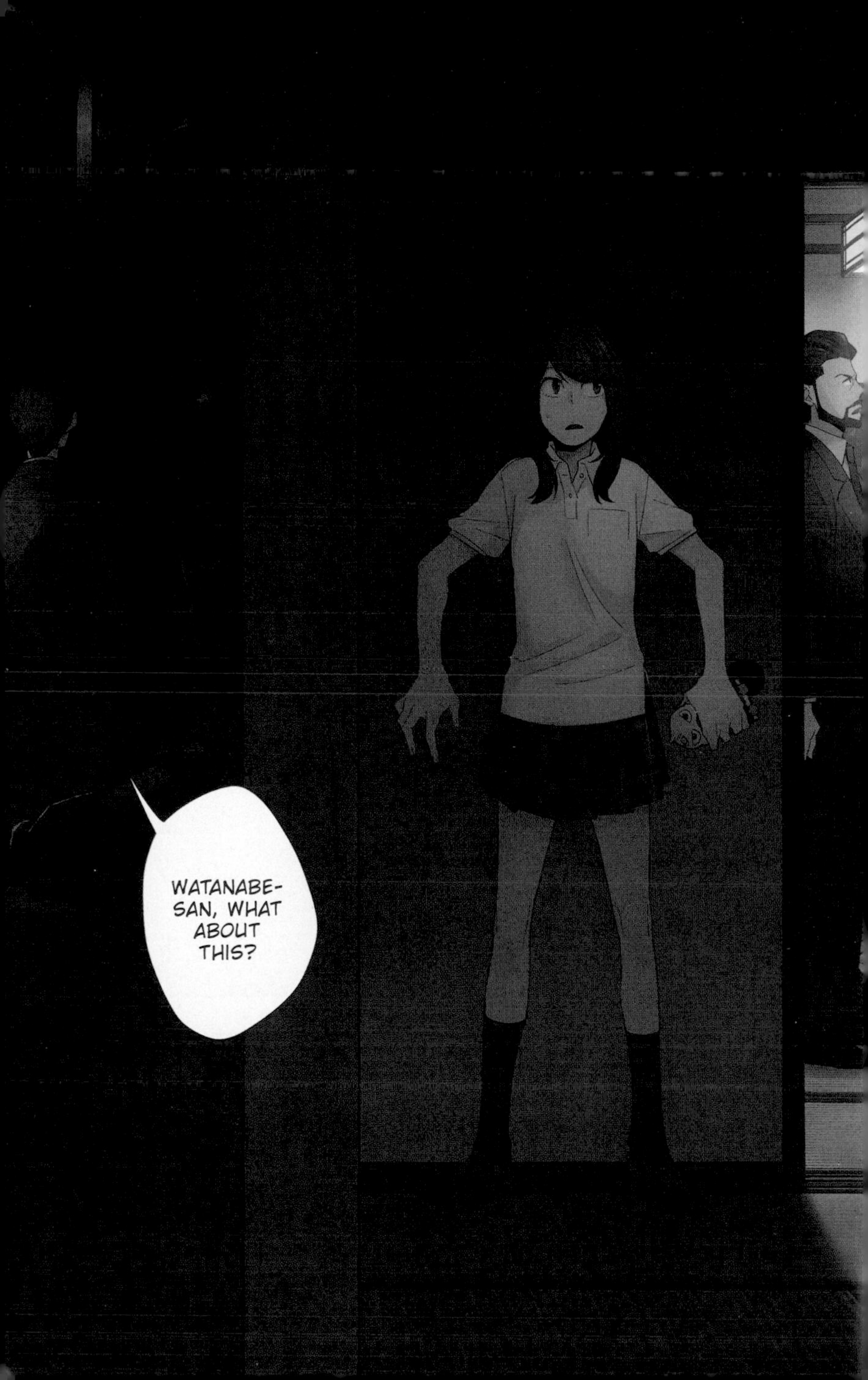
WATANABE-SAN, WHAT ABOUT THIS?

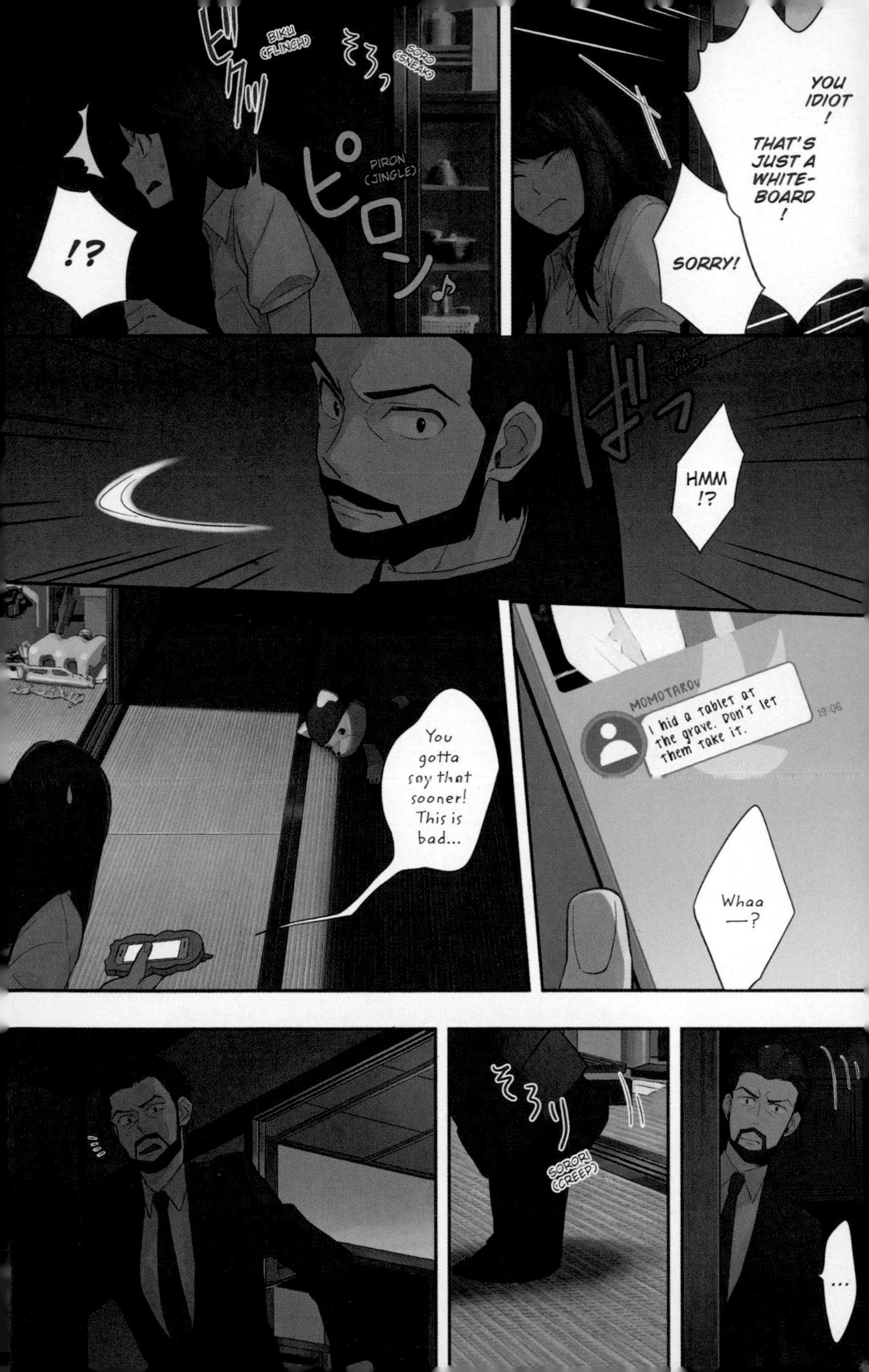
YOU IDIOT!
THAT'S JUST A WHITE-BOARD!
SORRY!
SORO (SNEAK)
BIKU (FLINCH)
PIRON (JINGLE)
!?
BA (WHIP)
HMM!?
MOMOTAROU
I hid a tablet at the grave. Don't let them take it.
19:06
Whaa—?
You gotta say that sooner! This is bad...
...
SORORI (CREEP)

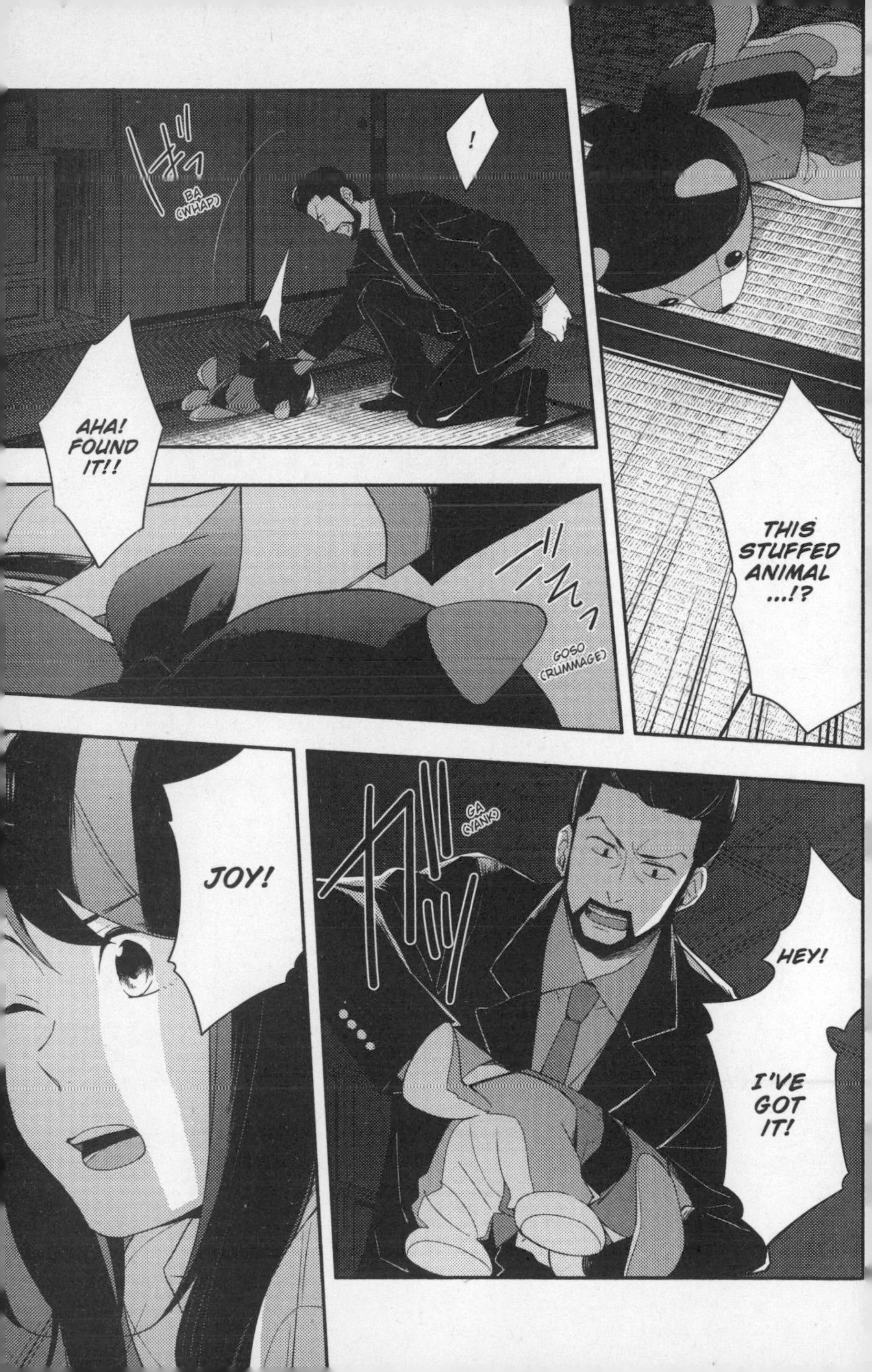
THIS STUFFED ANIMAL ...!?
!
BA (WHAP)
AHA! FOUND IT!!
GOSO (RUMMAGE)
GA (YANK)
HEY!
I'VE GOT IT!
JOY!

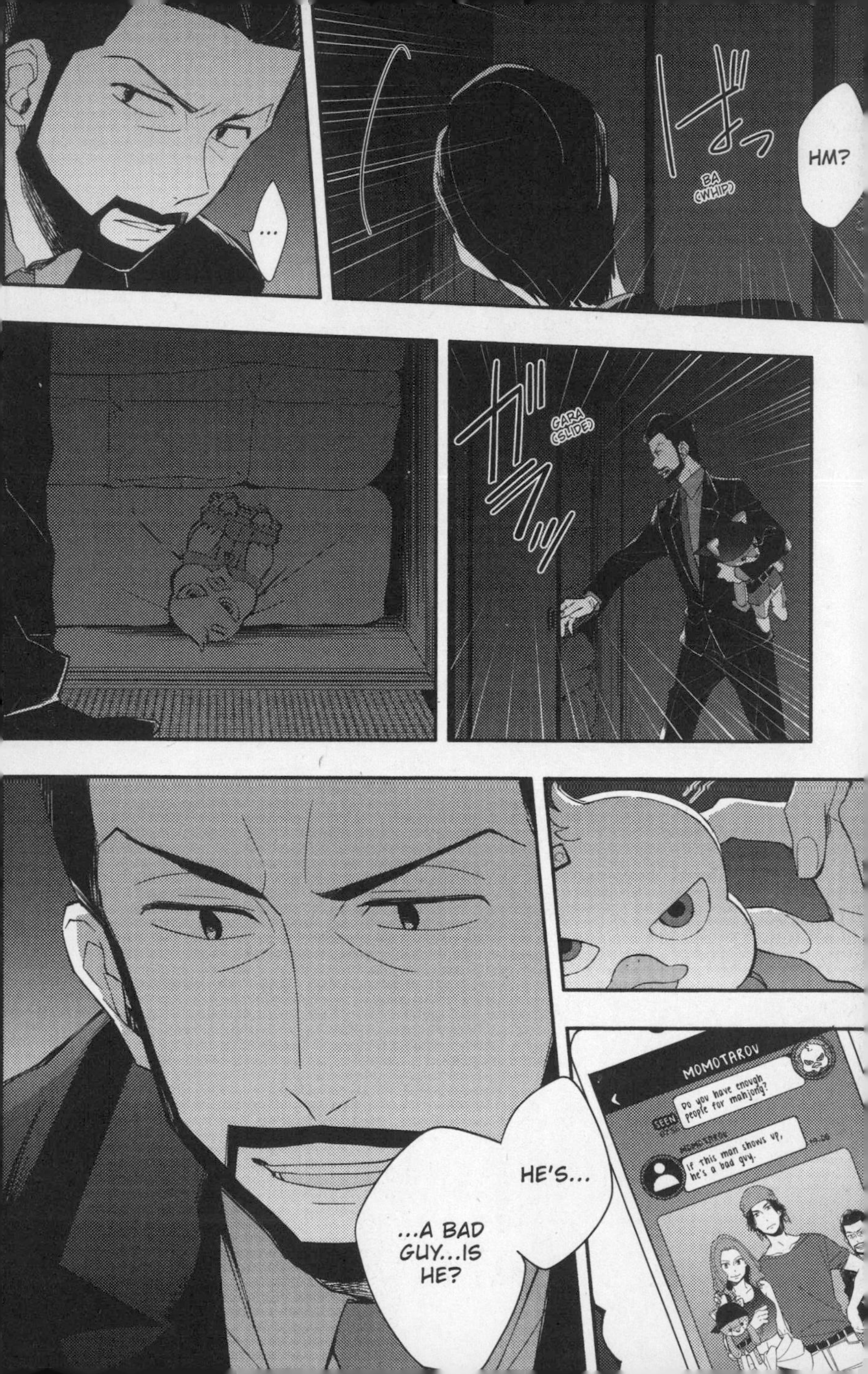
HM?
ぱっ
BA (WHIP)
...
ガラッ
GARA (SLIDE)
MOMOTAROU
Do you have enough people for mahjong?
SEEN
If this man shows up, he's a bad guy.
HE'S...
...A BAD GUY...IS HE?

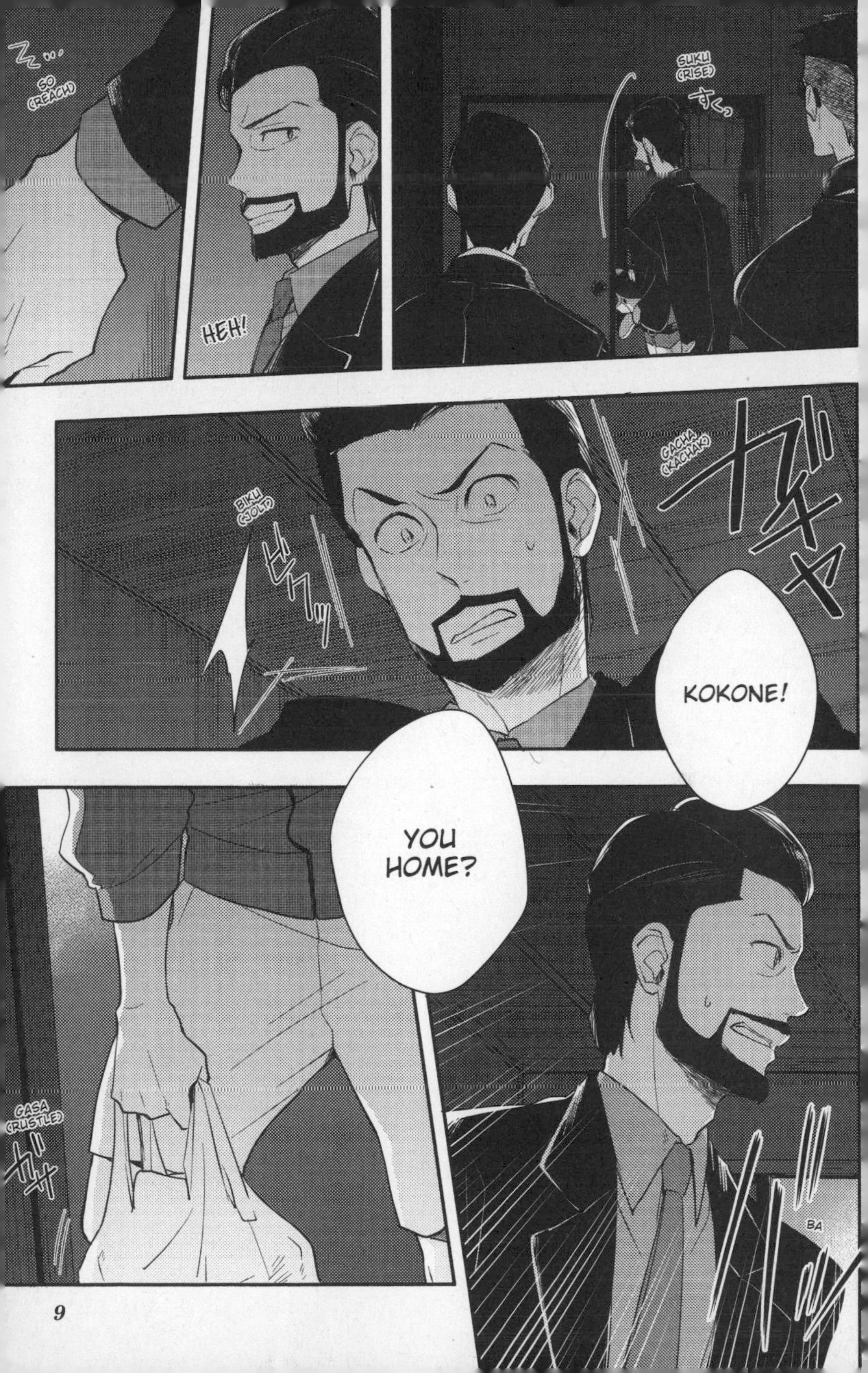

SUKU (RISE)
すくっ
HEH!
SO (REACH)
GACHA (KACHA)
ガチャ
BIKU (JOLT)
ビクッ
KOKONE!
YOU HOME?
BA
GASA (RUSTLE)
ガサ

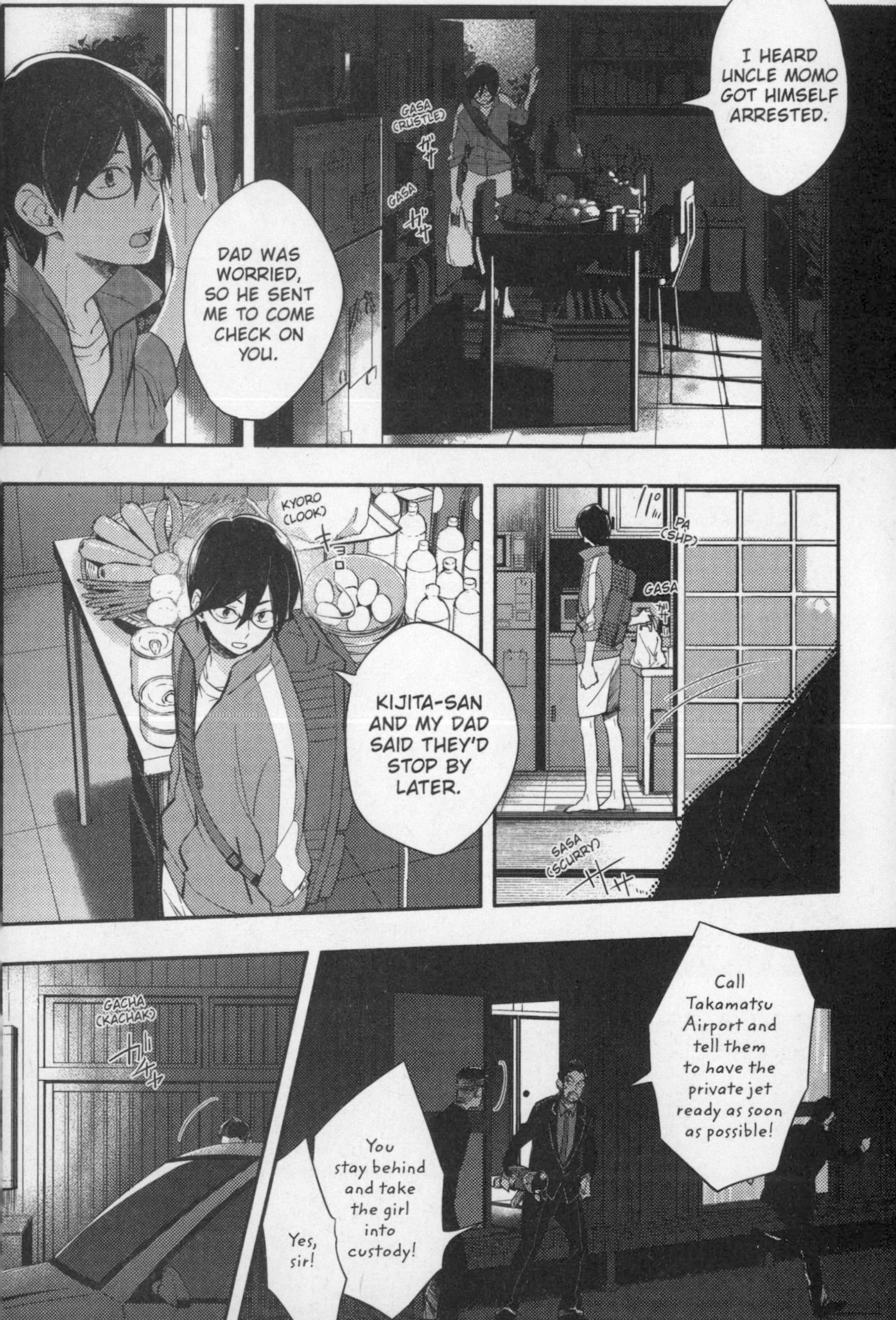
I HEARD UNCLE MOMO GOT HIMSELF ARRESTED.
GASA (RUSTLE)
GASA
DAD WAS WORRIED, SO HE SENT ME TO COME CHECK ON YOU.
PA (SHP)
GASA
SASA (SCURRY)
KYORO (LOOK)
KIJITA-SAN AND MY DAD SAID THEY'D STOP BY LATER.
Call Takamatsu Airport and tell them to have the private jet ready as soon as possible!
You stay behind and take the girl into custody!
Yes, sir!
GACHA (KACHAK)

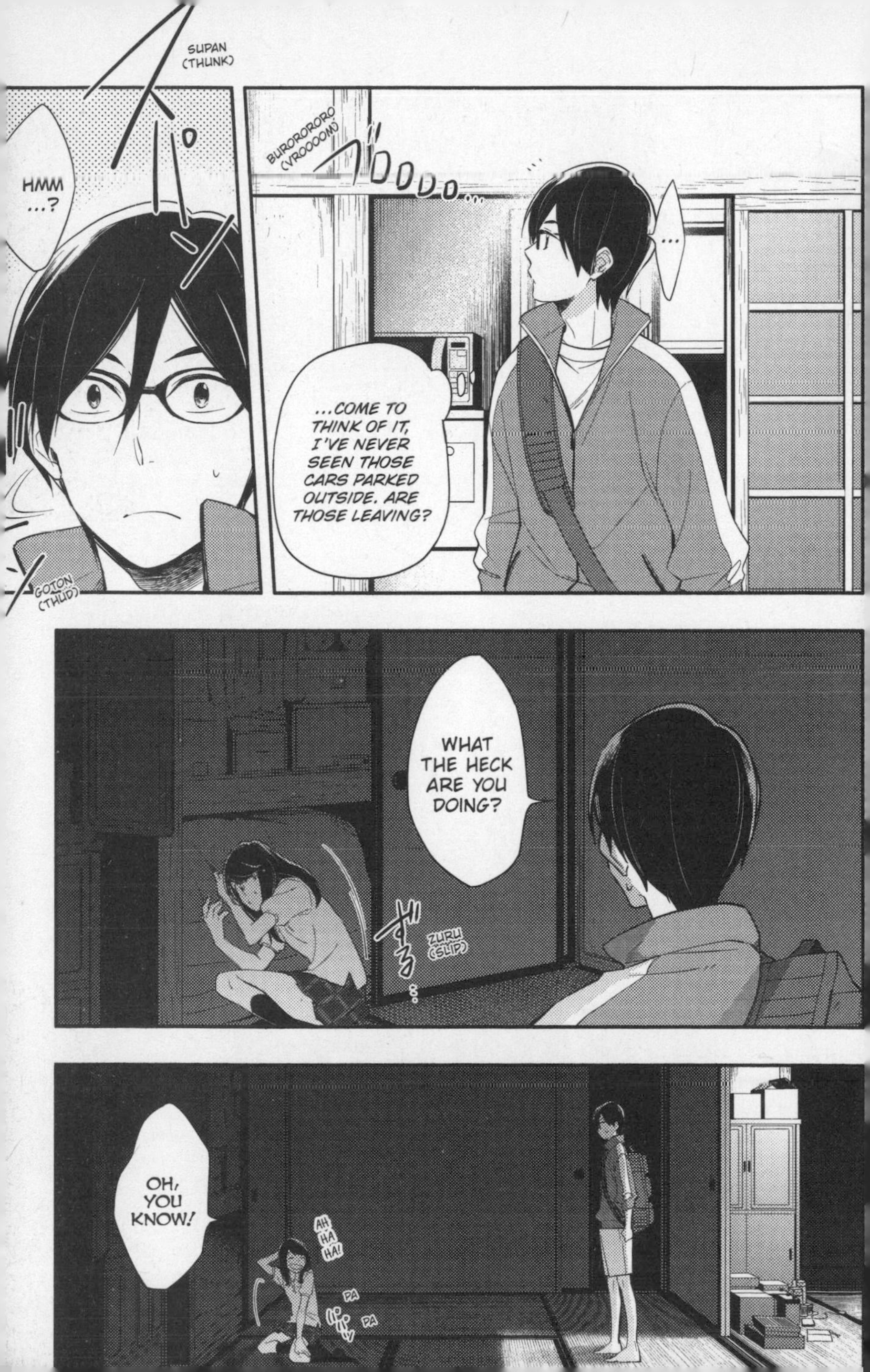
BUROROROR
(VROOOOM)
...
...COME TO THINK OF IT, I'VE NEVER SEEN THOSE CARS PARKED OUTSIDE. ARE THOSE LEAVING?
SUPAN
(THUNK)
HMM ...?
GOTON
(THUD)
WHAT THE HECK ARE YOU DOING?
ZURU
(SLIP)
OH, YOU KNOW!
AH HA HA!
PA
PA

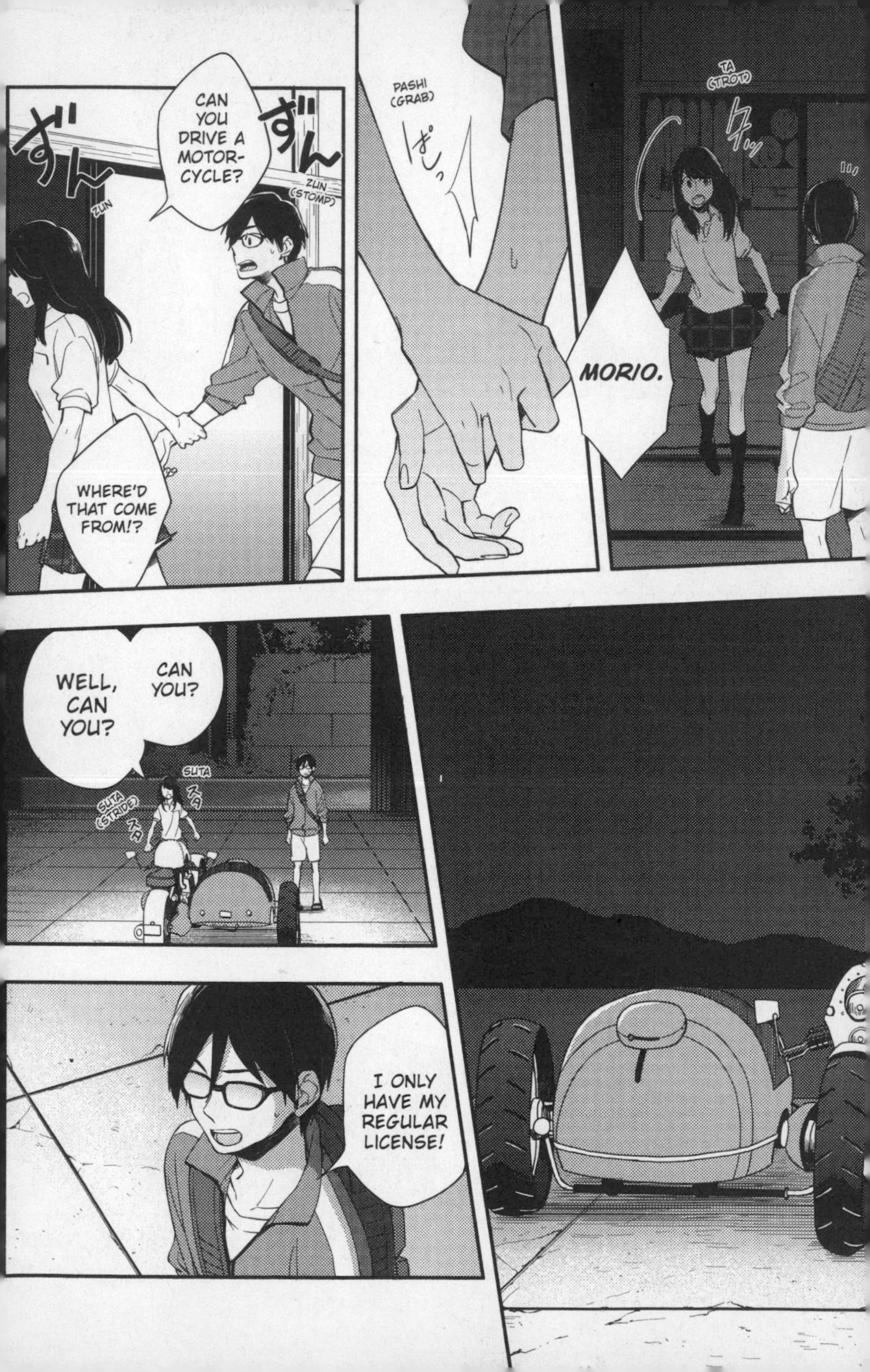

TA (STROT)
MORIO.
PASHI (GRAB)
ZUN (STOMP)
CAN YOU DRIVE A MOTOR-CYCLE?
ZUN
WHERE'D THAT COME FROM!?
CAN YOU?
WELL, CAN YOU?
SUTA
SUTA (STRIDE)
I ONLY HAVE MY REGULAR LICENSE!

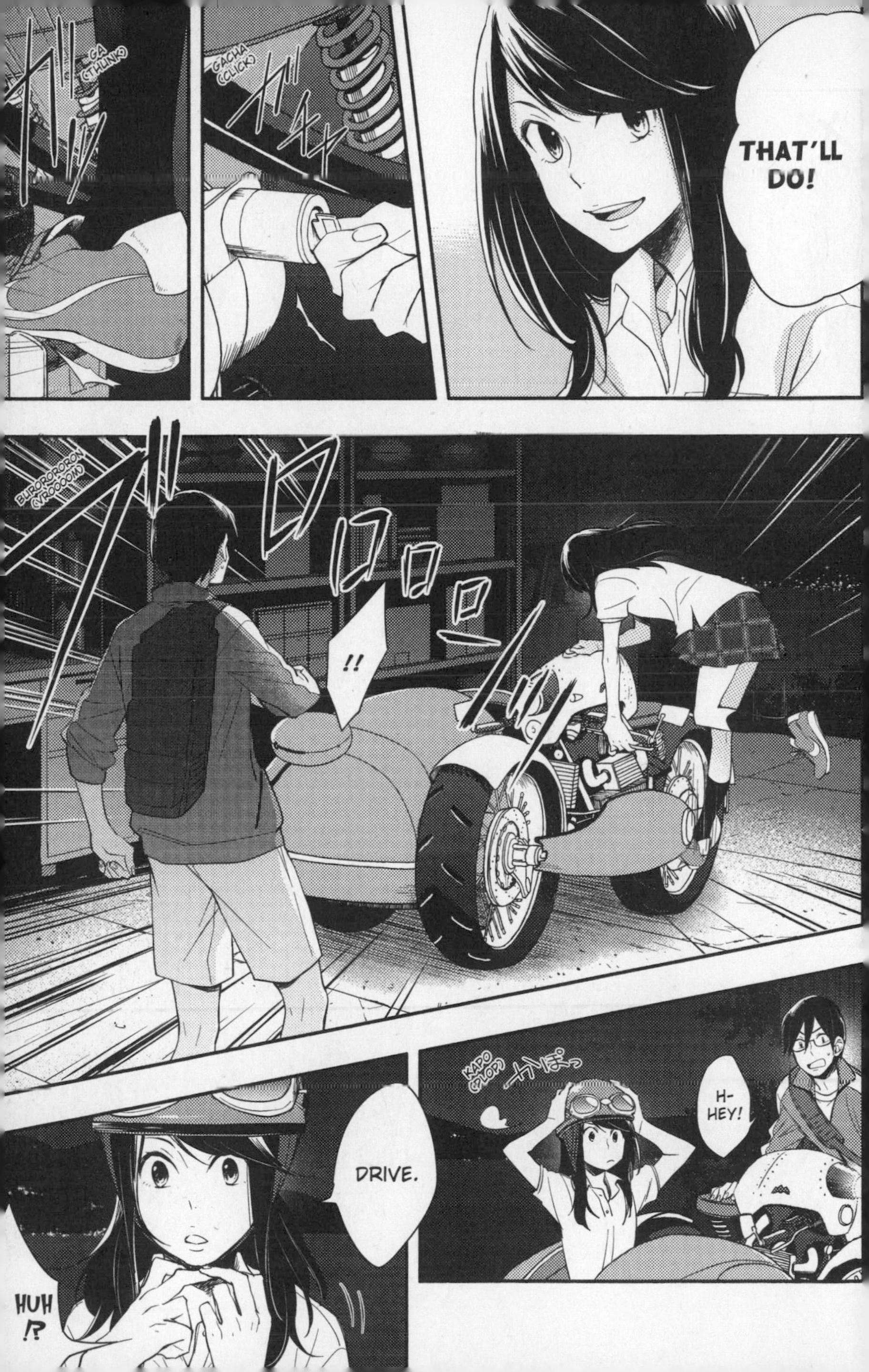
THAT'LL DO!
GACHA (CLICK)
GA (THUNK)
BURORORORON (VROOOOM)
!!
KAPO (PLOP)
H-HEY!
DRIVE.
HUH!?

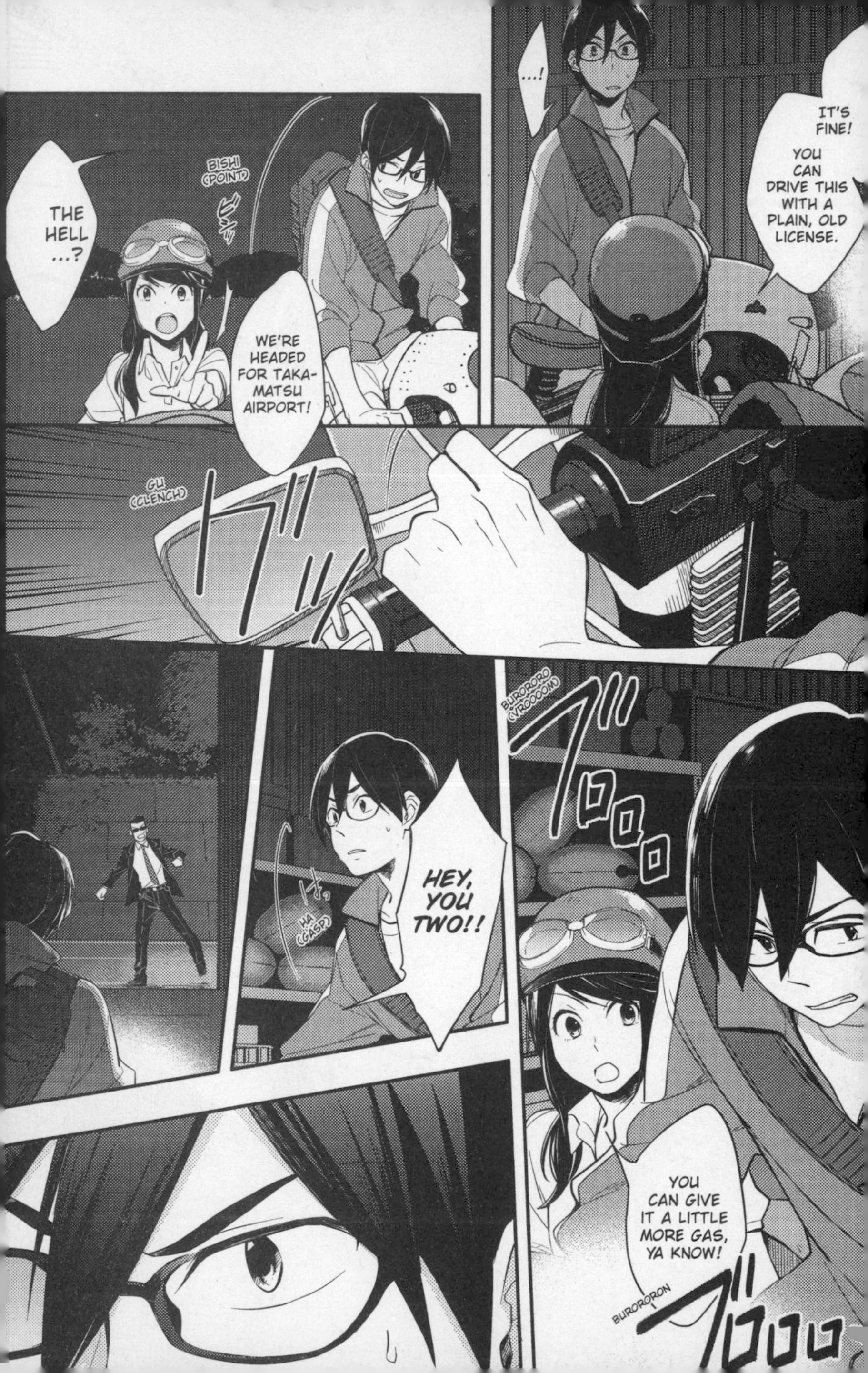
...!
IT'S FINE!
YOU CAN DRIVE THIS WITH A PLAIN, OLD LICENSE.
BISHI (POINT)
THE HELL ...?
WE'RE HEADED FOR TAKA-MATSU AIRPORT!
GU (CLENCH)
BURORORO (VROOOOM)
YOU CAN GIVE IT A LITTLE MORE GAS, YA KNOW!
BURORORON
HEY, YOU TWO!!
HA (GASP)

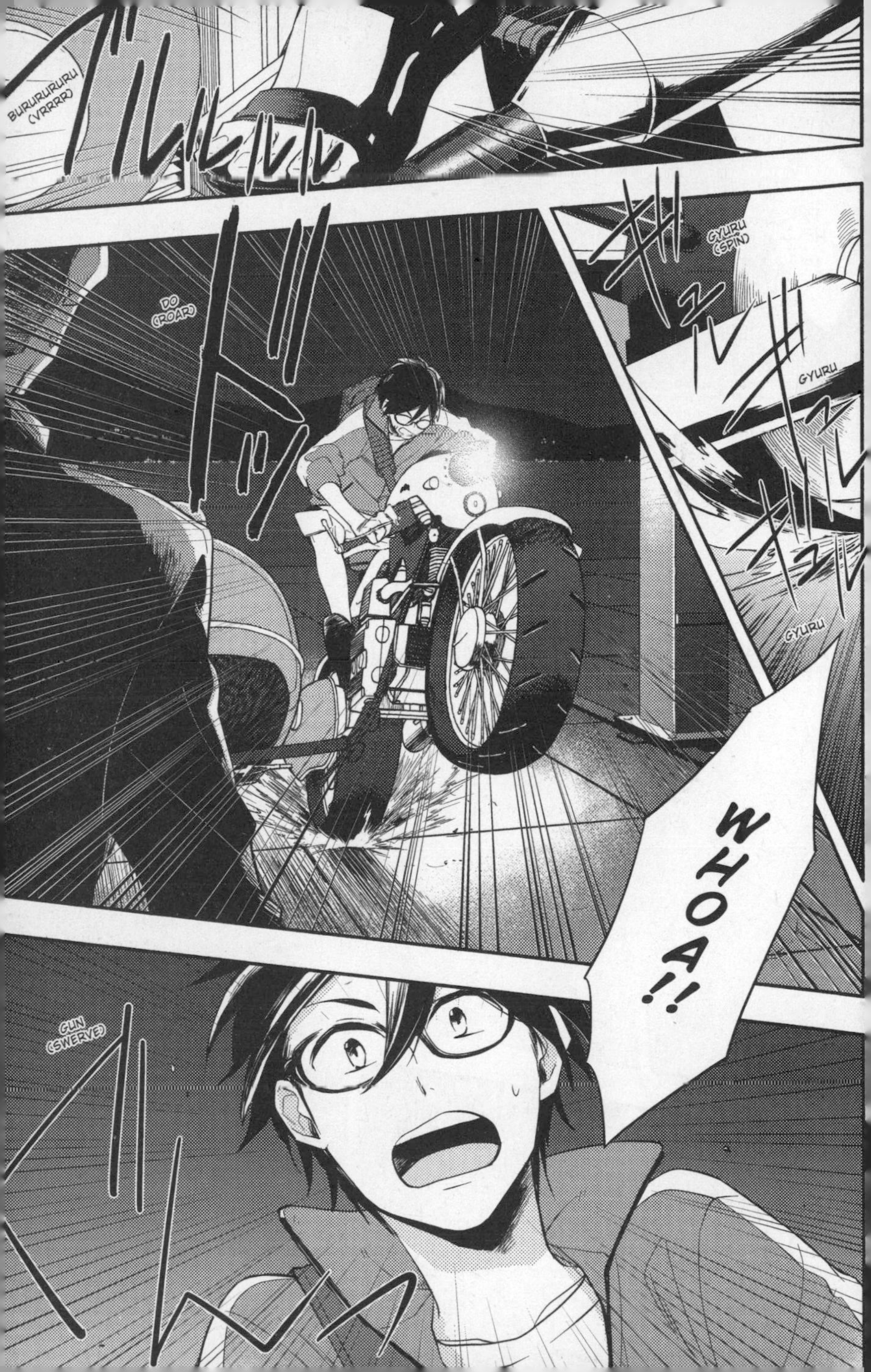
BURURURURU
(VRRRR)
GYURU
(SPIN)
GYURU
GYURU
DO
(ROAR)
WHOA!!
GUN
(SWERVE)

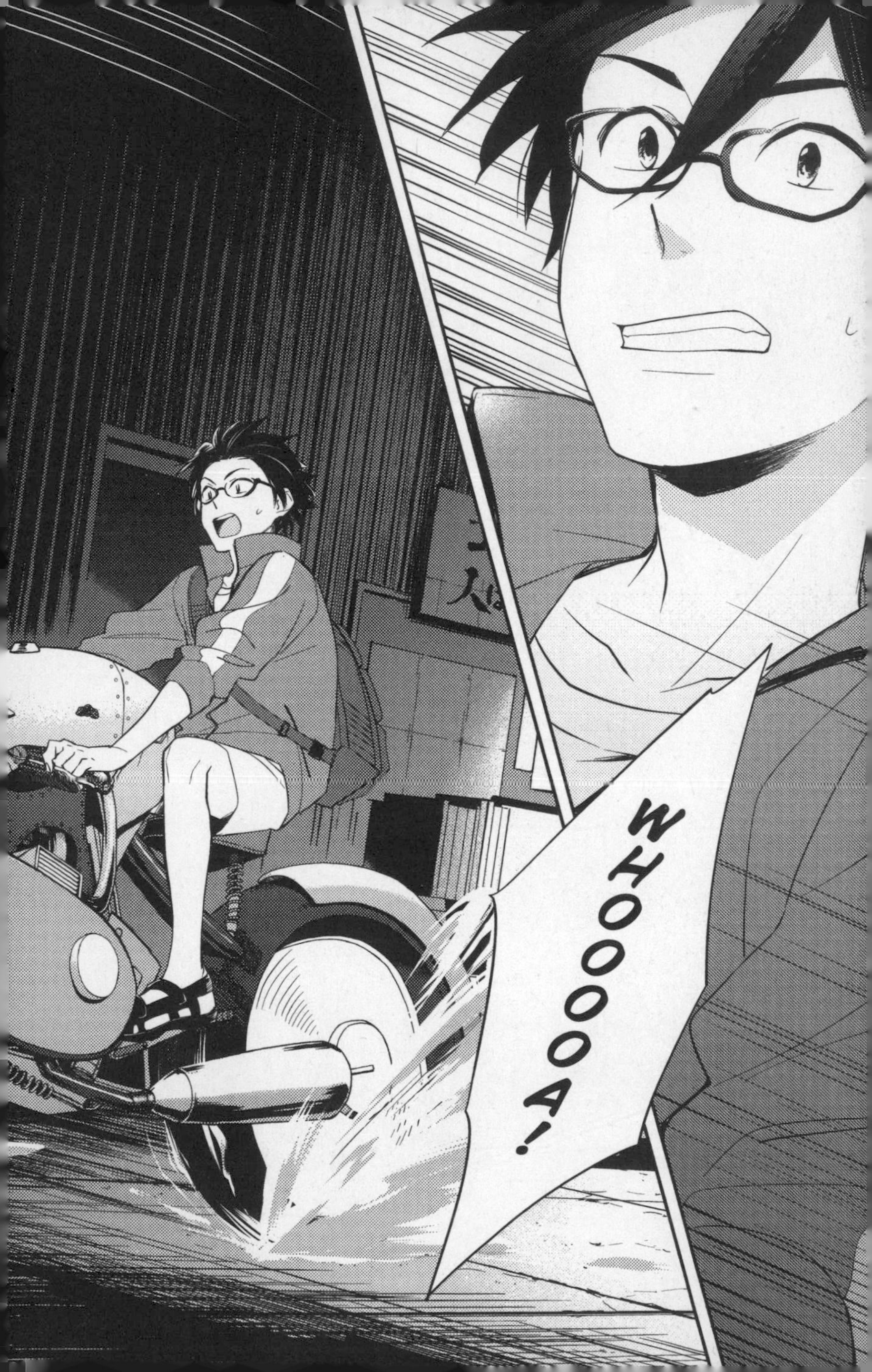
WHOOOOA!

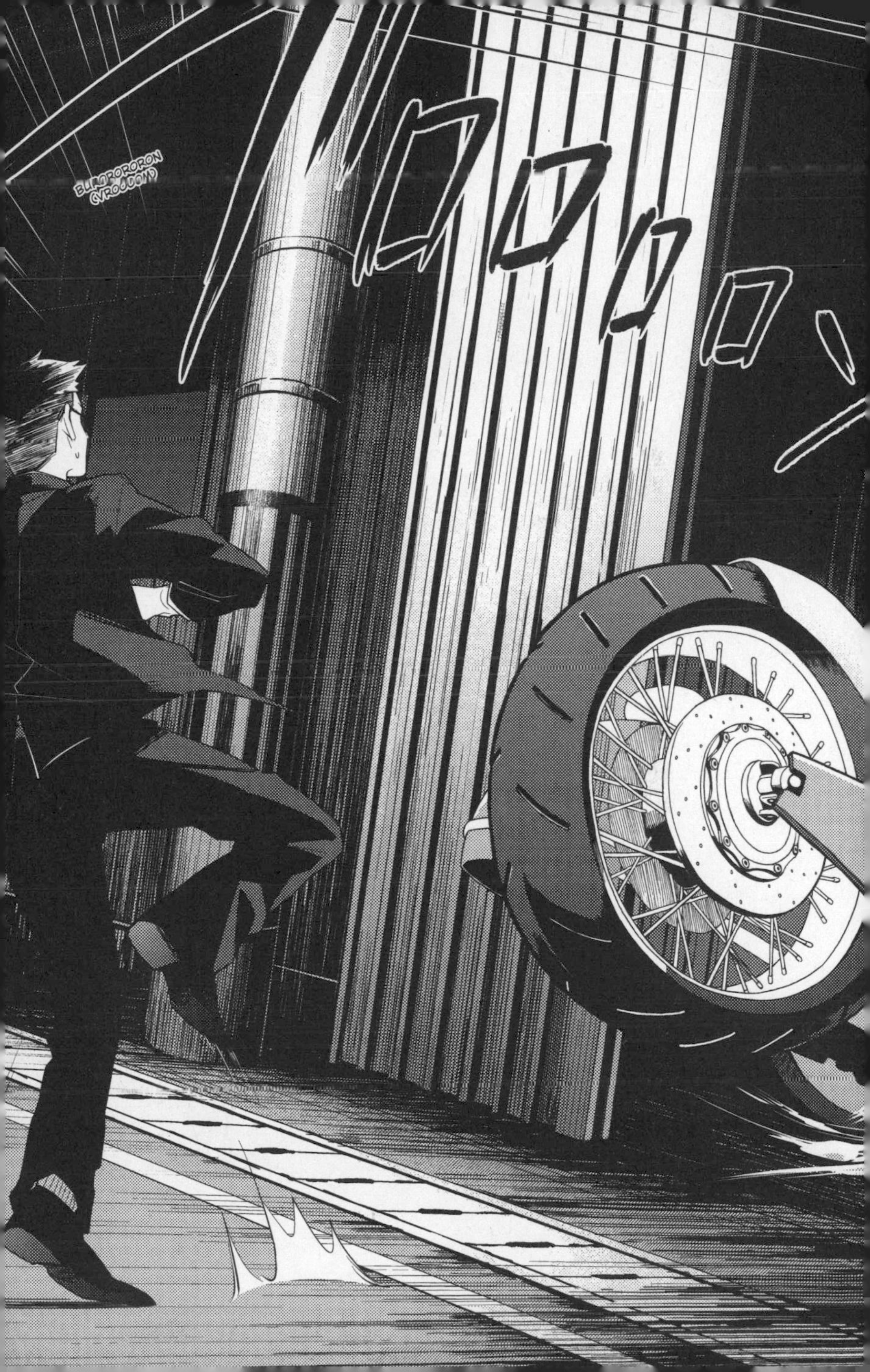
BURORORORON
(VROOOOM)

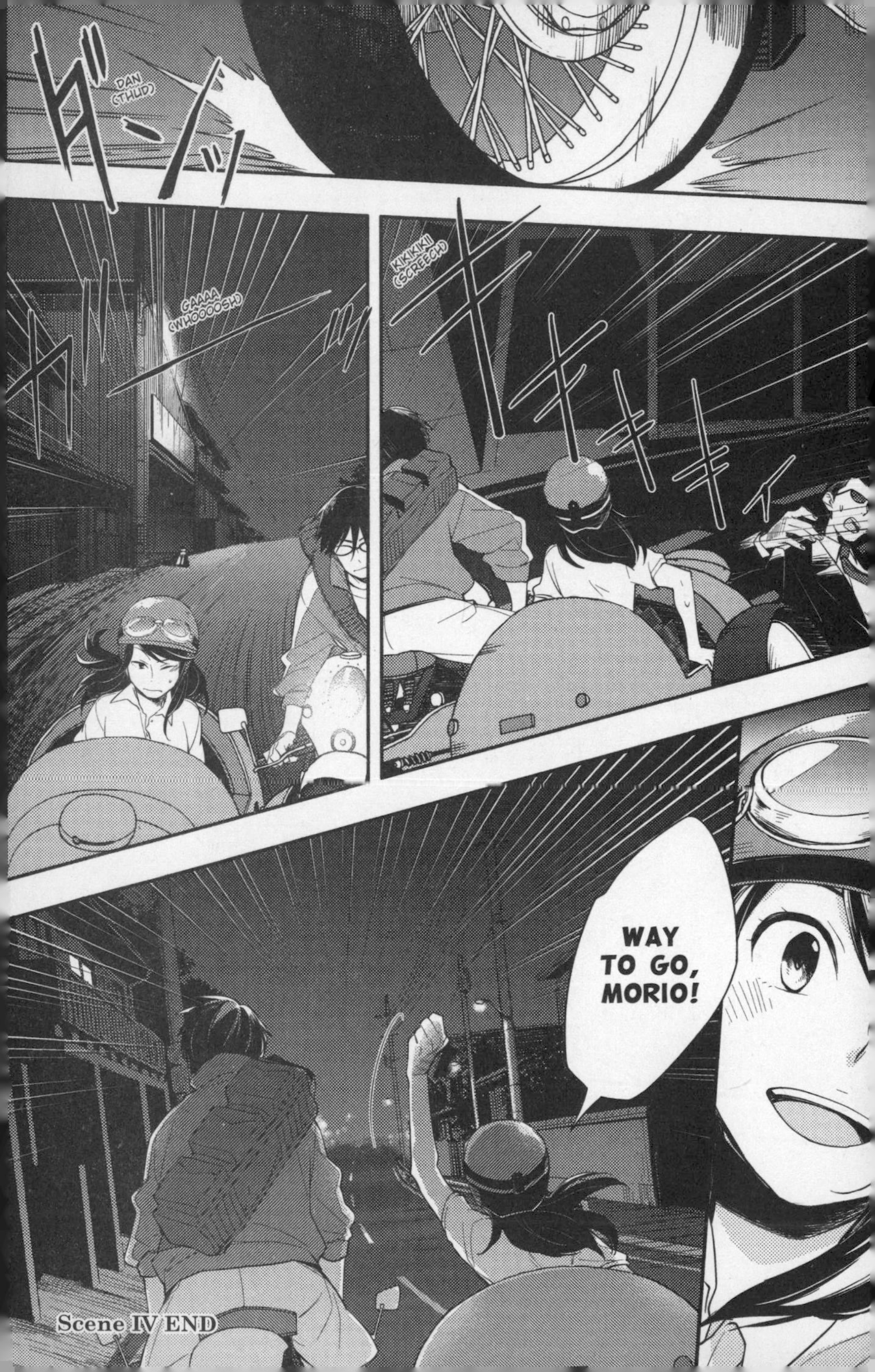
DAN (THUD)
KIKIKII (SCREECH)
GAAAA (WHOOOOSH)
WAY TO GO, MORIO!
Scene IV END

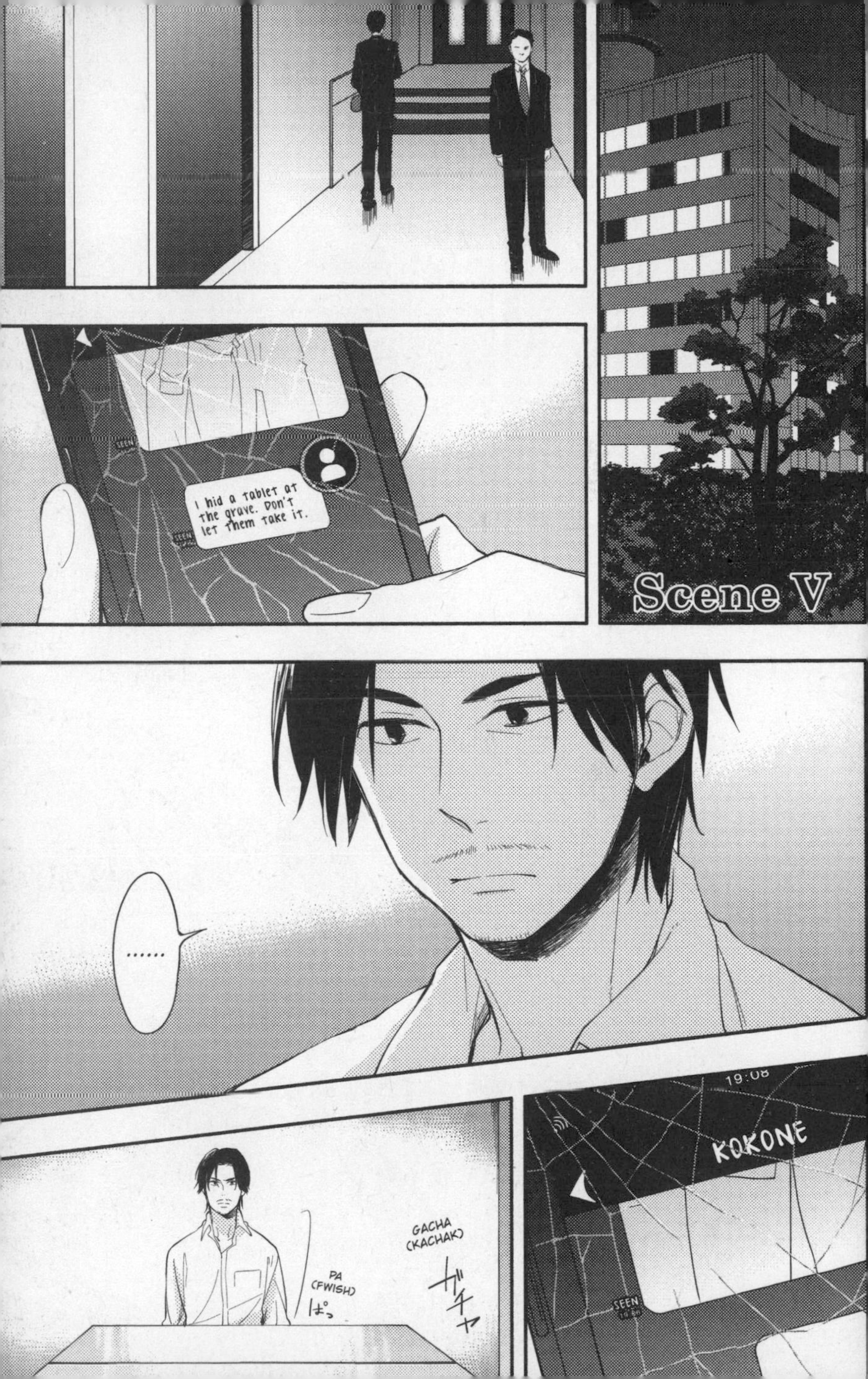
Scene V
I hid a tablet at the grave. Don't let them take it.
SEEN
......
19:08
KOKONE
SEEN
GACHA (KACHAK)
ガチャ
PA (FWISH)
ぱっ

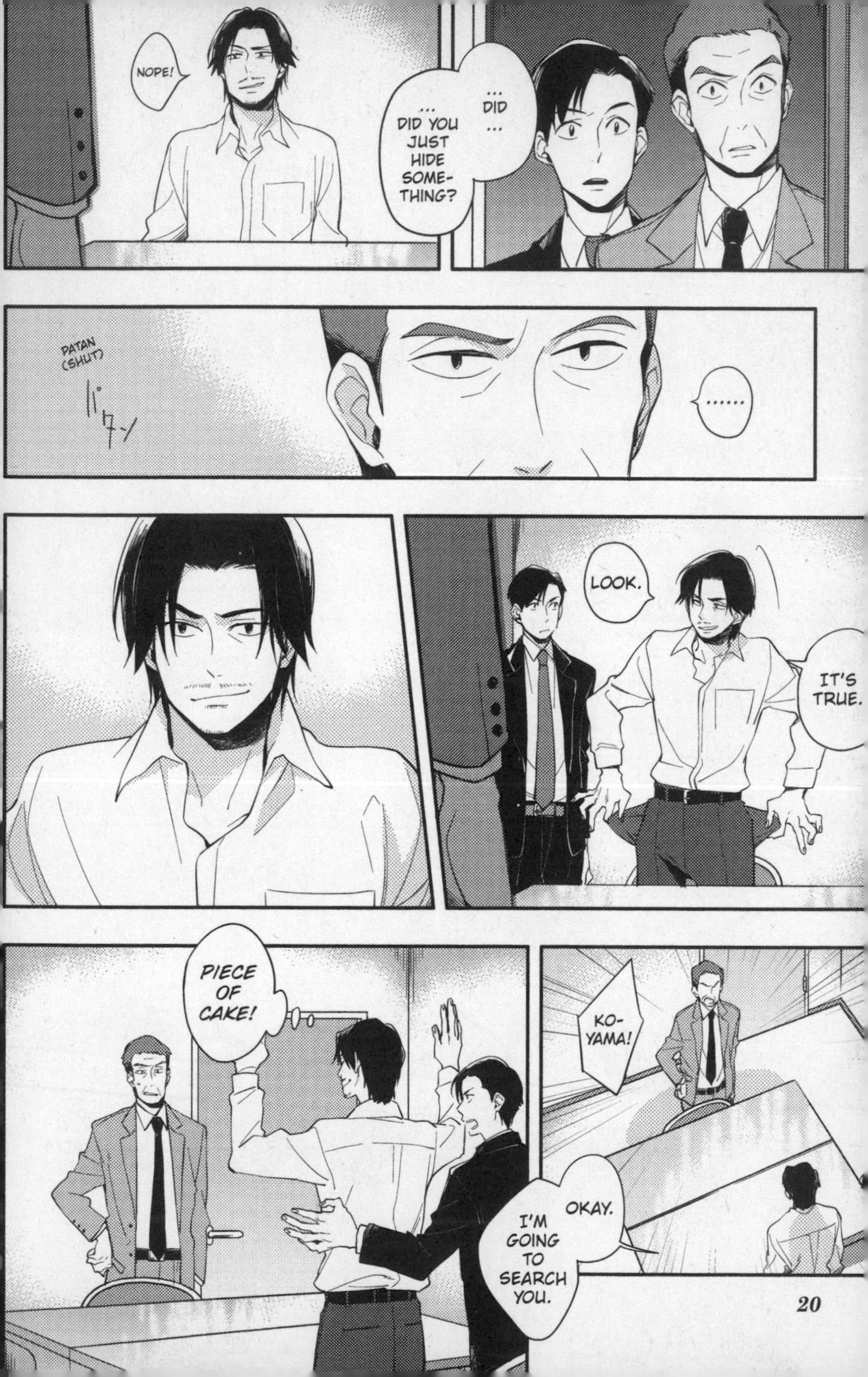
... DID ...
... DID YOU JUST HIDE SOMETHING?
NOPE!
......
PATAN (SHUT)
パタン
LOOK.
IT'S TRUE.
KO-YAMA!
OKAY. I'M GOING TO SEARCH YOU.
PIECE OF CAKE!

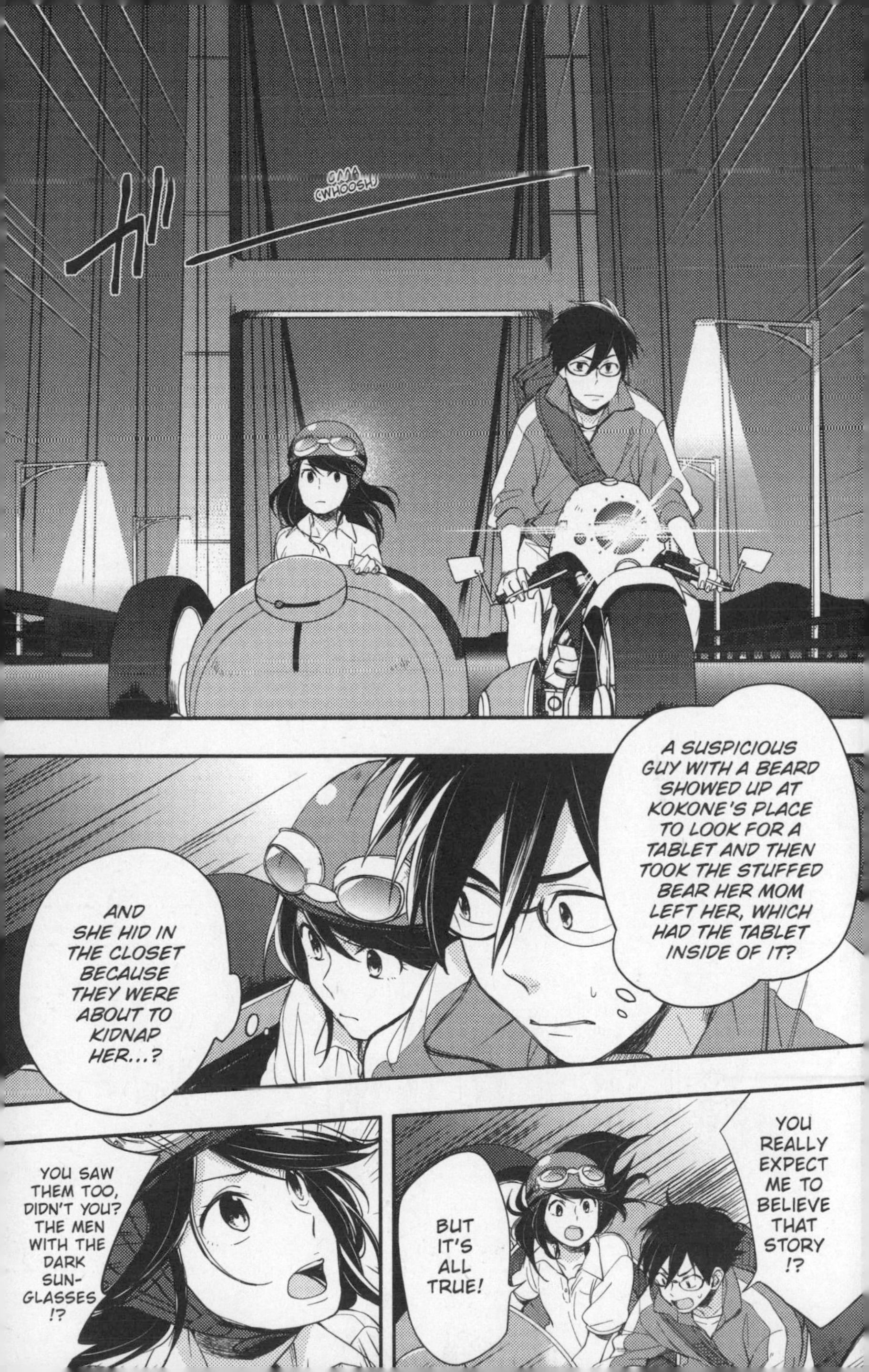
GAAA
(WHOOSH)
A SUSPICIOUS GUY WITH A BEARD SHOWED UP AT KOKONE'S PLACE TO LOOK FOR A TABLET AND THEN TOOK THE STUFFED BEAR HER MOM LEFT HER, WHICH HAD THE TABLET INSIDE OF IT?
AND SHE HID IN THE CLOSET BECAUSE THEY WERE ABOUT TO KIDNAP HER...?
YOU REALLY EXPECT ME TO BELIEVE THAT STORY !?
BUT IT'S ALL TRUE!
YOU SAW THEM TOO, DIDN'T YOU? THE MEN WITH THE DARK SUN-GLASSES !?

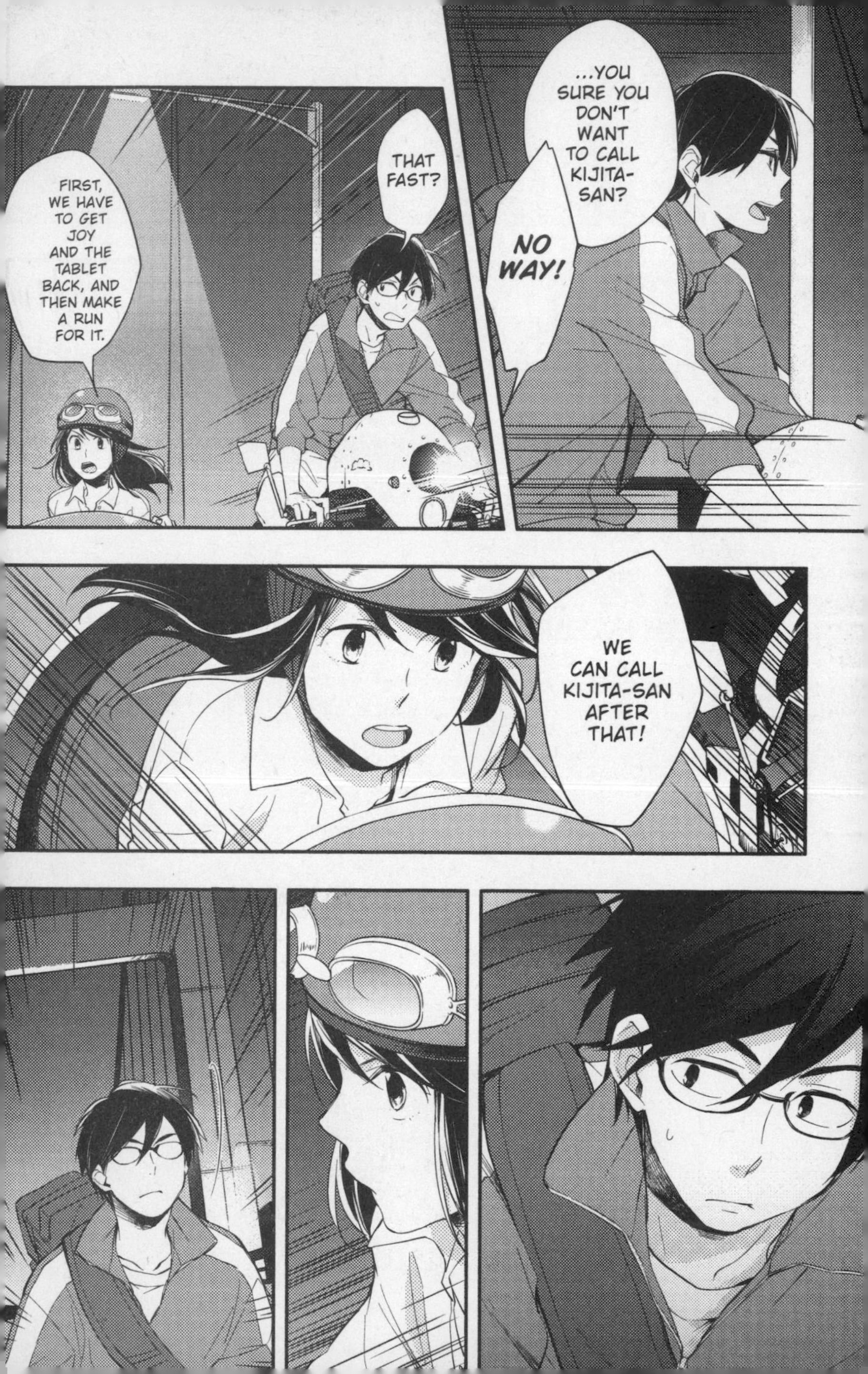
...YOU SURE YOU DON'T WANT TO CALL KIJITA-SAN?
NO WAY!
THAT FAST?
FIRST, WE HAVE TO GET JOY AND THE TABLET BACK, AND THEN MAKE A RUN FOR IT.
WE CAN CALL KIJITA-SAN AFTER THAT!

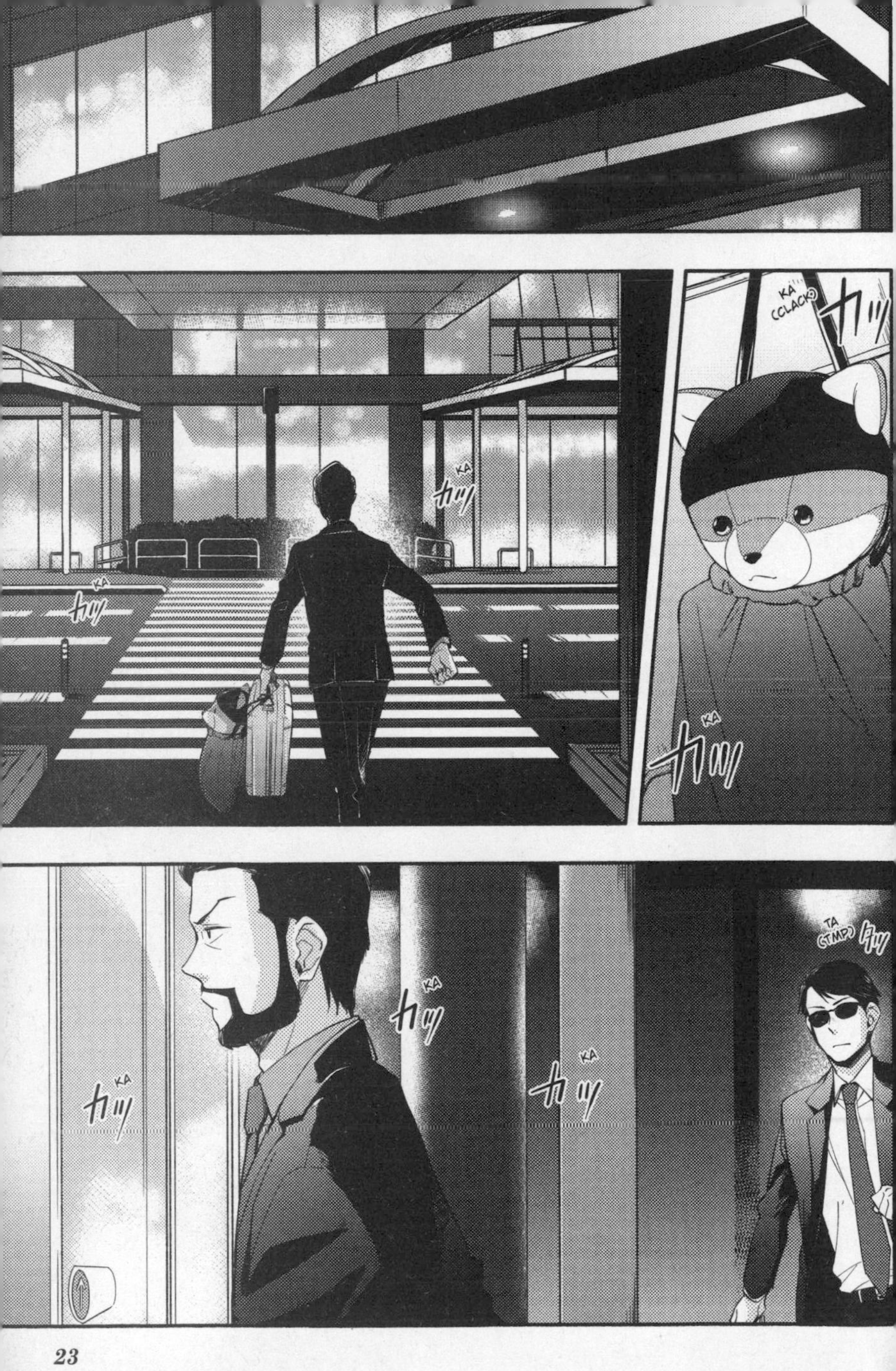
KA (CLACK)
カッ
KA
カッ
KA
カッ
KA
カッ
TA (TMP)
タッ
KA
カッ
KA
カッ
KA
カッ

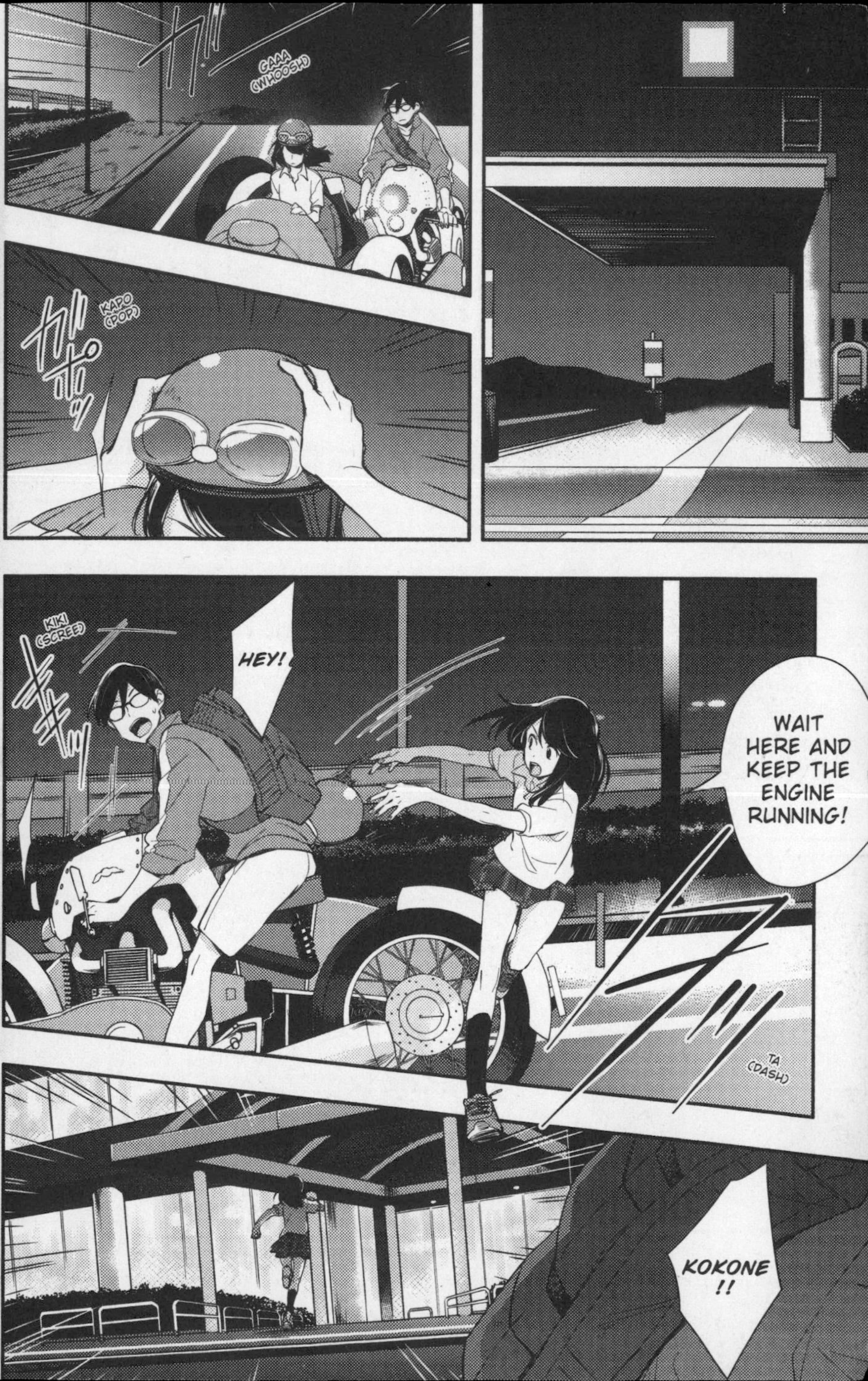
GAAA (WHOOSH)
KAPO (POP)
WAIT HERE AND KEEP THE ENGINE RUNNING!
HEY!
KIKI (SCREE)
TA (DASH)
KOKONE !!

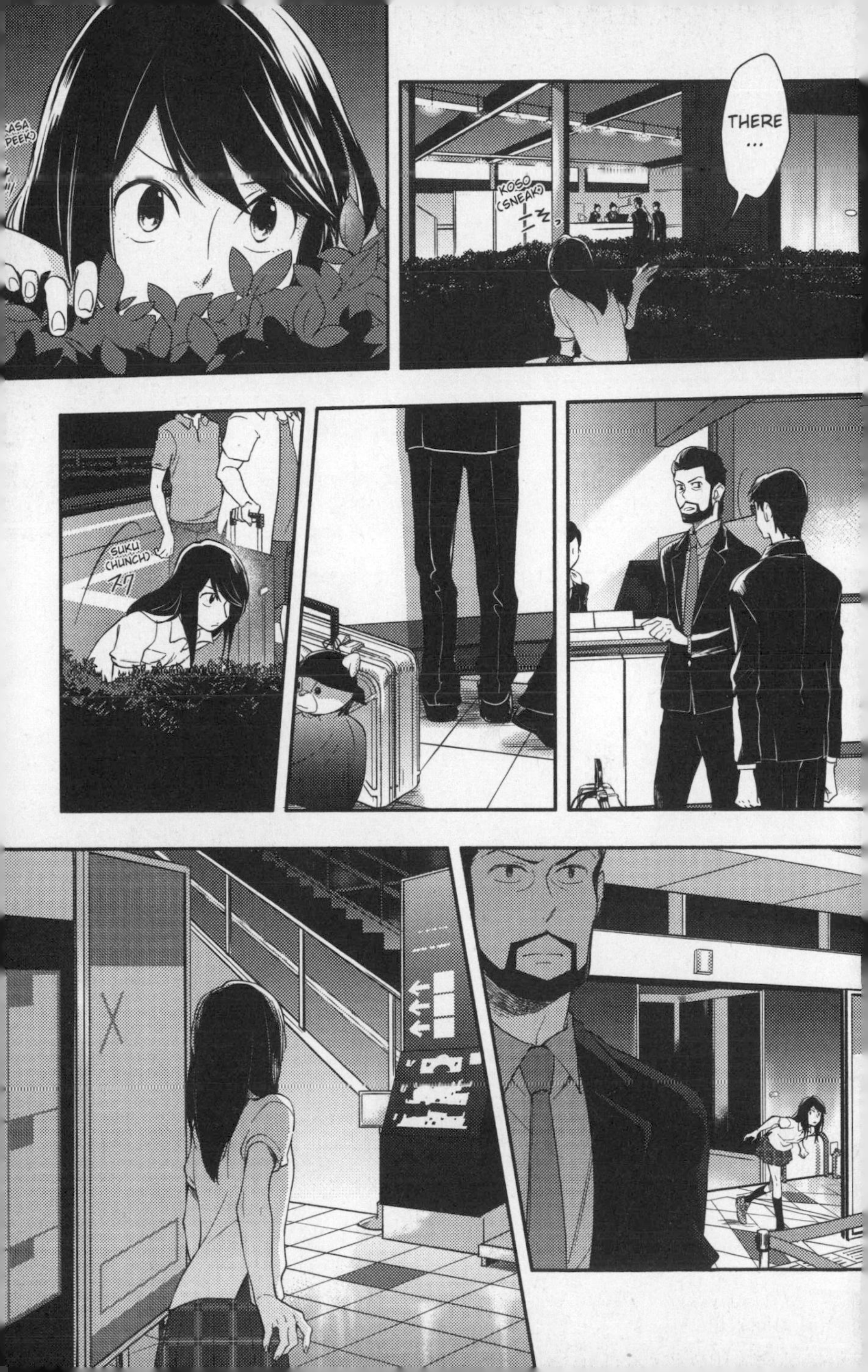
THERE ...
KOSO (SNEAK)
KASA
PEEK)
SUKU (HUNCH)
スク

GU
(GRAB)

!

SO
(SHF)

WHAAA!?

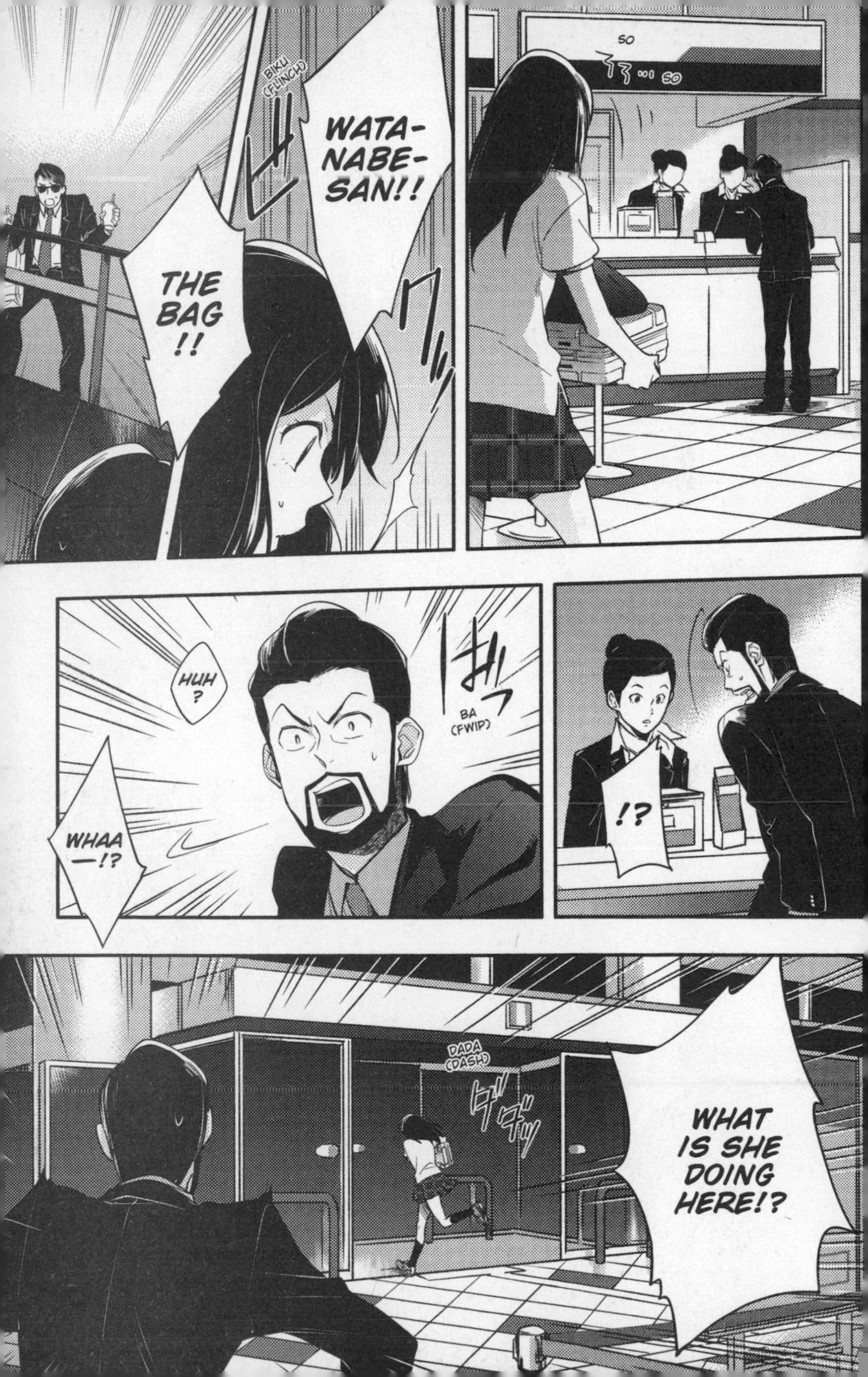
SO
SO
WATA-
NABE-
SAN!!
BIKU
(FLINCH)
THE
BAG
!!
!?
BA
(FWIP)
HUH
?
WHAA
—!?
WHAT
IS SHE
DOING
HERE!?
DADA
(DASH)

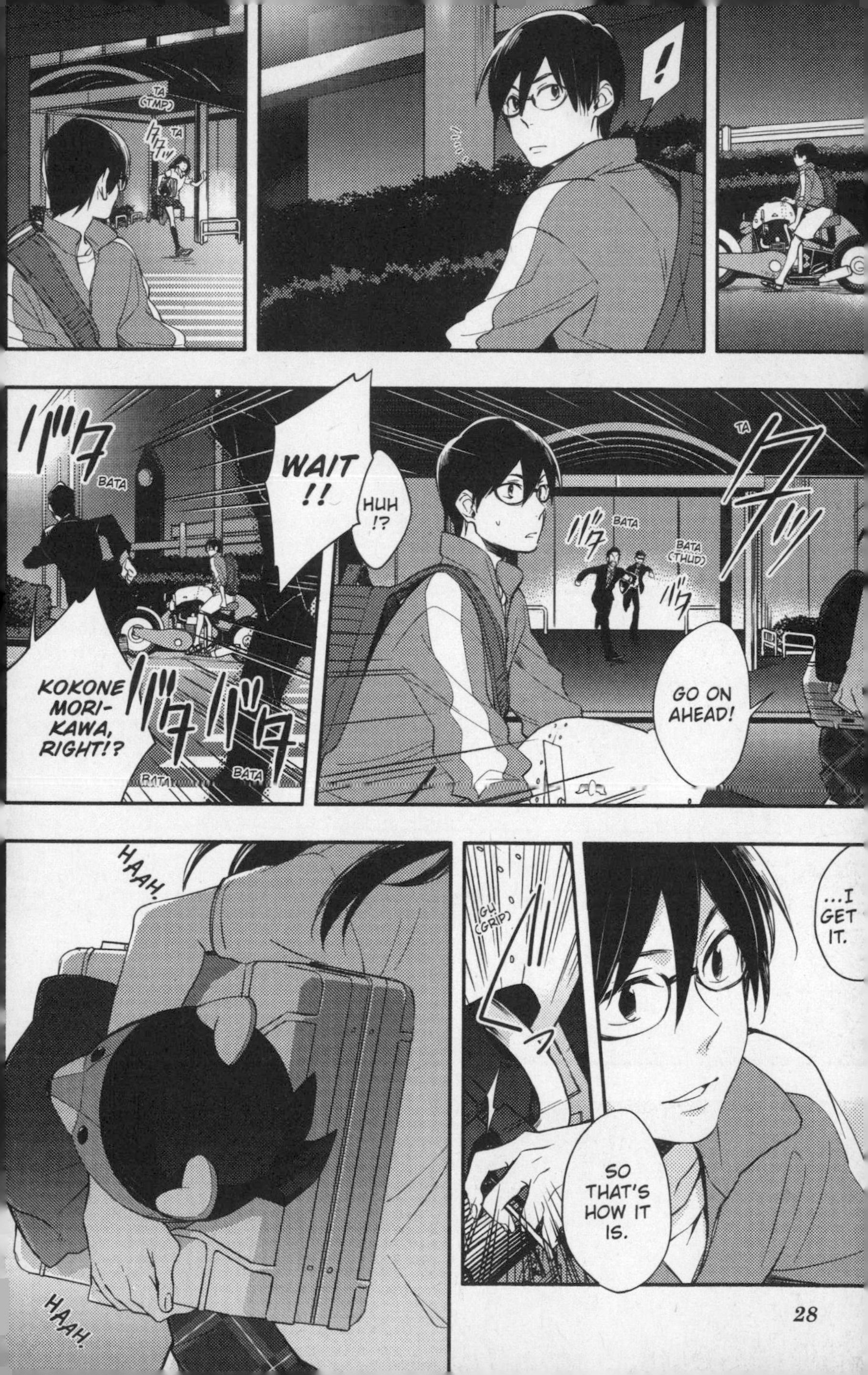
!
TA (TMP) TA
TA
BATA
BATA (THUD)
GO ON AHEAD!
HUH !?
WAIT !!
BATA
KOKONE MORI-KAWA, RIGHT!?
BATA
BATA
...I GET IT.
GU (GRIP)
SO THAT'S HOW IT IS.
HAAH.
HAAH.

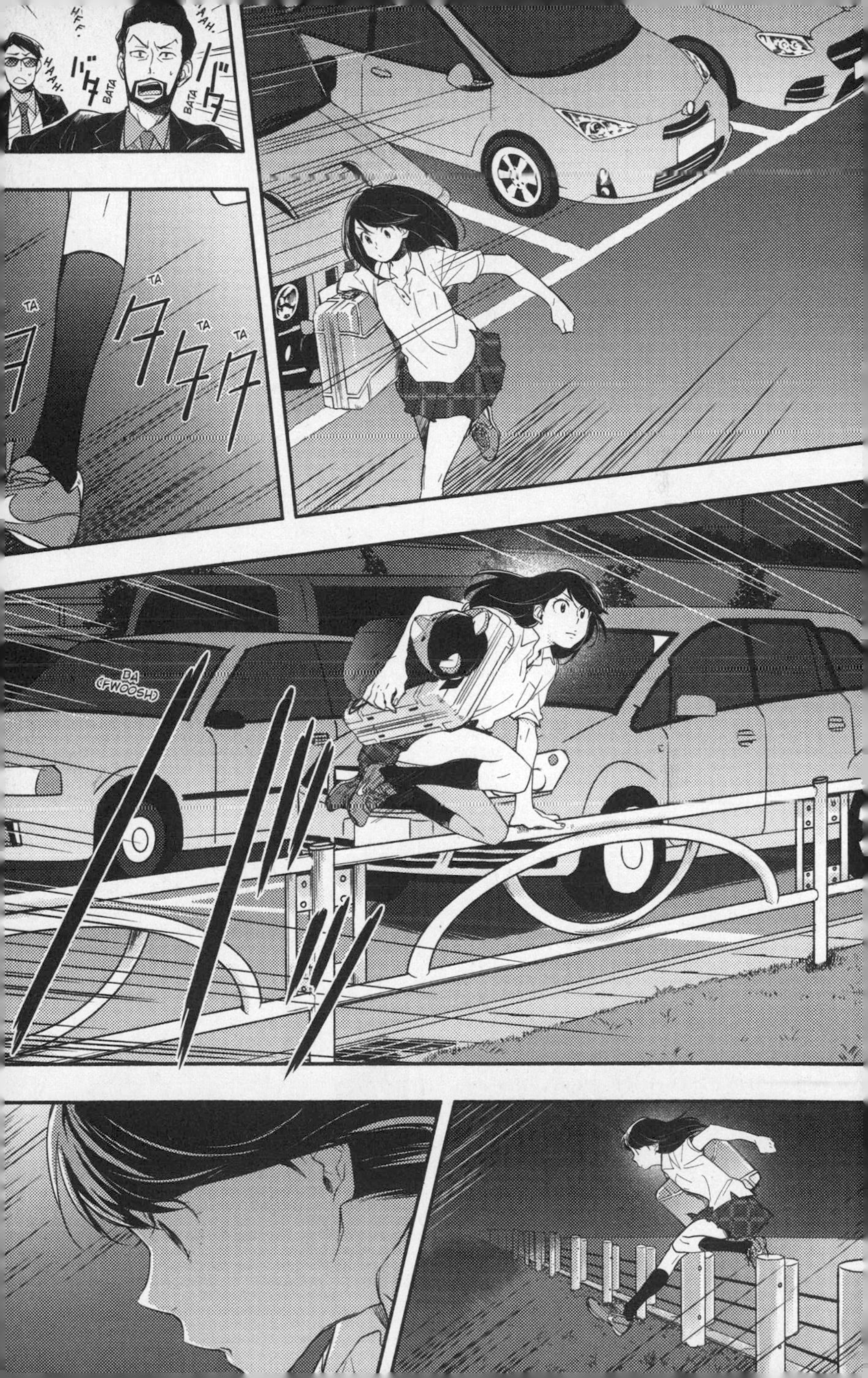
HAAH.
バタ BATA
HFF.
HAAH.
バタ BATA
タタタタ TA TA TA TA
BA (FWOOSH)

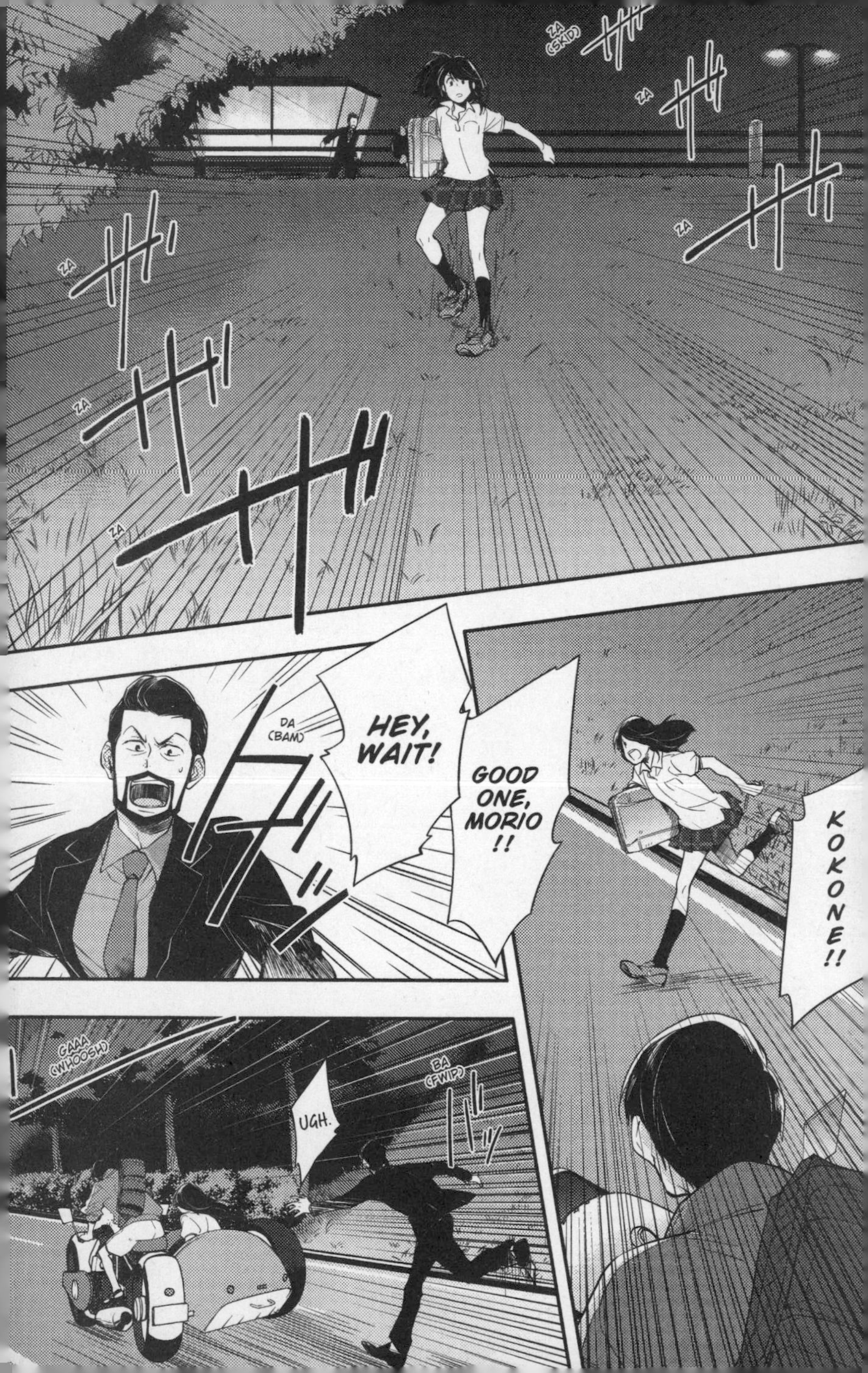
ZA (SKID)
ZA
ZA
ZA
ZA
ZA
KOKONE!!
GOOD ONE, MORIO!!
HEY, WAIT!
DA (BAM)
BA (FWIP)
UGH.
GAAA (WHOOSH)

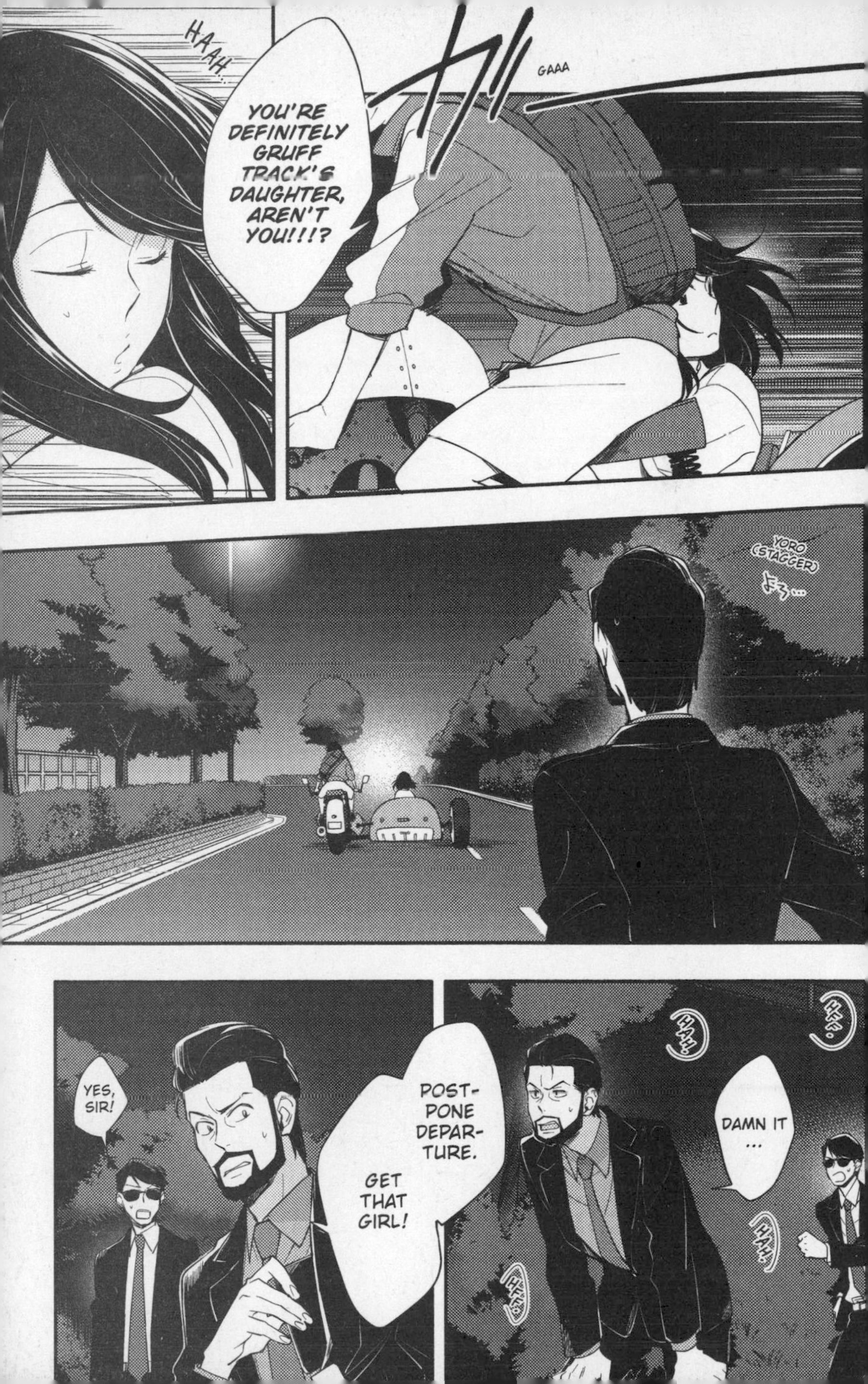
GAAA
HAAH...
YOU'RE DEFINITELY GRUFF TRACK'S DAUGHTER, AREN'T YOU!!!?
YORO (STAGGER)
よろ...
HFF.
HAH.
DAMN IT...
HAH.
HFF.
POST-PONE DEPAR-TURE.
GET THAT GIRL!
YES, SIR!

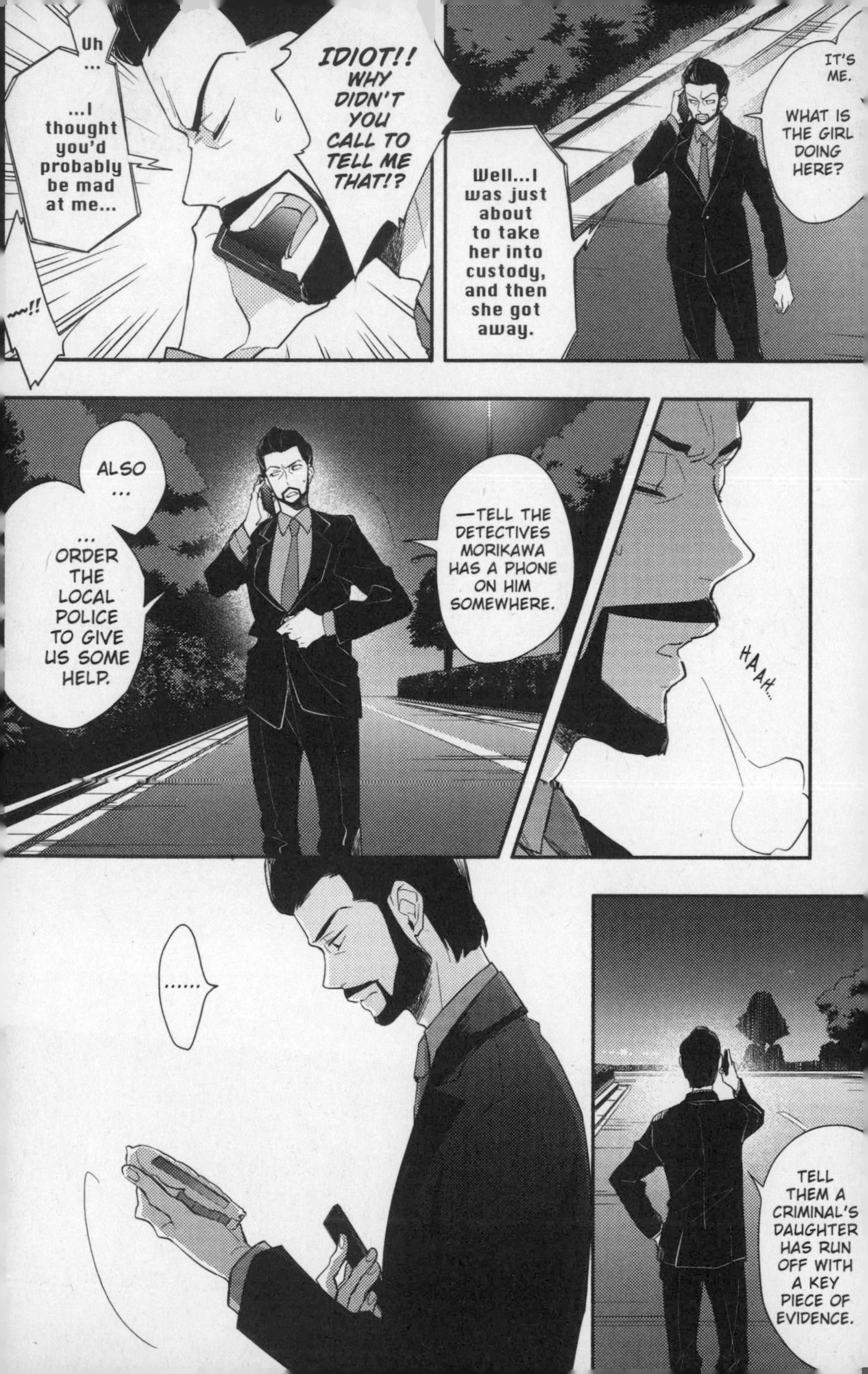
IT'S ME.
WHAT IS THE GIRL DOING HERE?
Well...I was just about to take her into custody, and then she got away.
IDIOT!! WHY DIDN'T YOU CALL TO TELL ME THAT!?
Uh ...
...I thought you'd probably be mad at me...
HAAAH...
—TELL THE DETECTIVES MORIKAWA HAS A PHONE ON HIM SOMEWHERE.
ALSO ...
... ORDER THE LOCAL POLICE TO GIVE US SOME HELP.
TELL THEM A CRIMINAL'S DAUGHTER HAS RUN OFF WITH A KEY PIECE OF EVIDENCE.
......

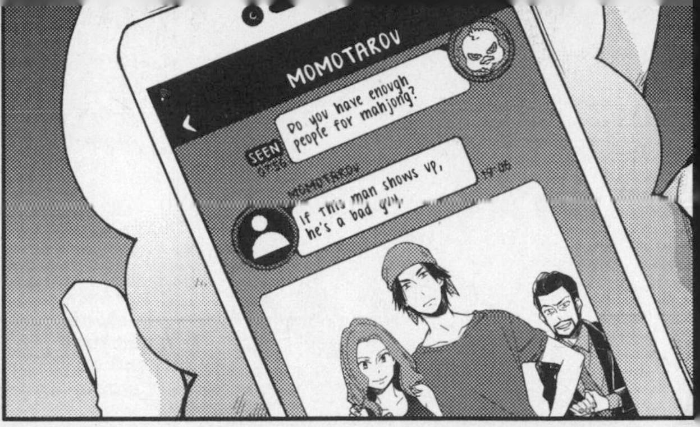
MOMOTAROU
Do you have enough people for mahjong?
SEEN
MOMOTAROU
If this man shows up, he's a bad guy.
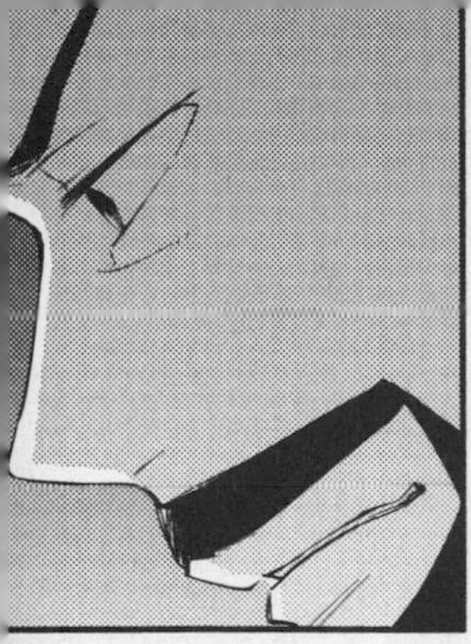
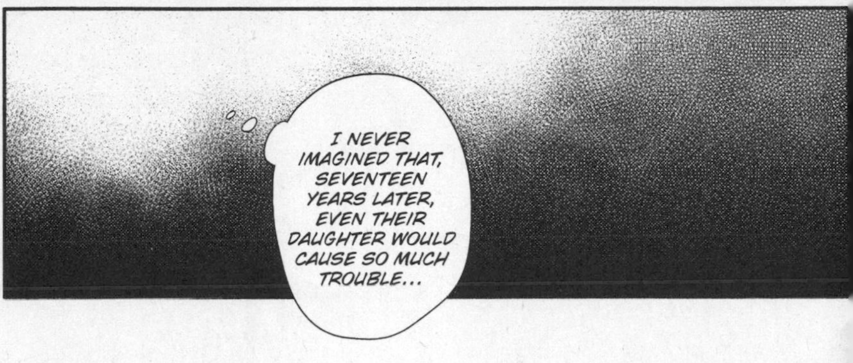
I NEVER IMAGINED THAT, SEVENTEEN YEARS LATER, EVEN THEIR DAUGHTER WOULD CAUSE SO MUCH TROUBLE...
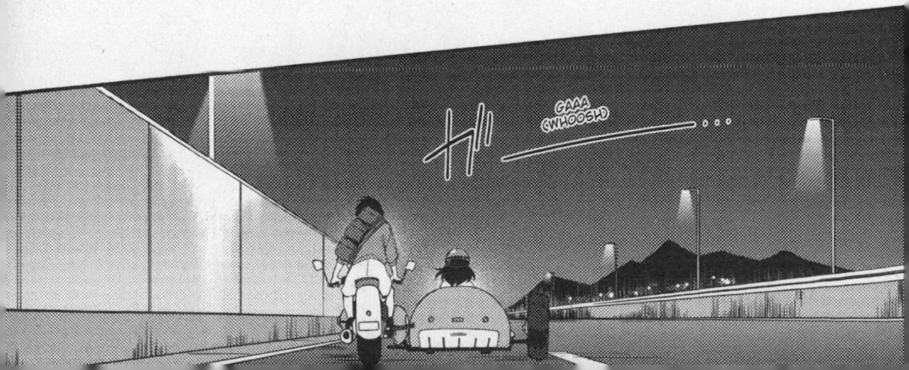
GAAA (WHOOSH)

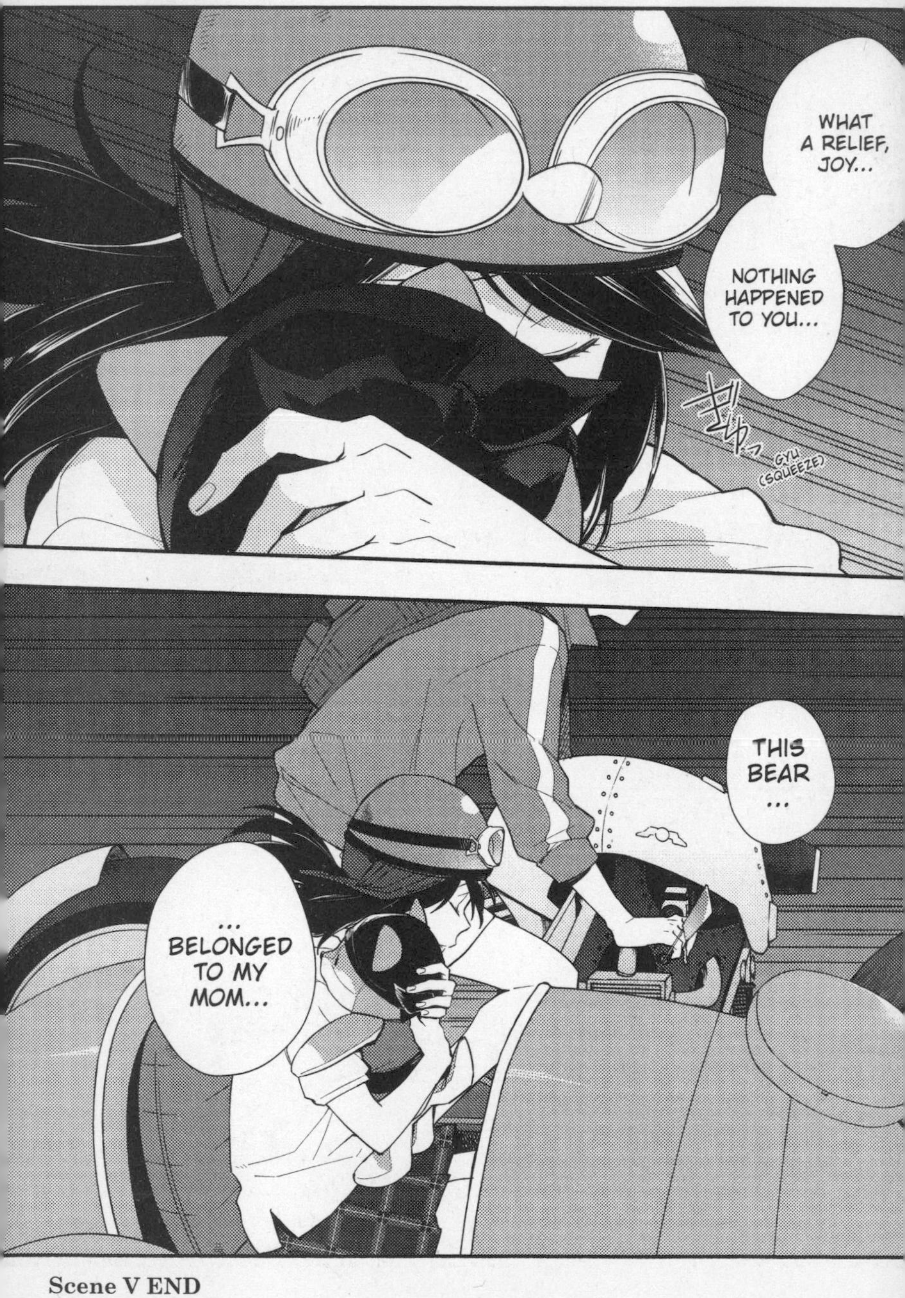
WHAT A RELIEF, JOY...
NOTHING HAPPENED TO YOU...
ぎゅっ
GYU (SQUEEZE)
THIS BEAR ...
... BELONGED TO MY MOM...

Scene V END

Scene VI

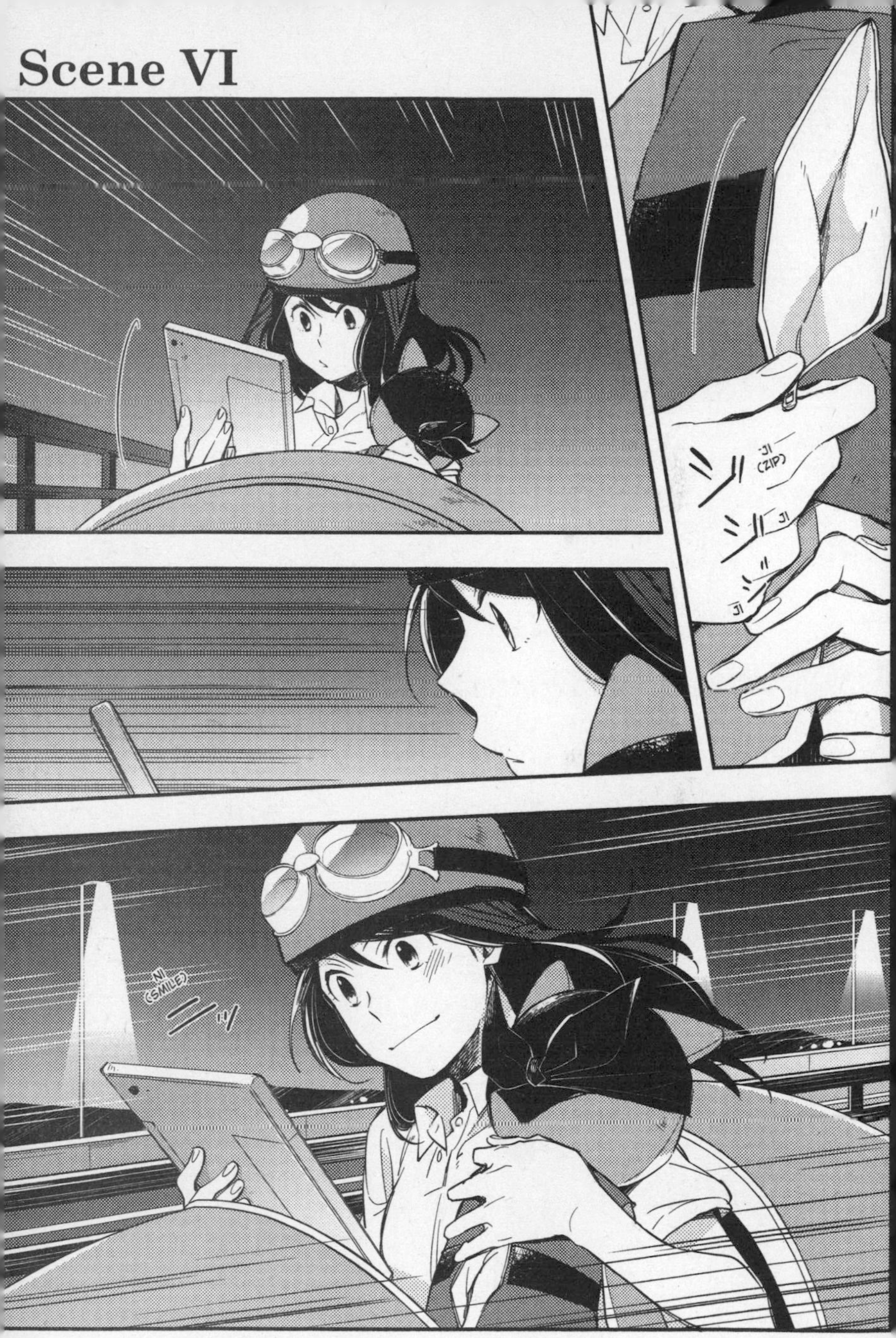
JI
(ZIP)
JI
JI
NI
(SMILE)

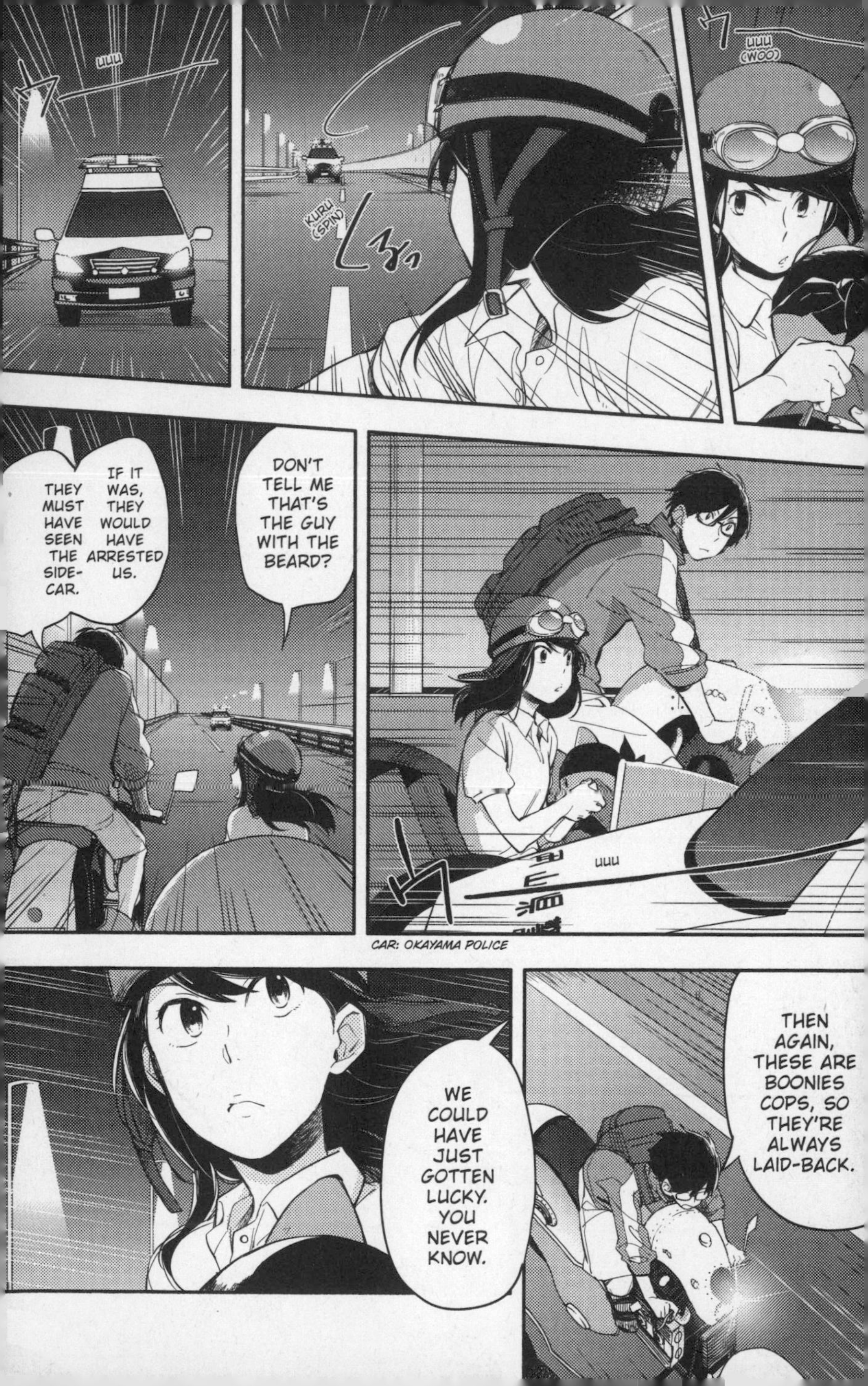
uuu (WOO)
KURU (SPIN)
uuu
uuu
CAR: OKAYAMA POLICE
DON'T TELL ME THAT'S THE GUY WITH THE BEARD?
IF IT WAS, THEY WOULD HAVE ARRESTED US.
THEY MUST HAVE SEEN THE SIDE-CAR.
THEN AGAIN, THESE ARE BOONIES COPS, SO THEY'RE ALWAYS LAID-BACK.
WE COULD HAVE JUST GOTTEN LUCKY. YOU NEVER KNOW.

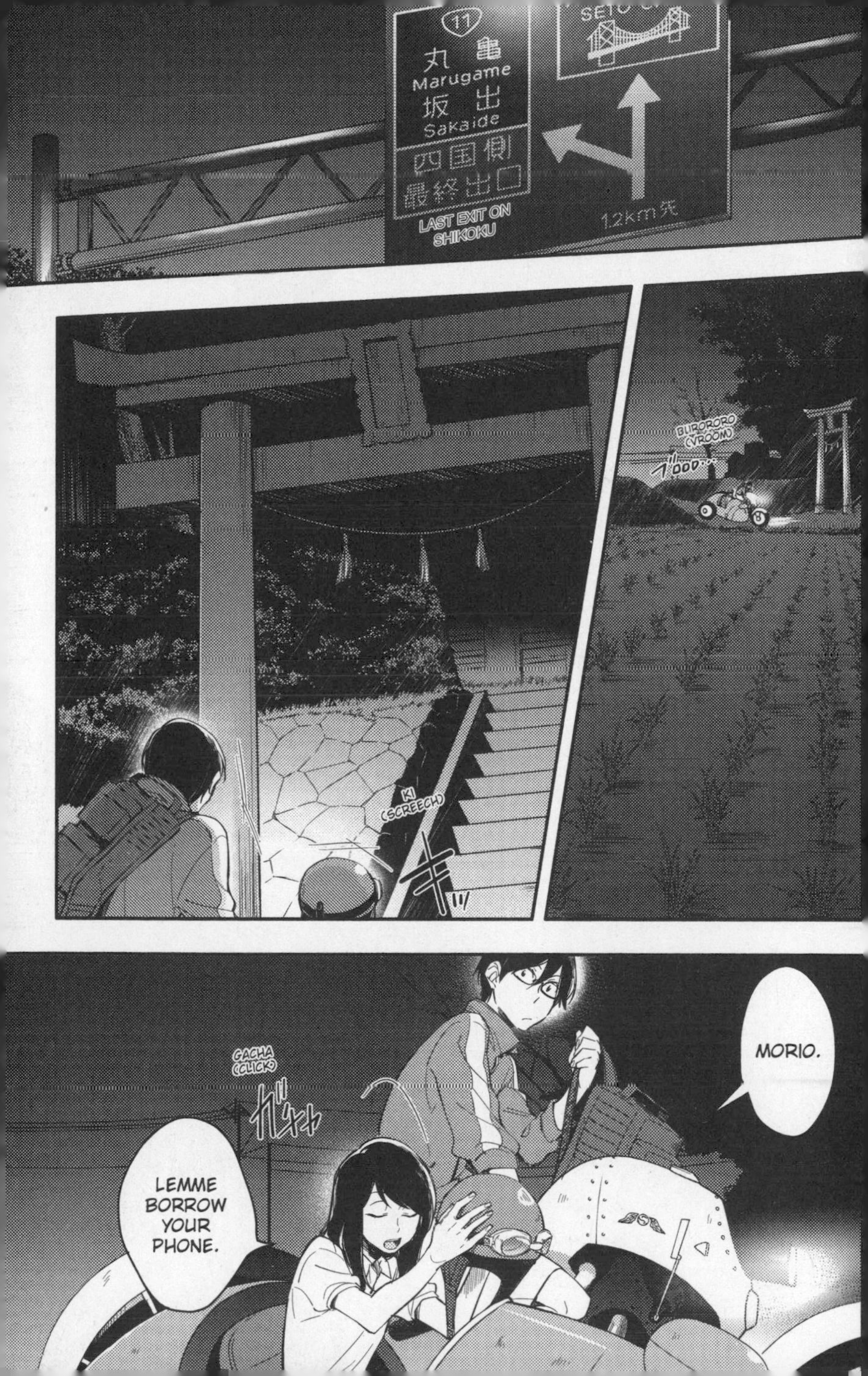
11
丸亀
Marugame
坂出
Sakaide
四国側
最終出口
LAST EXIT ON SHIKOKU
1.2km 先
BURORORO (VROOM)
KI (SCREECH)
MORIO.
GACHA (CLICK)
LEMME BORROW YOUR PHONE.

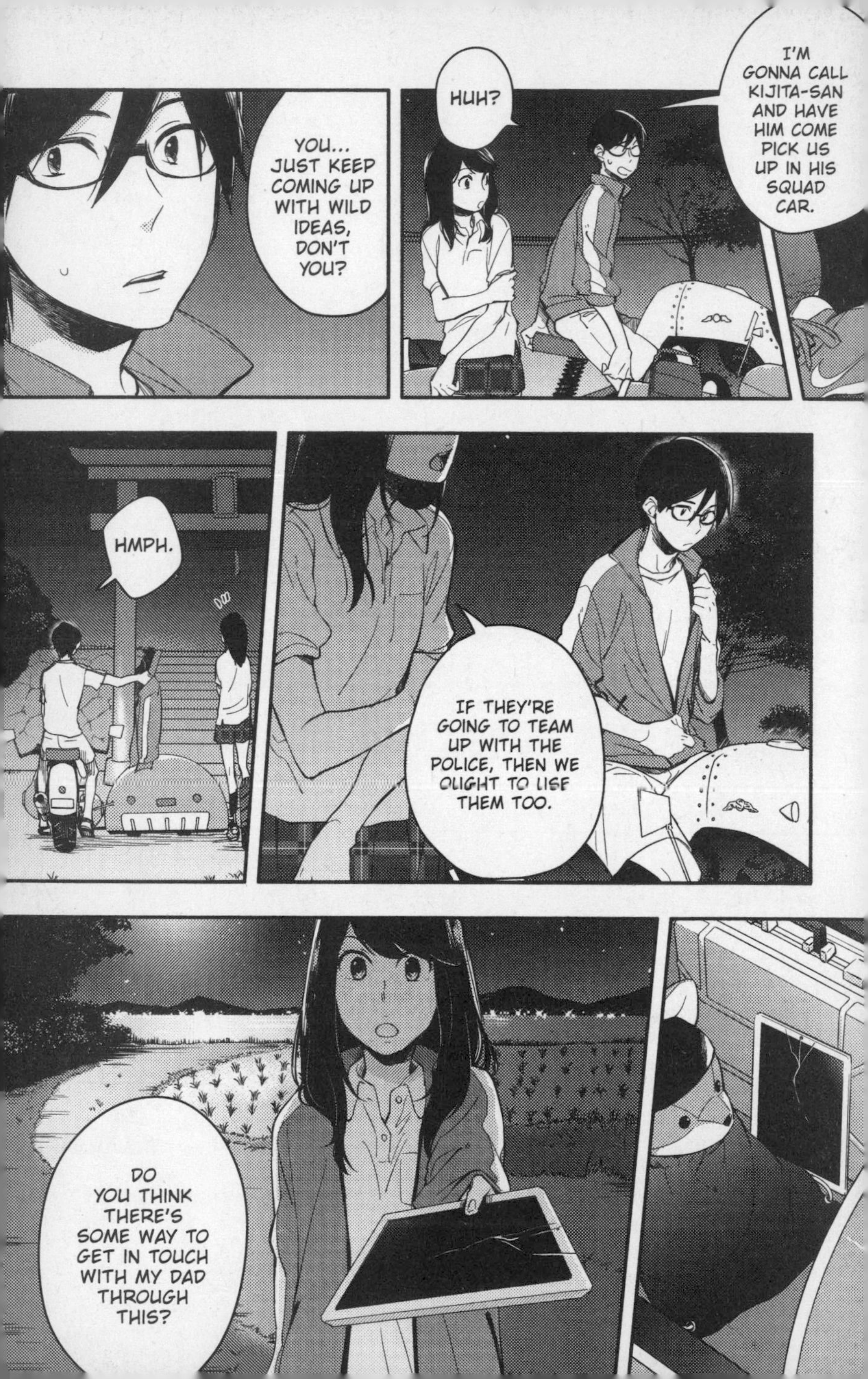
I'M GONNA CALL KIJITA-SAN AND HAVE HIM COME PICK US UP IN HIS SQUAD CAR.
HUH?
YOU... JUST KEEP COMING UP WITH WILD IDEAS, DON'T YOU?
IF THEY'RE GOING TO TEAM UP WITH THE POLICE, THEN WE OUGHT TO USE THEM TOO.
HMPH.
DO YOU THINK THERE'S SOME WAY TO GET IN TOUCH WITH MY DAD THROUGH THIS?

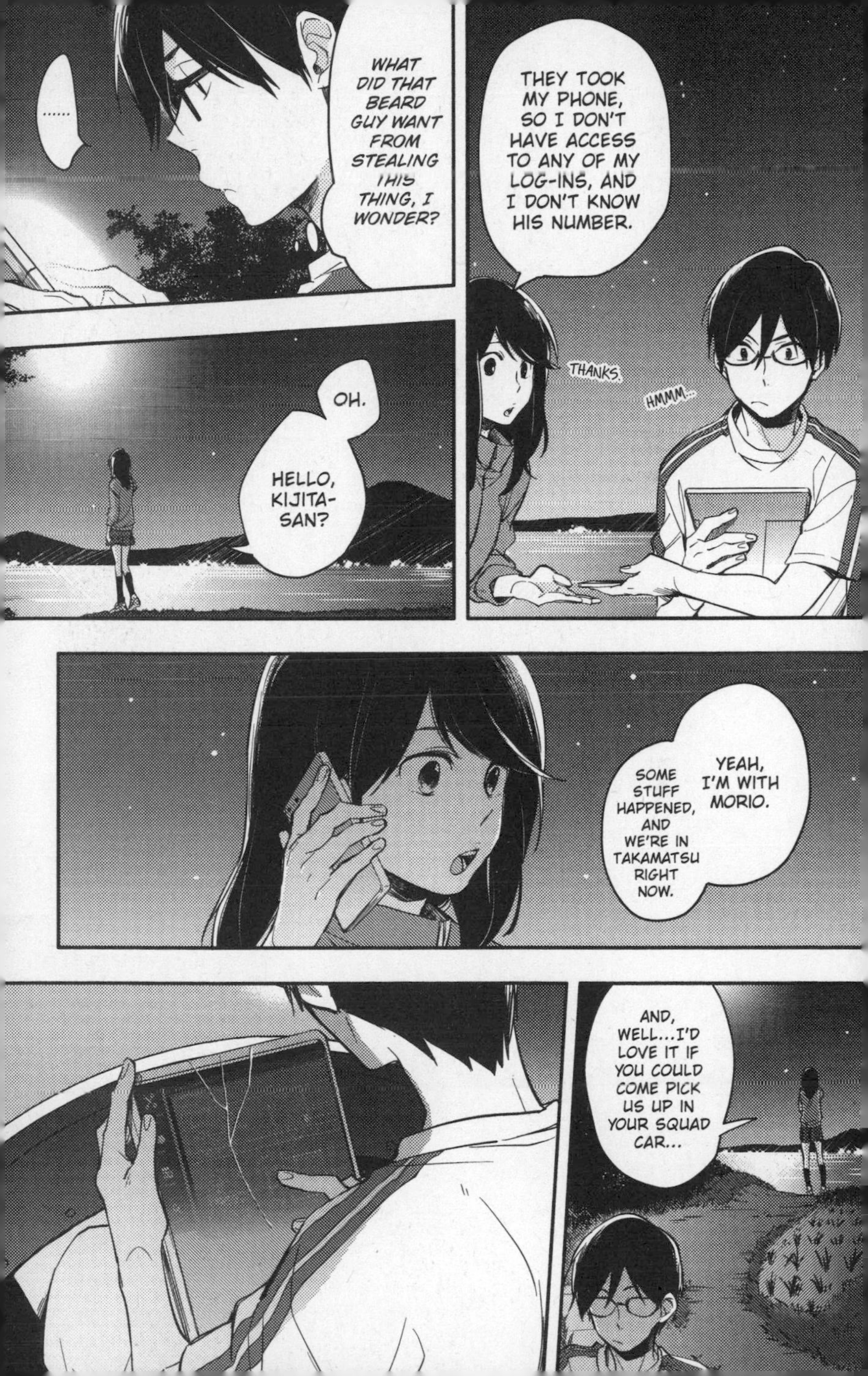
THEY TOOK MY PHONE, SO I DON'T HAVE ACCESS TO ANY OF MY LOG-INS, AND I DON'T KNOW HIS NUMBER.
THANKS.
HMMM...
WHAT DID THAT BEARD GUY WANT FROM STEALING THIS THING, I WONDER?
......
OH.
HELLO, KIJITA-SAN?
YEAH, I'M WITH MORIO.
SOME STUFF HAPPENED, AND WE'RE IN TAKAMATSU RIGHT NOW.
AND, WELL...I'D LOVE IT IF YOU COULD COME PICK US UP IN YOUR SQUAD CAR...

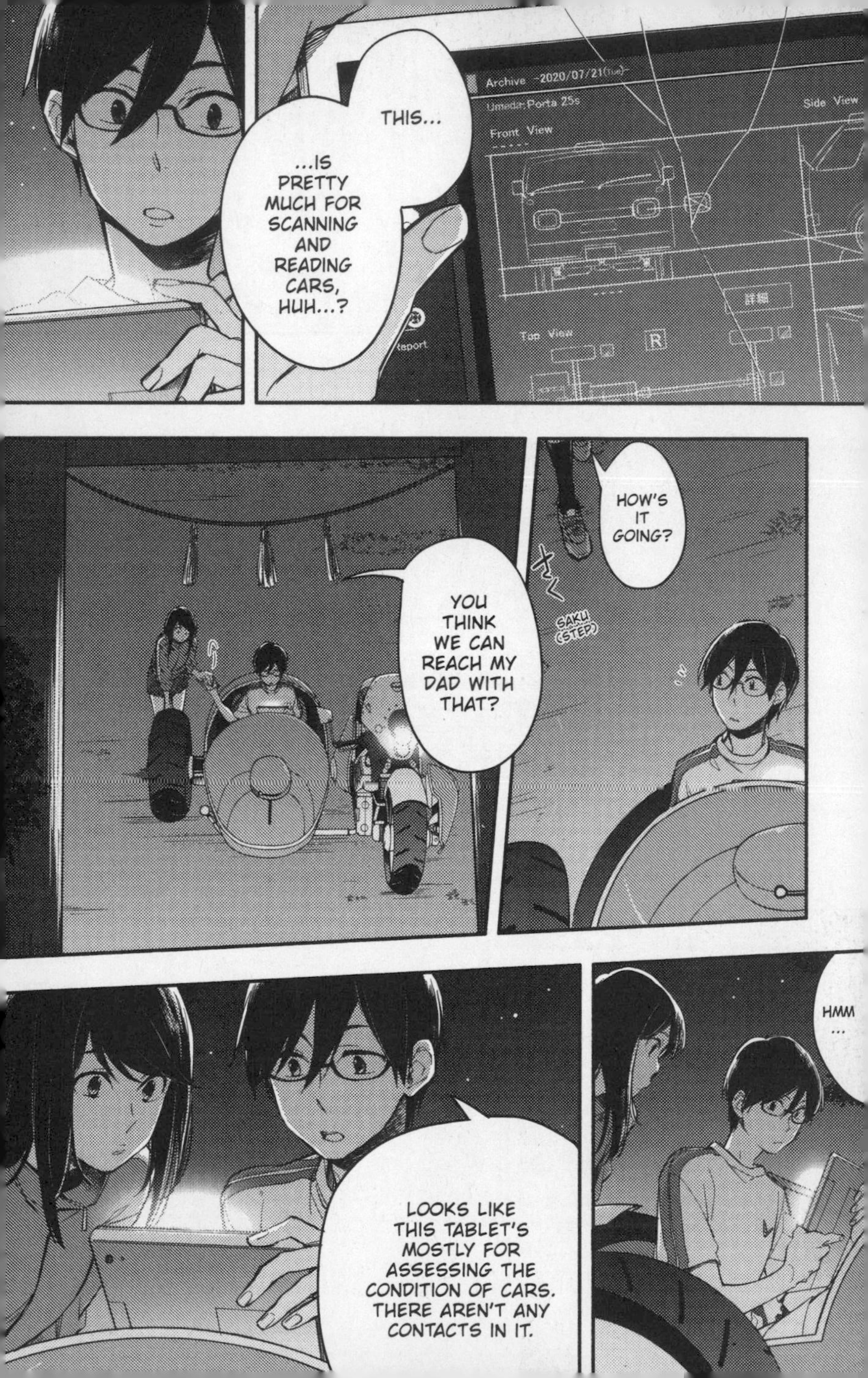
Archive -2020/07/21(Tue)-
Umeda:Porta 25s
Side View
Front View
詳細
Top View
R
Report
THIS...
...IS PRETTY MUCH FOR SCANNING AND READING CARS, HUH...?
HOW'S IT GOING?
SAKU (STEP)
YOU THINK WE CAN REACH MY DAD WITH THAT?
HMM...
LOOKS LIKE THIS TABLET'S MOSTLY FOR ASSESSING THE CONDITION OF CARS. THERE AREN'T ANY CONTACTS IN IT.

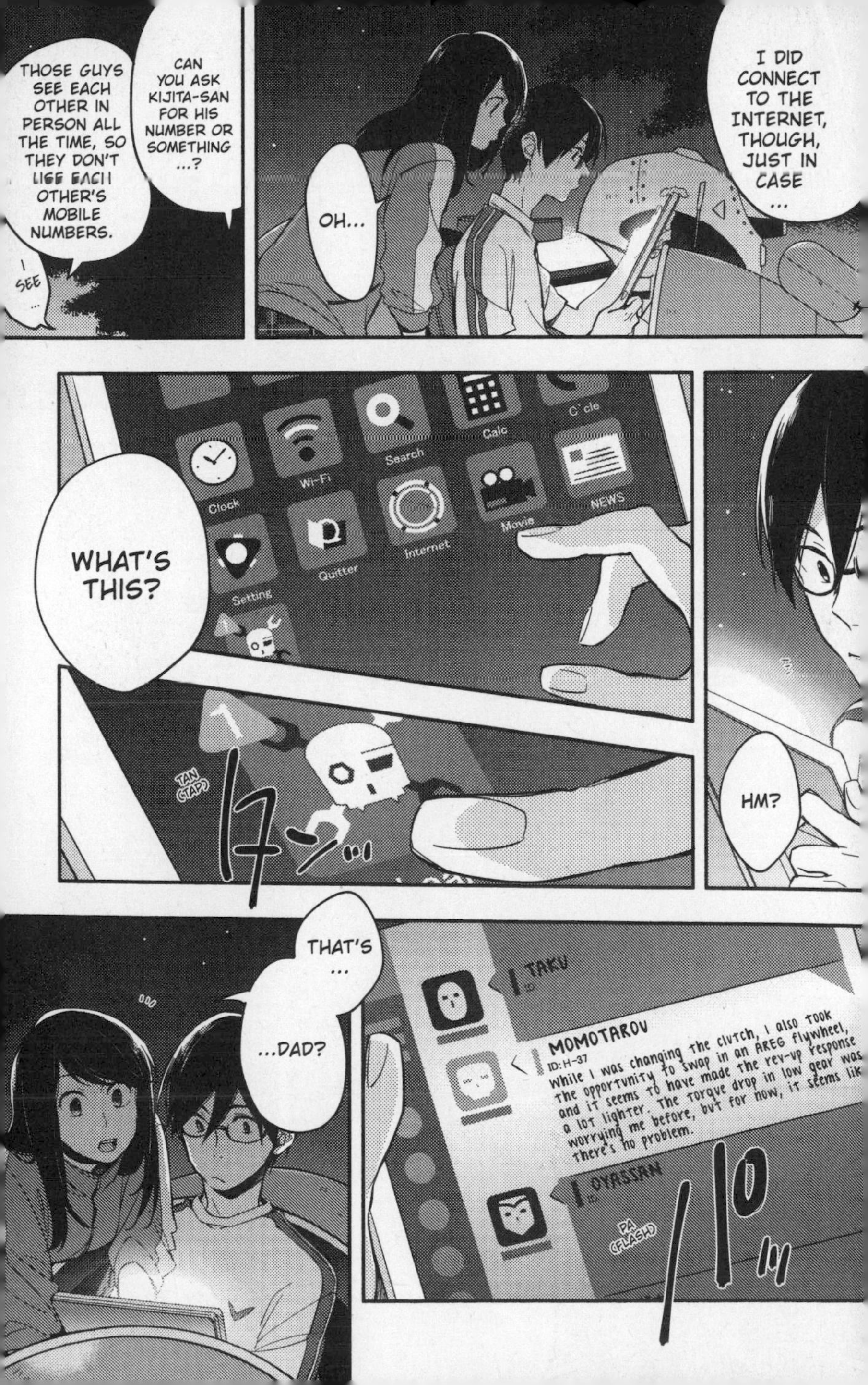
I DID CONNECT TO THE INTERNET, THOUGH, JUST IN CASE ...
OH...
CAN YOU ASK KIJITA-SAN FOR HIS NUMBER OR SOMETHING ...?
THOSE GUYS SEE EACH OTHER IN PERSON ALL THE TIME, SO THEY DON'T LIGE EACH OTHER'S MOBILE NUMBERS.
I SEE ...
HM?
Calc
C`cle
Search
Wi-Fi
Clock
NEWS
Movie
Internet
Quitter
Setting
WHAT'S THIS?
TAN (TAP)
TAKU
MOMOTAROU
ID: H-37
While I was changing the clutch, I also took the opportunity to swap in an AREG flywheel, and it seems to have made the rev-up response a lot lighter. The torque drop in low gear was worrying me before, but for now, it seems lik there's no problem.
OYASSAN
PA (FLASH)
THAT'S ...
...DAD?

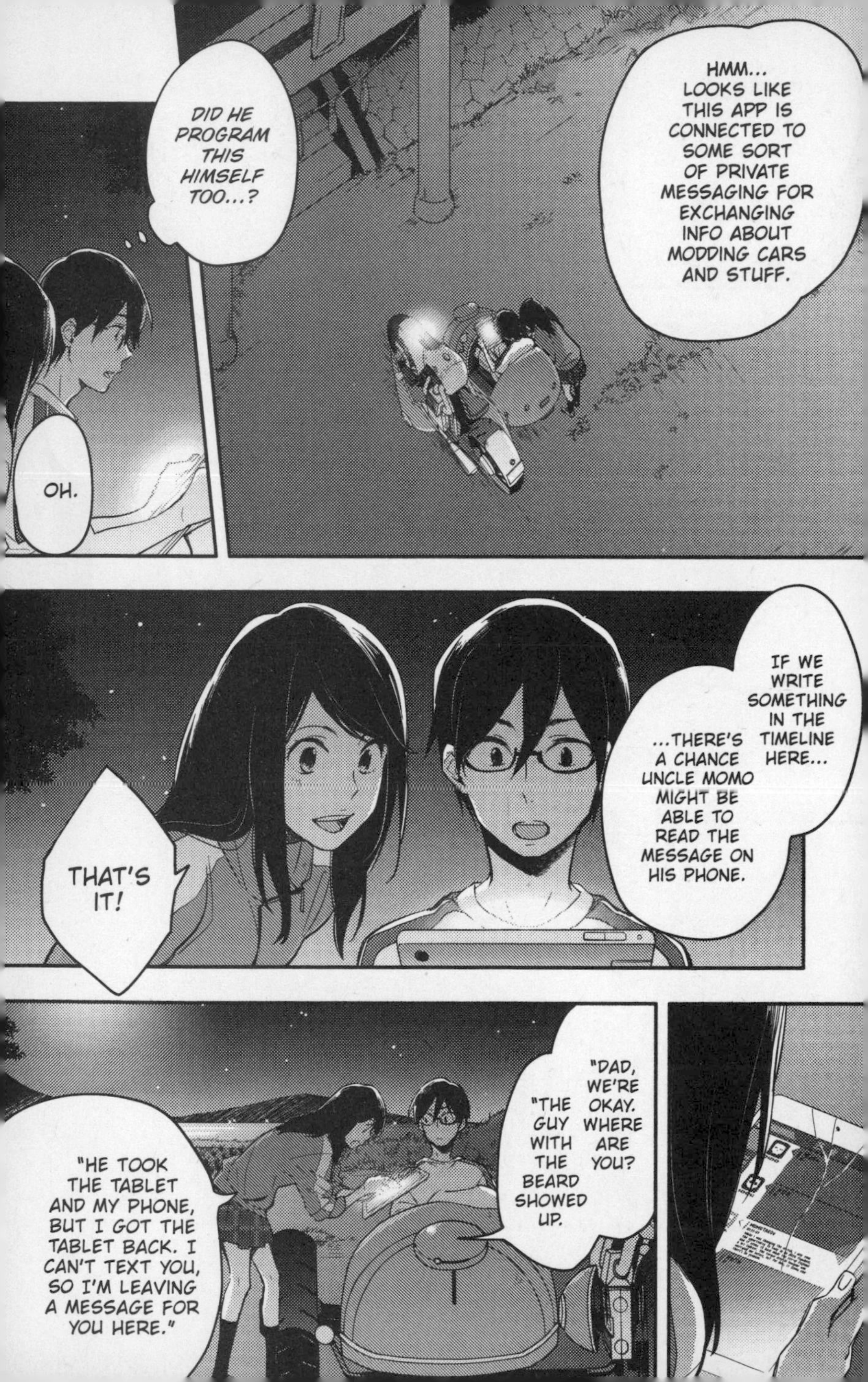
HMM... LOOKS LIKE THIS APP IS CONNECTED TO SOME SORT OF PRIVATE MESSAGING FOR EXCHANGING INFO ABOUT MODDING CARS AND STUFF.
DID HE PROGRAM THIS HIMSELF TOO...?
OH.
IF WE WRITE SOMETHING IN THE TIMELINE HERE...
...THERE'S A CHANCE UNCLE MOMO MIGHT BE ABLE TO READ THE MESSAGE ON HIS PHONE.
THAT'S IT!
"DAD, WE'RE OKAY. WHERE ARE YOU?
"THE GUY WITH THE BEARD SHOWED UP.
"HE TOOK THE TABLET AND MY PHONE, BUT I GOT THE TABLET BACK. I CAN'T TEXT YOU, SO I'M LEAVING A MESSAGE FOR YOU HERE."

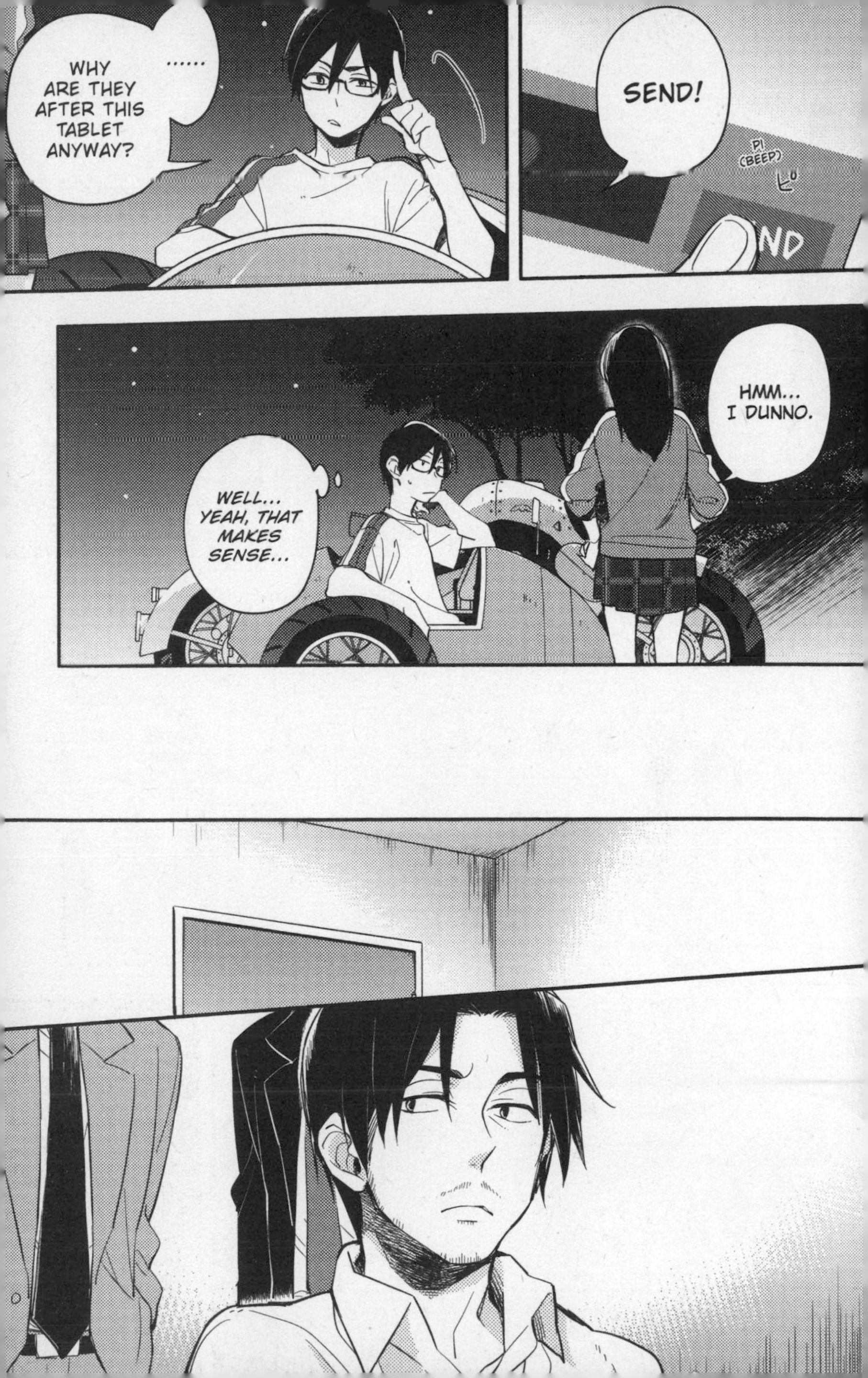
SEND!
PI (BEEP)
ピ
......
WHY ARE THEY AFTER THIS TABLET ANYWAY?
HMM... I DUNNO.
WELL... YEAH, THAT MAKES SENSE...

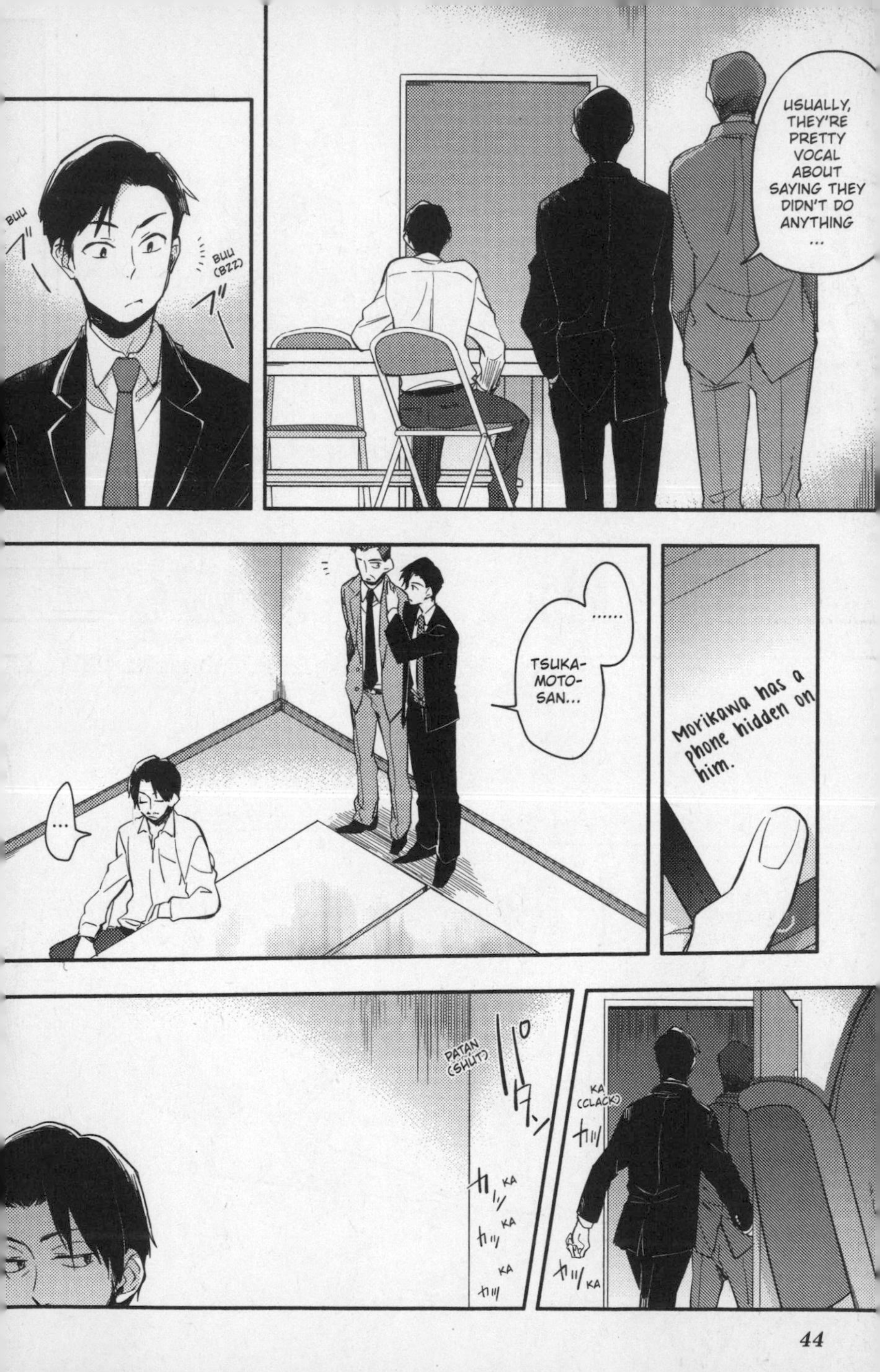
USUALLY, THEY'RE PRETTY VOCAL ABOUT SAYING THEY DIDN'T DO ANYTHING ...
BUU
BUU (BZZ)
Morikawa has a phone hidden on him.
......
TSUKA-MOTO-SAN...
...
KA (CLACK)
KA
PATAN (SHUT)
KA
KA
KA

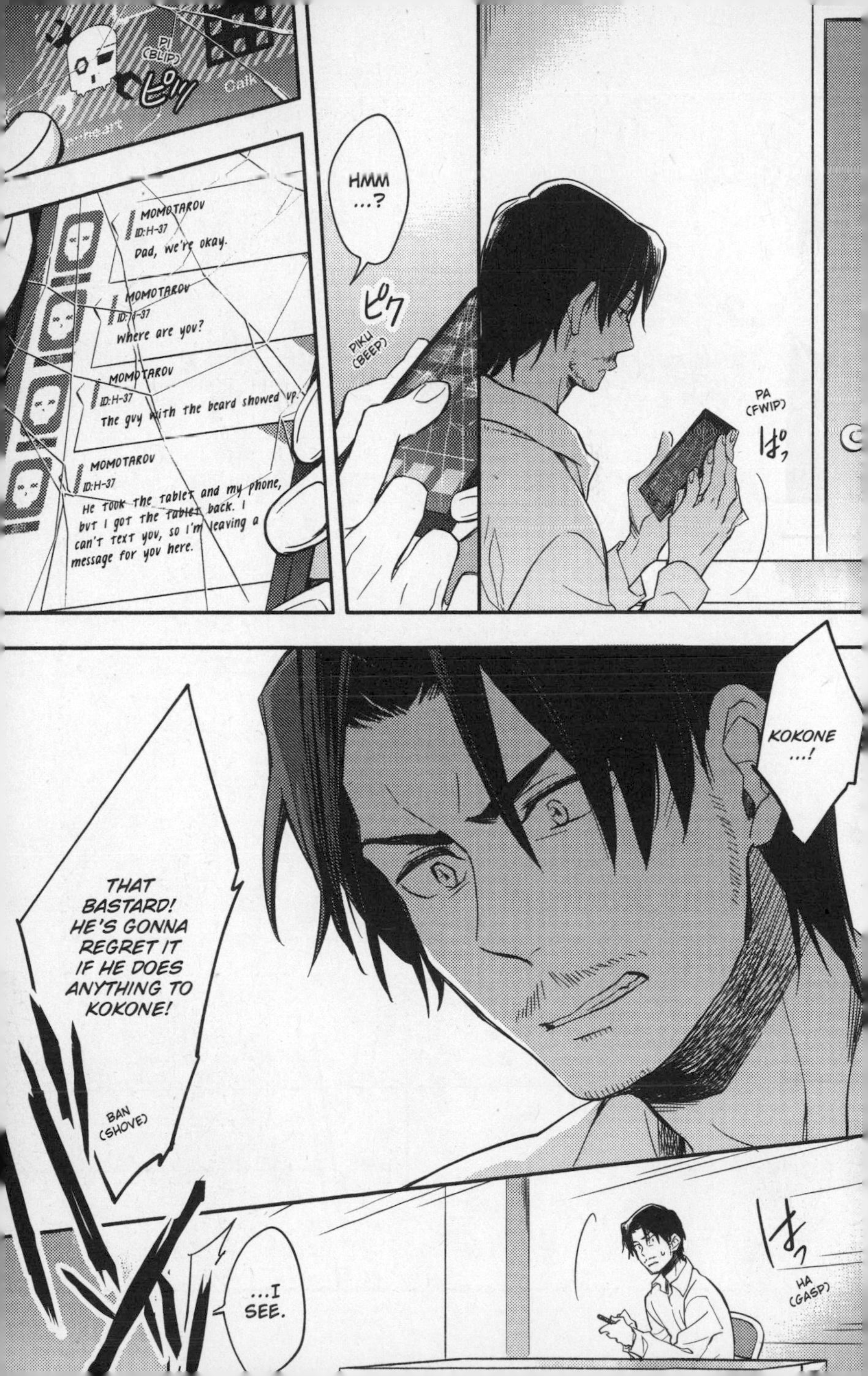
PA (FWIP)
ぱっ
HMM ...?
ピク
PIKU (BEEP)
PI (BLIP)
ピッ
Calk
MOMOTAROV
ID:H-37
Dad, we're okay.
MOMOTAROV
ID:H-37
Where are you?
MOMOTAROV
ID:H-37
The guy with the beard showed up.
MOMOTAROV
ID:H-37
He took the tablet and my phone, but I got the tablet back. I can't text you, so I'm leaving a message for you here.
KOKONE ...!
THAT BASTARD! HE'S GONNA REGRET IT IF HE DOES ANYTHING TO KOKONE!
BAN (SHOVE)
はっ
HA (GASP)
...I SEE.

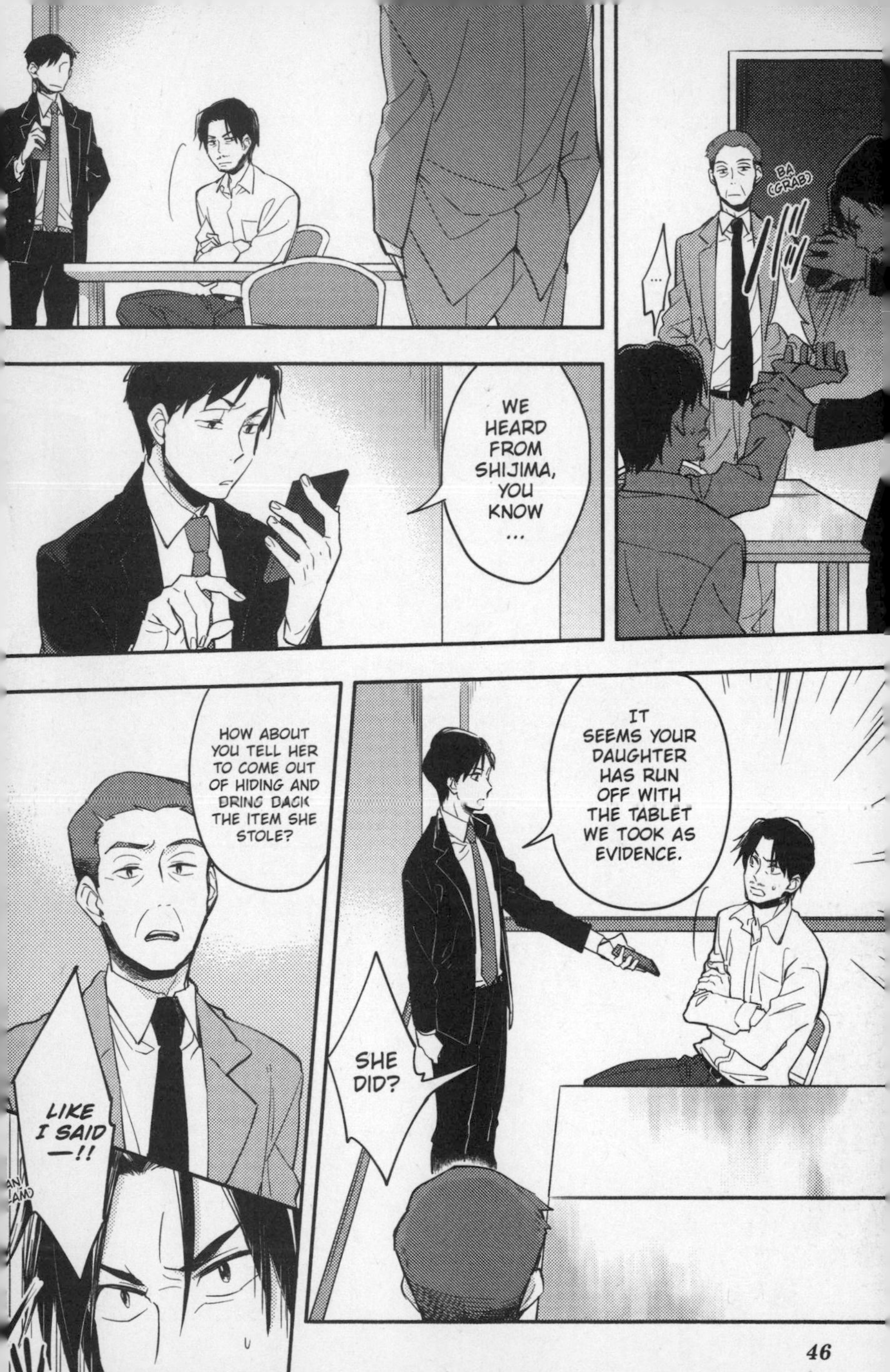
BA (GRAB)
...
WE HEARD FROM SHIJIMA, YOU KNOW...
IT SEEMS YOUR DAUGHTER HAS RUN OFF WITH THE TABLET WE TOOK AS EVIDENCE.
SHE DID?
HOW ABOUT YOU TELL HER TO COME OUT OF HIDING AND BRING BACK THE ITEM SHE STOLE?
LIKE I SAID—!!

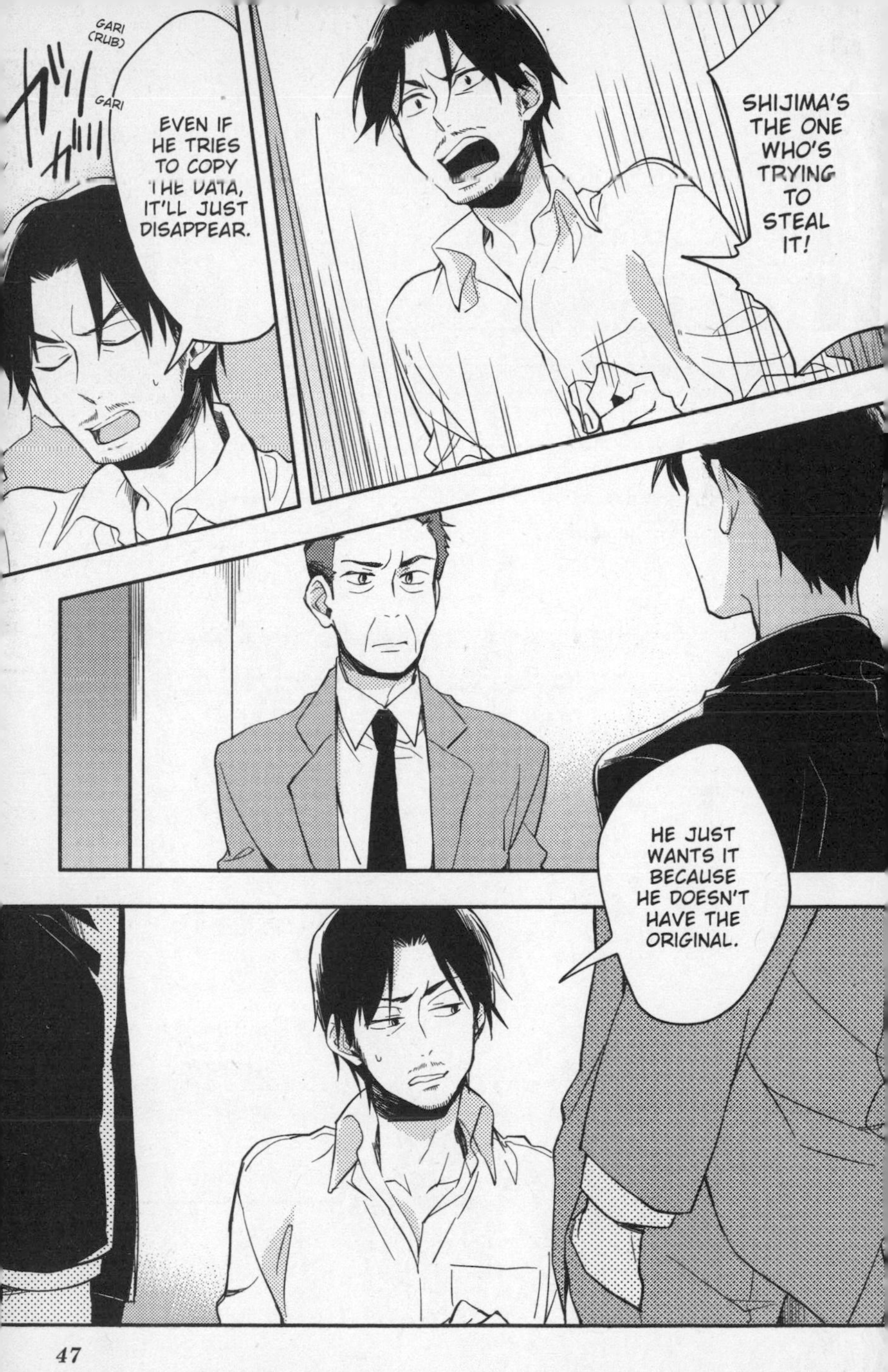
SHIJIMA'S THE ONE WHO'S TRYING TO STEAL IT!
GARI (RUB)
GARI
EVEN IF HE TRIES TO COPY THE DATA, IT'LL JUST DISAPPEAR.
HE JUST WANTS IT BECAUSE HE DOESN'T HAVE THE ORIGINAL.

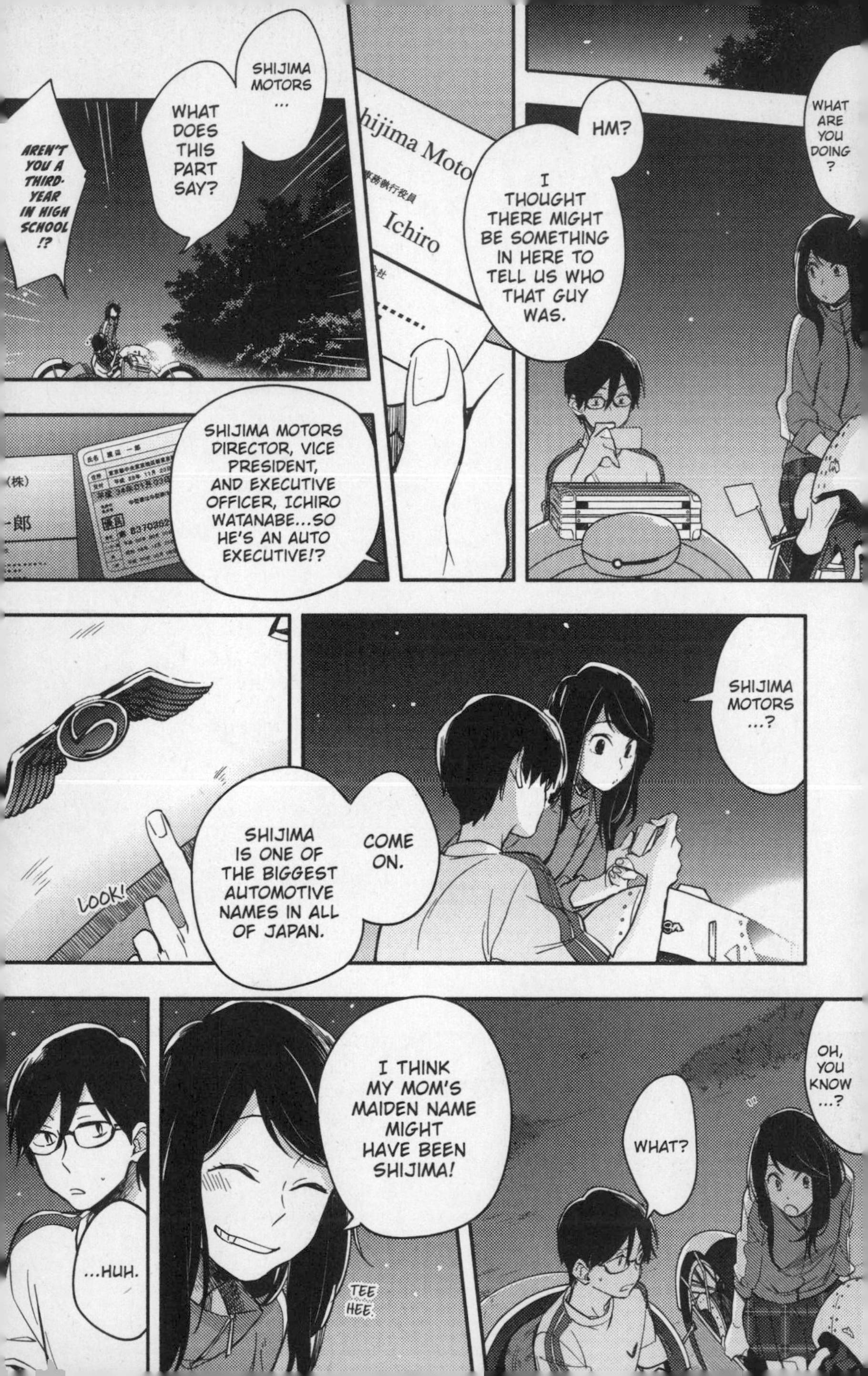

WHAT ARE YOU DOING?
HM?
I THOUGHT THERE MIGHT BE SOMETHING IN HERE TO TELL US WHO THAT GUY WAS.
hijima Moto
専務執行役員
Ichiro
SHIJIMA MOTORS...
WHAT DOES THIS PART SAY?
AREN'T YOU A THIRD-YEAR IN HIGH SCHOOL!?
SHIJIMA MOTORS DIRECTOR, VICE PRESIDENT, AND EXECUTIVE OFFICER, ICHIRO WATANABE...SO HE'S AN AUTO EXECUTIVE!?
SHIJIMA MOTORS...?
COME ON.
SHIJIMA IS ONE OF THE BIGGEST AUTOMOTIVE NAMES IN ALL OF JAPAN.
LOOK!
OH, YOU KNOW...?
WHAT?
I THINK MY MOM'S MAIDEN NAME MIGHT HAVE BEEN SHIJIMA!
TEE HEE.
...HUH.

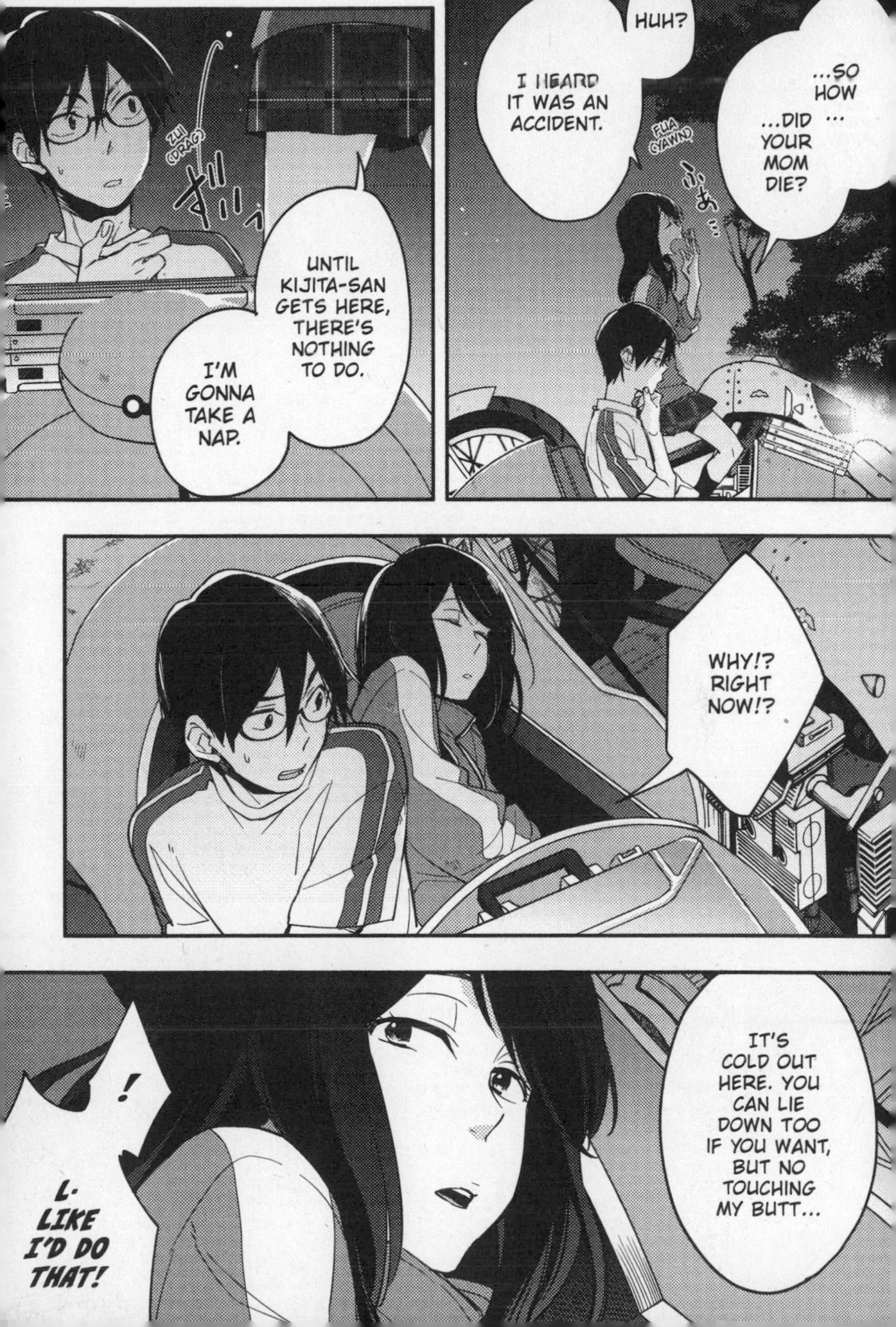
...SO HOW ...DID YOUR MOM DIE?
HUH?
I HEARD IT WAS AN ACCIDENT.
FUA (YAWN)
ふぁ…
UNTIL KIJITA-SAN GETS HERE, THERE'S NOTHING TO DO.
I'M GONNA TAKE A NAP.
ZUI (DRAG)
WHY!? RIGHT NOW!?
IT'S COLD OUT HERE. YOU CAN LIE DOWN TOO IF YOU WANT, BUT NO TOUCHING MY BUTT...
!
L-LIKE I'D DO THAT!

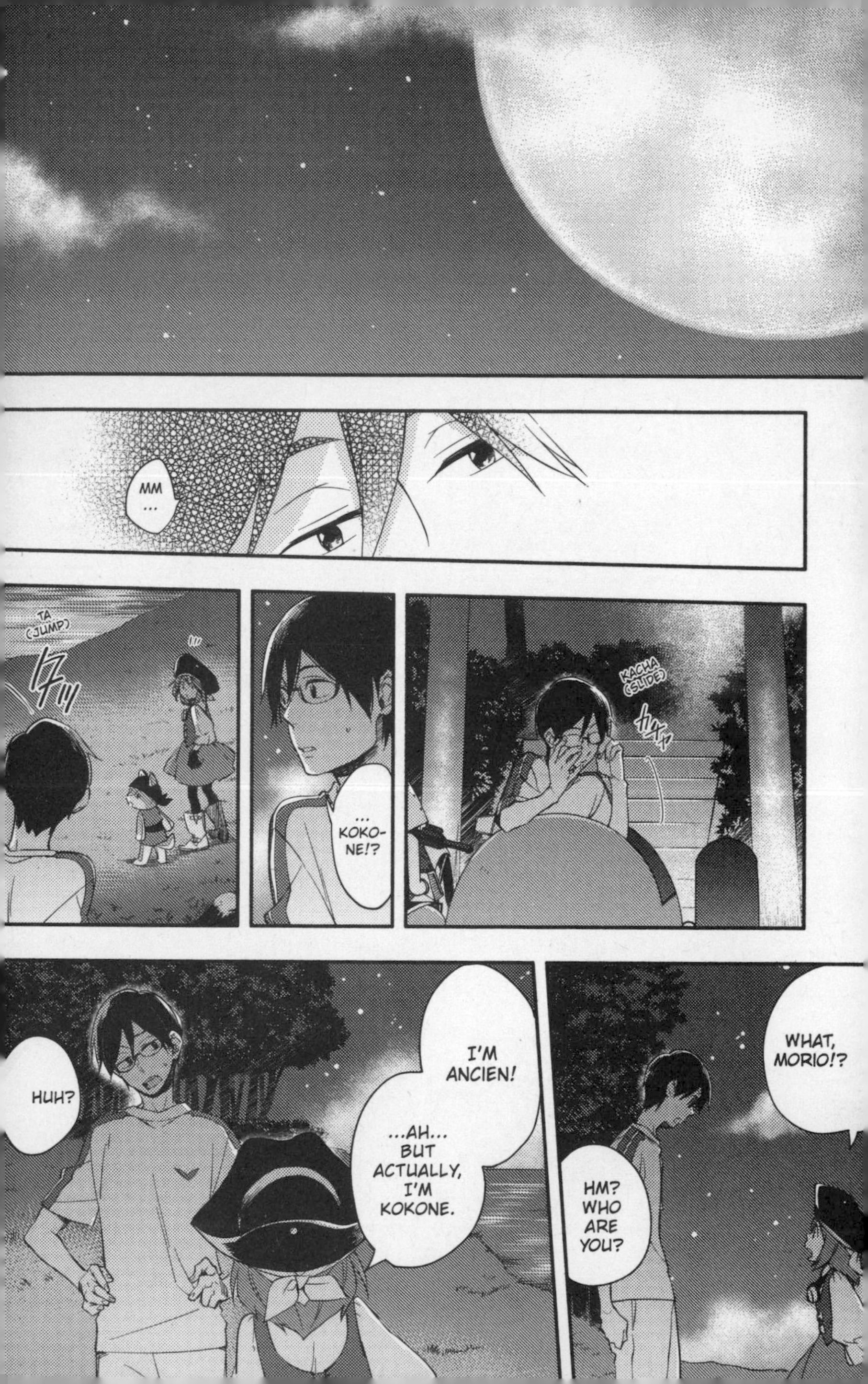
MM ...
KACHA (SLIDE)
... KOKONE!?
TA (JUMP)
WHAT, MORIO!?
HM? WHO ARE YOU?
I'M ANCIEN!
...AH... BUT ACTUALLY, I'M KOKONE.
HUH?

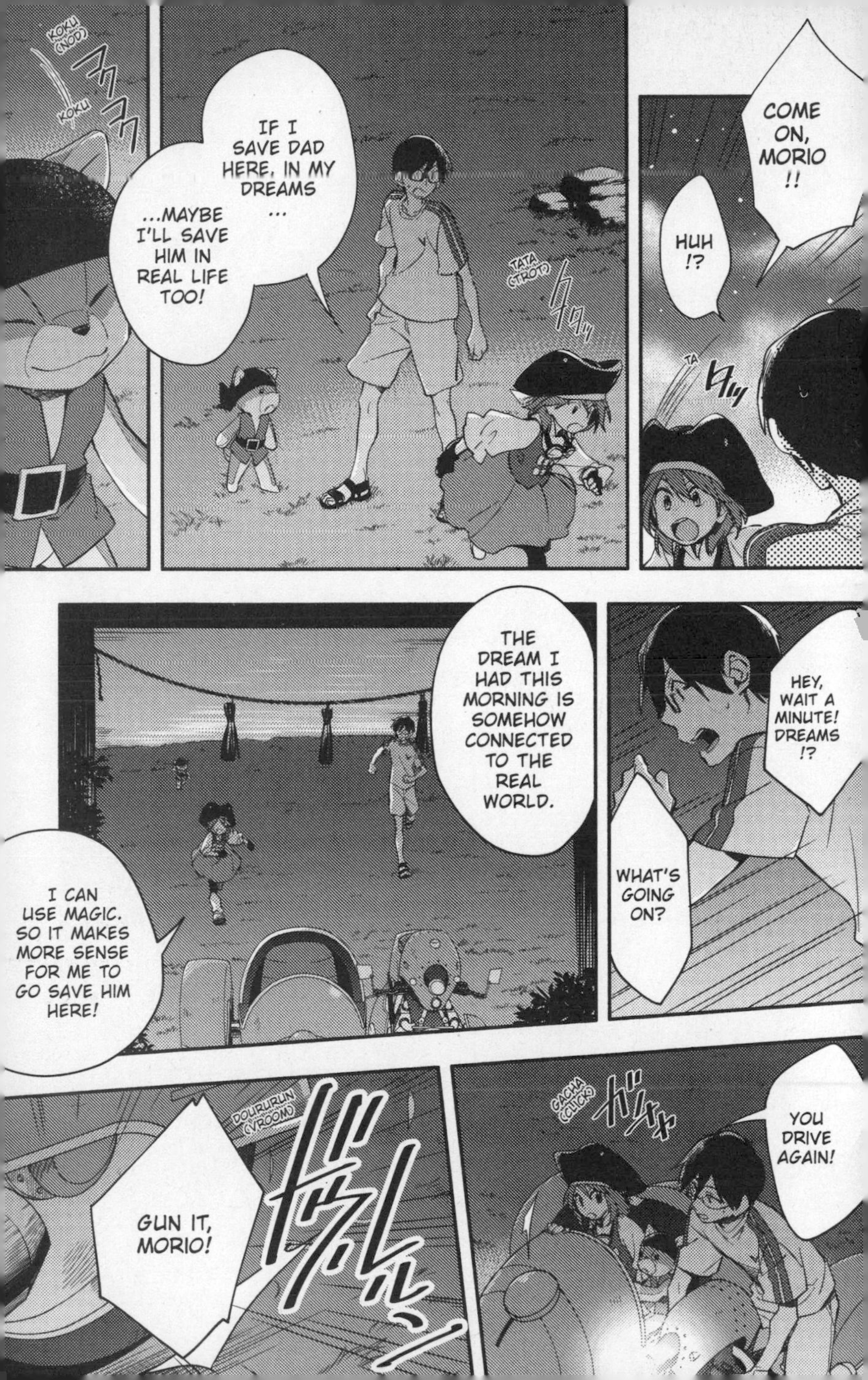
COME ON, MORIO!!
HUH!?
TA
IF I SAVE DAD HERE, IN MY DREAMS...
...MAYBE I'LL SAVE HIM IN REAL LIFE TOO!
TATA (TROT)
KOKU (NOD) KOKU
HEY, WAIT A MINUTE! DREAMS!?
WHAT'S GOING ON?
THE DREAM I HAD THIS MORNING IS SOMEHOW CONNECTED TO THE REAL WORLD.
I CAN USE MAGIC. SO IT MAKES MORE SENSE FOR ME TO GO SAVE HIM HERE!
GACHA (CLICK)
YOU DRIVE AGAIN!
DOURURUN (VROOM)
GUN IT, MORIO!

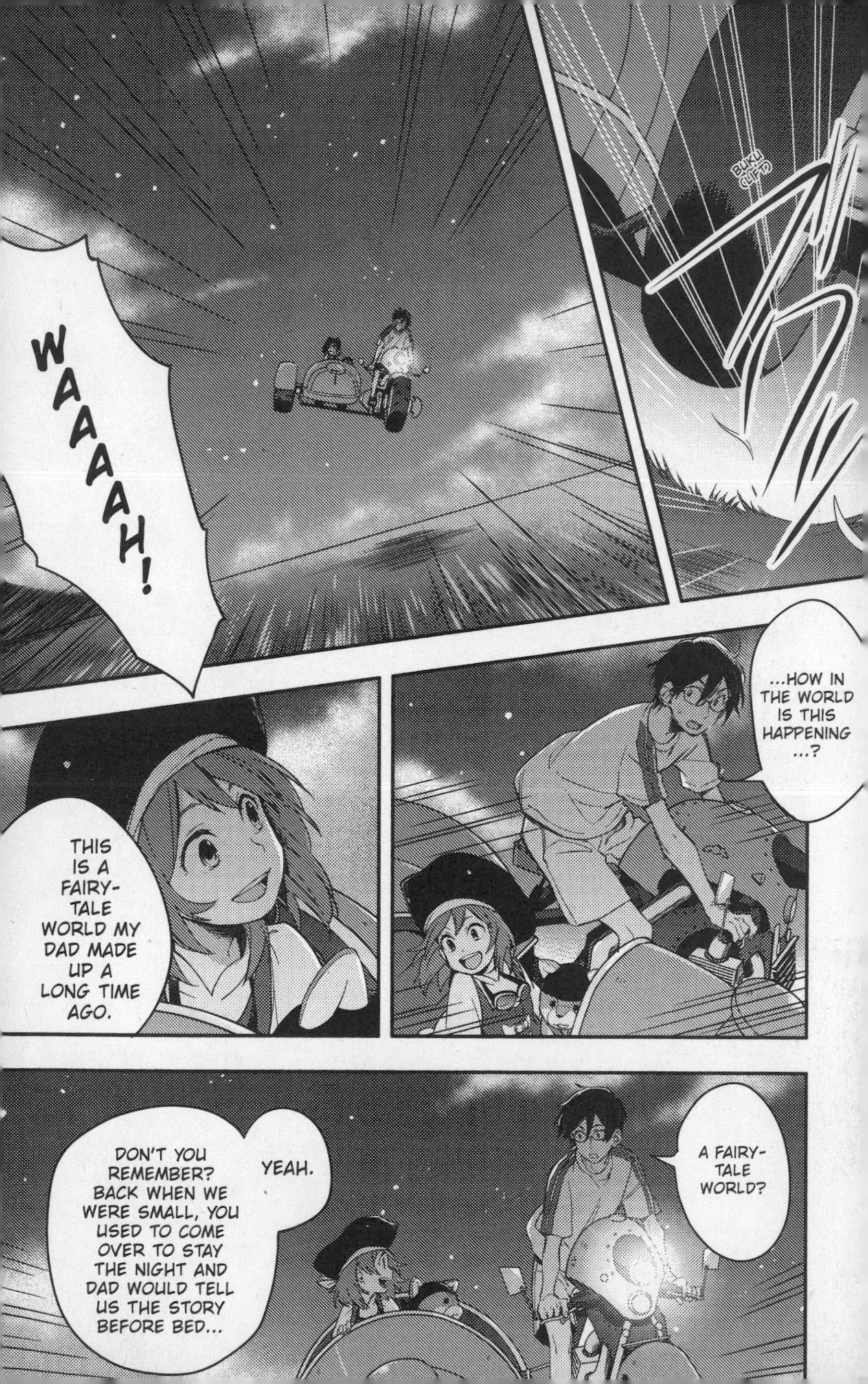
BUKU (LIFT)
WAAAAAH!
...HOW IN THE WORLD IS THIS HAPPENING ...?
THIS IS A FAIRY-TALE WORLD MY DAD MADE UP A LONG TIME AGO.
A FAIRY-TALE WORLD?
YEAH.
DON'T YOU REMEMBER? BACK WHEN WE WERE SMALL, YOU USED TO COME OVER TO STAY THE NIGHT AND DAD WOULD TELL US THE STORY BEFORE BED...

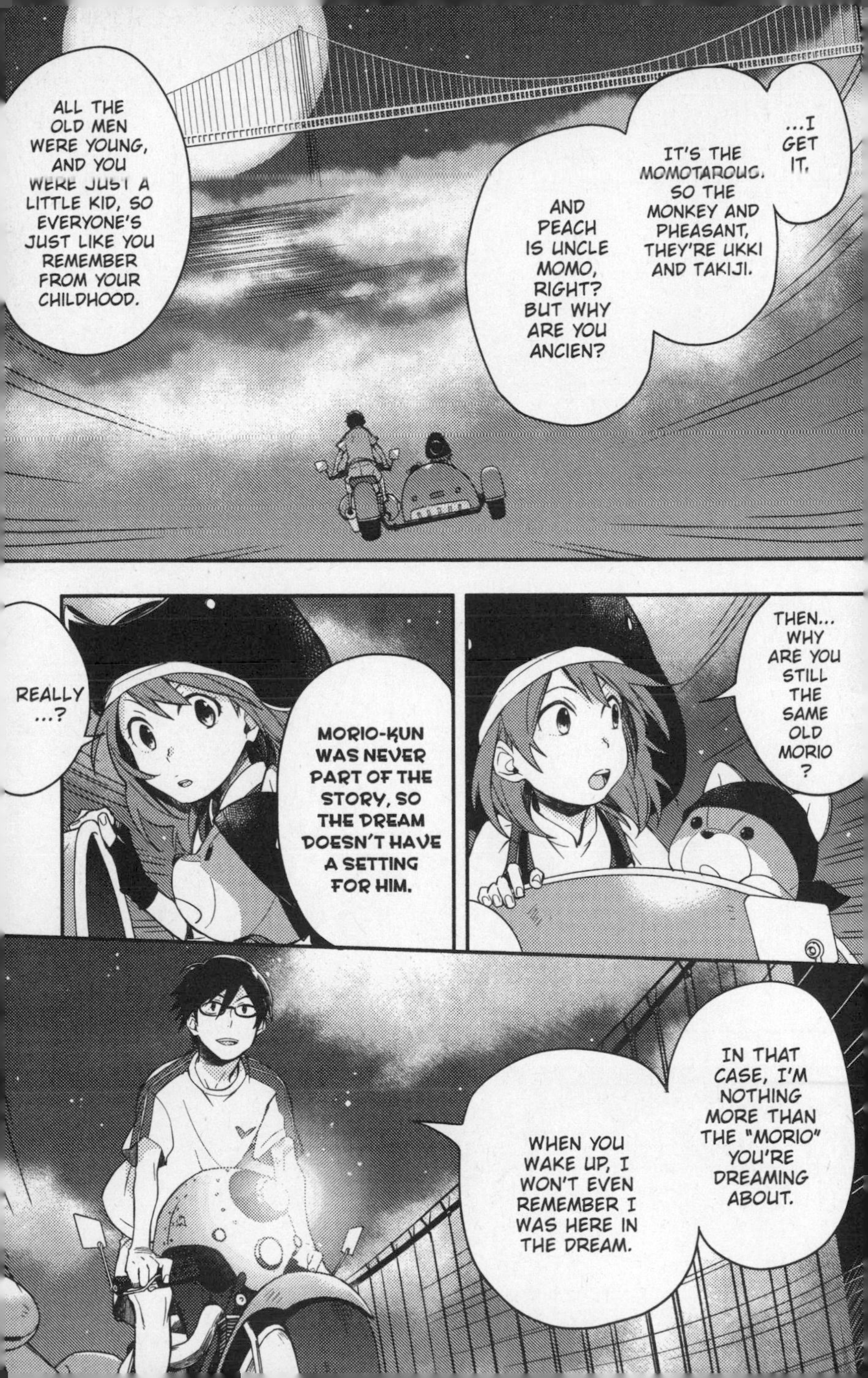

...I GET IT.
IT'S THE MOMOTAROUS. SO THE MONKEY AND PHEASANT, THEY'RE UKKI AND TAKIJI.
AND PEACH IS UNCLE MOMO, RIGHT? BUT WHY ARE YOU ANCIEN?
ALL THE OLD MEN WERE YOUNG, AND YOU WERE JUST A LITTLE KID, SO EVERYONE'S JUST LIKE YOU REMEMBER FROM YOUR CHILDHOOD.
THEN... WHY ARE YOU STILL THE SAME OLD MORIO?
MORIO-KUN WAS NEVER PART OF THE STORY, SO THE DREAM DOESN'T HAVE A SETTING FOR HIM.
REALLY...?
IN THAT CASE, I'M NOTHING MORE THAN THE "MORIO" YOU'RE DREAMING ABOUT.
WHEN YOU WAKE UP, I WON'T EVEN REMEMBER I WAS HERE IN THE DREAM.

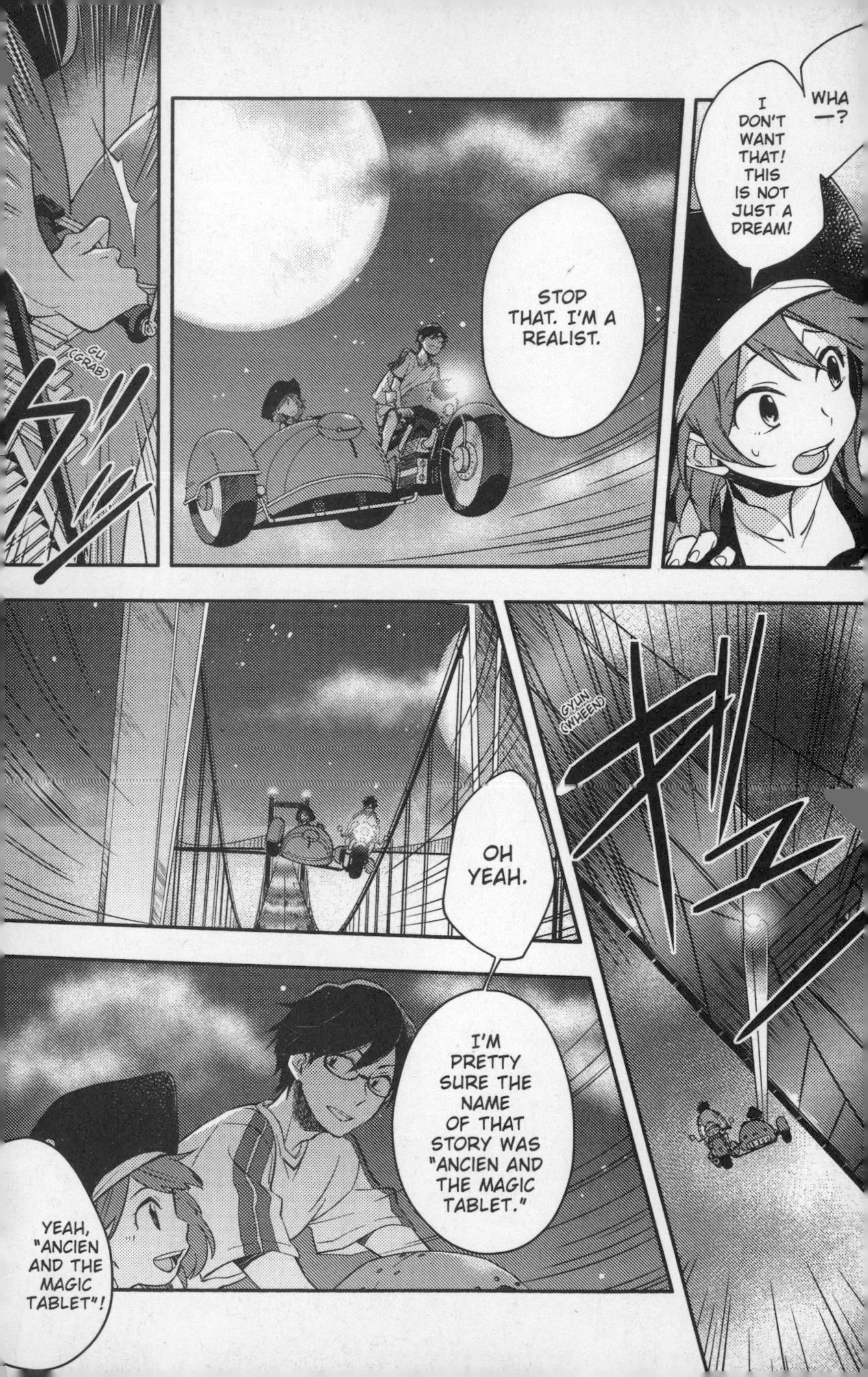
WHA—?
I DON'T WANT THAT! THIS IS NOT JUST A DREAM!
STOP THAT. I'M A REALIST.
GU (GRAB)
GYUN (WHEEN)
OH YEAH.
I'M PRETTY SURE THE NAME OF THAT STORY WAS "ANCIEN AND THE MAGIC TABLET."
YEAH, "ANCIEN AND THE MAGIC TABLET"!

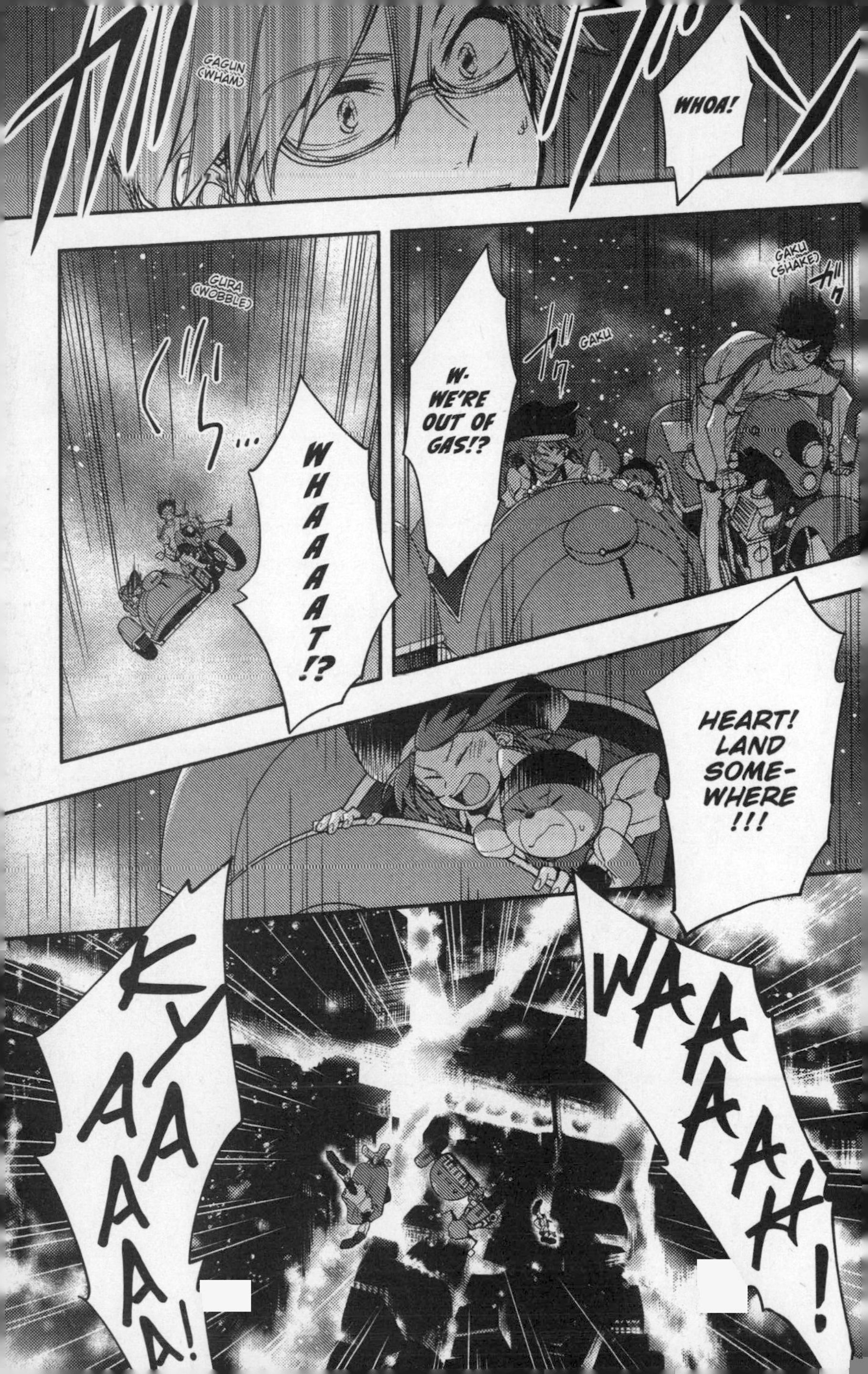
WHOA!
GAGUN (WHAM)
GAKU (SHAKE)
GAKU
W-WE'RE OUT OF GAS!?
GURA (WOBBLE)
...
WHAAAAAT!?
HEART! LAND SOMEWHERE!!!
WAAAAAH!
KYAAAAA!

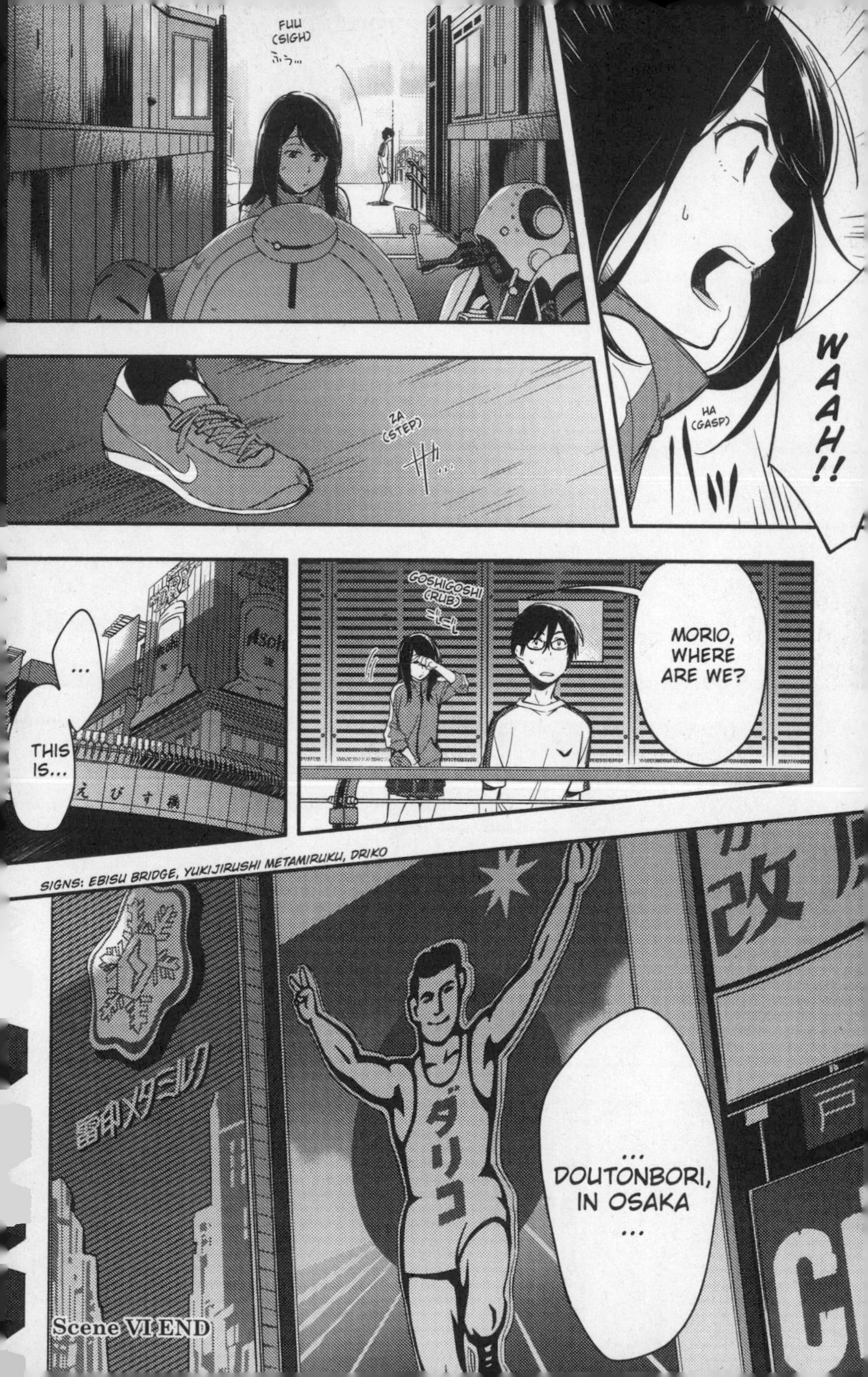
HA (GASP)
WAAAH!!
FUU (SIGH)
ふう…
ZA (STEP)
ザ…
GOSHIGOSHI (RUB)
ごしごし
MORIO, WHERE ARE WE?
…
THIS IS…
えびす橋
SIGNS: EBISU BRIDGE, YUKIJIRUSHI METAMIRUKU, DRIKO
雪印メタミルク
ダリコ
改
… DOUTONBORI, IN OSAKA …
Scene VI END

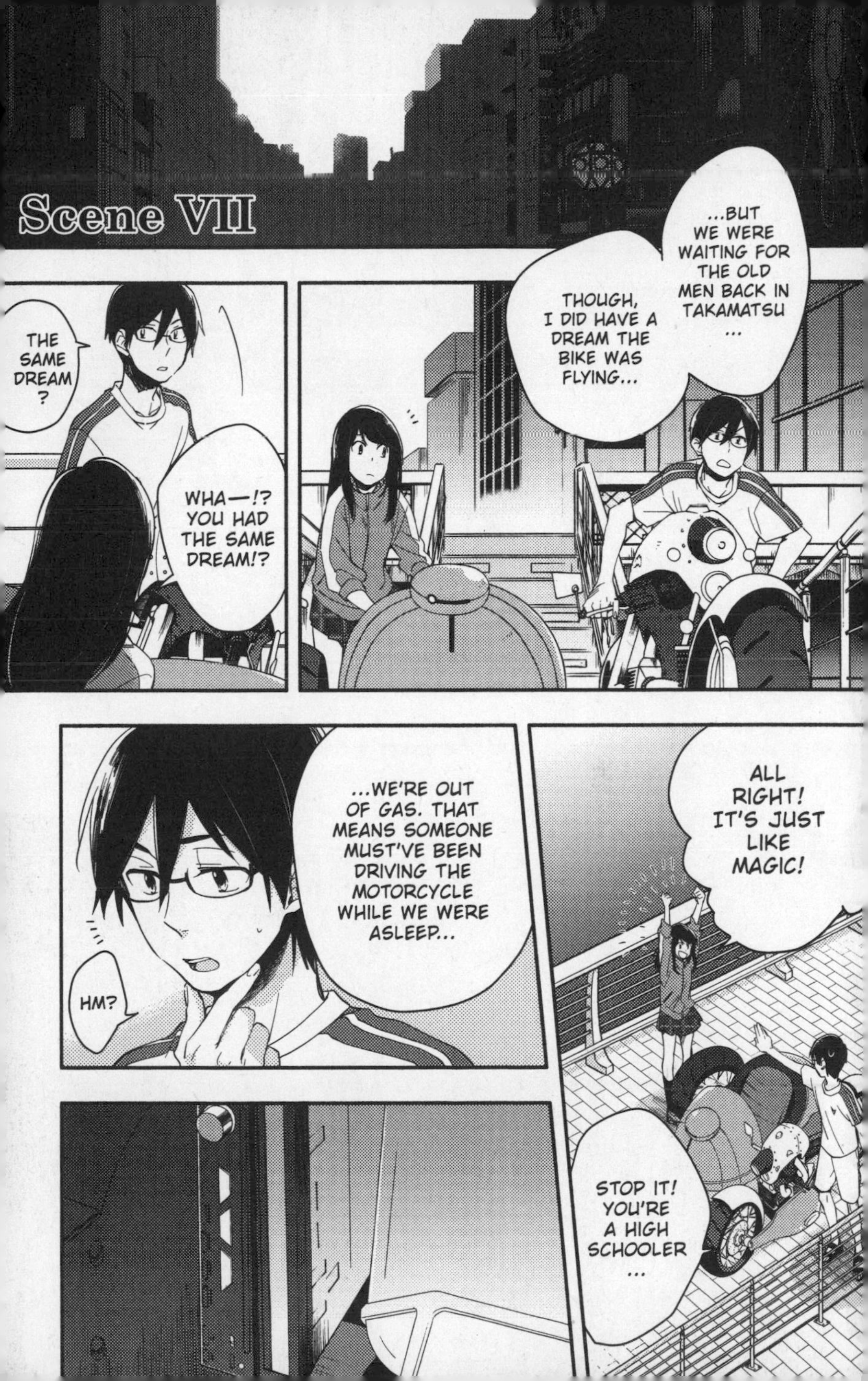
Scene VII
...BUT WE WERE WAITING FOR THE OLD MEN BACK IN TAKAMATSU ...
THOUGH, I DID HAVE A DREAM THE BIKE WAS FLYING...
WHA—!? YOU HAD THE SAME DREAM!?
THE SAME DREAM ?
ALL RIGHT! IT'S JUST LIKE MAGIC!
STOP IT! YOU'RE A HIGH SCHOOLER ...
...WE'RE OUT OF GAS. THAT MEANS SOMEONE MUST'VE BEEN DRIVING THE MOTORCYCLE WHILE WE WERE ASLEEP...
HM?

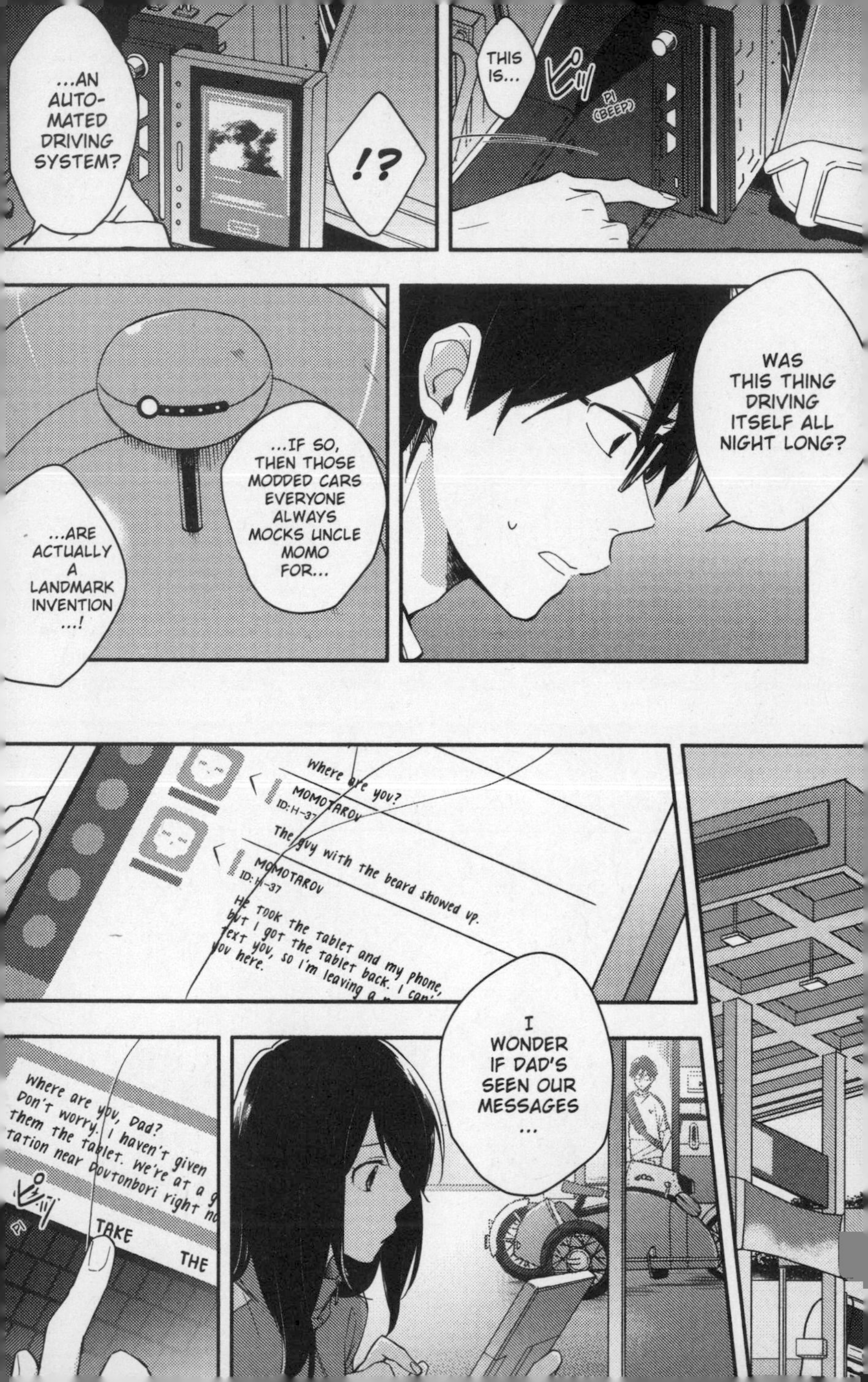
THIS IS...
ピッ
PI (BEEP)
!?
...AN AUTOMATED DRIVING SYSTEM?
WAS THIS THING DRIVING ITSELF ALL NIGHT LONG?
...IF SO, THEN THOSE MODDED CARS EVERYONE ALWAYS MOCKS UNCLE MOMO FOR...
...ARE ACTUALLY A LANDMARK INVENTION...!
I WONDER IF DAD'S SEEN OUR MESSAGES...
Where are you?
MOMOTAROV
ID: H-37
The guy with the beard showed up.
MOMOTAROV
ID: H-37
He took the tablet and my phone, but I got the tablet back. I can't text you, so I'm leaving a
you here.
Where are you, Dad? Don't worry. I haven't given them the tablet. We're at a g
tation near Dotonbori right n
ピッ
PI
TAKE
THE

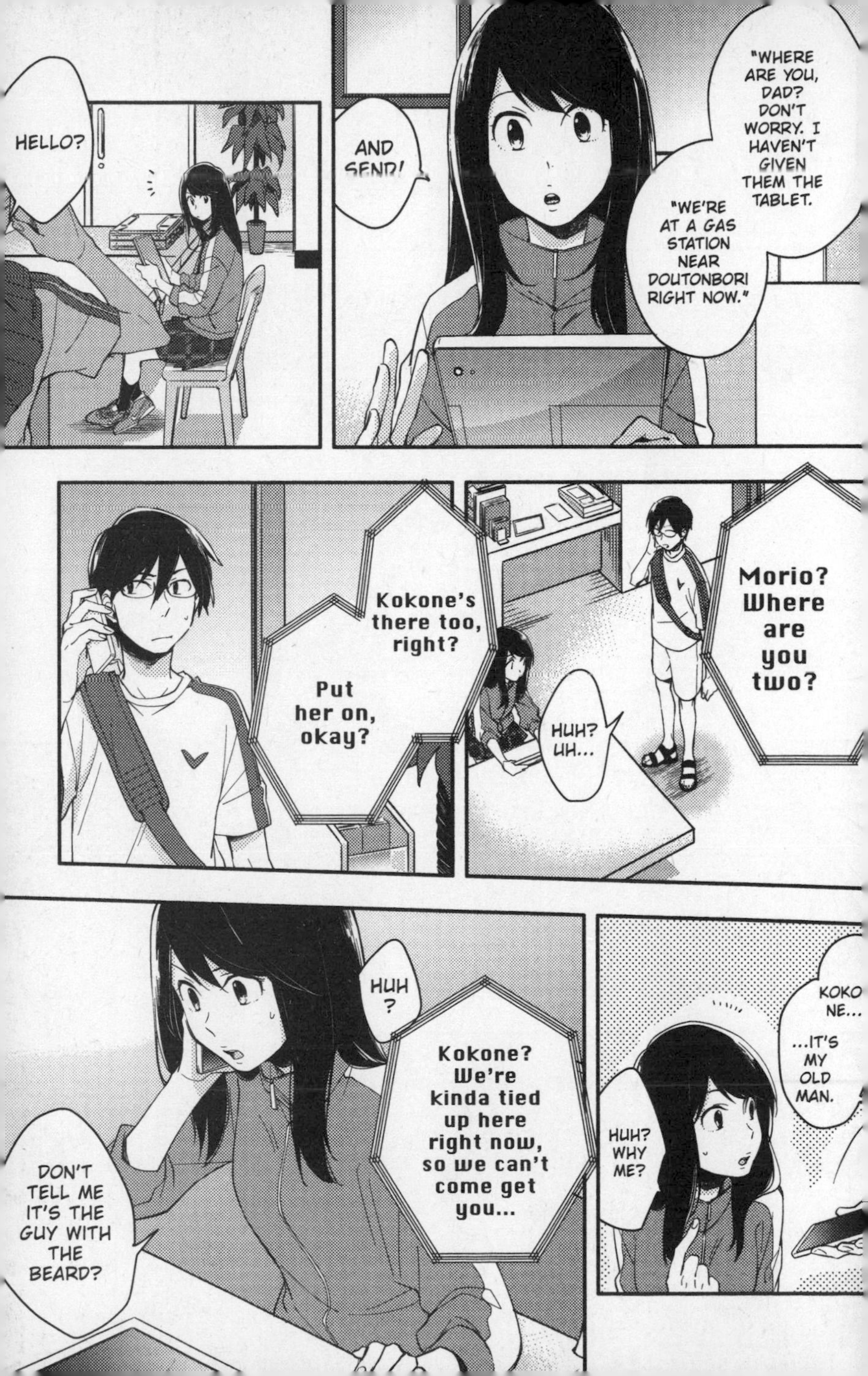
"WHERE ARE YOU, DAD? DON'T WORRY. I HAVEN'T GIVEN THEM THE TABLET.
"WE'RE AT A GAS STATION NEAR DOUTONBORI RIGHT NOW."
AND SEND!
HELLO?
Morio? Where are you two?
HUH? UH...
Kokone's there too, right?
Put her on, okay?
KOKONE...
...IT'S MY OLD MAN.
HUH? WHY ME?
HUH?
Kokone? We're kinda tied up here right now, so we can't come get you...
DON'T TELL ME IT'S THE GUY WITH THE BEARD?

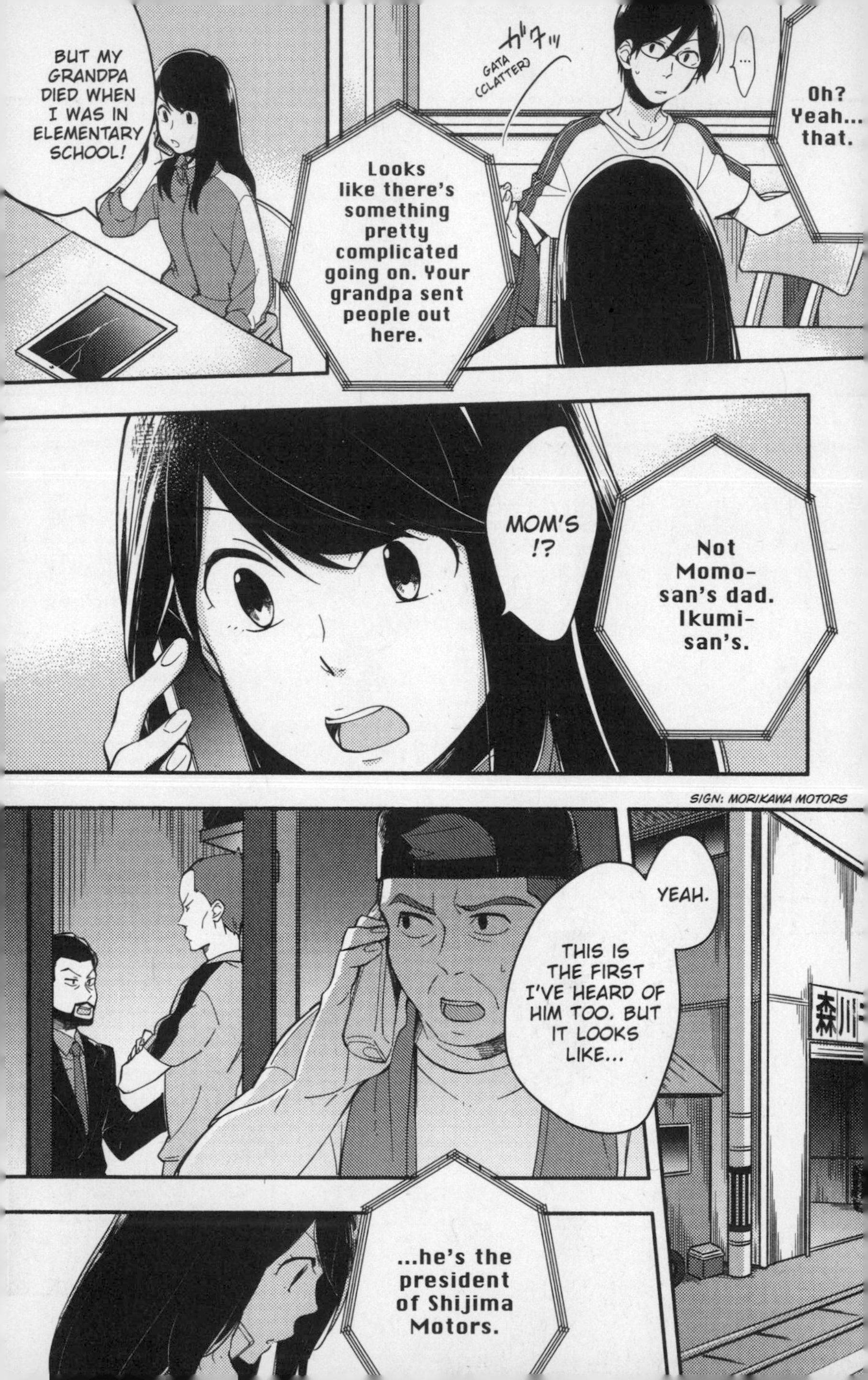
...
Oh? Yeah... that.
ガタッ
GATA (CLATTER)
Looks like there's something pretty complicated going on. Your grandpa sent people out here.
BUT MY GRANDPA DIED WHEN I WAS IN ELEMENTARY SCHOOL!
Not Momo-san's dad. Ikumi-san's.
MOM'S !?
SIGN: MORIKAWA MOTORS
森川
YEAH.
THIS IS THE FIRST I'VE HEARD OF HIM TOO. BUT IT LOOKS LIKE...
...he's the president of Shijima Motors.

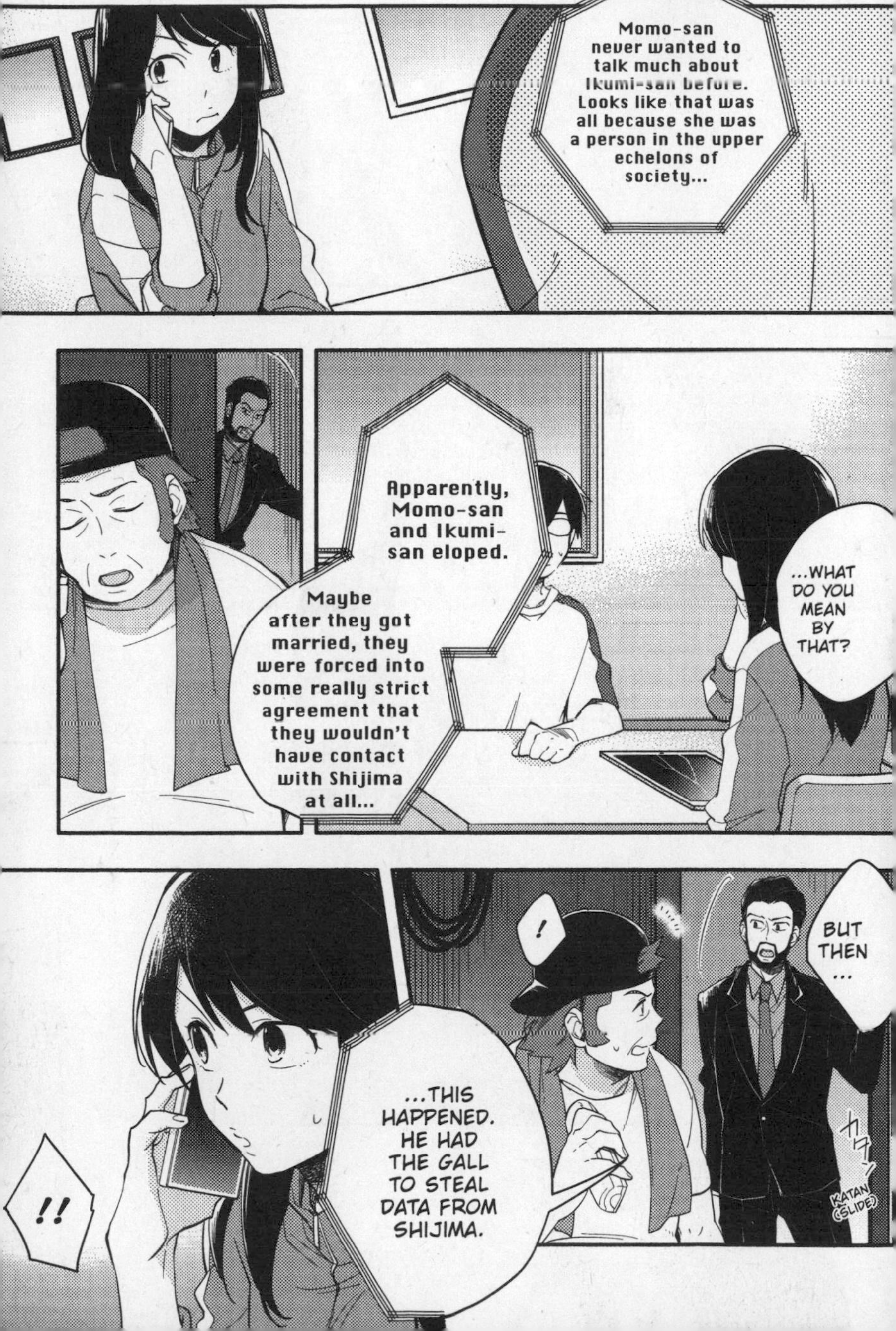
Momo-san never wanted to talk much about Ikumi-san before. Looks like that was all because she was a person in the upper echelons of society...
...WHAT DO YOU MEAN BY THAT?
Apparently, Momo-san and Ikumi-san eloped.
Maybe after they got married, they were forced into some really strict agreement that they wouldn't have contact with Shijima at all...
BUT THEN ...
!
KATAN (SLIDE)
...THIS HAPPENED. HE HAD THE GALL TO STEAL DATA FROM SHIJIMA.
!!

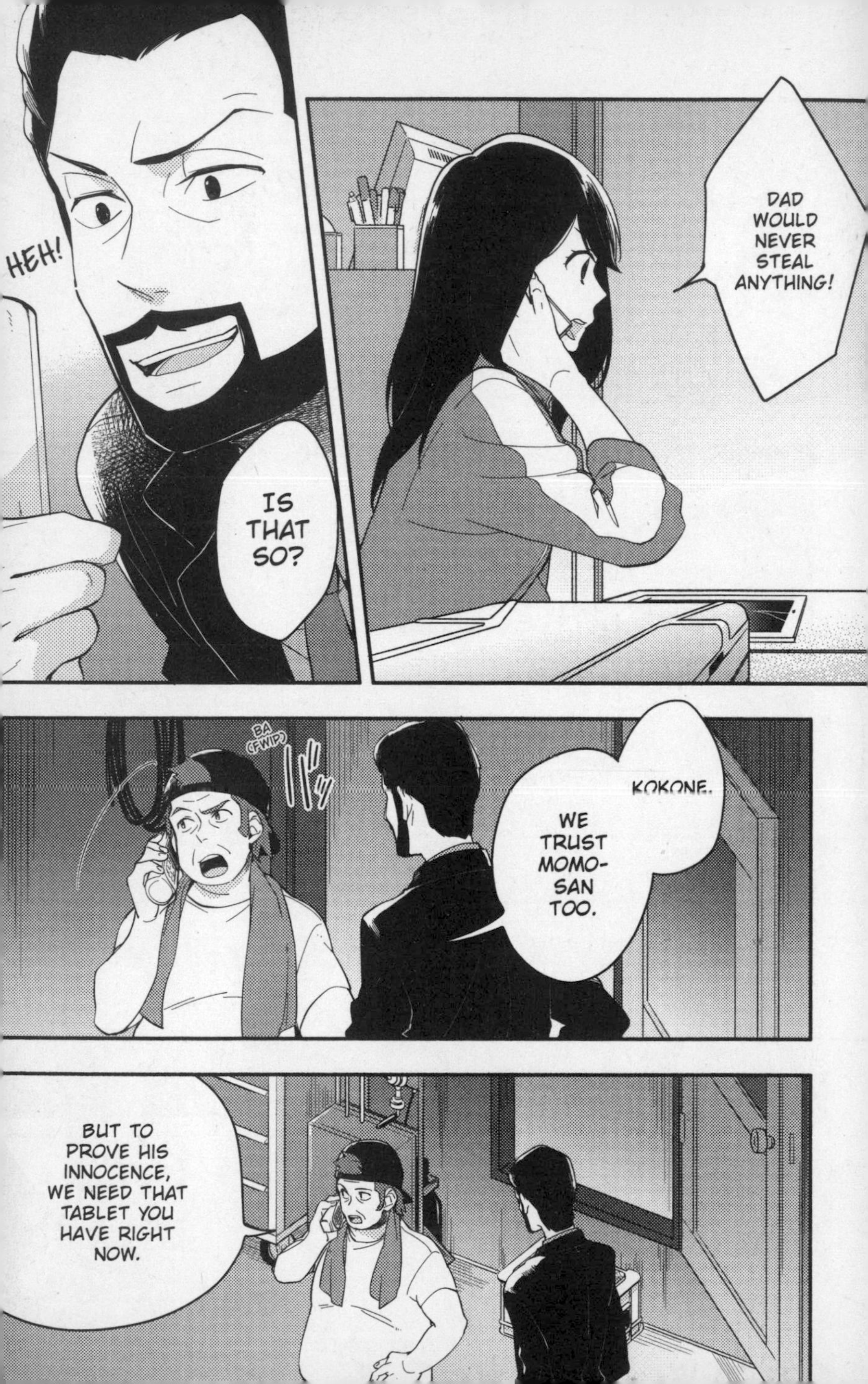
DAD WOULD NEVER STEAL ANYTHING!
HEH!
IS THAT SO?
KOKONE.
WE TRUST MOMO-SAN TOO.
BA (FWIP)
BUT TO PROVE HIS INNOCENCE, WE NEED THAT TABLET YOU HAVE RIGHT NOW.

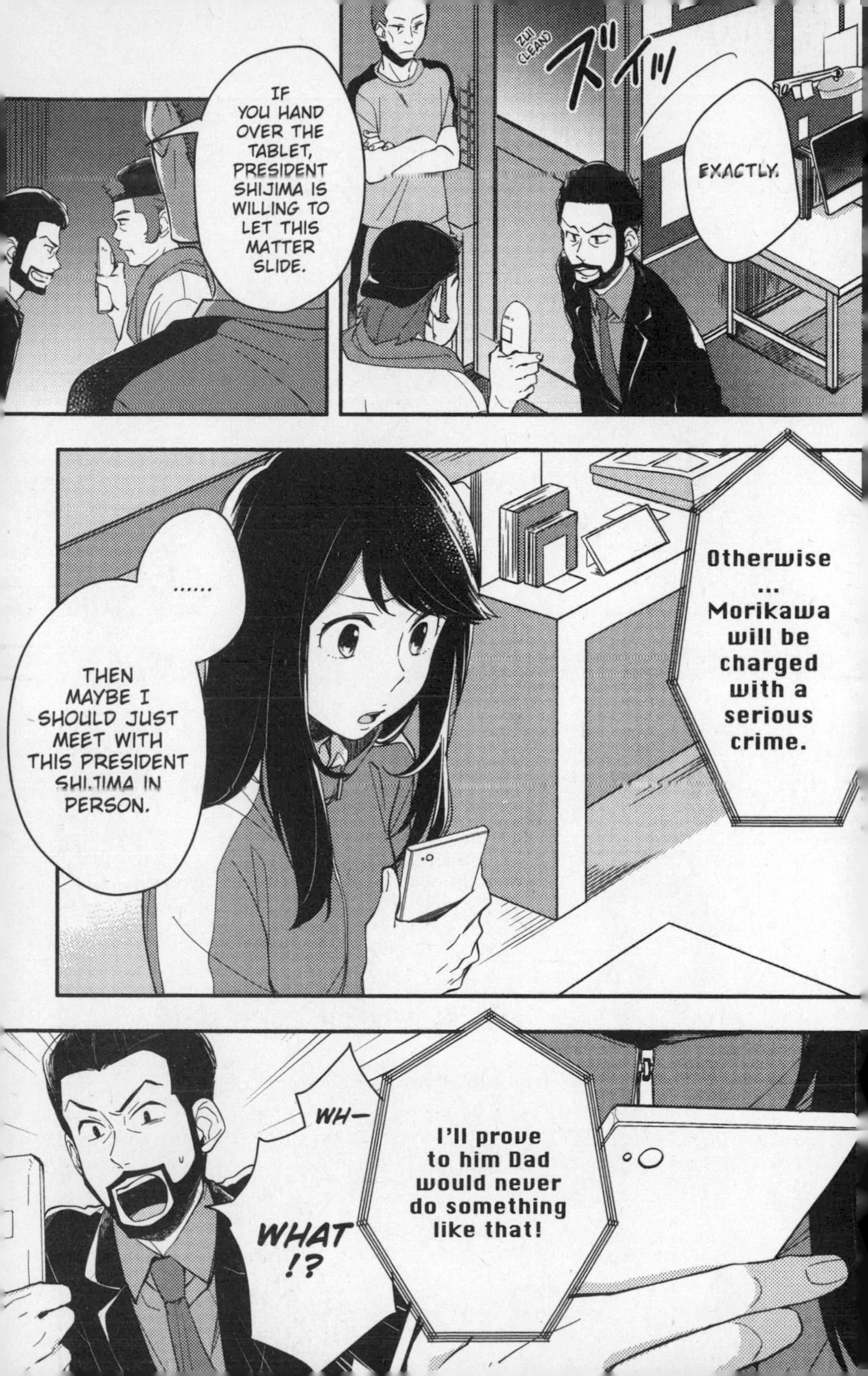
EXACTLY.
ZUI (LEAN)
IF YOU HAND OVER THE TABLET, PRESIDENT SHIJIMA IS WILLING TO LET THIS MATTER SLIDE.
Otherwise ... Morikawa will be charged with a serious crime.
......
THEN MAYBE I SHOULD JUST MEET WITH THIS PRESIDENT SHIJIMA IN PERSON.
I'll prove to him Dad would never do something like that!
WH—
WHAT !?

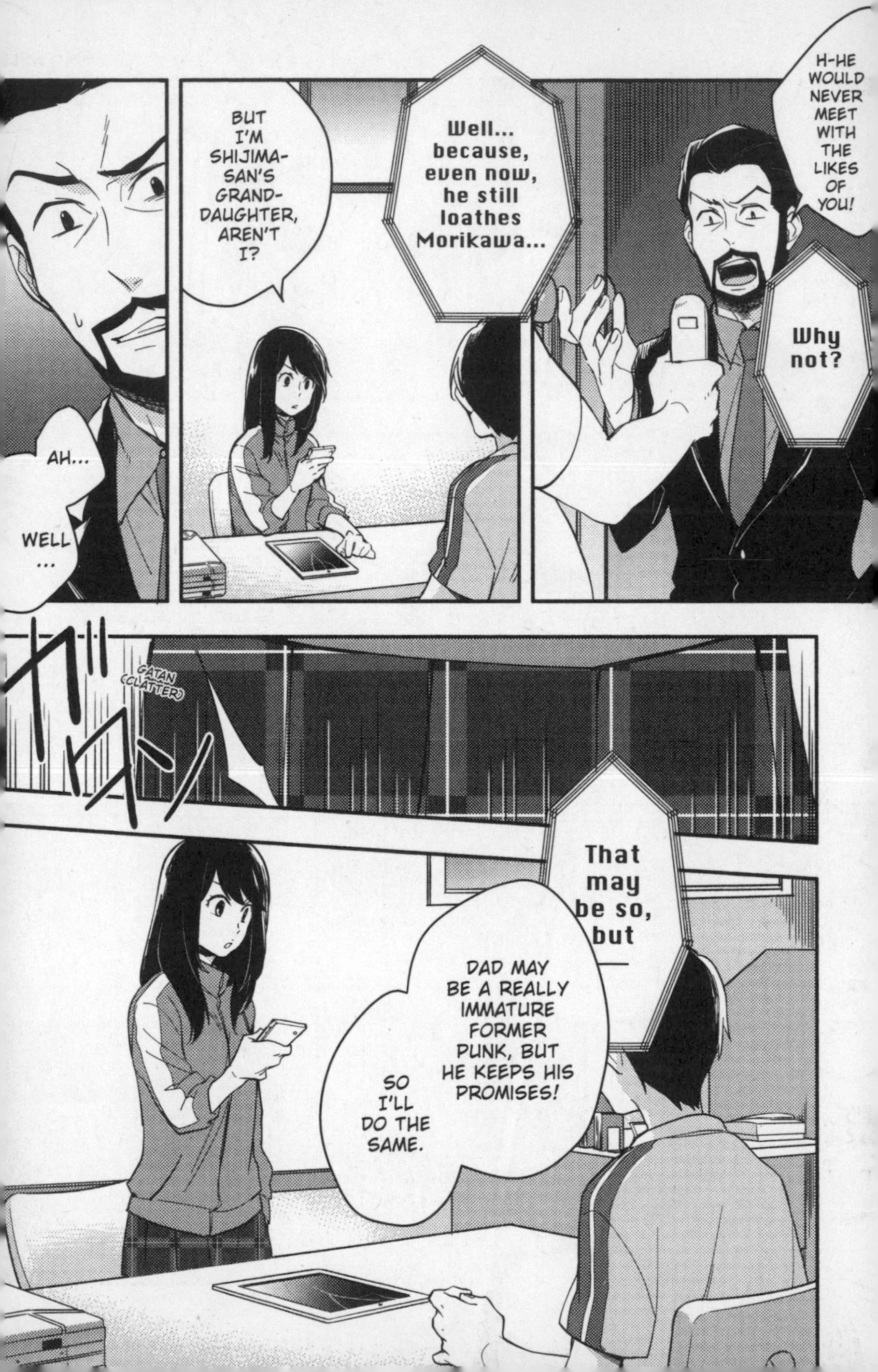
H-HE WOULD NEVER MEET WITH THE LIKES OF YOU!
Why not?
Well... because, even now, he still loathes Morikawa...
BUT I'M SHIJIMA-SAN'S GRAND-DAUGHTER, AREN'T I?
AH...
WELL ...
GATAN (CLATTER)
That may be so, but—
DAD MAY BE A REALLY IMMATURE FORMER PUNK, BUT HE KEEPS HIS PROMISES!
SO I'LL DO THE SAME.

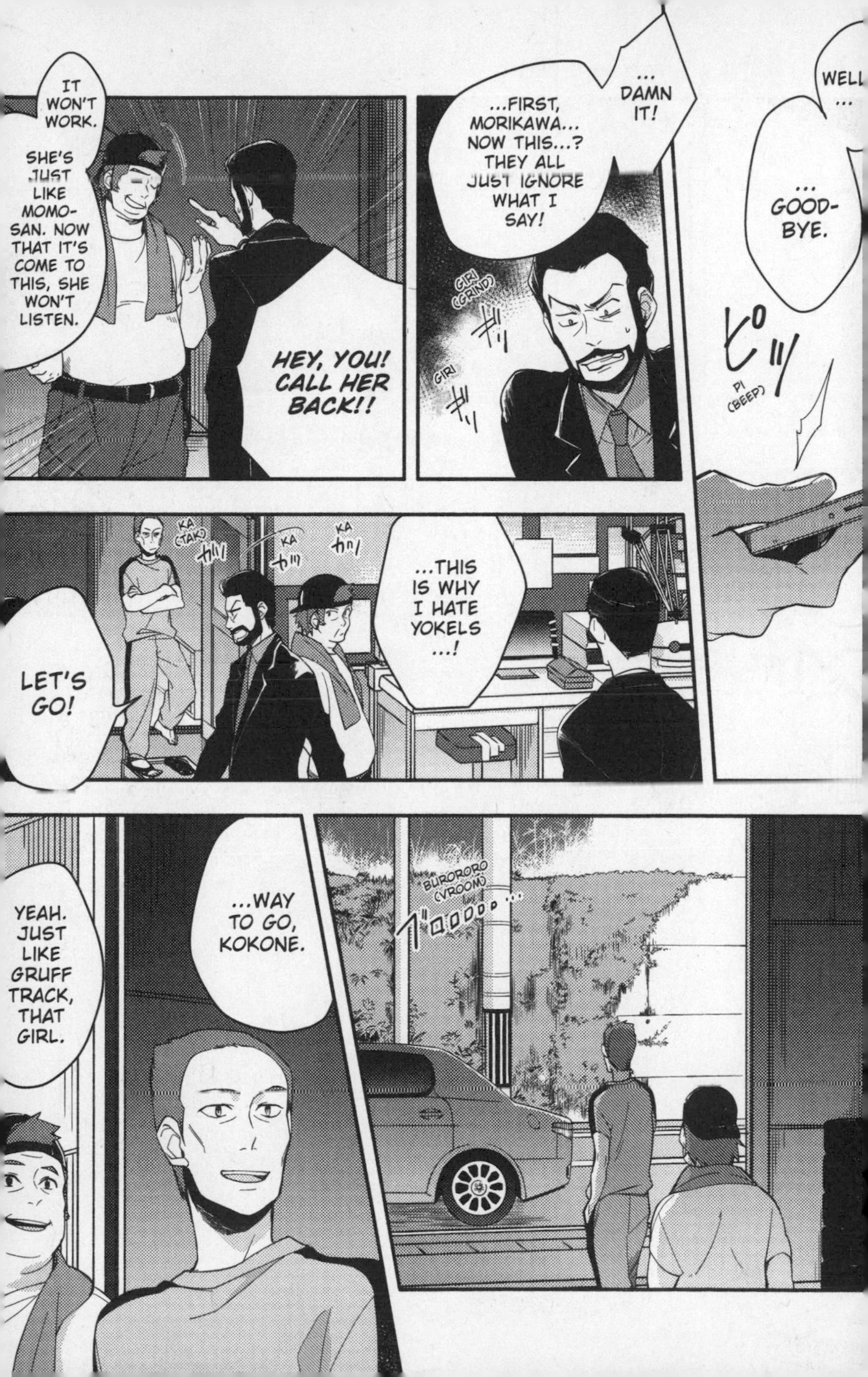
WELL...
...GOOD-BYE.
PI (BEEP)
...DAMN IT!
...FIRST, MORIKAWA... NOW THIS...? THEY ALL JUST IGNORE WHAT I SAY!
GIRI (GRIND)
GIRI
HEY, YOU! CALL HER BACK!!
IT WON'T WORK.
SHE'S JUST LIKE MOMO-SAN. NOW THAT IT'S COME TO THIS, SHE WON'T LISTEN.
...THIS IS WHY I HATE YOKELS...!
KA
KA
KA (TAK)
LET'S GO!
BURORORO (VROOM)
...WAY TO GO, KOKONE.
YEAH. JUST LIKE GRUFF TRACK, THAT GIRL.

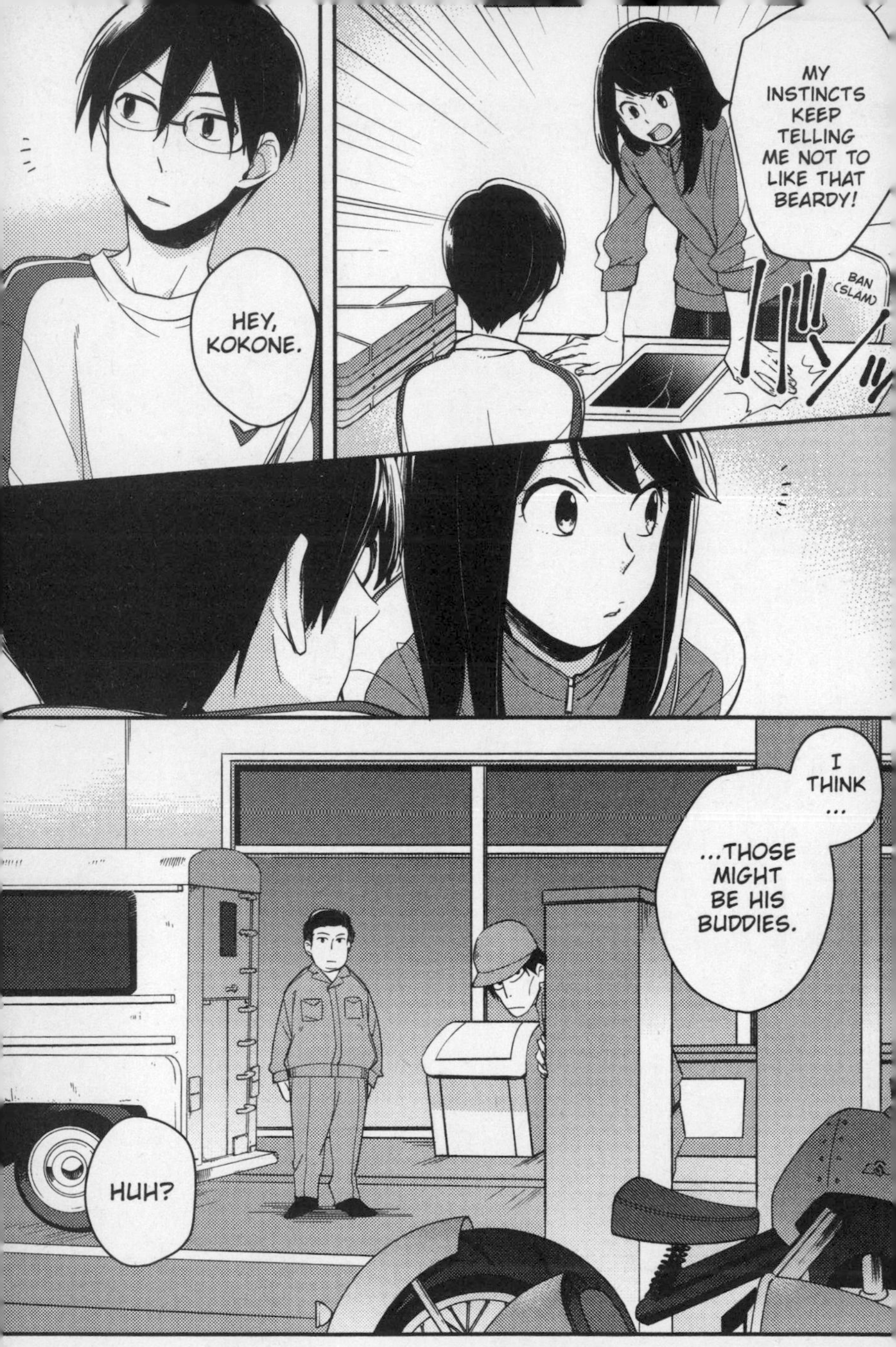
MY INSTINCTS KEEP TELLING ME NOT TO LIKE THAT BEARDY!
BAN (SLAM)
HEY, KOKONE.
I THINK ...
...THOSE MIGHT BE HIS BUDDIES.
HUH?

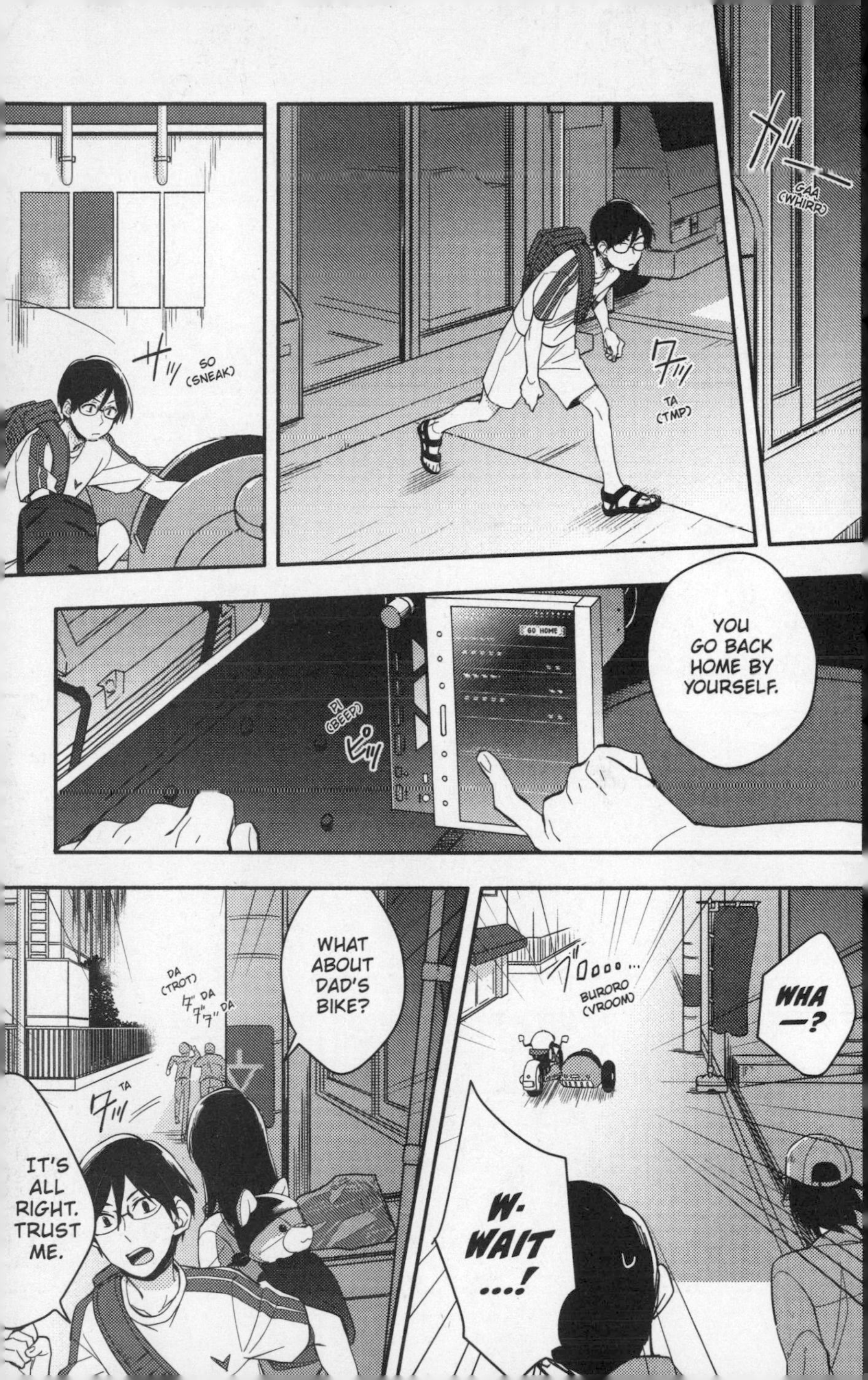
GAA (WHIRR)
TA (TMP)
SO (SNEAK)
YOU GO BACK HOME BY YOURSELF.
GO HOME
PI (BEEP)
BURORO (VROOM)
WHA—?
W-WAIT ...!
WHAT ABOUT DAD'S BIKE?
DA (TROT) DA DA
TA
IT'S ALL RIGHT. TRUST ME.

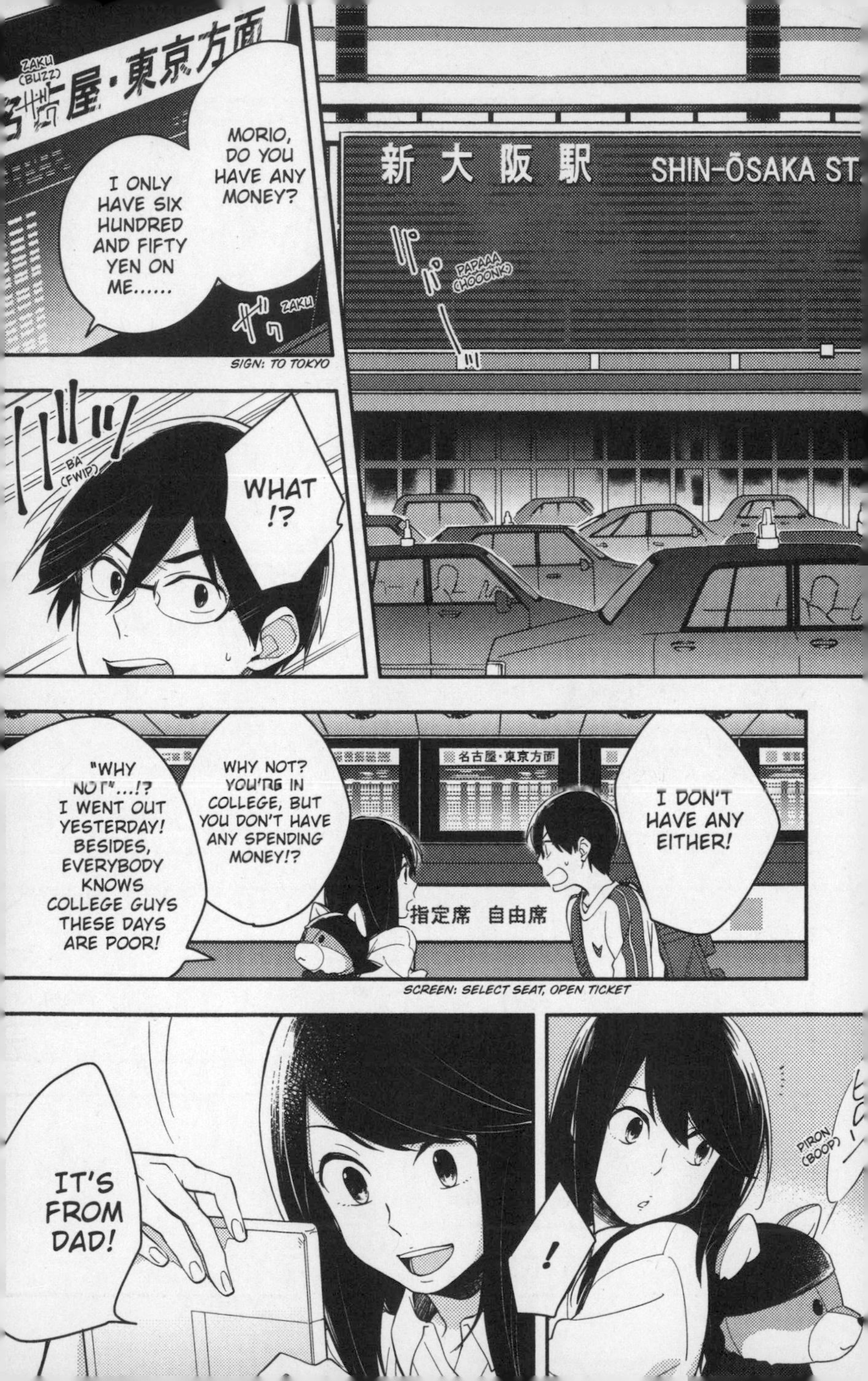
新大阪駅
SHIN-ŌSAKA ST
PAPAAA (HOOONK)
名古屋・東京方面
ZAKU (BUZZ)
MORIO, DO YOU HAVE ANY MONEY?
I ONLY HAVE SIX HUNDRED AND FIFTY YEN ON ME......
ZAKU
SIGN: TO TOKYO
BA (FWIP)
WHAT !?
I DON'T HAVE ANY EITHER!
名古屋・東京方面
WHY NOT? YOU'RE IN COLLEGE, BUT YOU DON'T HAVE ANY SPENDING MONEY!?
"WHY NOT"...!? I WENT OUT YESTERDAY! BESIDES, EVERYBODY KNOWS COLLEGE GUYS THESE DAYS ARE POOR!
指定席 自由席
SCREEN: SELECT SEAT, OPEN TICKET
PIRON (BOOP)
!
IT'S FROM DAD!

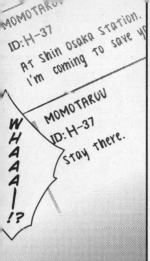

WHAAA!?

"KO-KONE, WHERE ARE YOU RIGHT NOW?"

MOMOTAROU
ID:H-37

Where are yo
Don't worry.
them the t
station near

MOMOTAROU
ID:H-37

Kokone, where are you right now?

"AT SHIN OSAKA STATION. I'M COMING TO SAVE YOU."

"WE DON'T HAVE ANY MONEY, SO WE CAN'T GET TICKETS FOR THE BULLET TRAIN.

"I'M WITH MORIO.

"WHERE ARE YOU?"

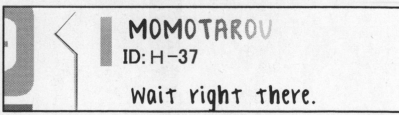

MOMOTAROU
ID: H-37

Wait right there.

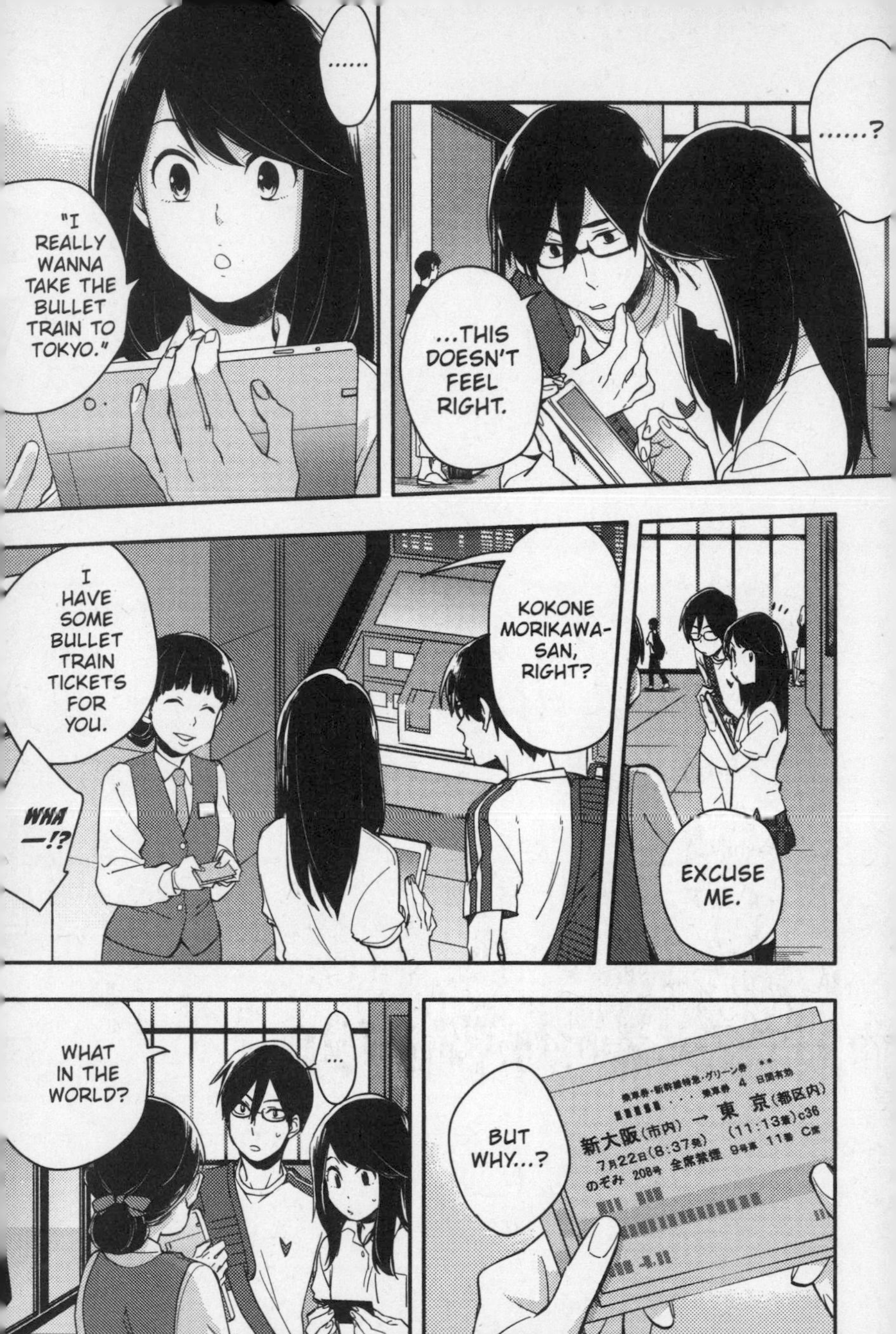
......?
...THIS DOESN'T FEEL RIGHT.
......
"I REALLY WANNA TAKE THE BULLET TRAIN TO TOKYO."
EXCUSE ME.
KOKONE MORIKAWA-SAN, RIGHT?
I HAVE SOME BULLET TRAIN TICKETS FOR YOU.
WHA—!?
新大阪(市内) → 東京(都区内)
7月22日(8:37発) (11:13着) c36
のぞみ 208号 全席禁煙 9号車 11番 C席
BUT WHY...?
...
WHAT IN THE WORLD?

TICKET: SHIN OSAKA STATION TO TOKYO STATION

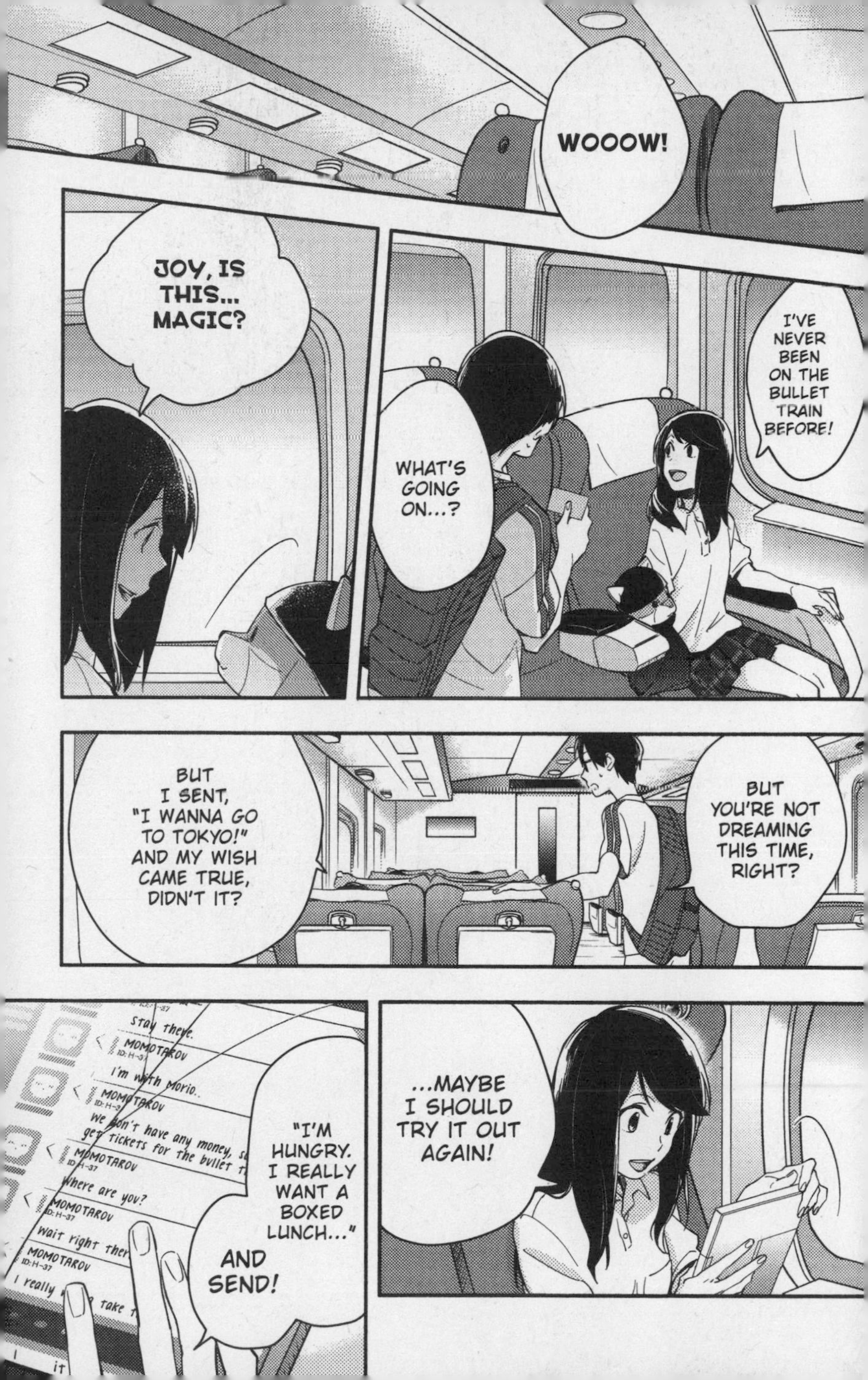
WOOOW!
I'VE NEVER BEEN ON THE BULLET TRAIN BEFORE!
WHAT'S GOING ON...?
JOY, IS THIS... MAGIC?
BUT YOU'RE NOT DREAMING THIS TIME, RIGHT?
BUT I SENT, "I WANNA GO TO TOKYO!" AND MY WISH CAME TRUE, DIDN'T IT?
...MAYBE I SHOULD TRY IT OUT AGAIN!
Stay there.
MOMOTAROV
I'm with Morio.
MOMOTAROV
MOMOTAROV
Where are you?
MOMOTAROV
MOMOTAROV
"I'M HUNGRY. I REALLY WANT A BOXED LUNCH..."
AND SEND!

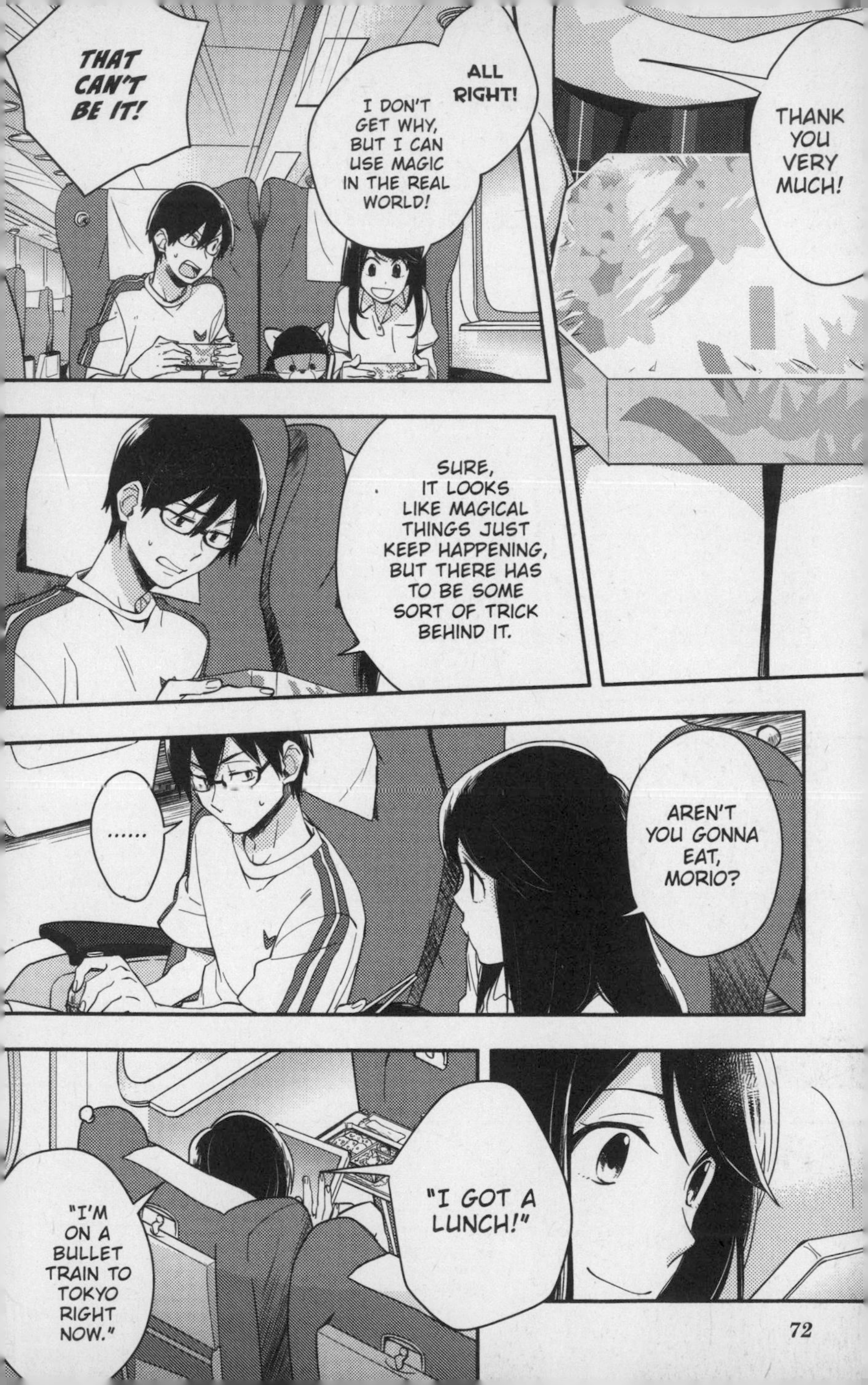
THANK YOU VERY MUCH!
ALL RIGHT!
I DON'T GET WHY, BUT I CAN USE MAGIC IN THE REAL WORLD!
THAT CAN'T BE IT!
SURE, IT LOOKS LIKE MAGICAL THINGS JUST KEEP HAPPENING, BUT THERE HAS TO BE SOME SORT OF TRICK BEHIND IT.
AREN'T YOU GONNA EAT, MORIO?
......
"I GOT A LUNCH!"
"I'M ON A BULLET TRAIN TO TOKYO RIGHT NOW."

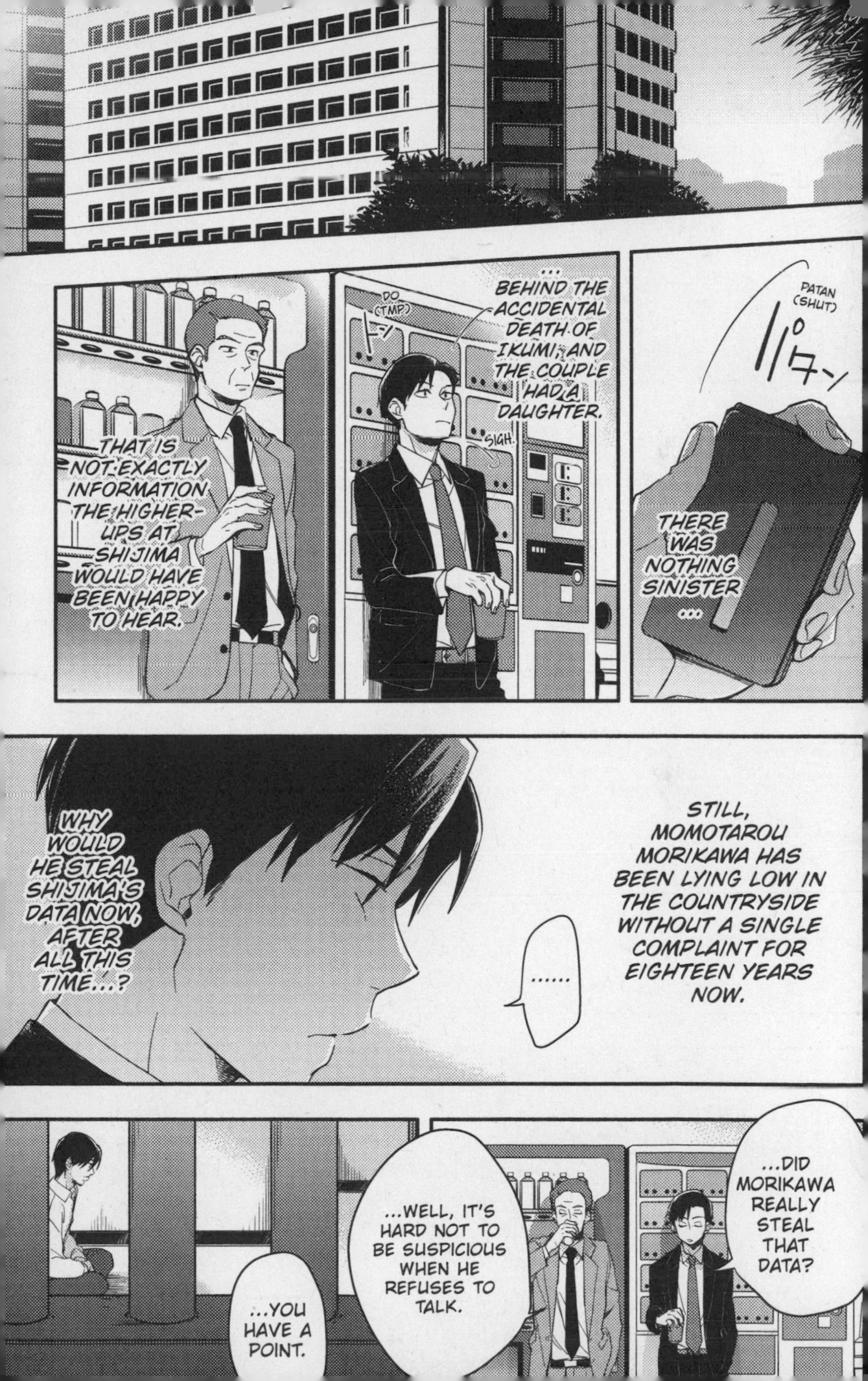
PATAN (SHUT)
THERE WAS NOTHING SINISTER ...
DO (TMP)
... BEHIND THE ACCIDENTAL DEATH OF IKUMI, AND THE COUPLE HAD A DAUGHTER.
SIGH
THAT IS NOT EXACTLY INFORMATION THE HIGHER-UPS AT SHIJIMA WOULD HAVE BEEN HAPPY TO HEAR.
STILL, MOMOTAROU MORIKAWA HAS BEEN LYING LOW IN THE COUNTRYSIDE WITHOUT A SINGLE COMPLAINT FOR EIGHTEEN YEARS NOW.
......
WHY WOULD HE STEAL SHIJIMA'S DATA NOW, AFTER ALL THIS TIME...?
...DID MORIKAWA REALLY STEAL THAT DATA?
...WELL, IT'S HARD NOT TO BE SUSPICIOUS WHEN HE REFUSES TO TALK.
...YOU HAVE A POINT.

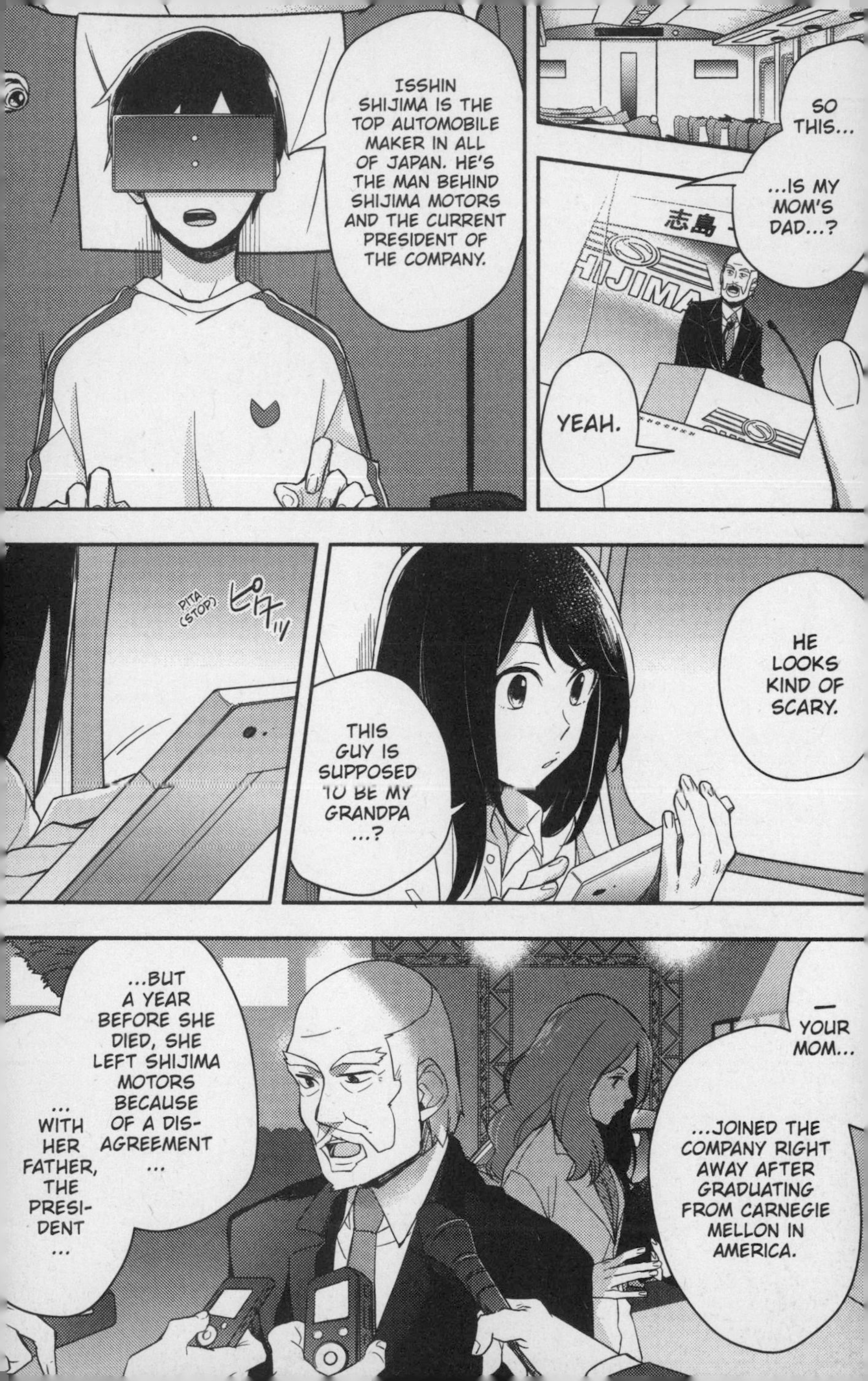
SO THIS...
...IS MY MOM'S DAD...?
YEAH.
ISSHIN SHIJIMA IS THE TOP AUTOMOBILE MAKER IN ALL OF JAPAN. HE'S THE MAN BEHIND SHIJIMA MOTORS AND THE CURRENT PRESIDENT OF THE COMPANY.
HE LOOKS KIND OF SCARY.
THIS GUY IS SUPPOSED TO BE MY GRANDPA ...?
PITA (STOP)
ピタッ
— YOUR MOM...
...JOINED THE COMPANY RIGHT AWAY AFTER GRADUATING FROM CARNEGIE MELLON IN AMERICA.
...BUT A YEAR BEFORE SHE DIED, SHE LEFT SHIJIMA MOTORS BECAUSE OF A DIS-AGREEMENT ...
... WITH HER FATHER, THE PRESI-DENT ...

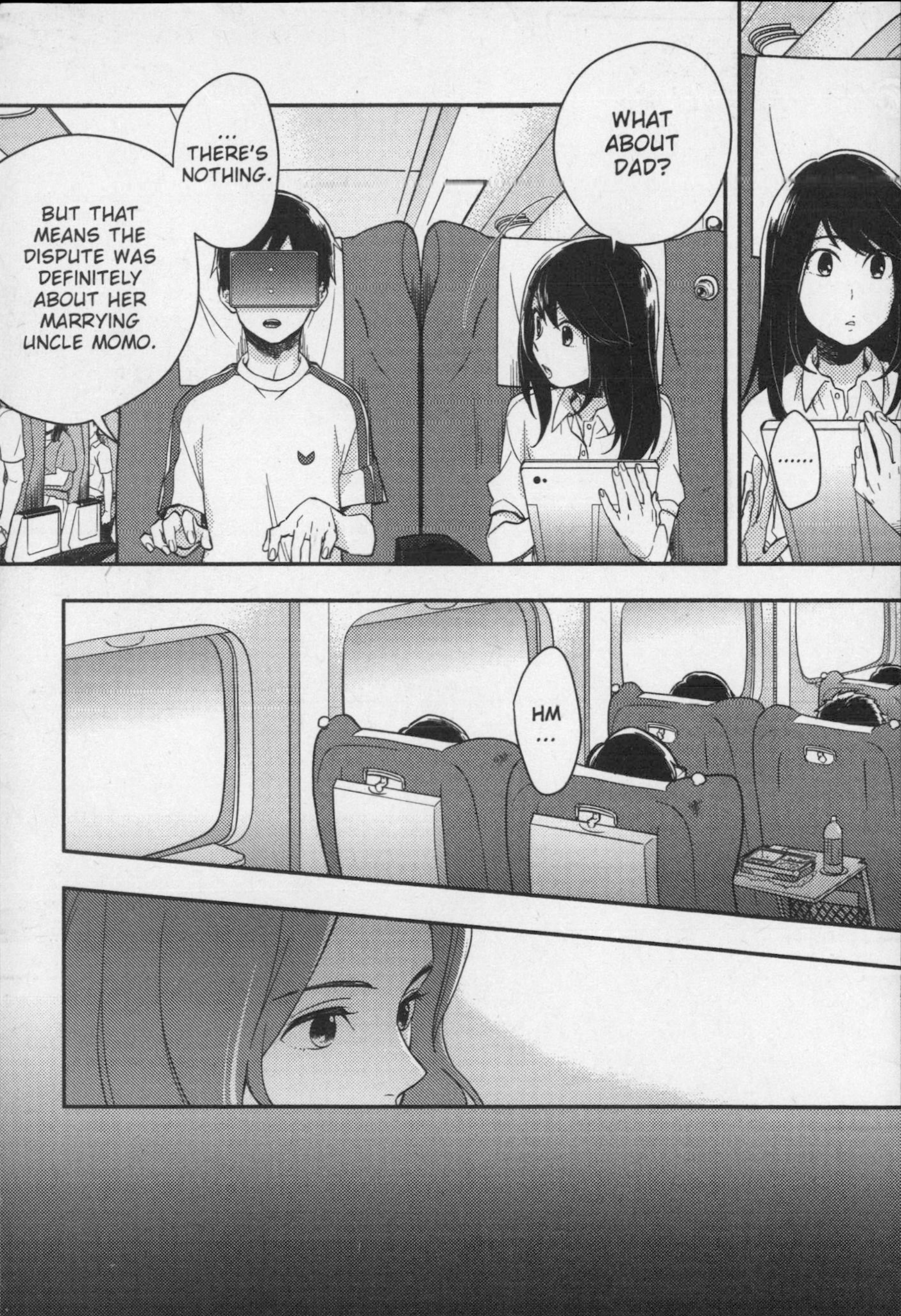
......
WHAT ABOUT DAD?
... THERE'S NOTHING.
BUT THAT MEANS THE DISPUTE WAS DEFINITELY ABOUT HER MARRYING UNCLE MOMO.
HM ...

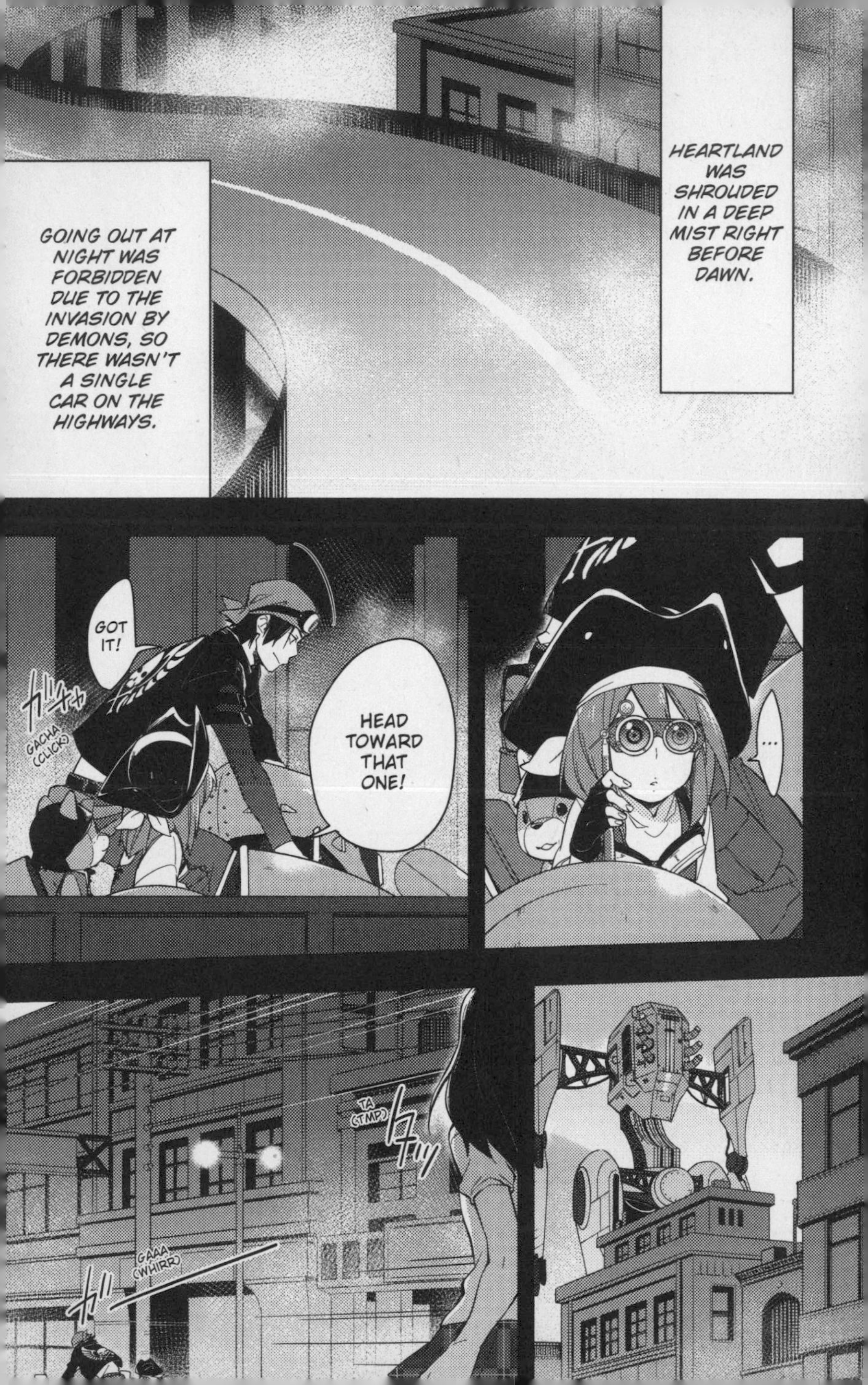
HEARTLAND WAS SHROUDED IN A DEEP MIST RIGHT BEFORE DAWN.
GOING OUT AT NIGHT WAS FORBIDDEN DUE TO THE INVASION BY DEMONS, SO THERE WASN'T A SINGLE CAR ON THE HIGHWAYS.
...
HEAD TOWARD THAT ONE!
GOT IT!
GACHA (CLICK)
TA (STMP)
GAAA (WHIRR)

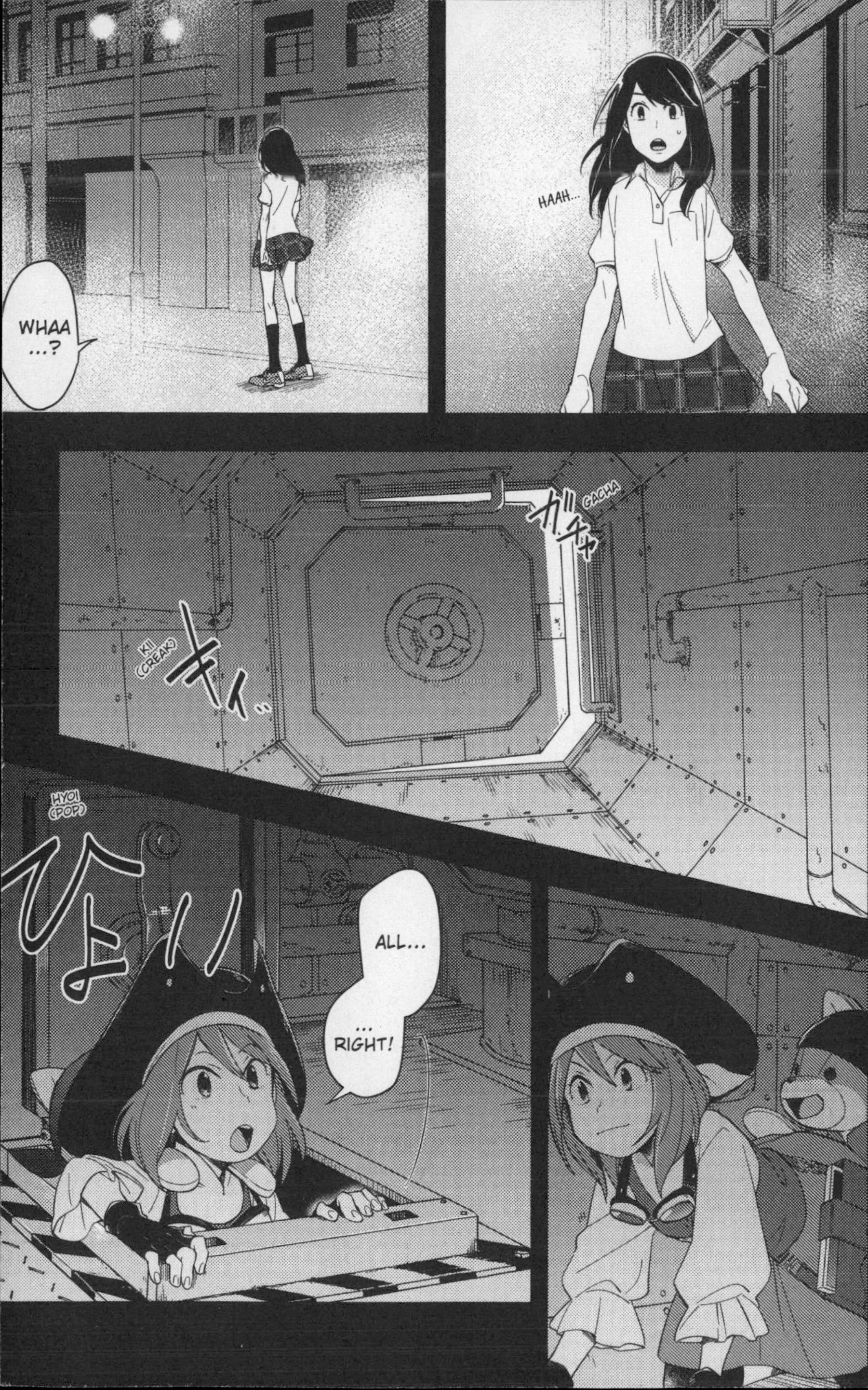
HAAH...
WHAA ...?
ガチャ
GACHA
キィ..
KII (CREAK)
ひょい
HYOI (POP)
ALL...
... RIGHT!

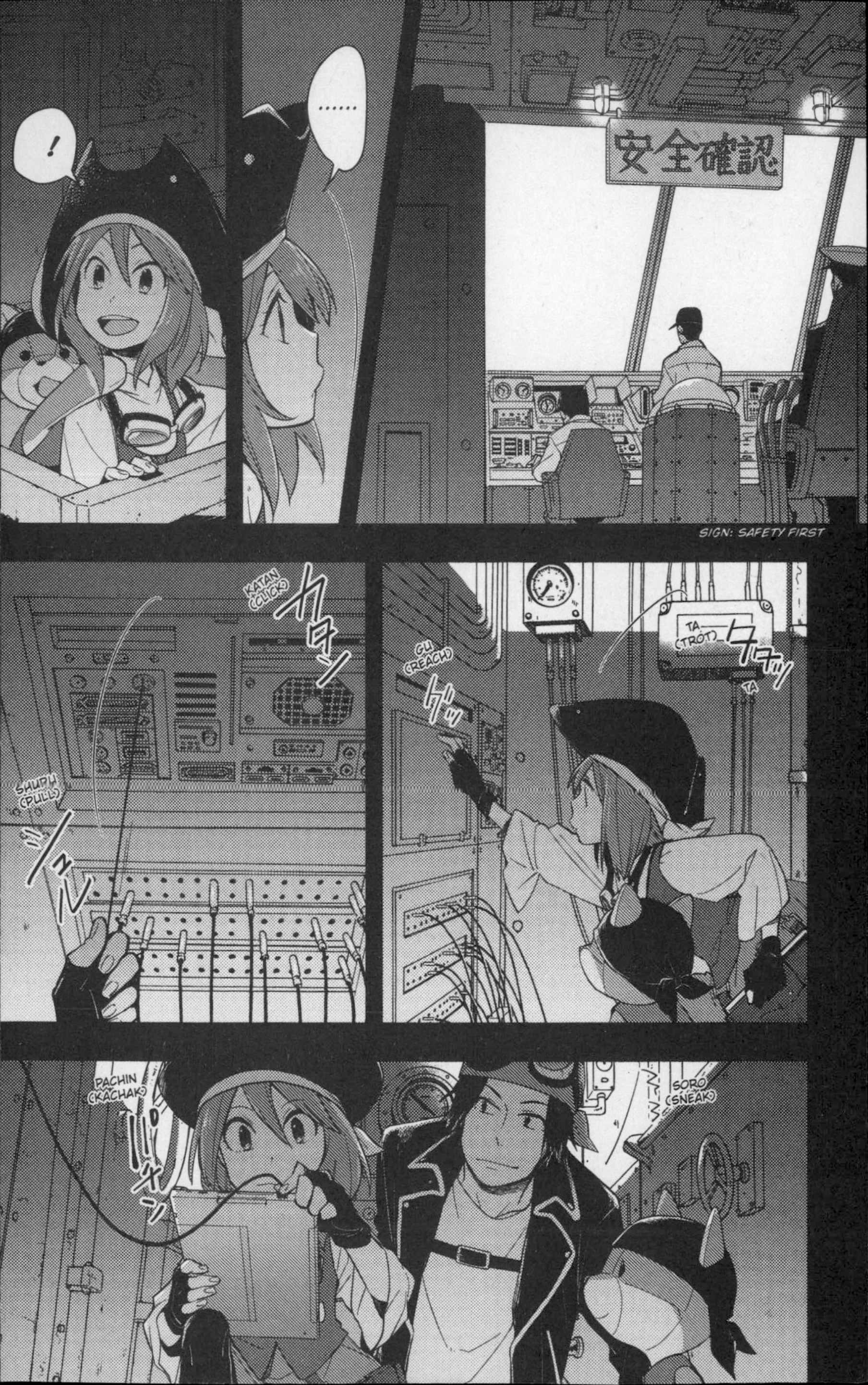
安全確認
SIGN: SAFETY FIRST
……
!
TA (TROT)
タタッ
TA
GU (REACH)
グッ
KATAN (CLICK)
カタン
SHURU (PULLS)
シュル
SORO (SNEAK)
PACHIN (KACHAK)
パチン

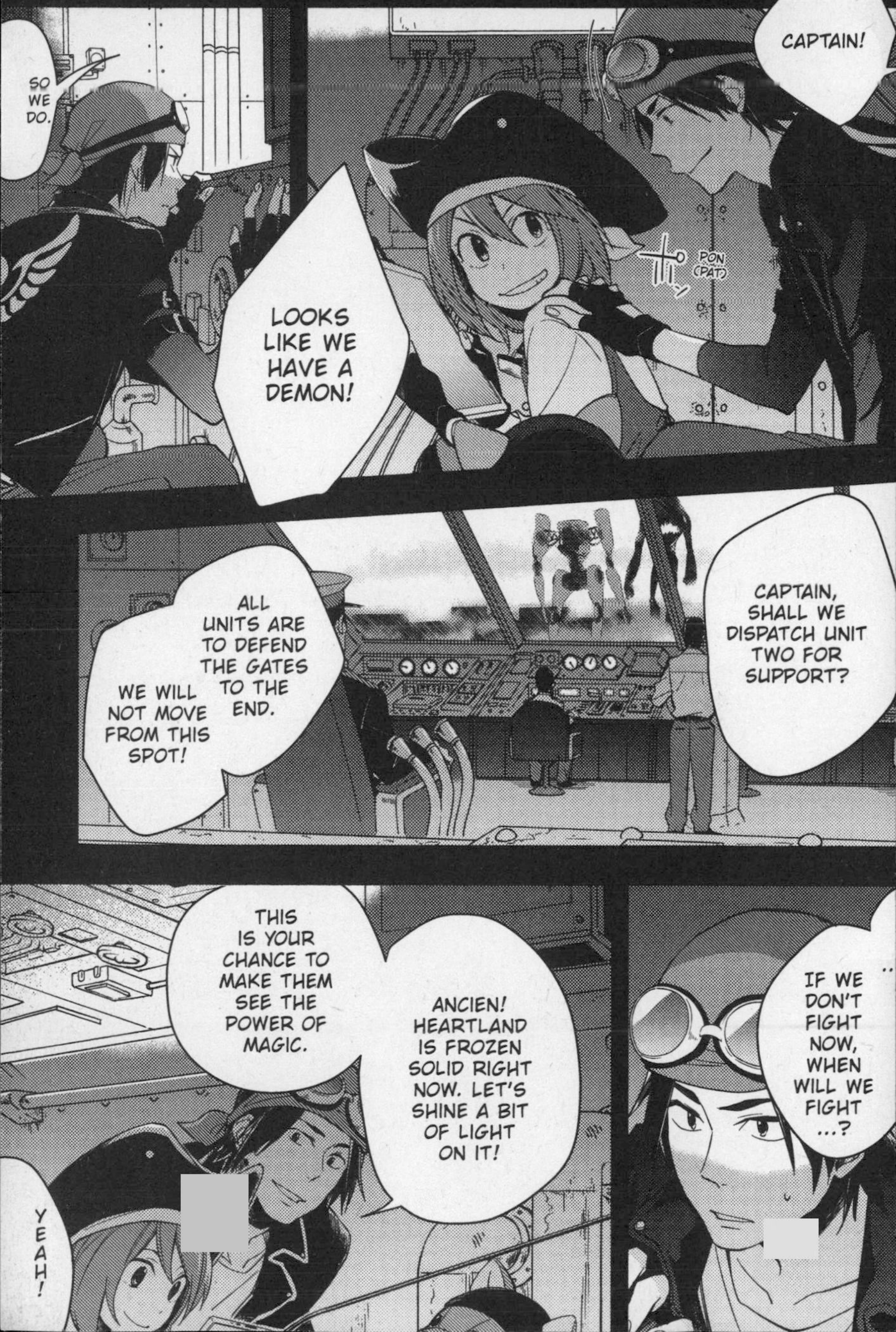
CAPTAIN!
PON (PAT)
LOOKS LIKE WE HAVE A DEMON!
SO WE DO.
CAPTAIN, SHALL WE DISPATCH UNIT TWO FOR SUPPORT?
ALL UNITS ARE TO DEFEND THE GATES TO THE END.
WE WILL NOT MOVE FROM THIS SPOT!
IF WE DON'T FIGHT NOW, WHEN WILL WE FIGHT ...?
ANCIEN! HEARTLAND IS FROZEN SOLID RIGHT NOW. LET'S SHINE A BIT OF LIGHT ON IT!
THIS IS YOUR CHANCE TO MAKE THEM SEE THE POWER OF MAGIC.
YEAH!

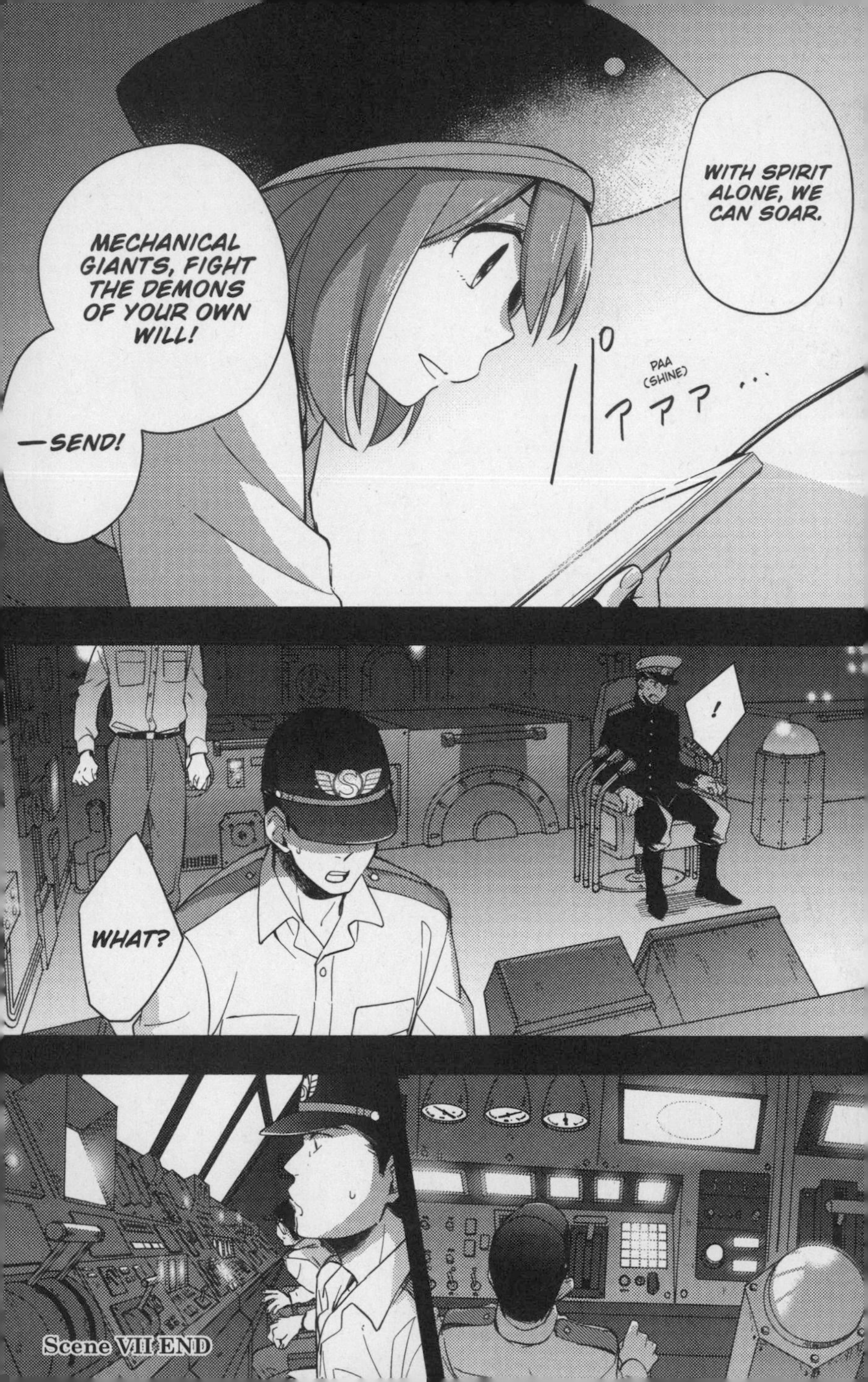
WITH SPIRIT ALONE, WE CAN SOAR.
PAA (SHINE)
パアアア…
MECHANICAL GIANTS, FIGHT THE DEMONS OF YOUR OWN WILL!
—SEND!
!
WHAT?
Scene VII END

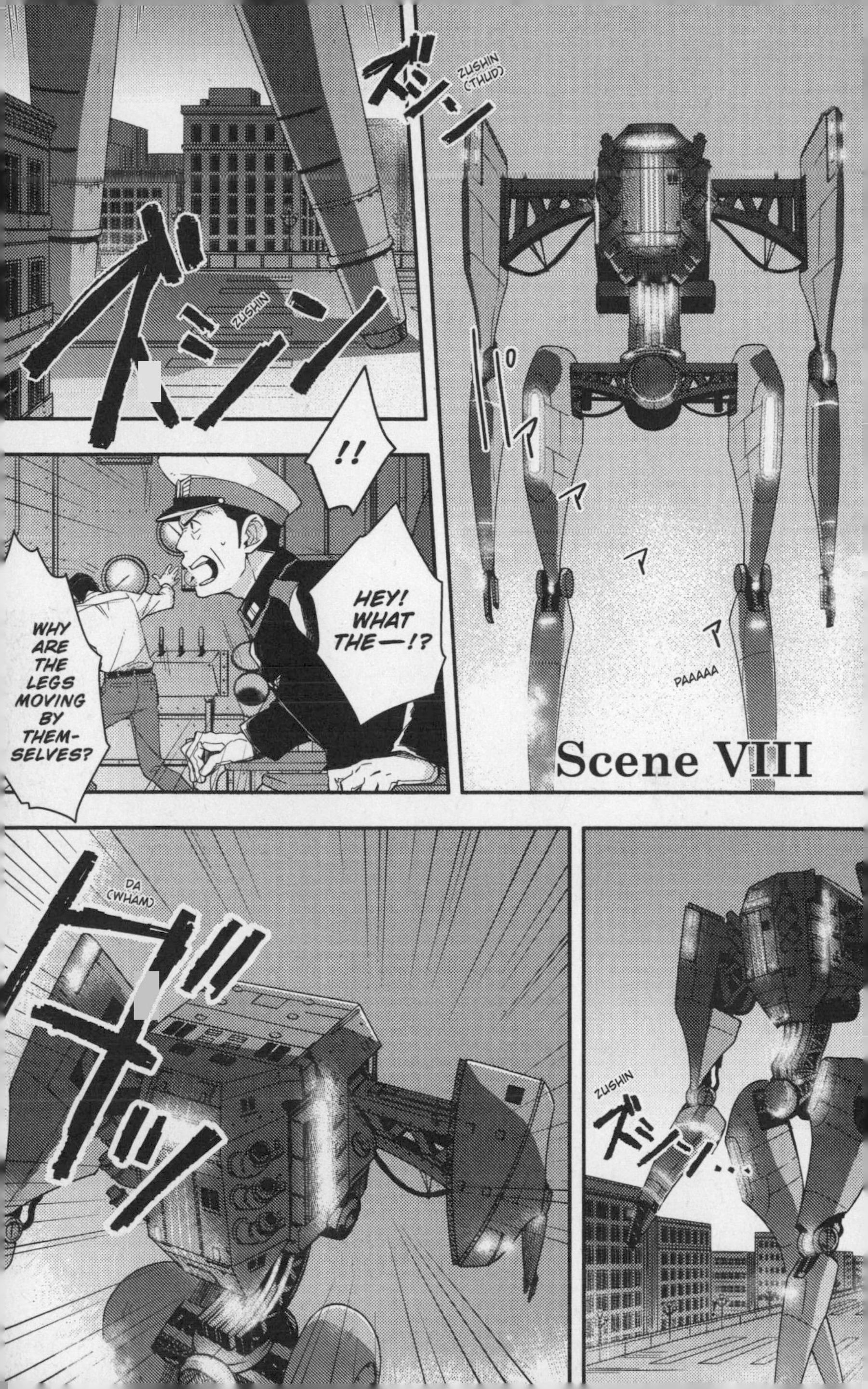
ZUSHIN (THUD)
PAAAAA
Scene VIII
ZUSHIN
!!
HEY! WHAT THE—!?
WHY ARE THE LEGS MOVING BY THEMSELVES?
ZUSHIN
DA (WHAM)

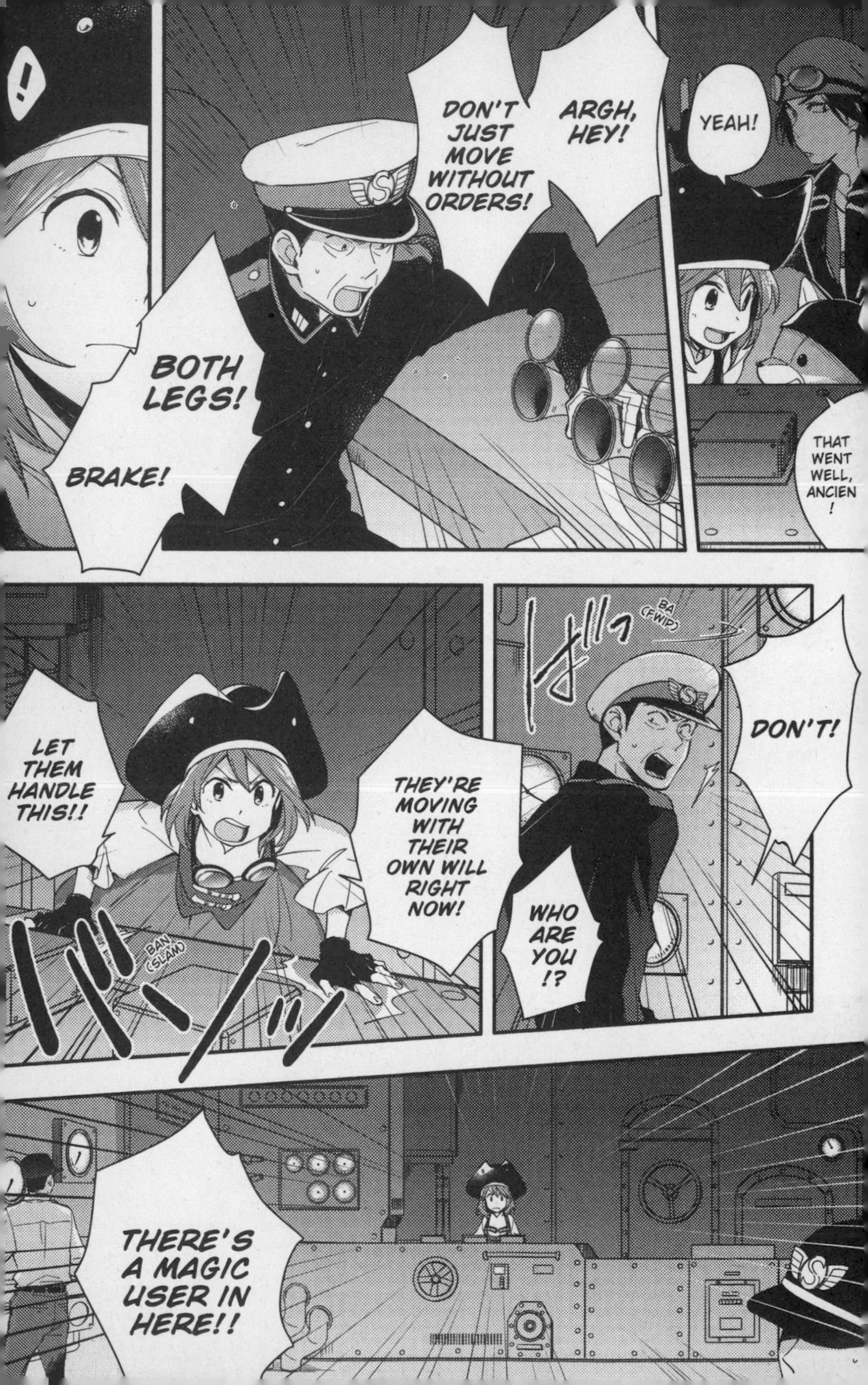
YEAH!
THAT WENT WELL, ANCIEN!
ARGH, HEY!
DON'T JUST MOVE WITHOUT ORDERS!
!
BOTH LEGS!
BRAKE!
BA (FWIP)
DON'T!
WHO ARE YOU!?
THEY'RE MOVING WITH THEIR OWN WILL RIGHT NOW!
LET THEM HANDLE THIS!!
BAN (SLAM)
THERE'S A MAGIC USER IN HERE!!

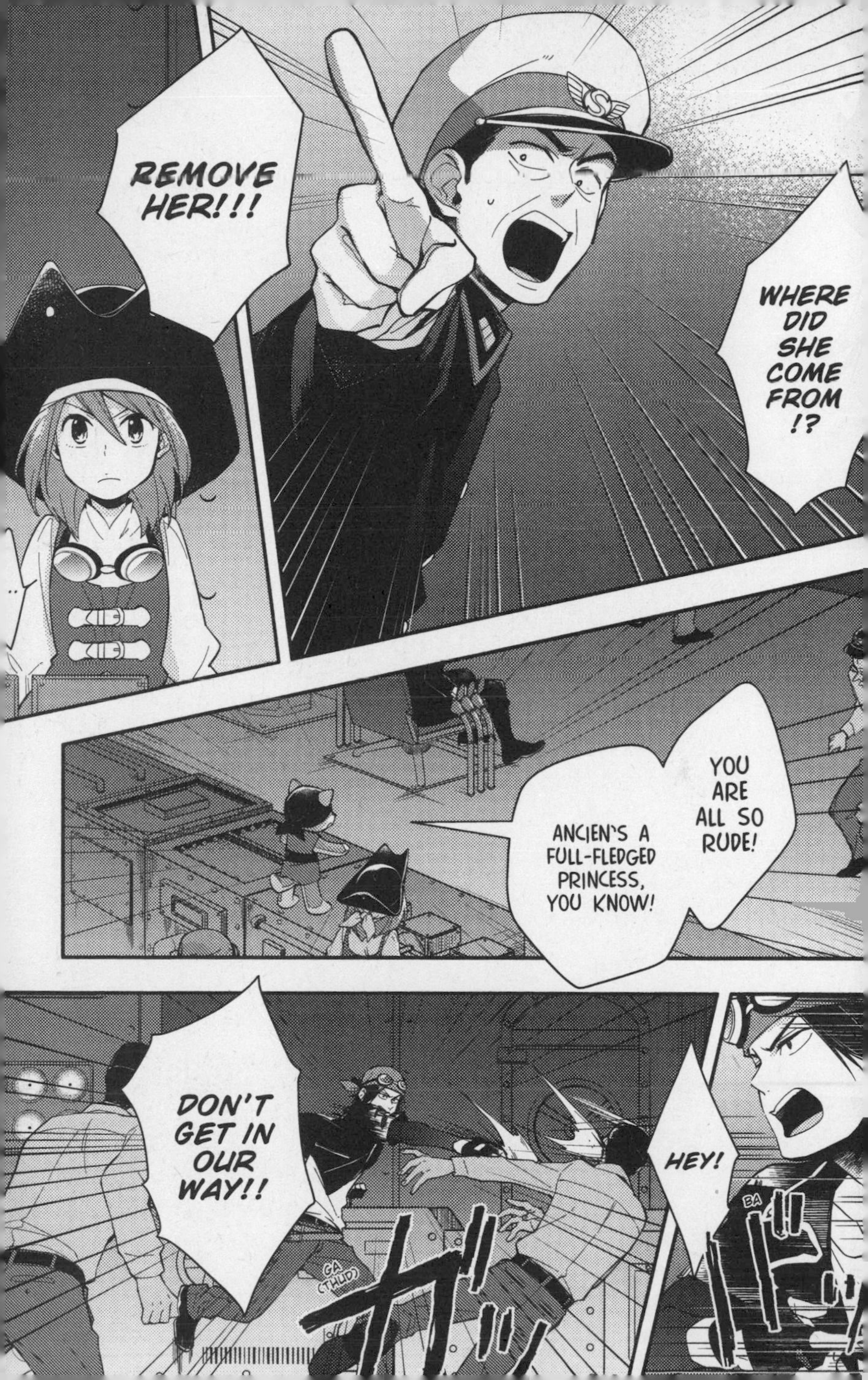
WHERE DID SHE COME FROM!?
REMOVE HER!!!
...
YOU ARE ALL SO RUDE!
ANCIEN'S A FULL-FLEDGED PRINCESS, YOU KNOW!
HEY!
BA
DON'T GET IN OUR WAY!!
GA (THUD)

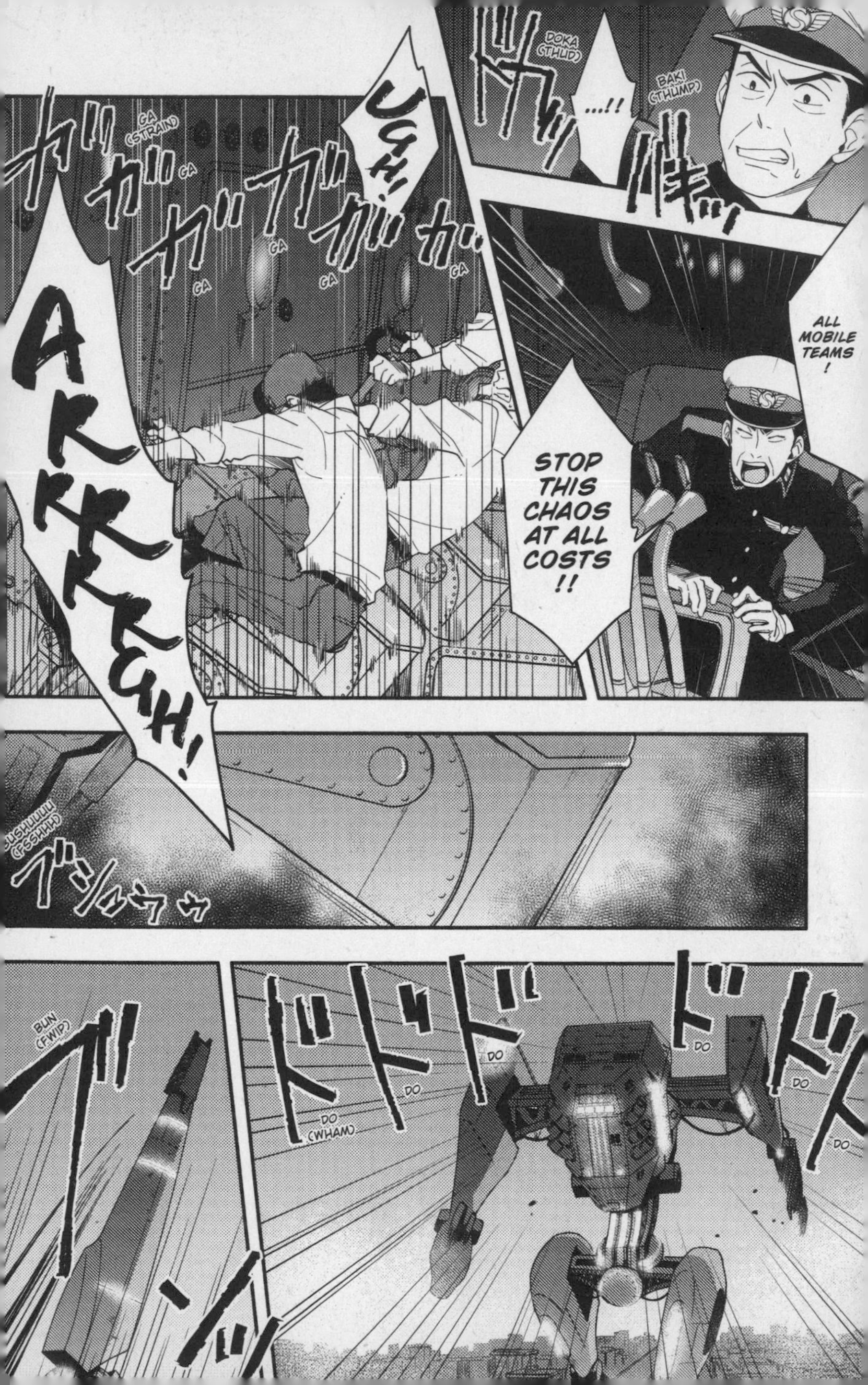
DOKA (THUD)
...!!
BAKI (THUMP)
ALL MOBILE TEAMS!
STOP THIS CHAOS AT ALL COSTS!!
GA (STRAIN)
GA
GA
GA
GA
GA
UGH!
ARKKKKUGH!
USHUUUU (FSSHHH)
DO
DO
DO
DO
DO (WHAM)
DO
BUN (FWIP)

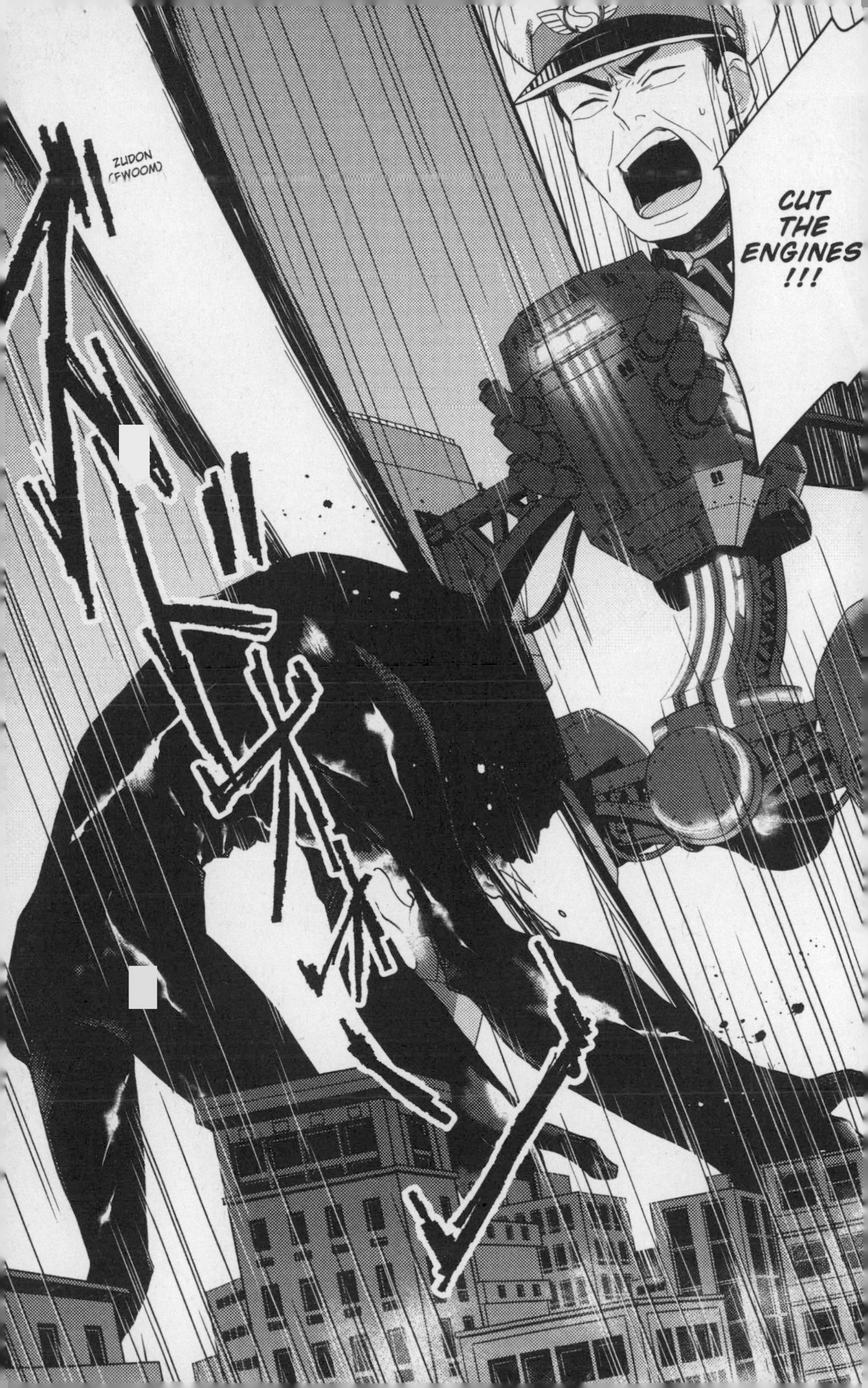
CUT THE ENGINES!!!
ZUDON (FWOOM)

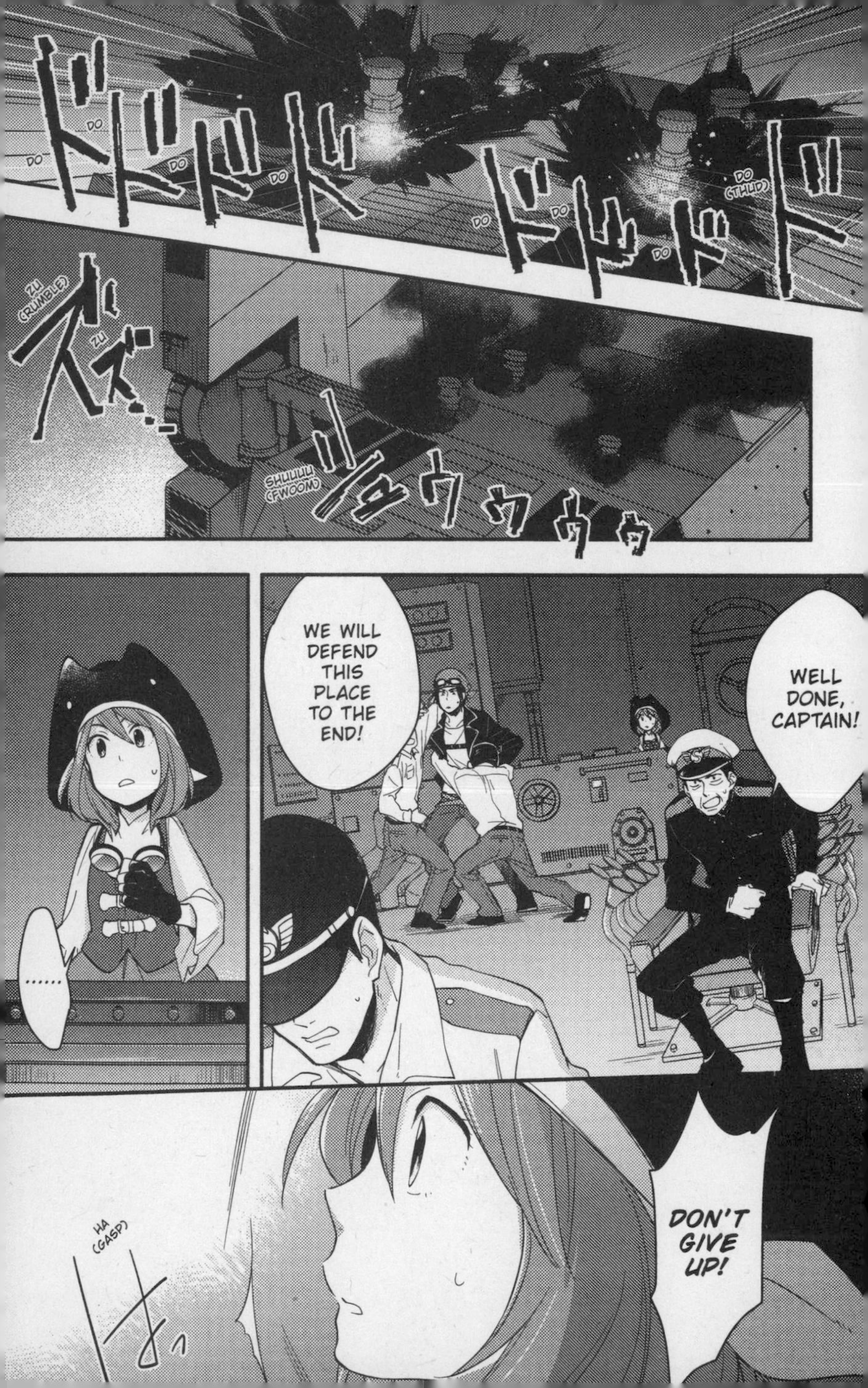
DO (THUD)
DO
DO
DO
DO
DO
DO
DO
ZU (RUMBLE)
ZU
SHUUUU (FWOOM)
WELL DONE, CAPTAIN!
WE WILL DEFEND THIS PLACE TO THE END!
......
DON'T GIVE UP!
HA (GASP)

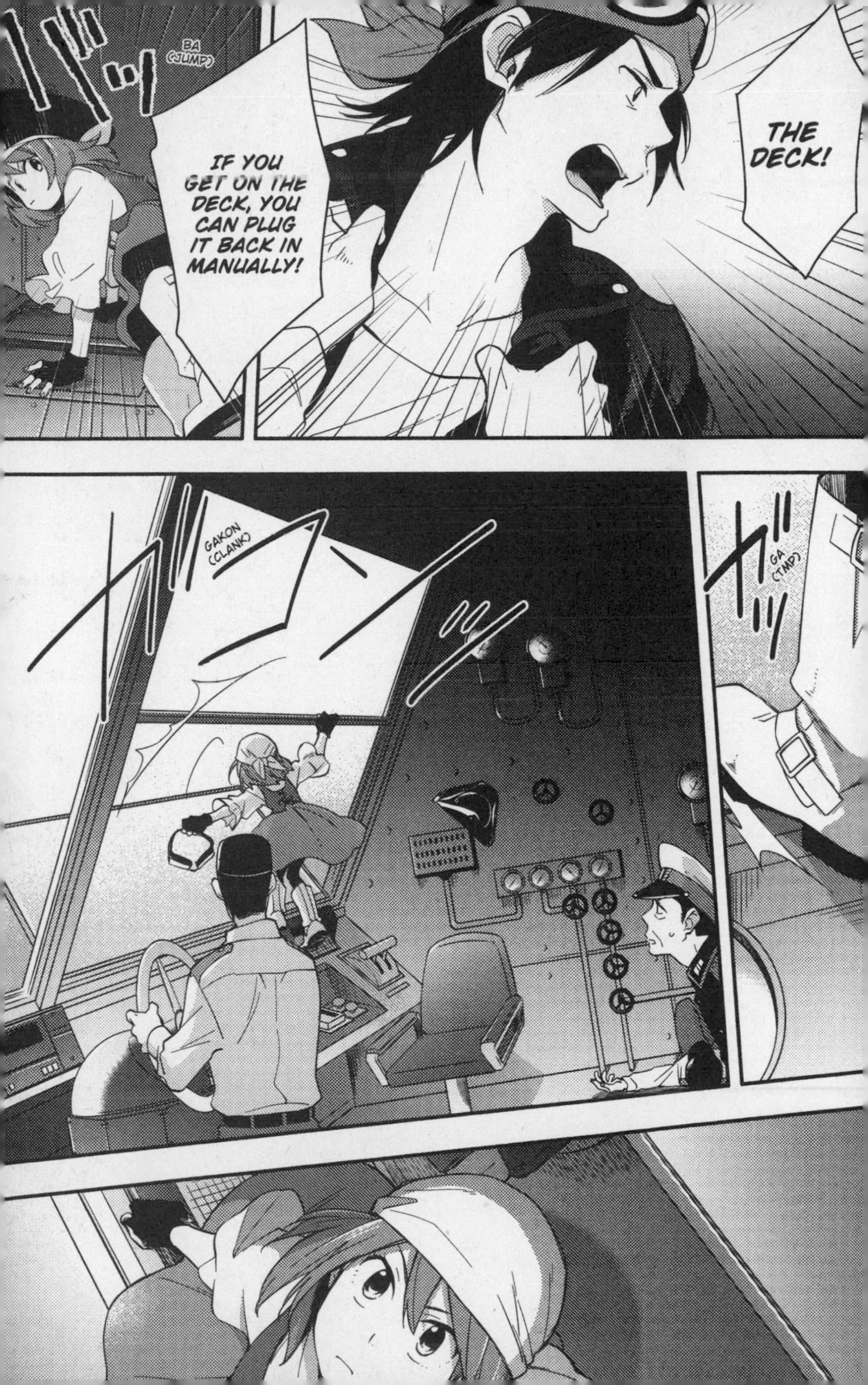
THE DECK!
IF YOU GET ON THE DECK, YOU CAN PLUG IT BACK IN MANUALLY!
BA (JUMP)
GA (TMP)
GAKON (CLANK)

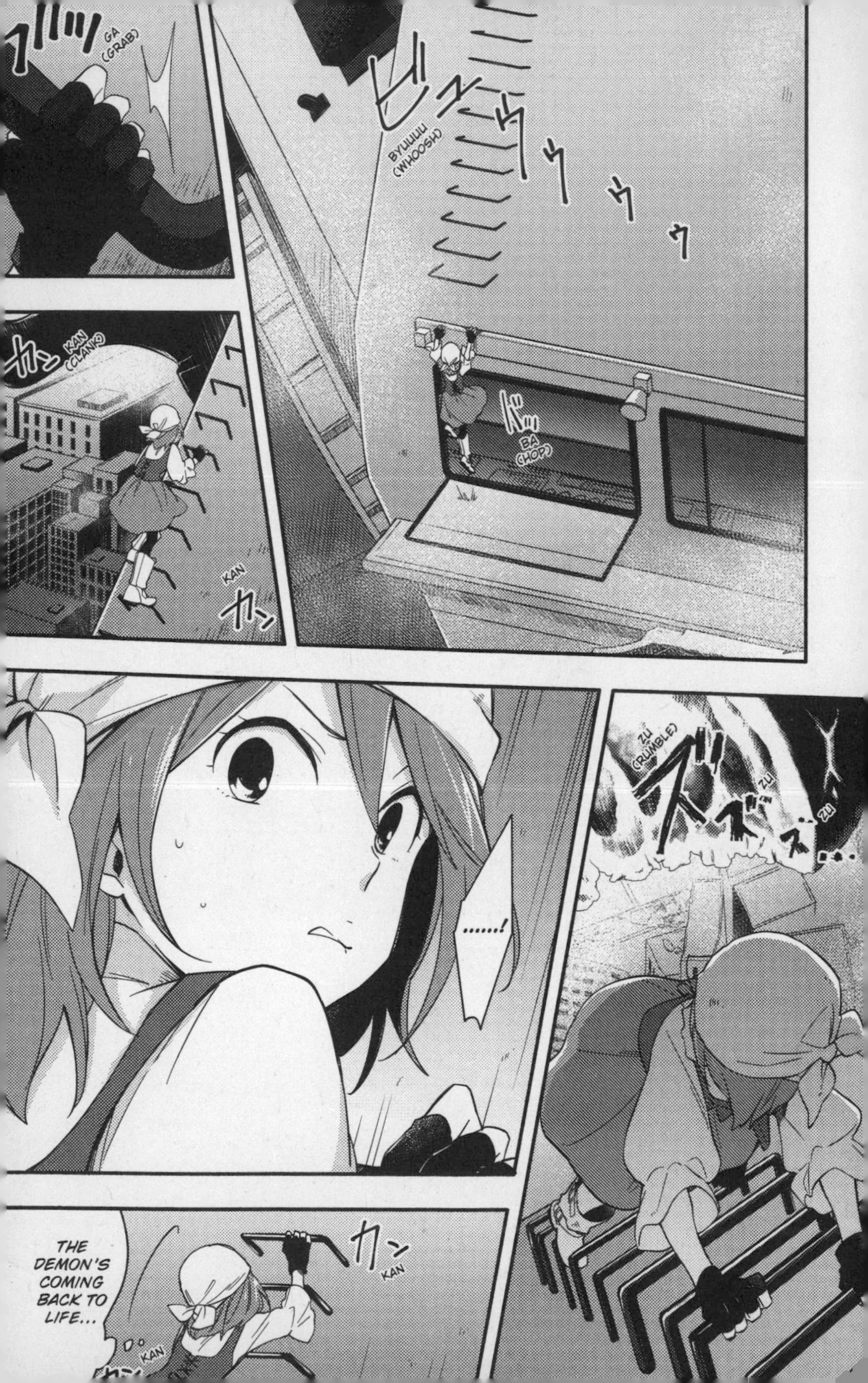

BYUUUU (WHOOSH)
BA (HOP)
GA (GRAB)
KAN (CLANK)
KAN
ZU (RUMBLE)
ZU
ZU
......!
KAN
THE DEMON'S COMING BACK TO LIFE...
KAN

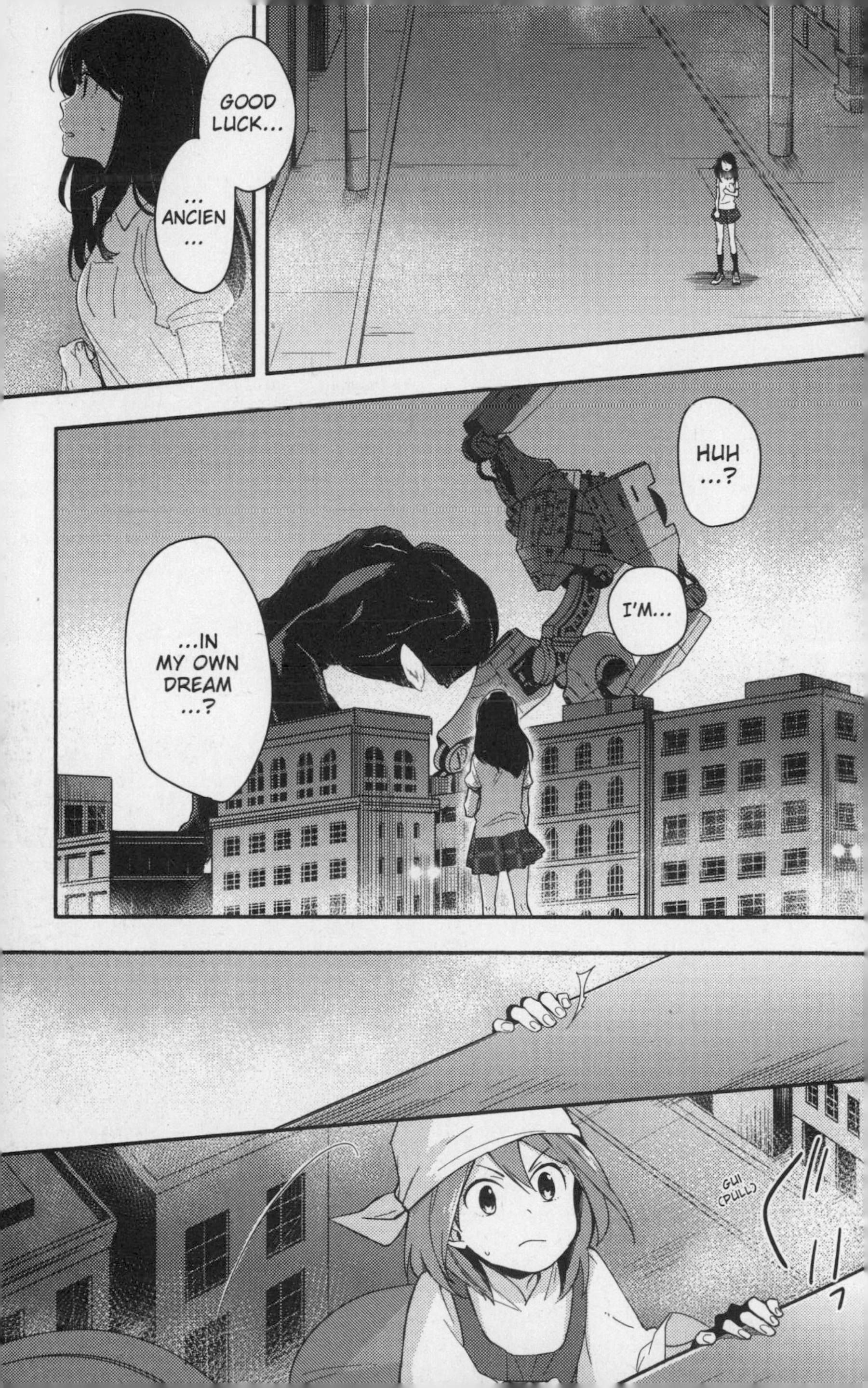
GOOD LUCK...
...ANCIEN...
HUH...?
I'M...
...IN MY OWN DREAM...?
GUI (PULL)

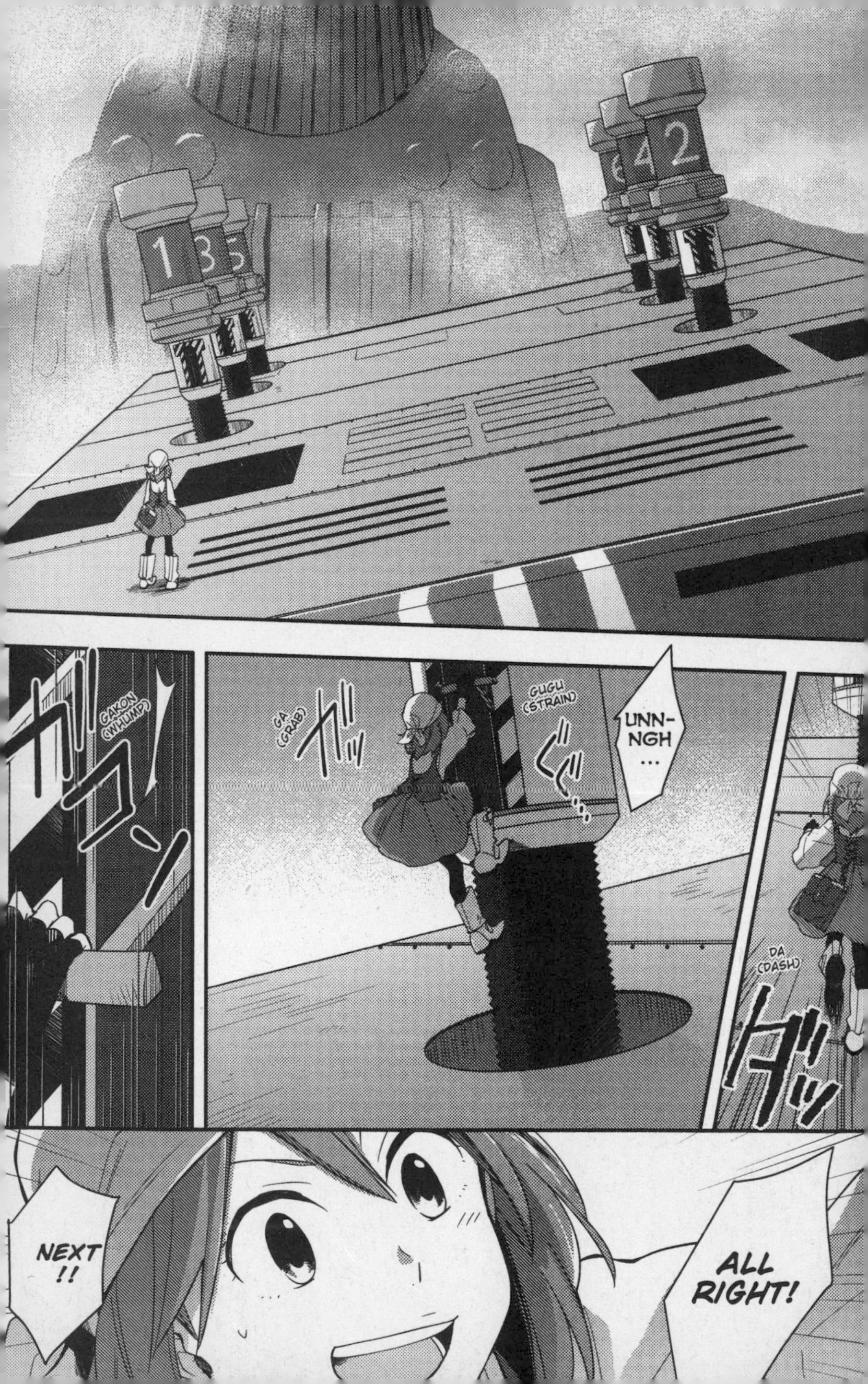
DA (DASH)
UNN-NGH...
GUGU (STRAIN)
GA (GRAB)
GAKON (WHUMP)
ALL RIGHT!
NEXT!!

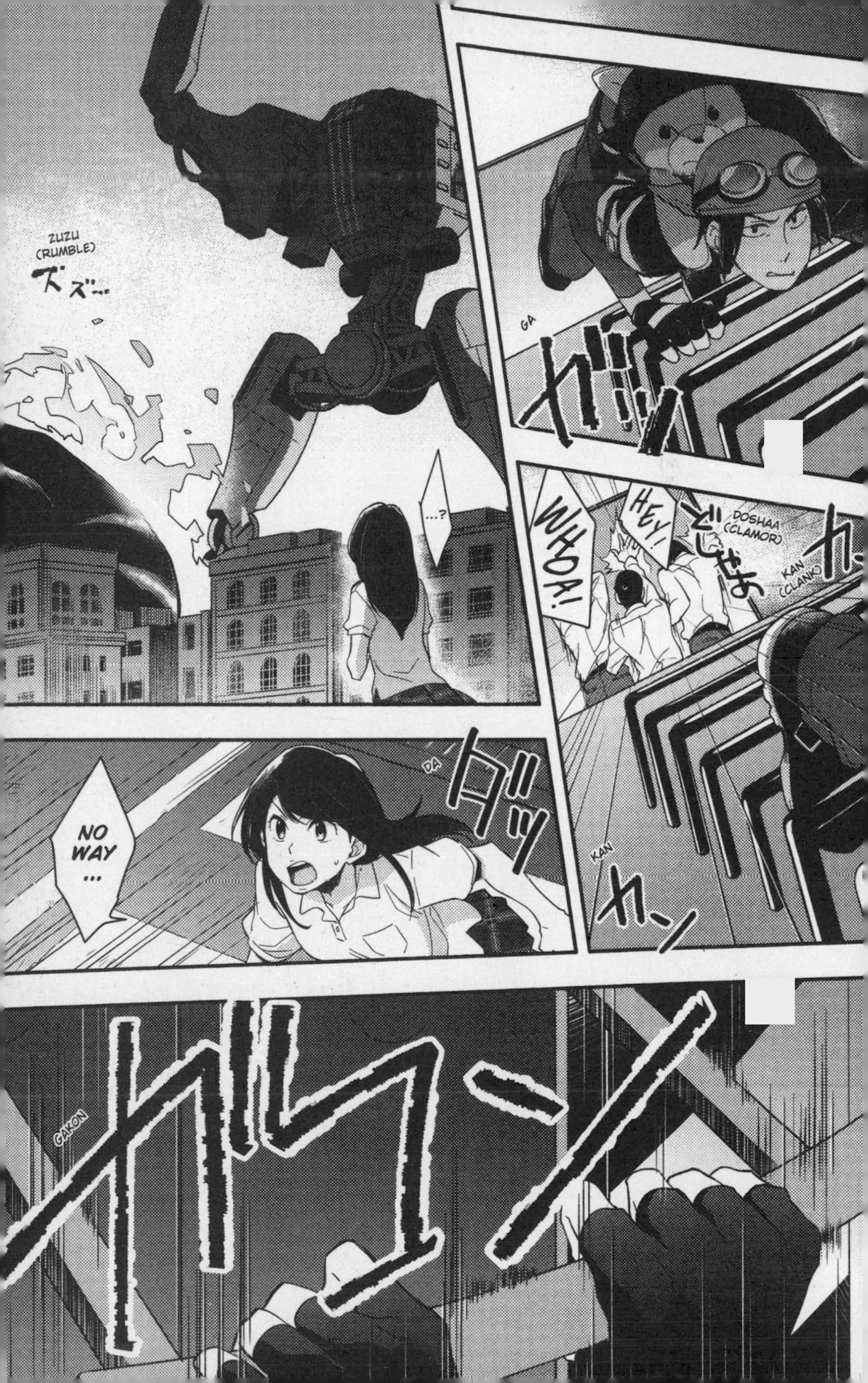
GA
ZUZU (RUMBLE)
...?
HEY!
WHOA!!
DOSHAA (CLAMOR)
KAN (CLANK)
KAN
DA
NO WAY ...
GAKON

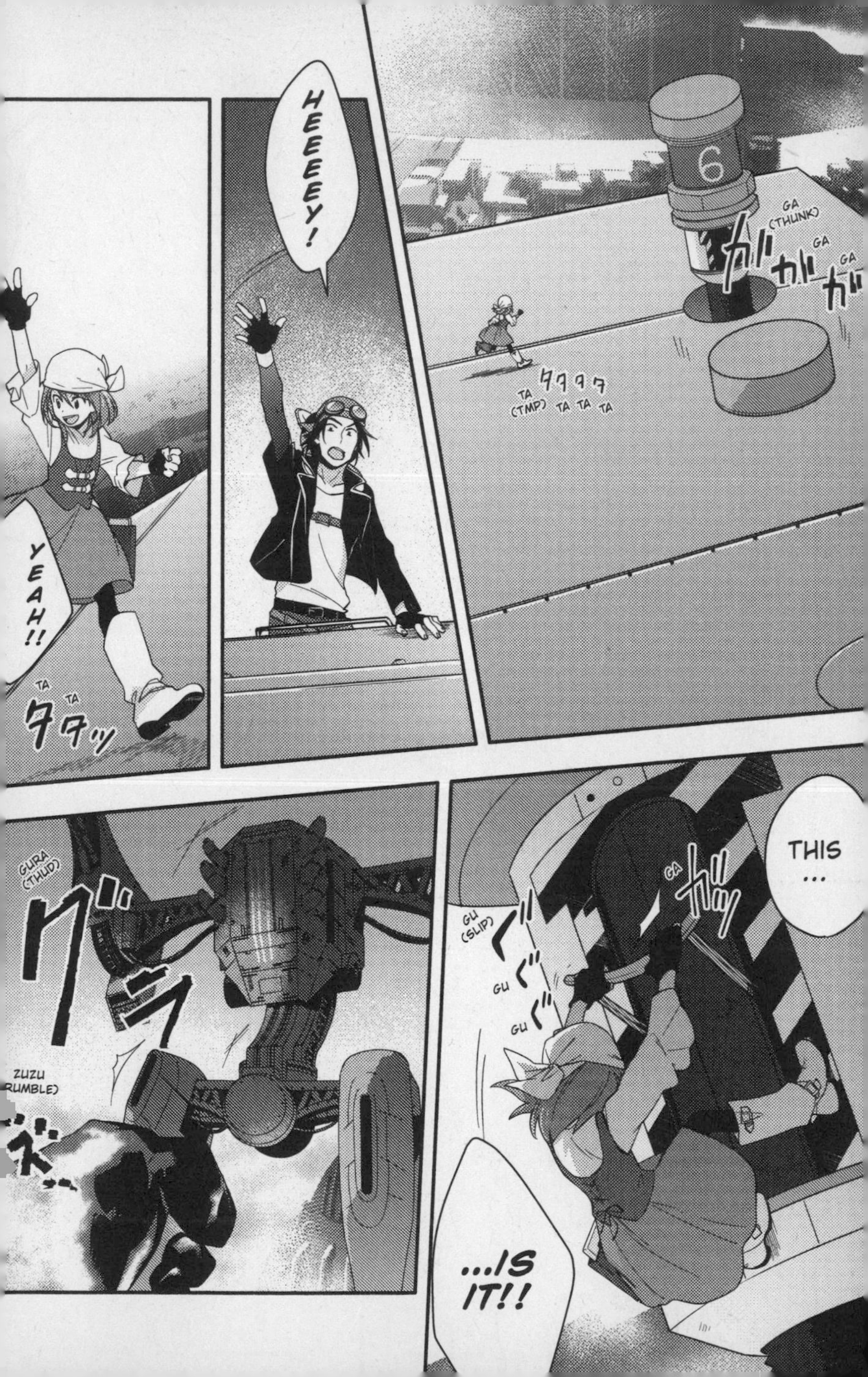
GA (THUNK)
GA
GA
TA (TMP) TA TA TA
タタタタ
HEEEEEY!
YEAH!!
TA TA
タタッ
THIS ...
GA
GU (SLIP)
GU
GU
...IS IT!!
GURA (THUD)
ZUZU (RUMBLE)

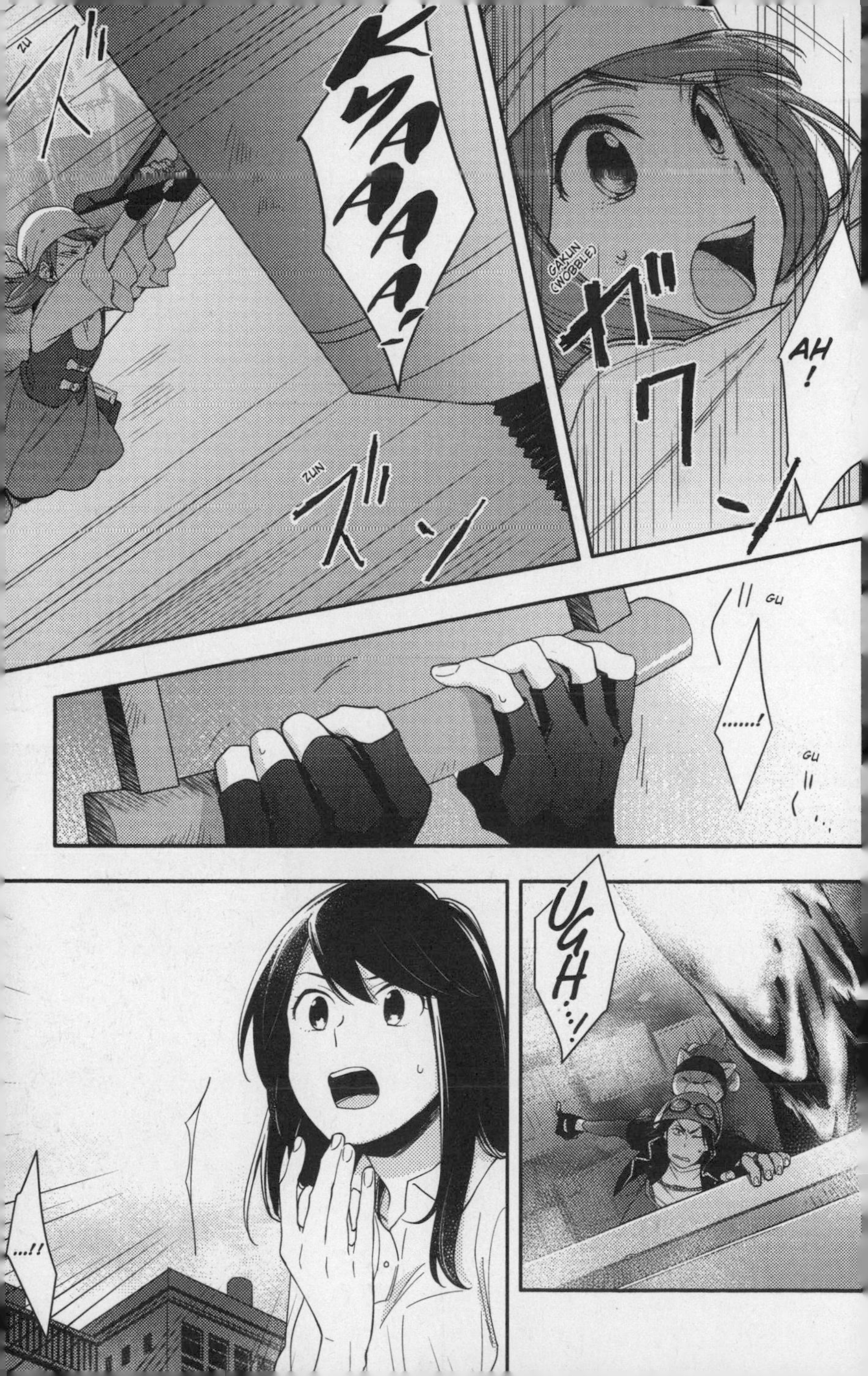
GAKUN (WOBBLE)
AH!
ZU
KWAAAA!
ZUN
GU
......!
GU
UGH...!
...!!

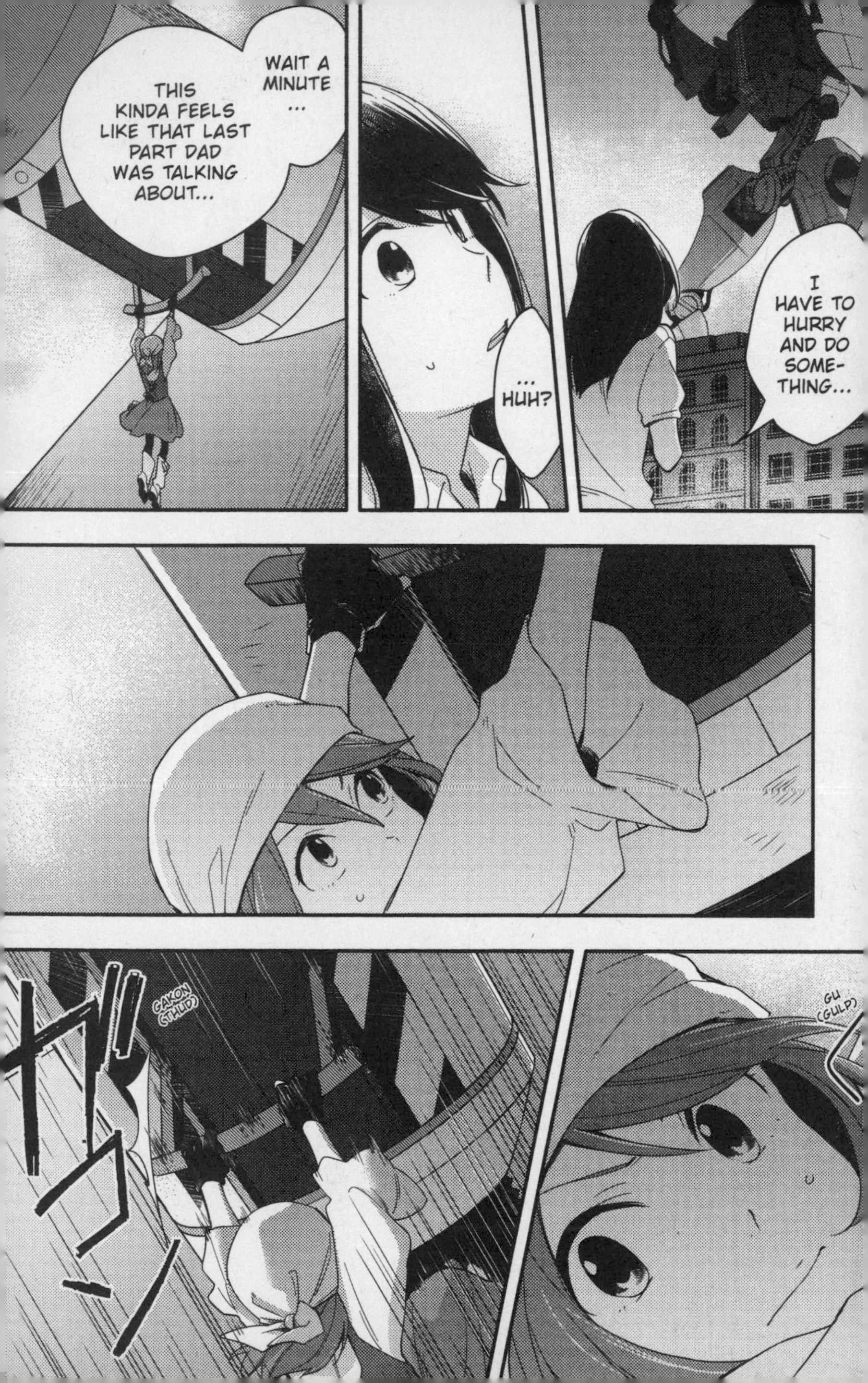
I HAVE TO HURRY AND DO SOME-THING...
... HUH?
WAIT A MINUTE ...
THIS KINDA FEELS LIKE THAT LAST PART DAD WAS TALKING ABOUT...
GU (GULP)
GAKON (THUD)

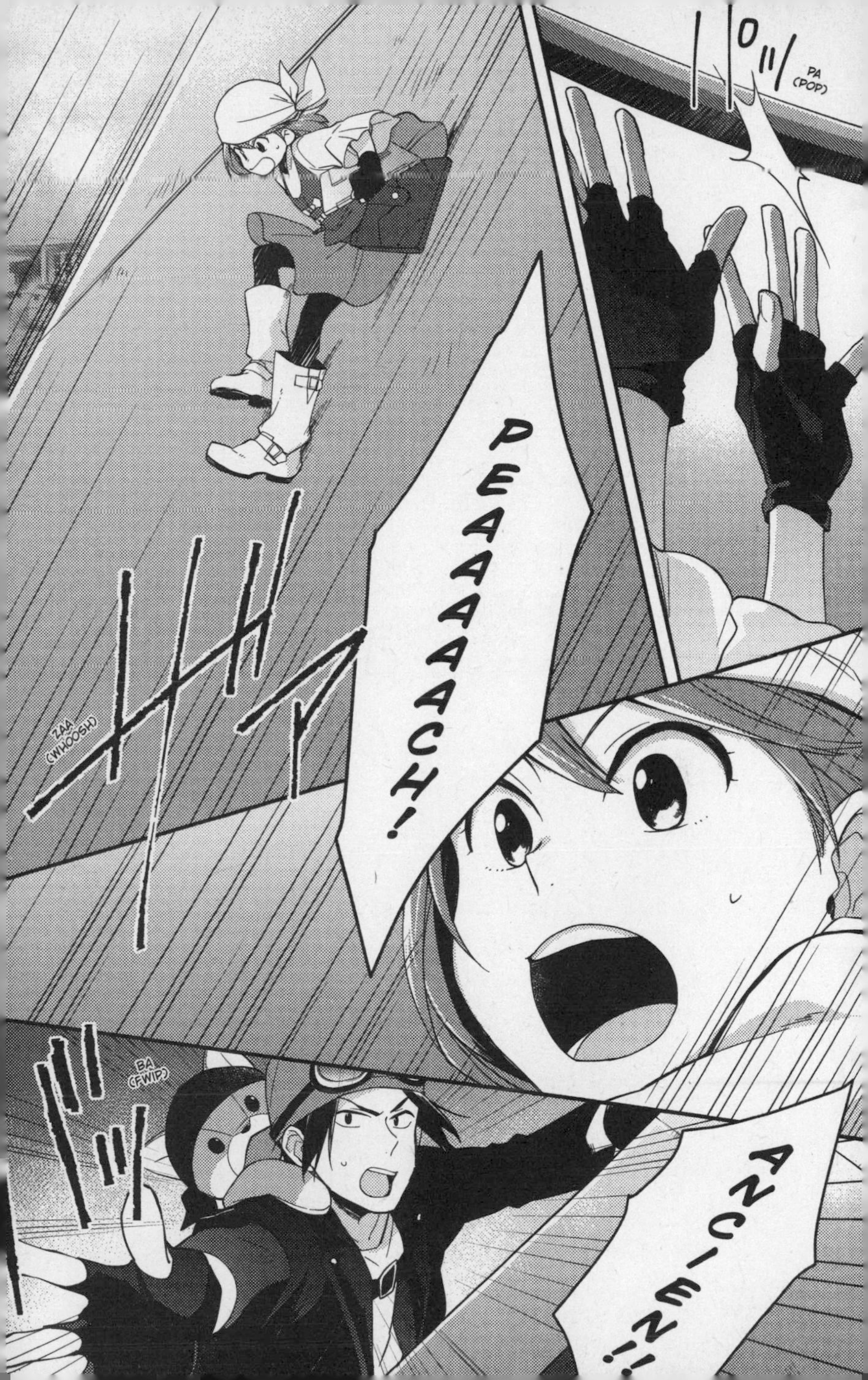
PA
(POP)
ZAA
(WHOOSH)
PEAAAAAACH!
ANC—IEN!!
BA
(FWIP)

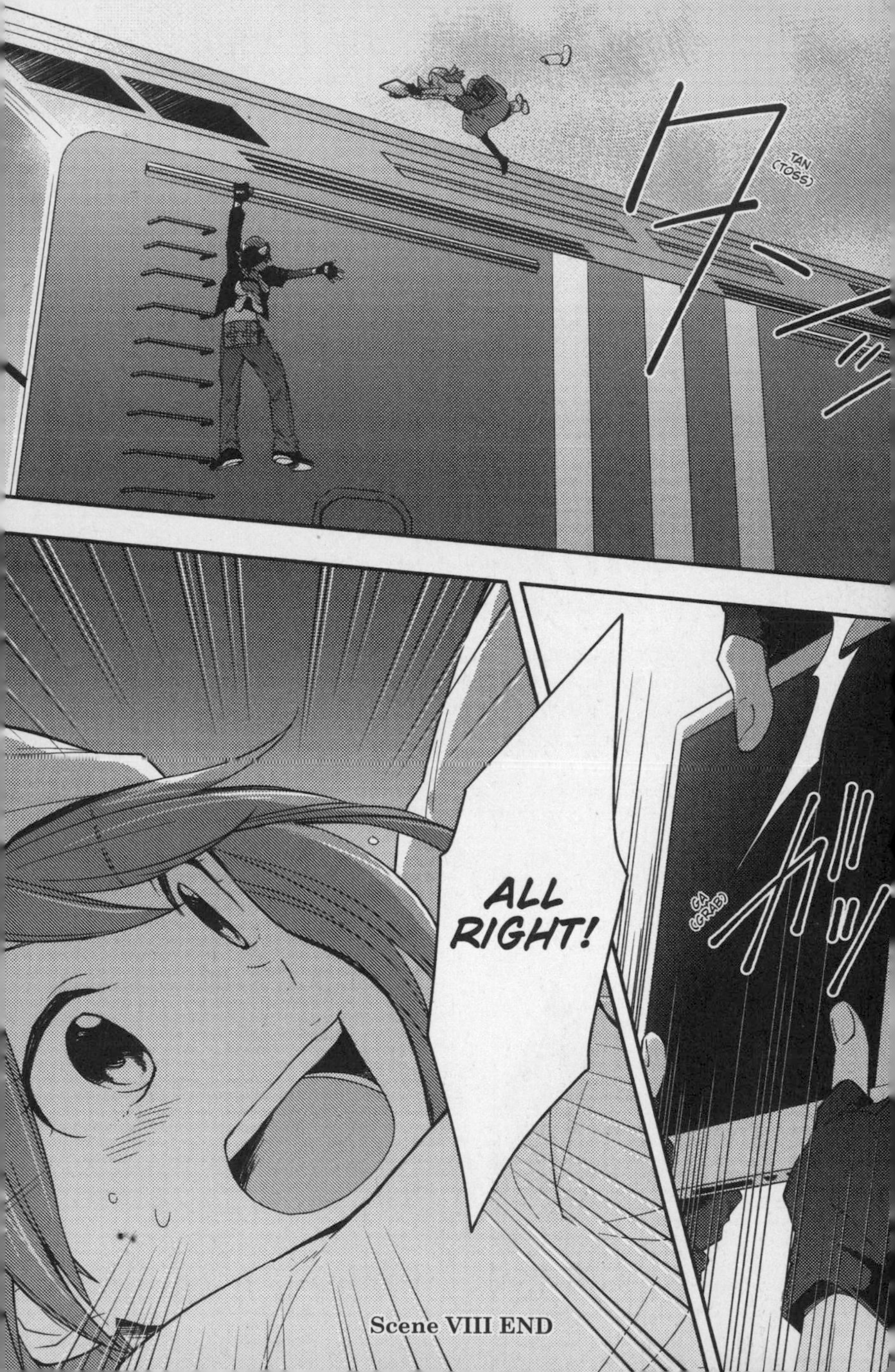
TAN (TOSS)
GA (GRAB)
ALL RIGHT!

Scene VIII END

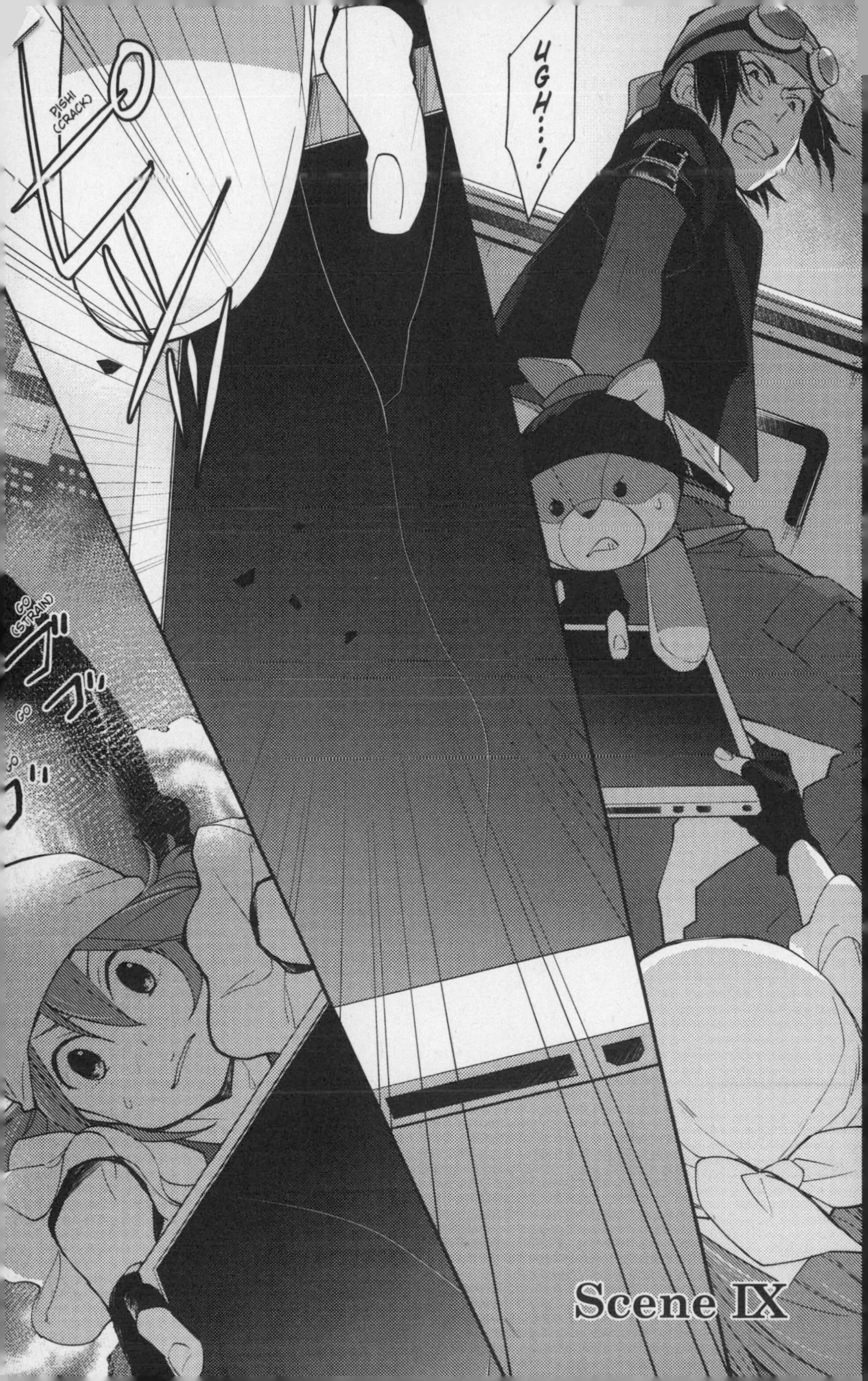
UGH...!
PISHI (CRACK)
GO (STRAIN)
GO
GO

Scene IX

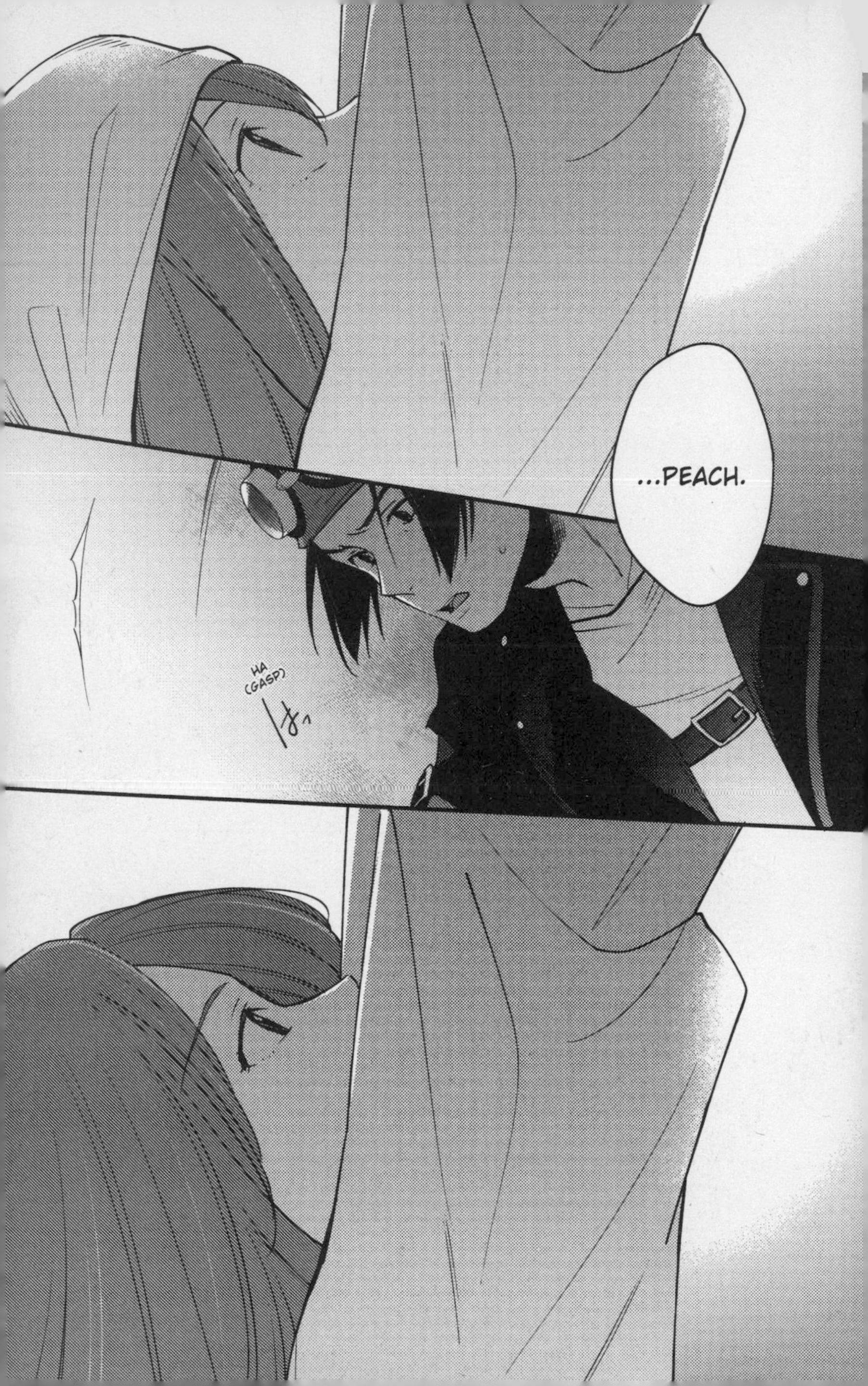
...PEACH.
HA (GASP)
はっ

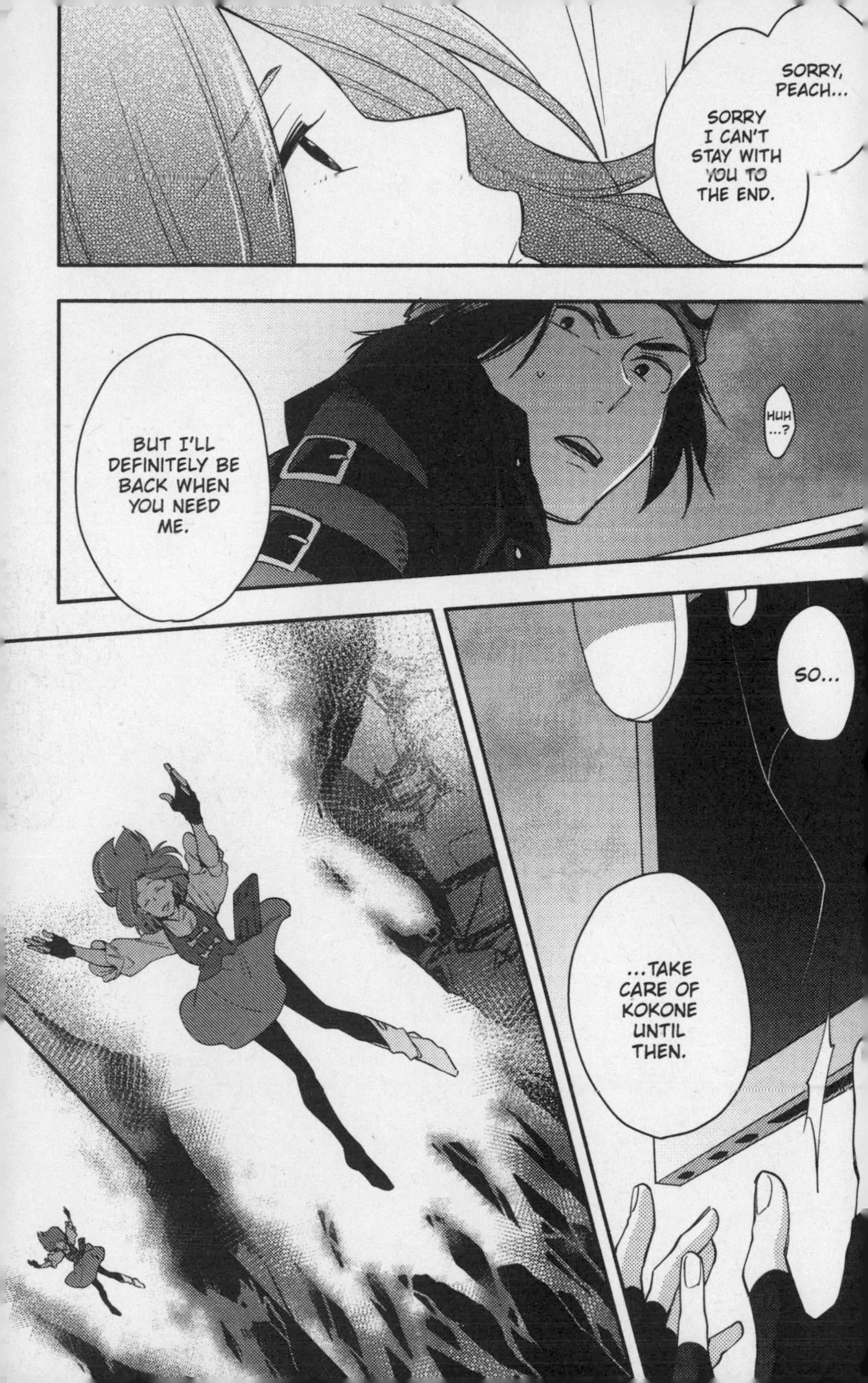
SORRY, PEACH...
SORRY I CAN'T STAY WITH YOU TO THE END.
HUH ...?
BUT I'LL DEFINITELY BE BACK WHEN YOU NEED ME.
SO...
...TAKE CARE OF KOKONE UNTIL THEN.

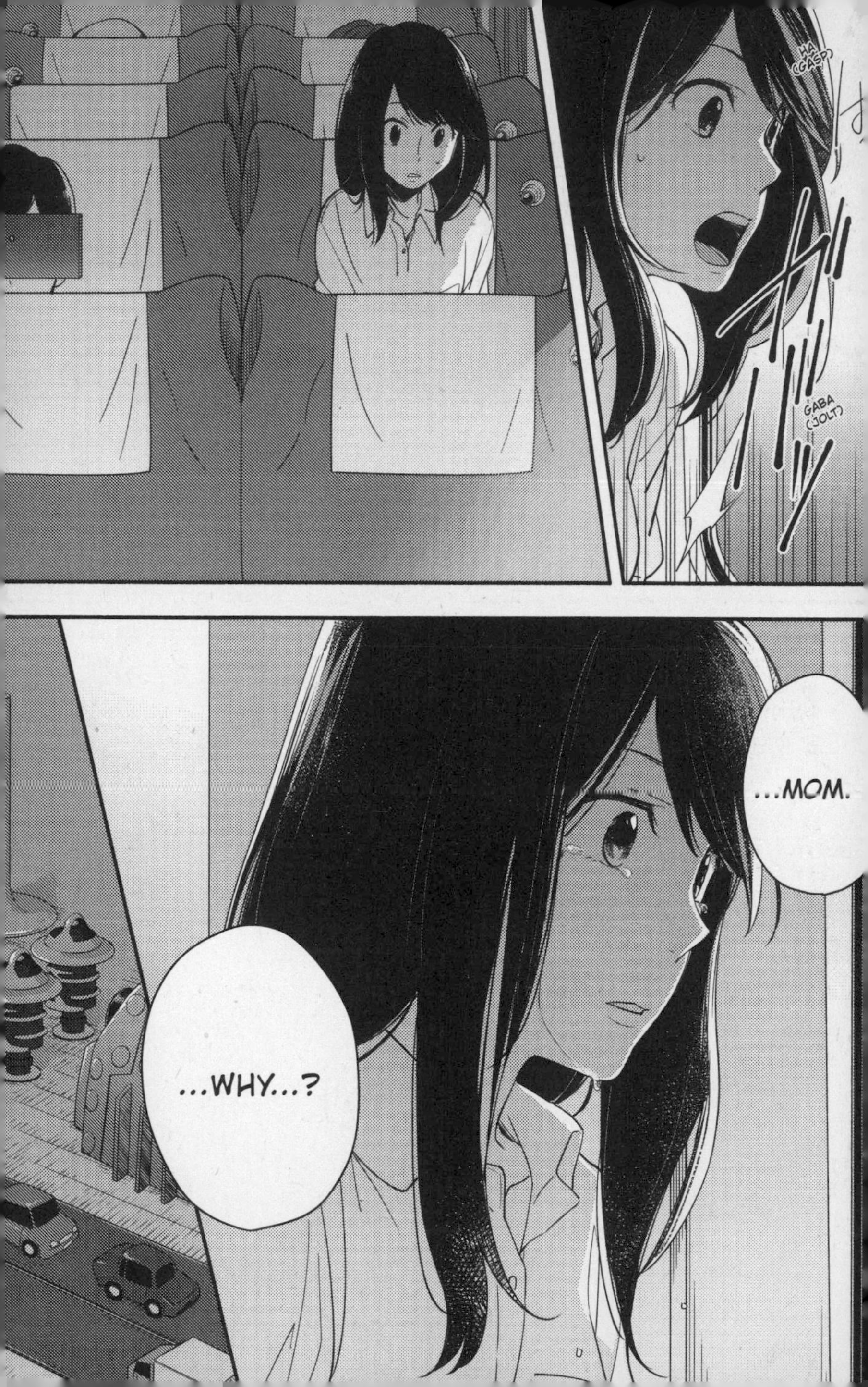
HA (GASP)
GABA (JOLT)
...MOM.
...WHY...?

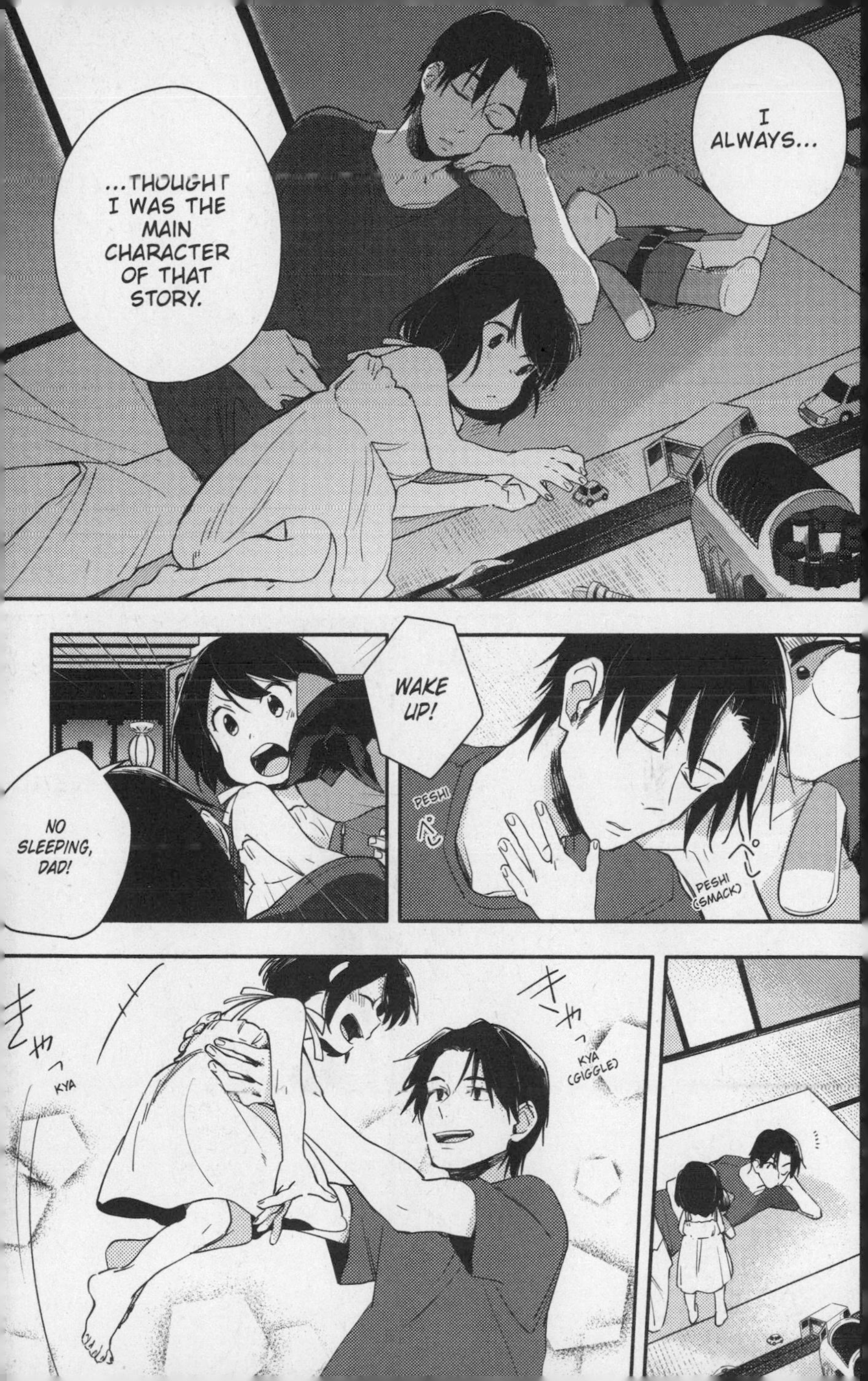
I ALWAYS...
...THOUGHT I WAS THE MAIN CHARACTER OF THAT STORY.
PESHI (SMACK)
PESHI
WAKE UP!
NO SLEEPING, DAD!
...
KYA (GIGGLE)
KYA

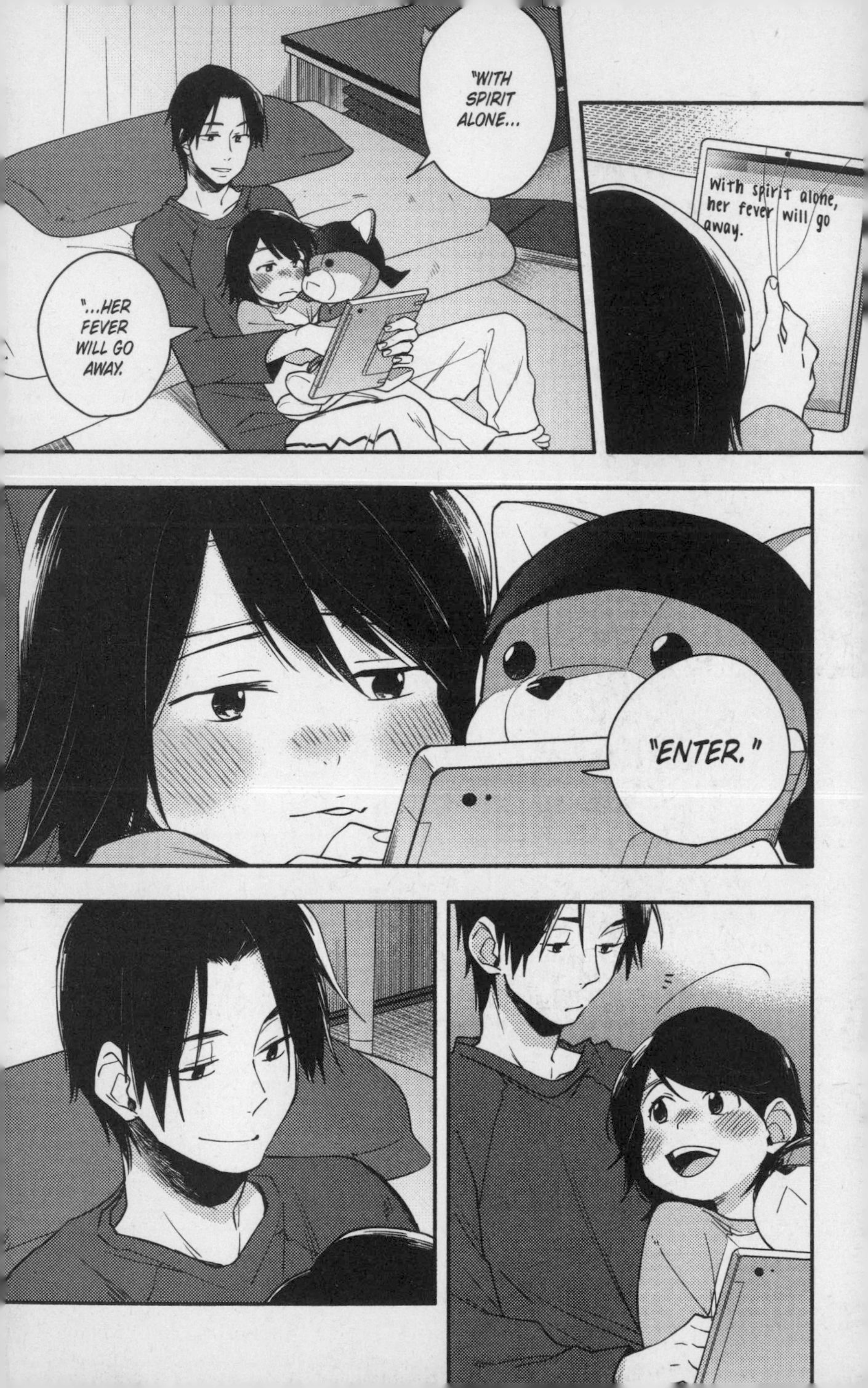
With spirit alone, her fever will go away.
"WITH SPIRIT ALONE...
"...HER FEVER WILL GO AWAY.
"ENTER."

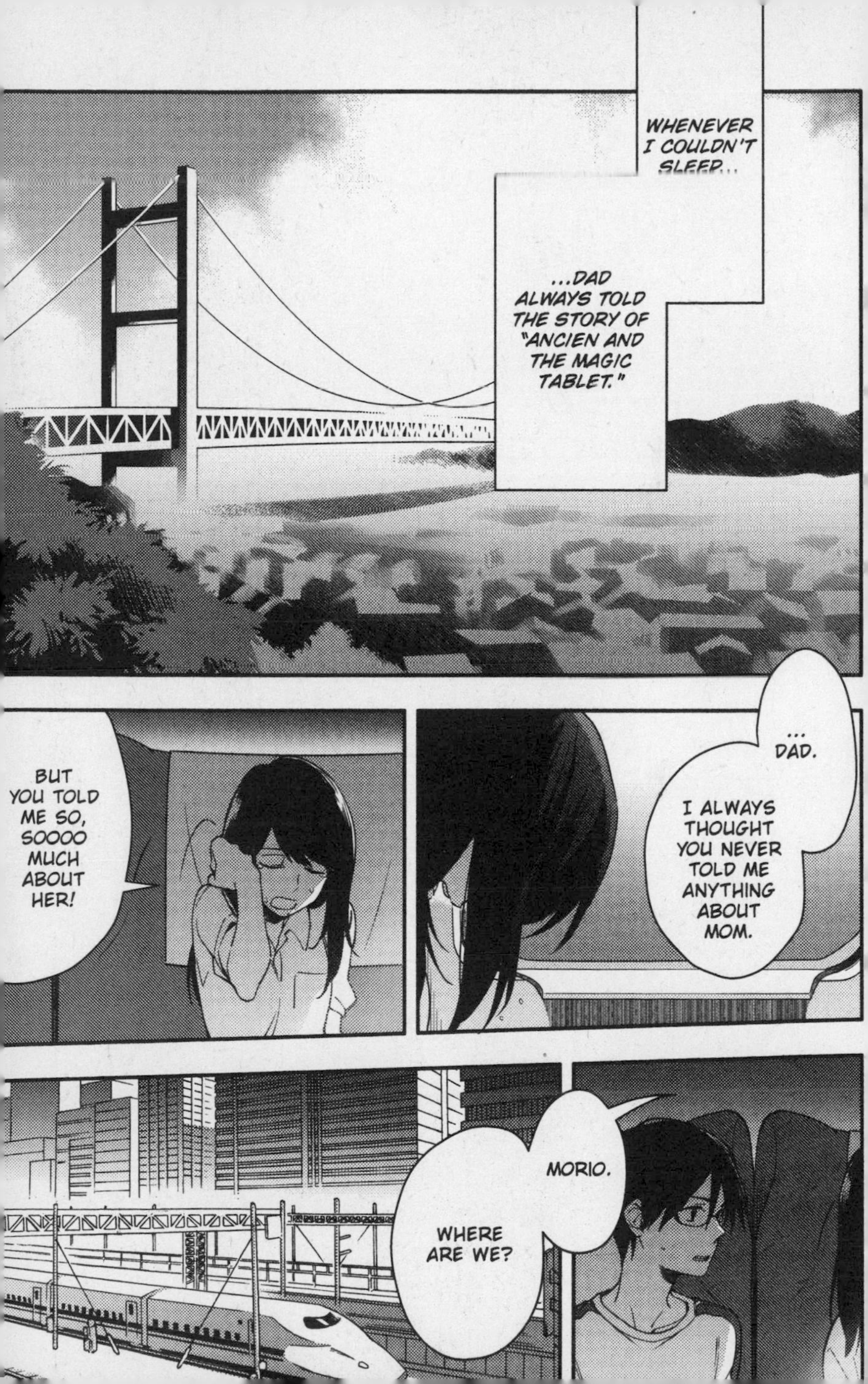
WHENEVER I COULDN'T SLEEP...
...DAD ALWAYS TOLD THE STORY OF "ANCIEN AND THE MAGIC TABLET."
... DAD.
I ALWAYS THOUGHT YOU NEVER TOLD ME ANYTHING ABOUT MOM.
BUT YOU TOLD ME SO, SOOOO MUCH ABOUT HER!
MORIO.
WHERE ARE WE?

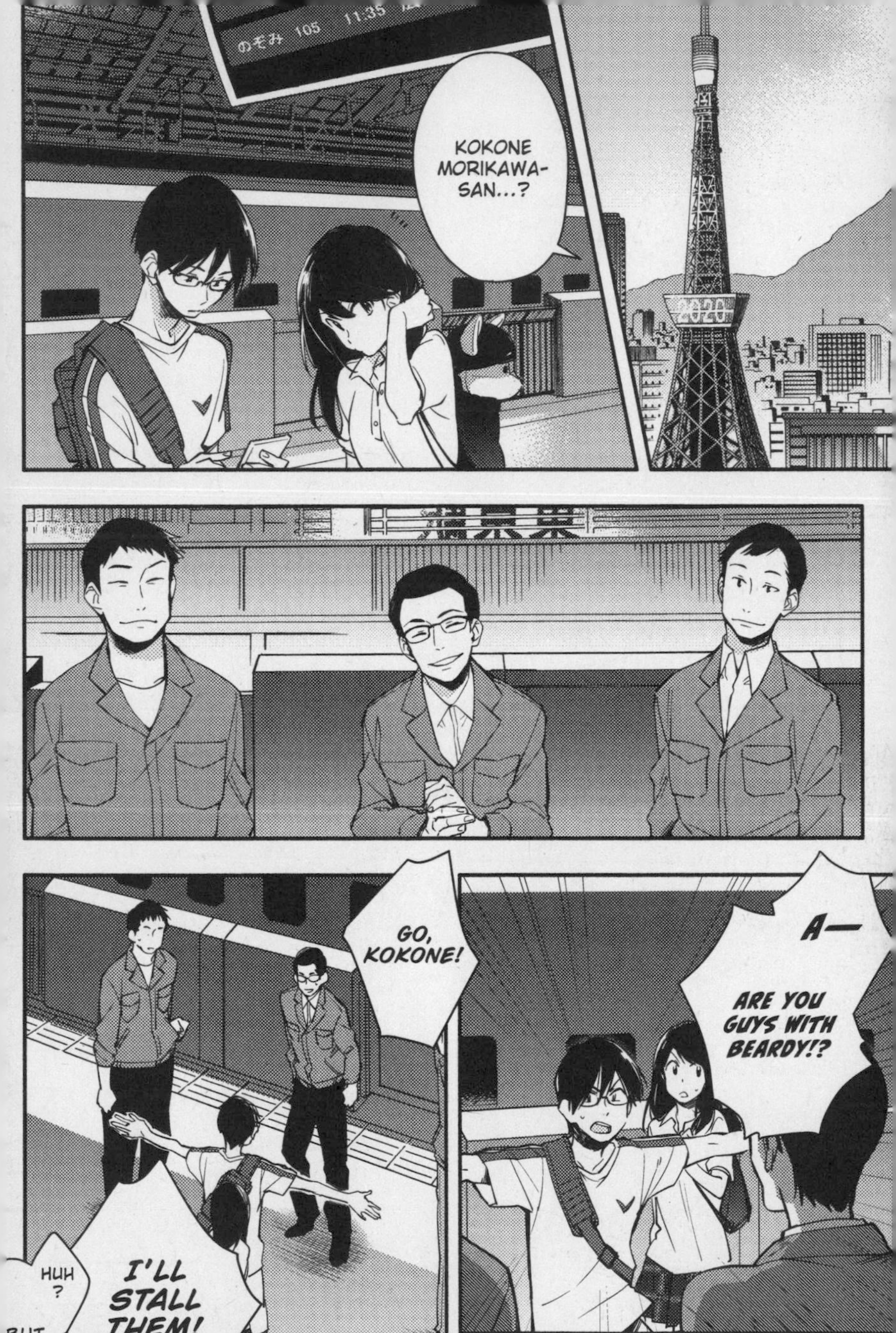
2020
のぞみ 105 11:35
KOKONE MORIKAWA-SAN...?
A—
ARE YOU GUYS WITH BEARDY!?
GO, KOKONE!
I'LL STALL THEM!
HUH? BUT...

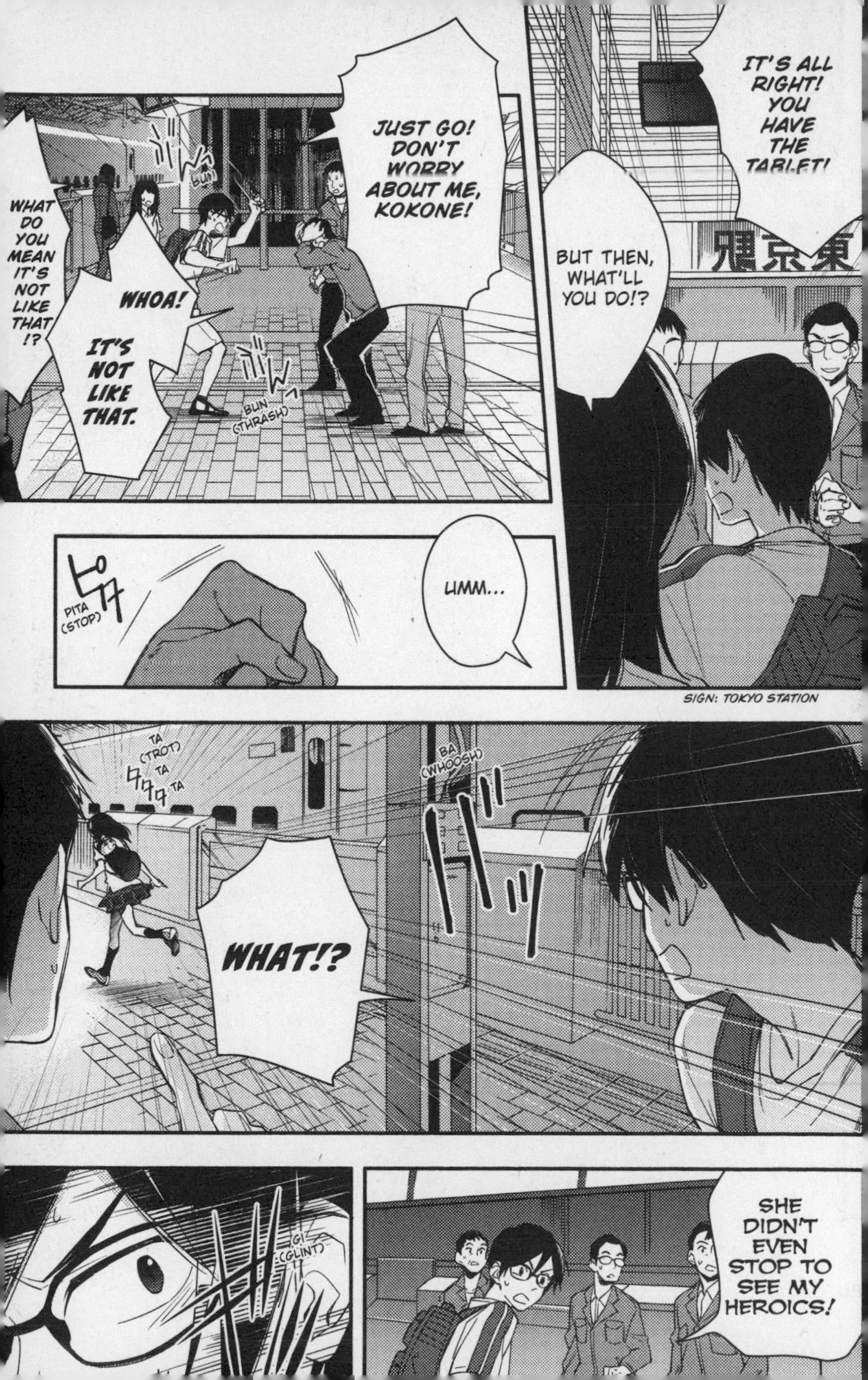
IT'S ALL RIGHT! YOU HAVE THE TABLET!
BUT THEN, WHAT'LL YOU DO!?
SIGN: TOKYO STATION
JUST GO! DON'T WORRY ABOUT ME, KOKONE!
BUN
WHOA!
IT'S NOT LIKE THAT.
WHAT DO YOU MEAN IT'S NOT LIKE THAT!?
BUN (THRASH)
UMM...
PITA (STOP)
BA (WHOOSH)
WHAT!?
TA (TROT) TA TA
SHE DIDN'T EVEN STOP TO SEE MY HEROICS!
GI (GLINT)

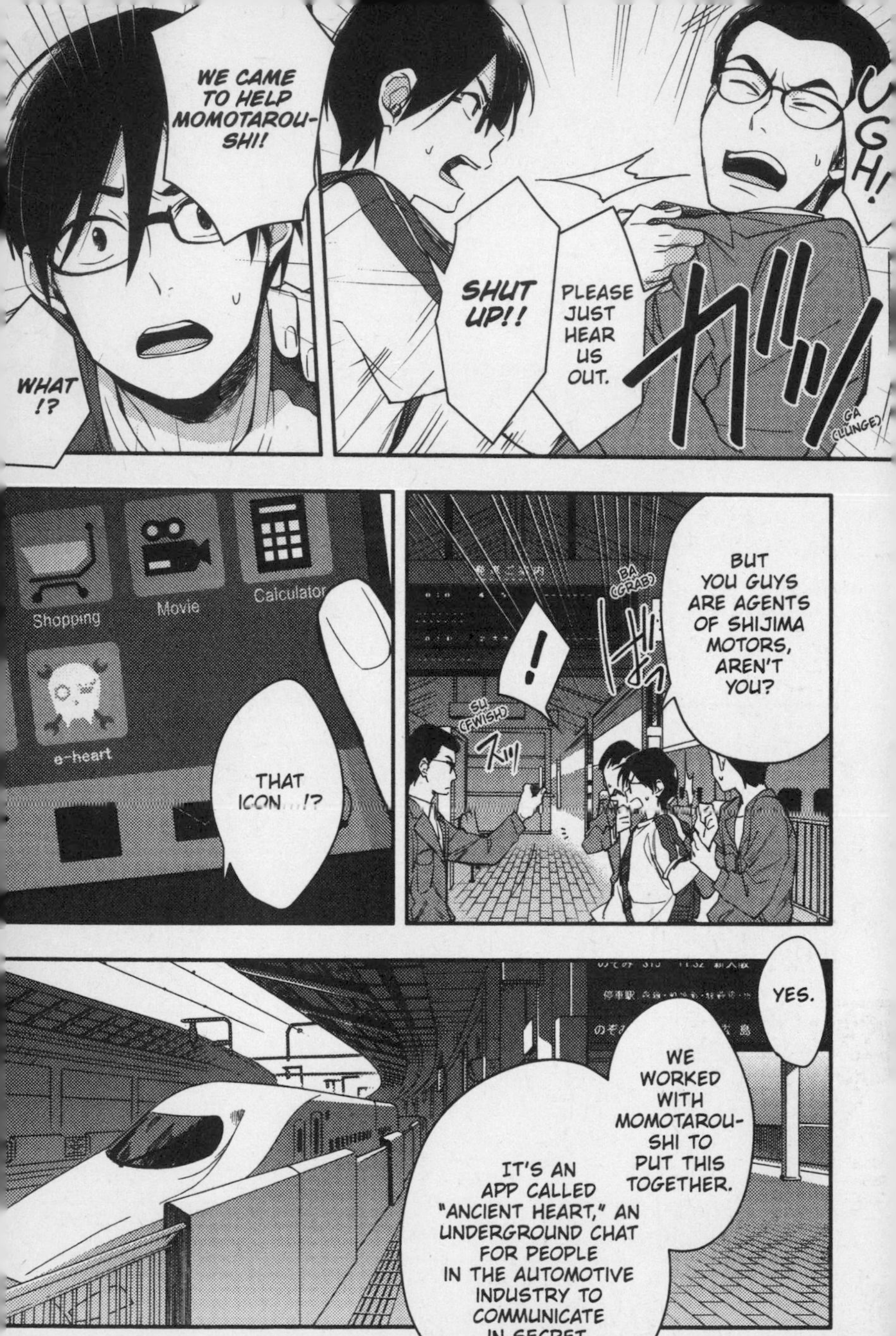
UGH!
GA (LUNGE)
PLEASE JUST HEAR US OUT.
SHUT UP!!
WE CAME TO HELP MOMOTAROU-SHI!
WHAT!?
BUT YOU GUYS ARE AGENTS OF SHIJIMA MOTORS, AREN'T YOU?
BA (GRAB)
!
SU (FWISH)
THAT ICON...!?
Calculator
Movie
Shopping
e-heart
YES.
WE WORKED WITH MOMOTAROU-SHI TO PUT THIS TOGETHER.
IT'S AN APP CALLED "ANCIENT HEART," AN UNDERGROUND CHAT FOR PEOPLE IN THE AUTOMOTIVE INDUSTRY TO COMMUNICATE IN SECRET.

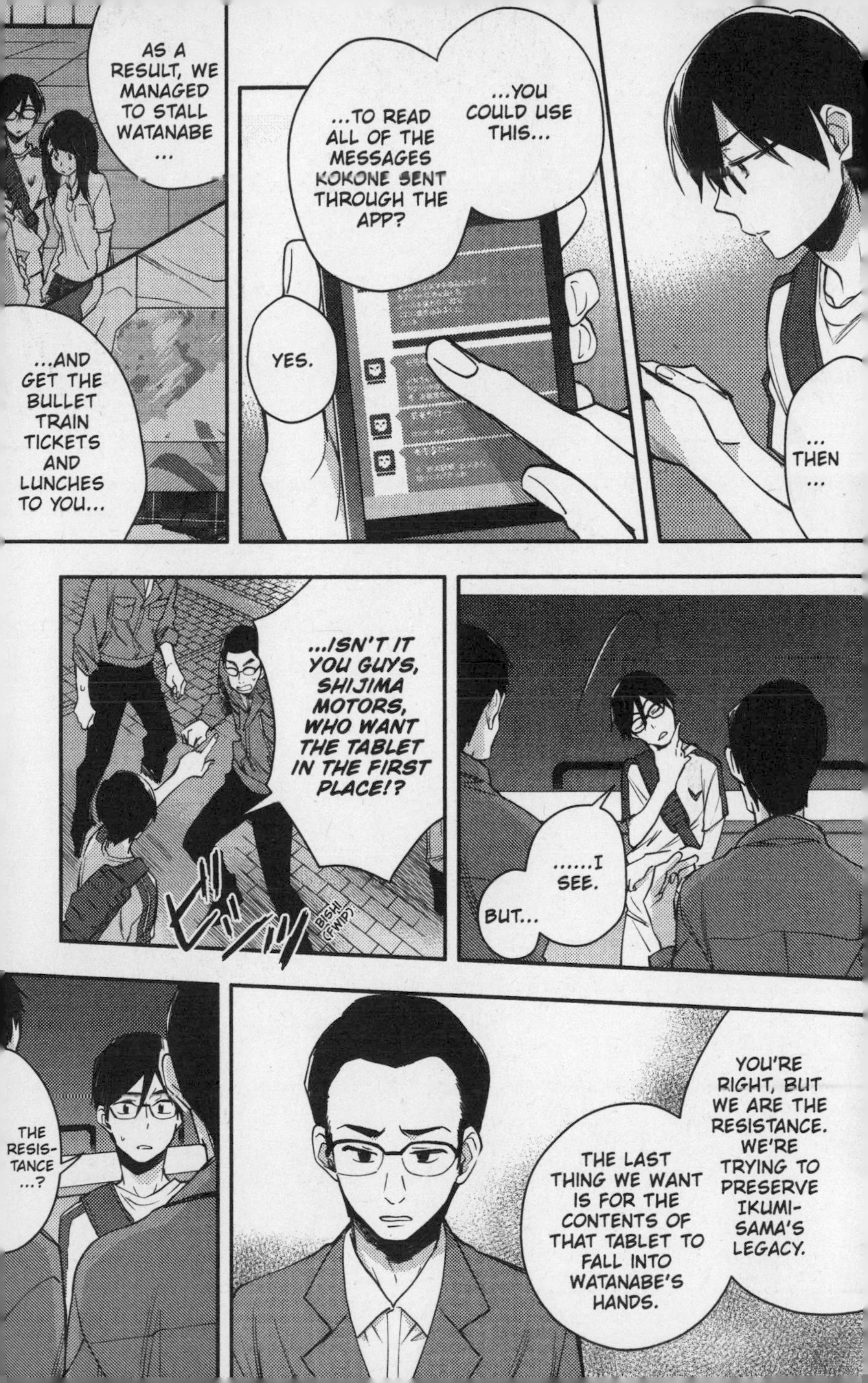
...THEN...
...YOU COULD USE THIS...
...TO READ ALL OF THE MESSAGES KOKONE SENT THROUGH THE APP?
YES.
AS A RESULT, WE MANAGED TO STALL WATANABE...
...AND GET THE BULLET TRAIN TICKETS AND LUNCHES TO YOU...
......I SEE.
BUT...
...ISN'T IT YOU GUYS, SHIJIMA MOTORS, WHO WANT THE TABLET IN THE FIRST PLACE!?
BISHI (FWIP)
YOU'RE RIGHT, BUT WE ARE THE RESISTANCE. WE'RE TRYING TO PRESERVE IKUMI-SAMA'S LEGACY.
THE LAST THING WE WANT IS FOR THE CONTENTS OF THAT TABLET TO FALL INTO WATANABE'S HANDS.
THE RESISTANCE...?

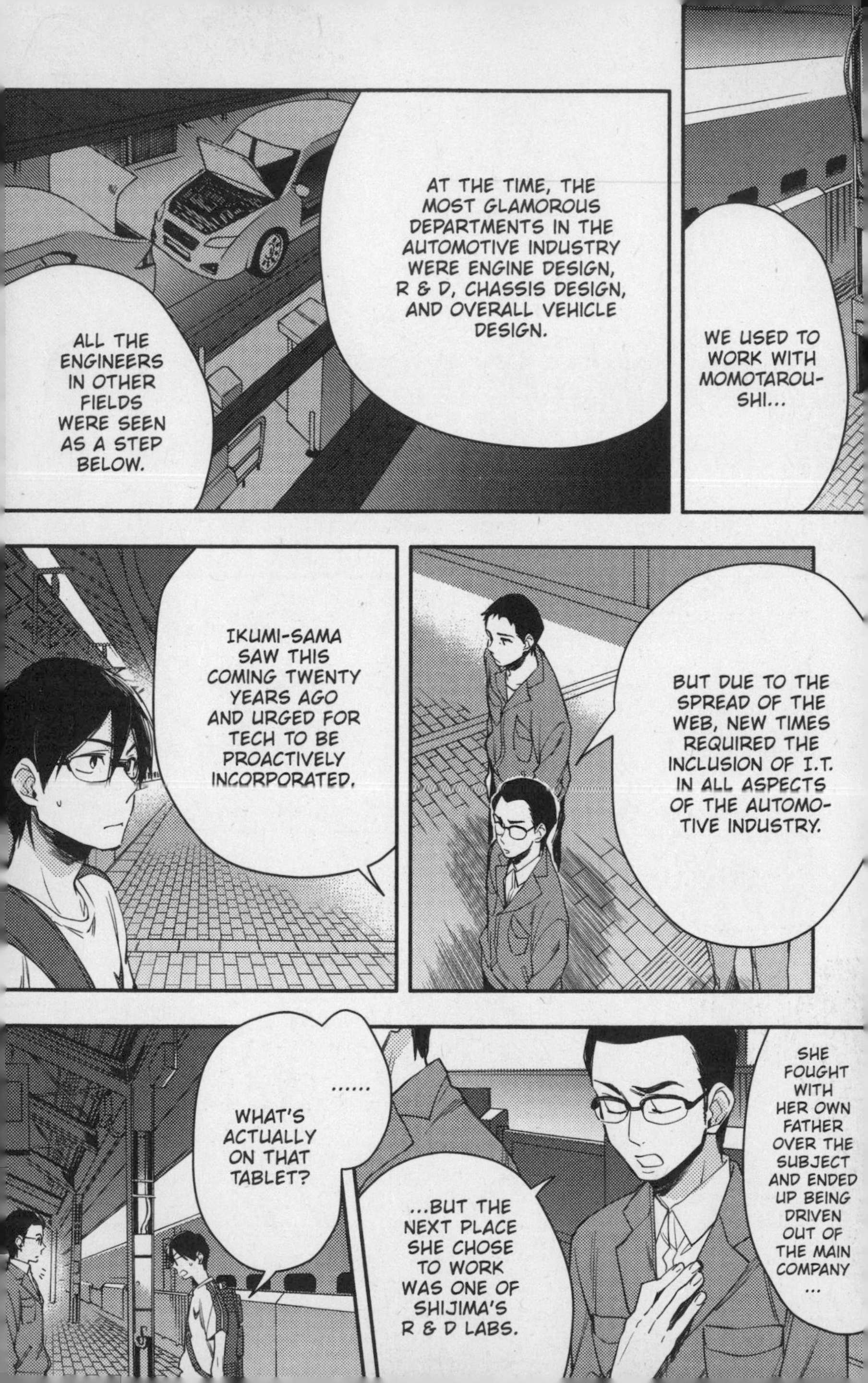

WE USED TO WORK WITH MOMOTAROU-SHI...
AT THE TIME, THE MOST GLAMOROUS DEPARTMENTS IN THE AUTOMOTIVE INDUSTRY WERE ENGINE DESIGN, R & D, CHASSIS DESIGN, AND OVERALL VEHICLE DESIGN.
ALL THE ENGINEERS IN OTHER FIELDS WERE SEEN AS A STEP BELOW.
BUT DUE TO THE SPREAD OF THE WEB, NEW TIMES REQUIRED THE INCLUSION OF I.T. IN ALL ASPECTS OF THE AUTOMOTIVE INDUSTRY.
IKUMI-SAMA SAW THIS COMING TWENTY YEARS AGO AND URGED FOR TECH TO BE PROACTIVELY INCORPORATED.
SHE FOUGHT WITH HER OWN FATHER OVER THE SUBJECT AND ENDED UP BEING DRIVEN OUT OF THE MAIN COMPANY...
...BUT THE NEXT PLACE SHE CHOSE TO WORK WAS ONE OF SHIJIMA'S R & D LABS.
......
WHAT'S ACTUALLY ON THAT TABLET?

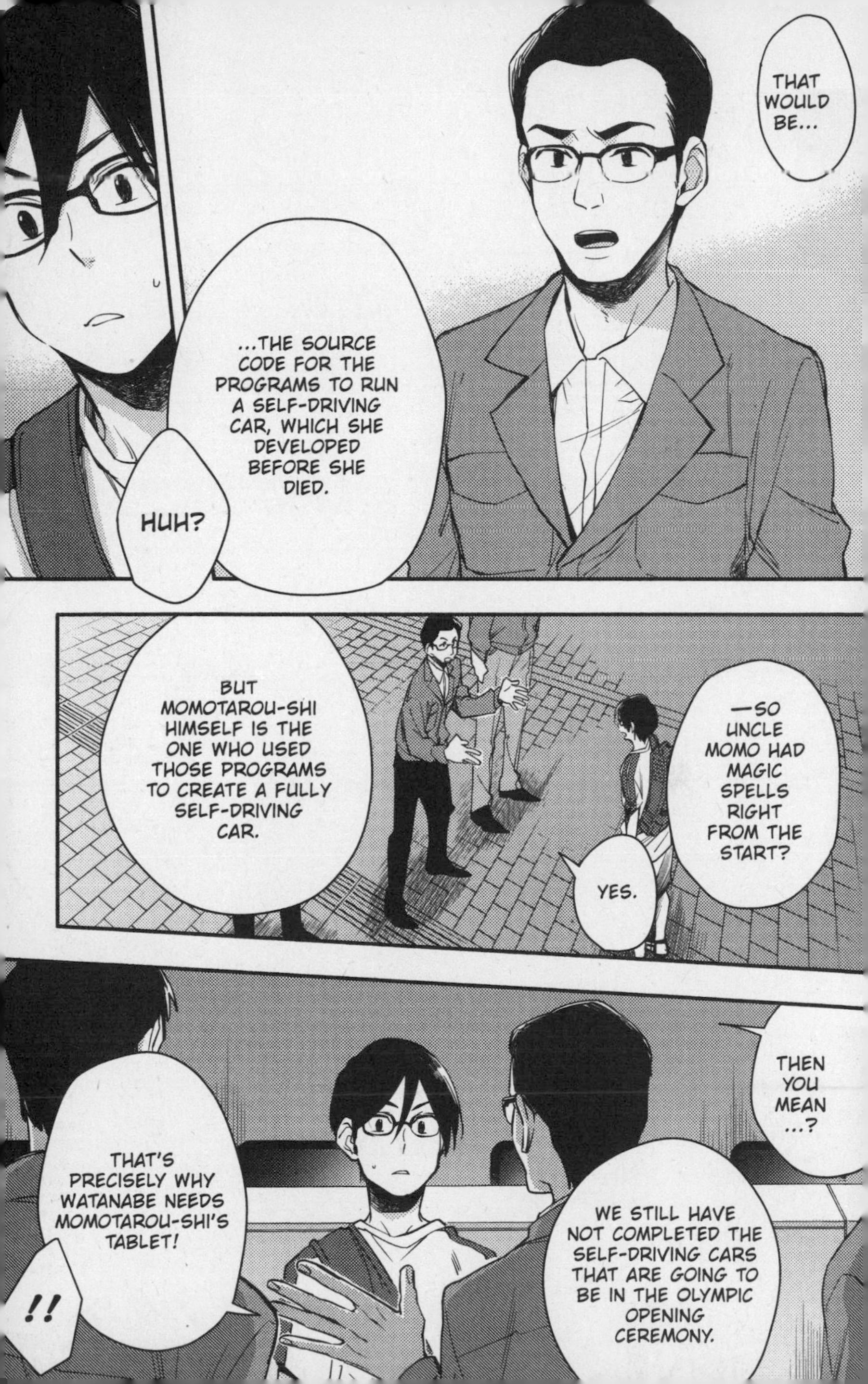
THAT WOULD BE...
...THE SOURCE CODE FOR THE PROGRAMS TO RUN A SELF-DRIVING CAR, WHICH SHE DEVELOPED BEFORE SHE DIED.
HUH?
—SO UNCLE MOMO HAD MAGIC SPELLS RIGHT FROM THE START?
YES.
BUT MOMOTAROU-SHI HIMSELF IS THE ONE WHO USED THOSE PROGRAMS TO CREATE A FULLY SELF-DRIVING CAR.
THEN YOU MEAN ...?
WE STILL HAVE NOT COMPLETED THE SELF-DRIVING CARS THAT ARE GOING TO BE IN THE OLYMPIC OPENING CEREMONY.
THAT'S PRECISELY WHY WATANABE NEEDS MOMOTAROU-SHI'S TABLET!
!!

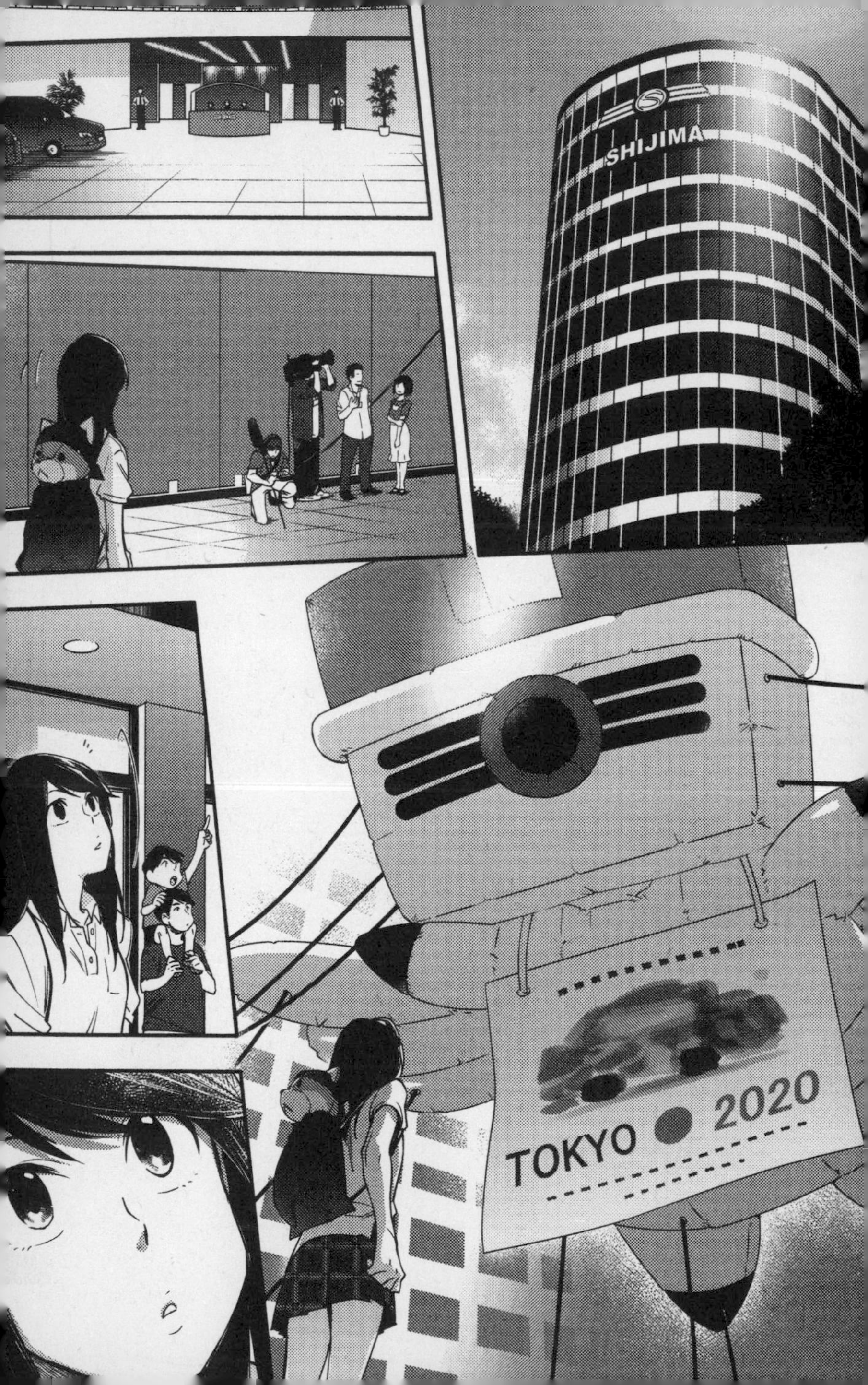
SHIJIMA
TOKYO 2020

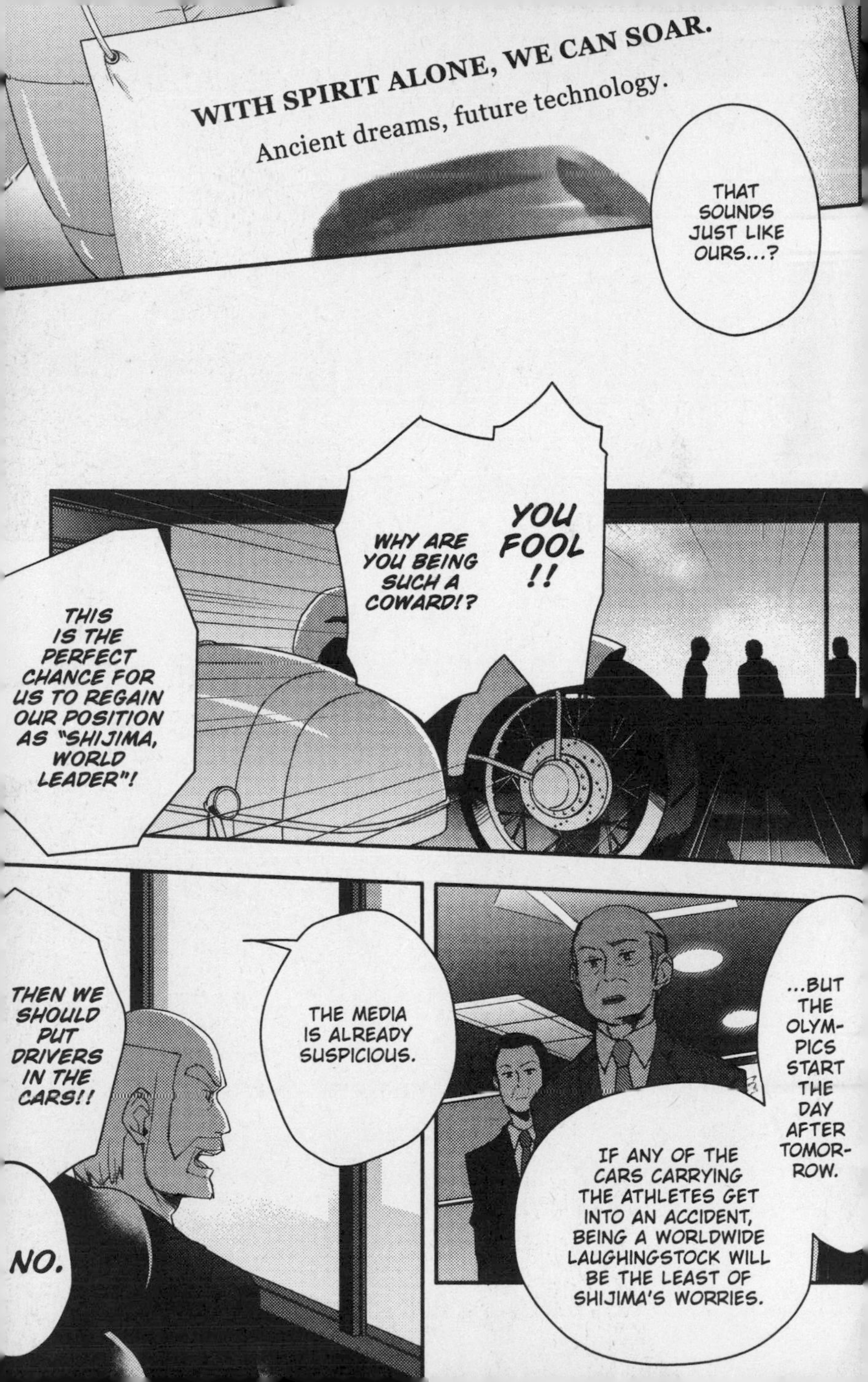
WITH SPIRIT ALONE, WE CAN SOAR.
Ancient dreams, future technology.
THAT SOUNDS JUST LIKE OURS...?
YOU FOOL!!
WHY ARE YOU BEING SUCH A COWARD!?
THIS IS THE PERFECT CHANCE FOR US TO REGAIN OUR POSITION AS "SHIJIMA, WORLD LEADER"!
...BUT THE OLYMPICS START THE DAY AFTER TOMORROW.
IF ANY OF THE CARS CARRYING THE ATHLETES GET INTO AN ACCIDENT, BEING A WORLDWIDE LAUGHINGSTOCK WILL BE THE LEAST OF SHIJIMA'S WORRIES.
THE MEDIA IS ALREADY SUSPICIOUS.
THEN WE SHOULD PUT DRIVERS IN THE CARS!!
NO.

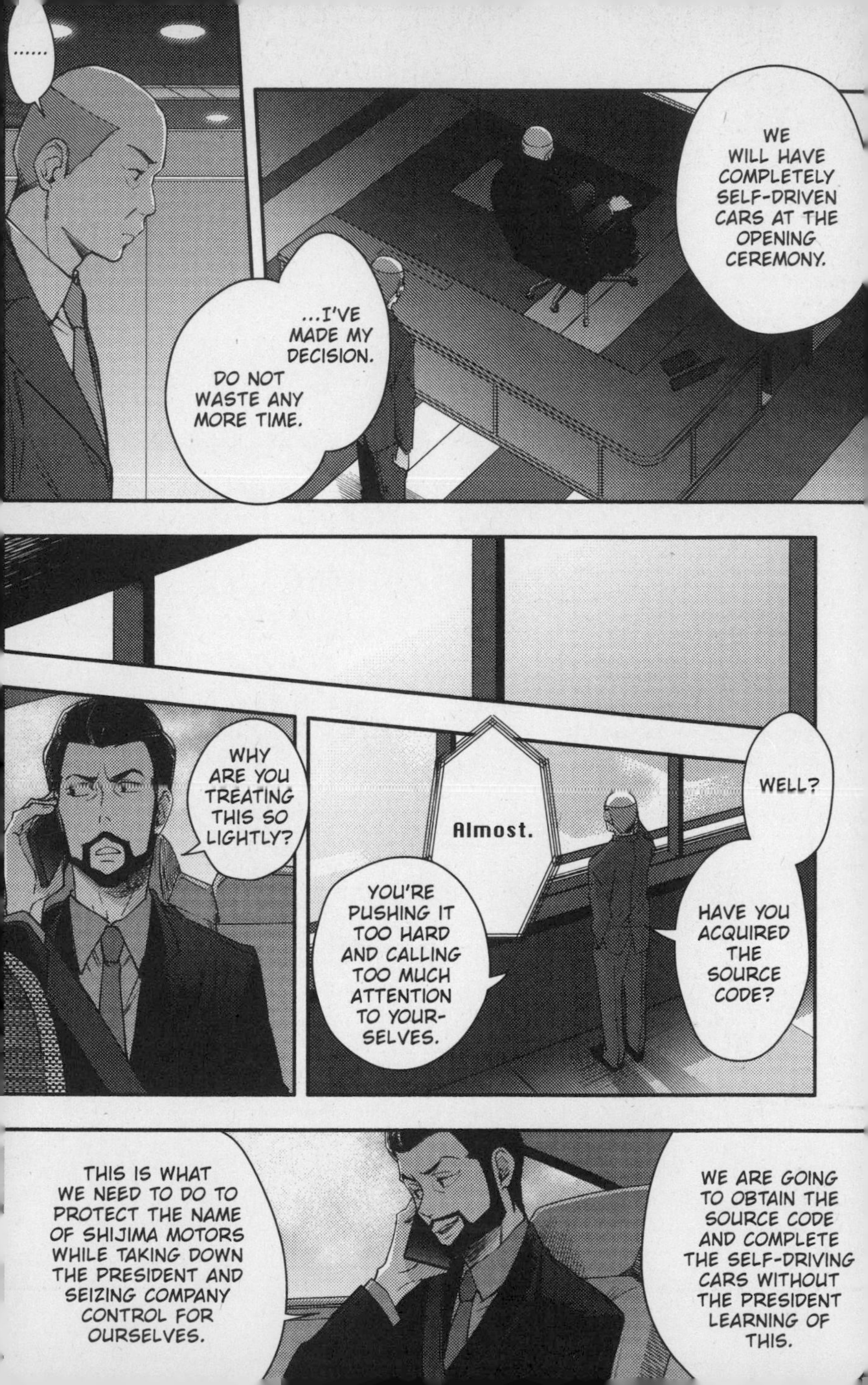
WE WILL HAVE COMPLETELY SELF-DRIVEN CARS AT THE OPENING CEREMONY.
...I'VE MADE MY DECISION.
DO NOT WASTE ANY MORE TIME.
......
WELL?
HAVE YOU ACQUIRED THE SOURCE CODE?
Almost.
YOU'RE PUSHING IT TOO HARD AND CALLING TOO MUCH ATTENTION TO YOUR-SELVES.
WHY ARE YOU TREATING THIS SO LIGHTLY?
WE ARE GOING TO OBTAIN THE SOURCE CODE AND COMPLETE THE SELF-DRIVING CARS WITHOUT THE PRESIDENT LEARNING OF THIS.
THIS IS WHAT WE NEED TO DO TO PROTECT THE NAME OF SHIJIMA MOTORS WHILE TAKING DOWN THE PRESIDENT AND SEIZING COMPANY CONTROL FOR OURSELVES.

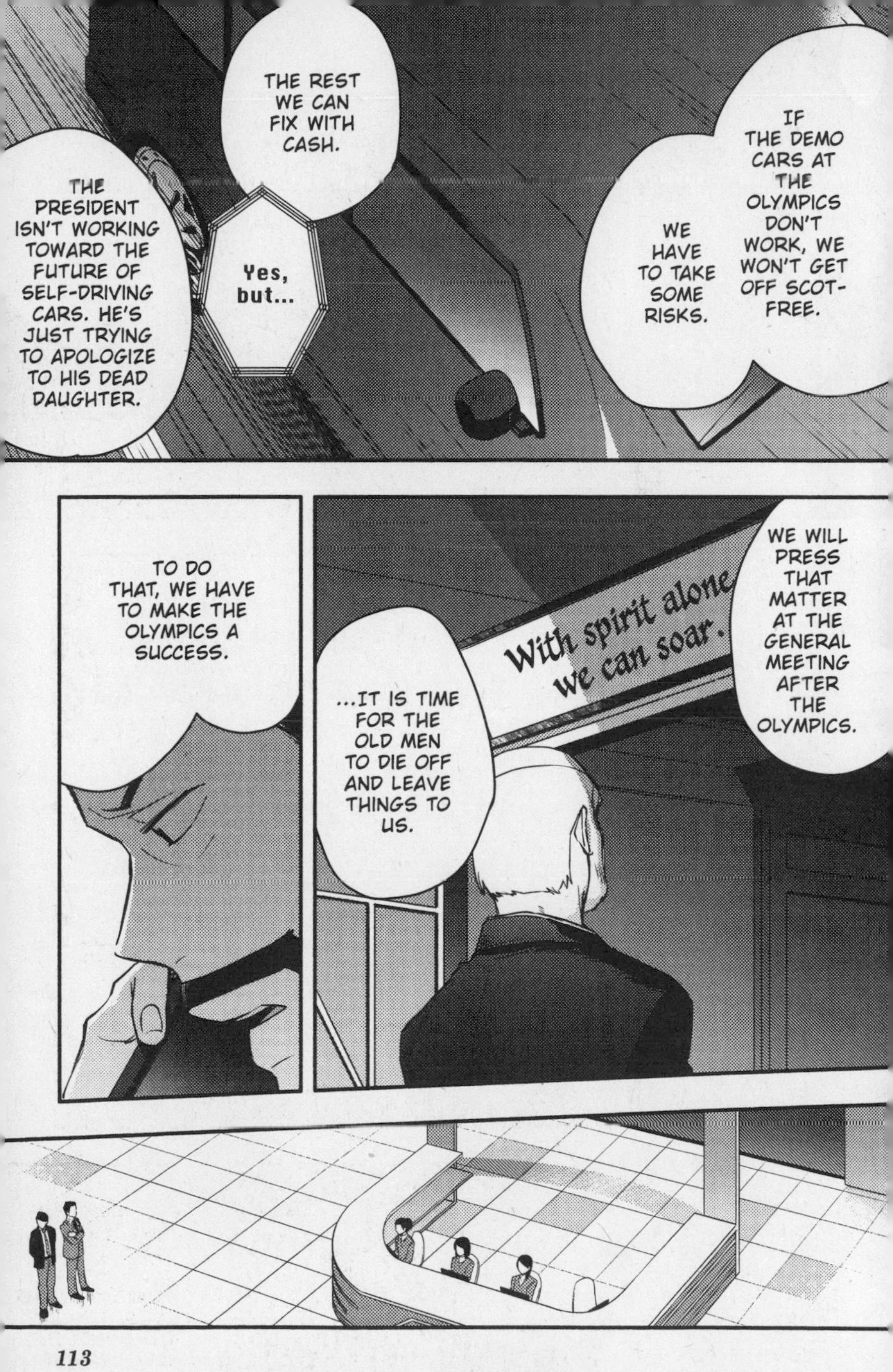
IF THE DEMO CARS AT THE OLYMPICS DON'T WORK, WE WON'T GET OFF SCOT-FREE.
WE HAVE TO TAKE SOME RISKS.
THE REST WE CAN FIX WITH CASH.
Yes, but...
THE PRESIDENT ISN'T WORKING TOWARD THE FUTURE OF SELF-DRIVING CARS. HE'S JUST TRYING TO APOLOGIZE TO HIS DEAD DAUGHTER.
WE WILL PRESS THAT MATTER AT THE GENERAL MEETING AFTER THE OLYMPICS.
With spirit alone we can soar.
...IT IS TIME FOR THE OLD MEN TO DIE OFF AND LEAVE THINGS TO US.
TO DO THAT, WE HAVE TO MAKE THE OLYMPICS A SUCCESS.

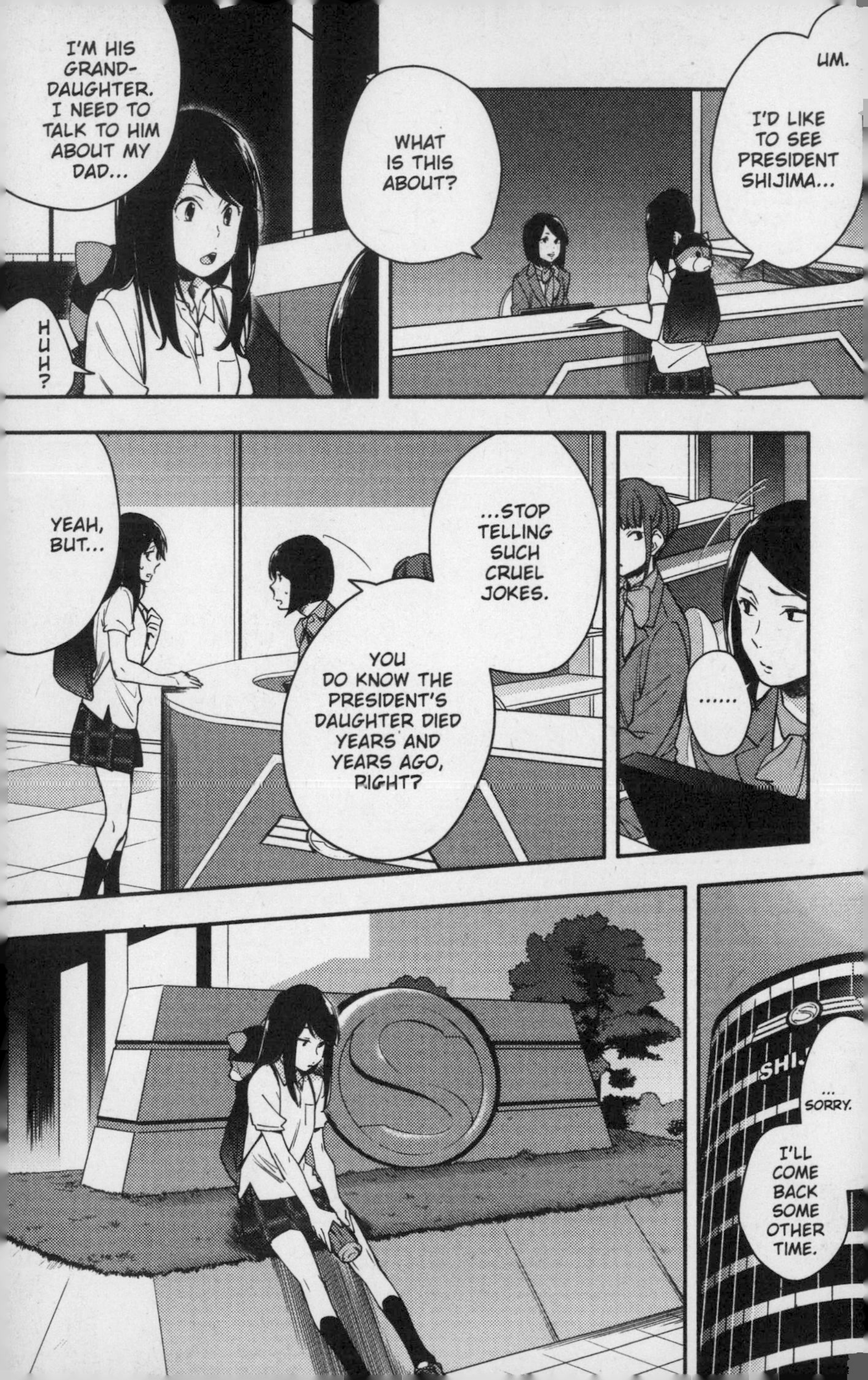
UM.
I'D LIKE TO SEE PRESIDENT SHIJIMA...
WHAT IS THIS ABOUT?
I'M HIS GRAND-DAUGHTER. I NEED TO TALK TO HIM ABOUT MY DAD...
HUH?
......
...STOP TELLING SUCH CRUEL JOKES.
YOU DO KNOW THE PRESIDENT'S DAUGHTER DIED YEARS AND YEARS AGO, RIGHT?
YEAH, BUT...
... SORRY.
I'LL COME BACK SOME OTHER TIME.

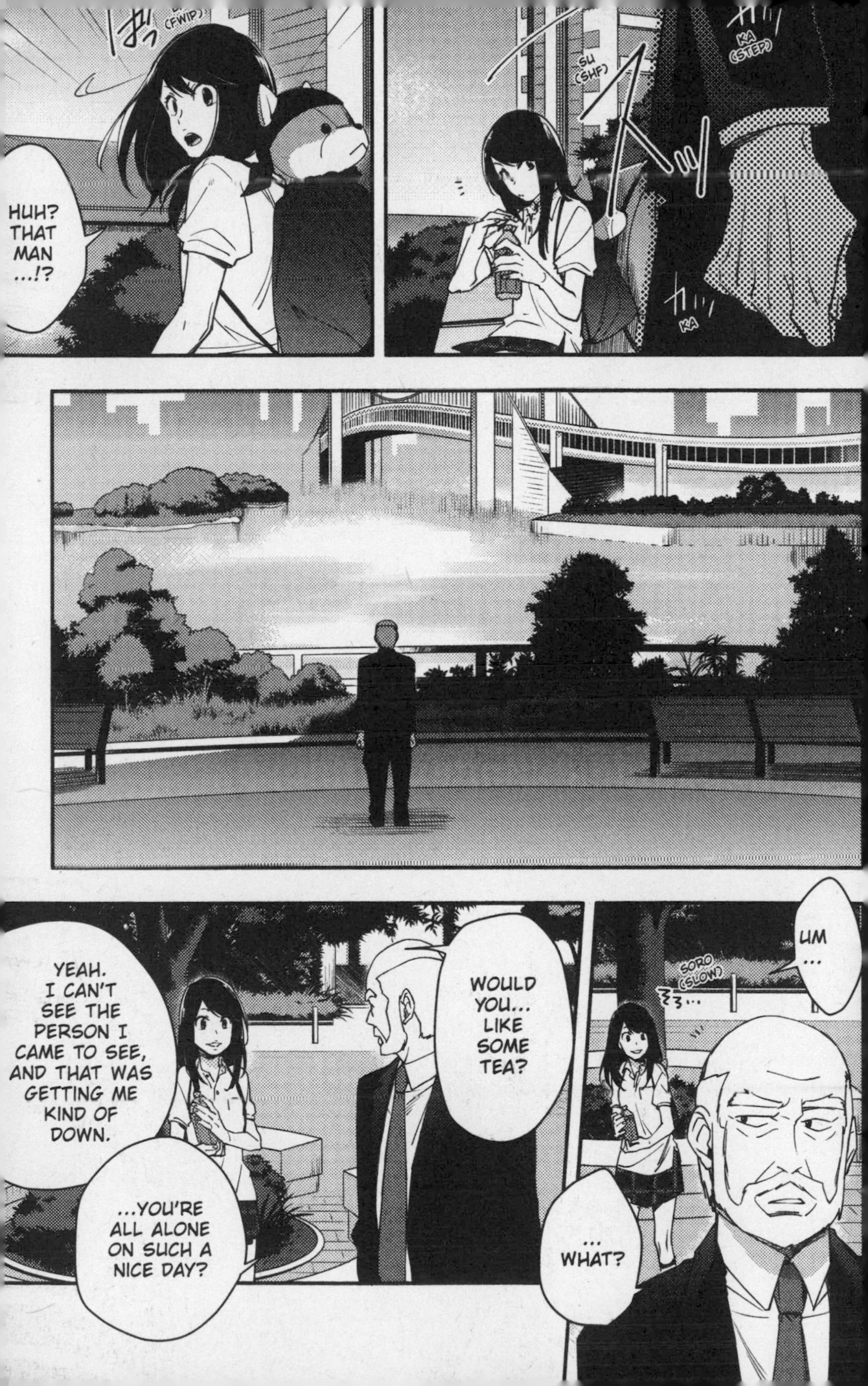
KA (STEP)
SU (SHF)
KA
(FWIP)
HUH? THAT MAN ...!?
UM ...
SORO (SLOW)
... WHAT?
WOULD YOU... LIKE SOME TEA?
...YOU'RE ALL ALONE ON SUCH A NICE DAY?
YEAH. I CAN'T SEE THE PERSON I CAME TO SEE, AND THAT WAS GETTING ME KIND OF DOWN.

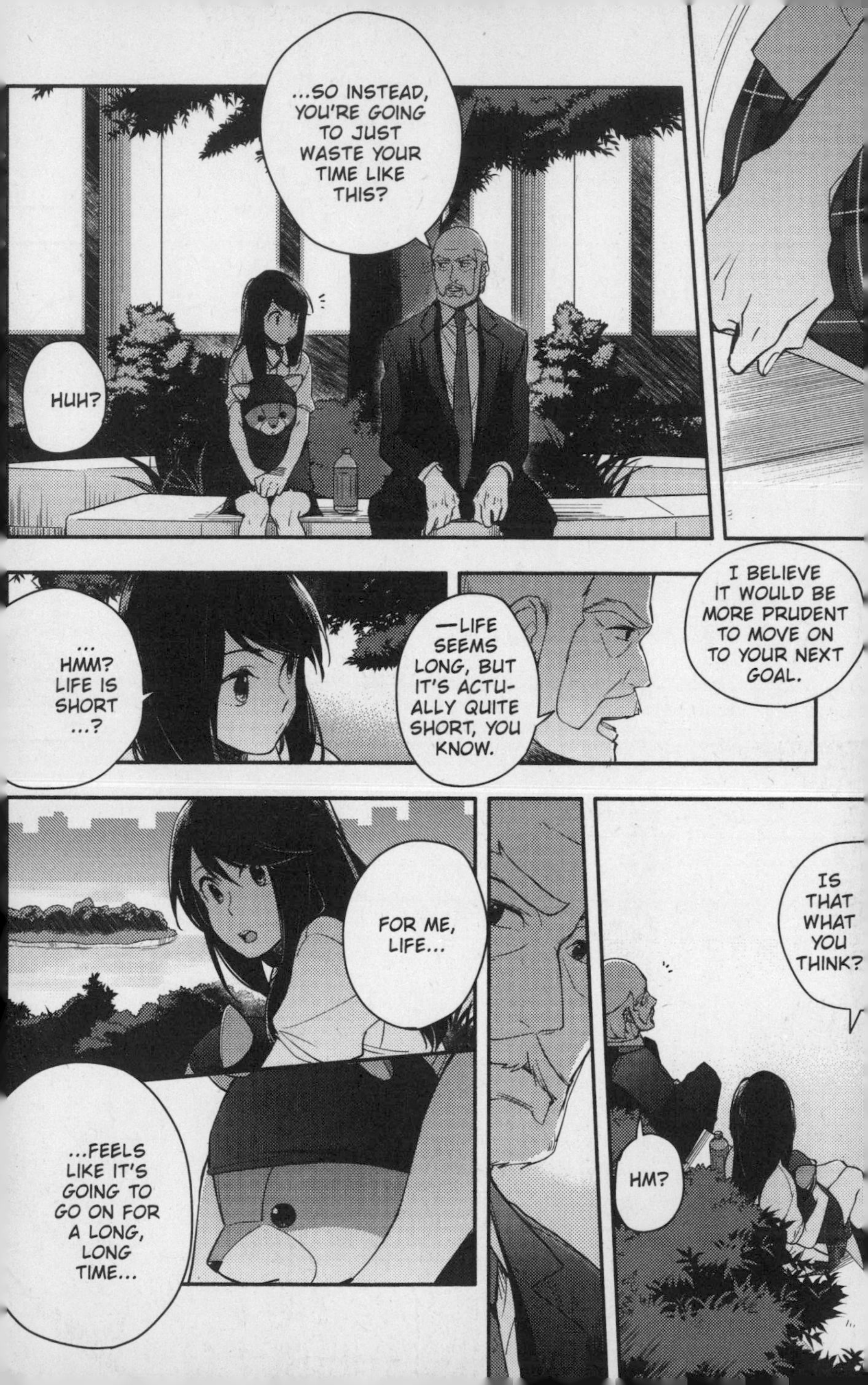
...SO INSTEAD, YOU'RE GOING TO JUST WASTE YOUR TIME LIKE THIS?
HUH?
I BELIEVE IT WOULD BE MORE PRUDENT TO MOVE ON TO YOUR NEXT GOAL.
—LIFE SEEMS LONG, BUT IT'S ACTUALLY QUITE SHORT, YOU KNOW.
... HMM? LIFE IS SHORT ...?
IS THAT WHAT YOU THINK?
HM?
FOR ME, LIFE...
...FEELS LIKE IT'S GOING TO GO ON FOR A LONG, LONG TIME...

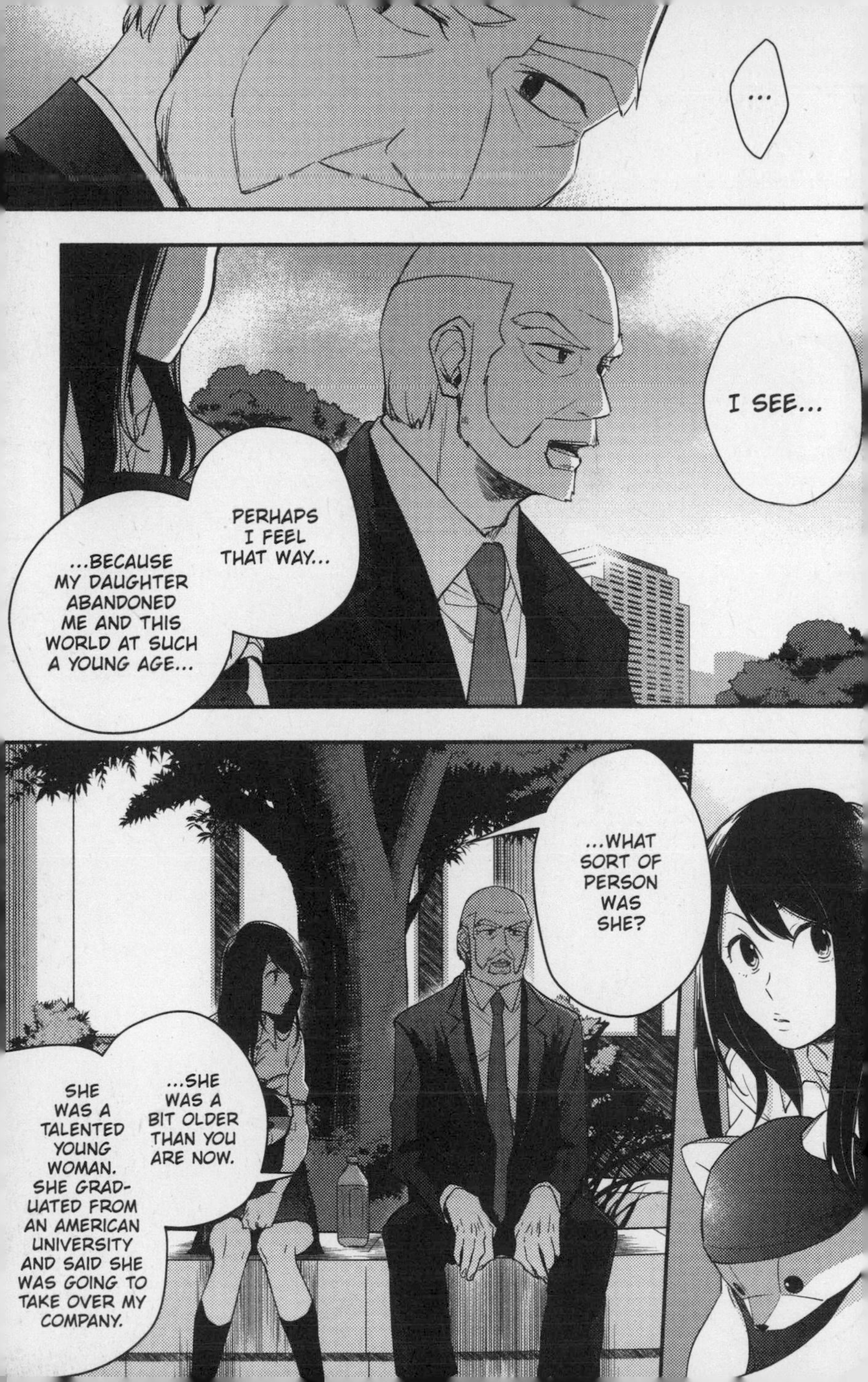
...
I SEE...
PERHAPS I FEEL THAT WAY...
...BECAUSE MY DAUGHTER ABANDONED ME AND THIS WORLD AT SUCH A YOUNG AGE...
...WHAT SORT OF PERSON WAS SHE?
...SHE WAS A BIT OLDER THAN YOU ARE NOW.
SHE WAS A TALENTED YOUNG WOMAN. SHE GRAD-UATED FROM AN AMERICAN UNIVERSITY AND SAID SHE WAS GOING TO TAKE OVER MY COMPANY.

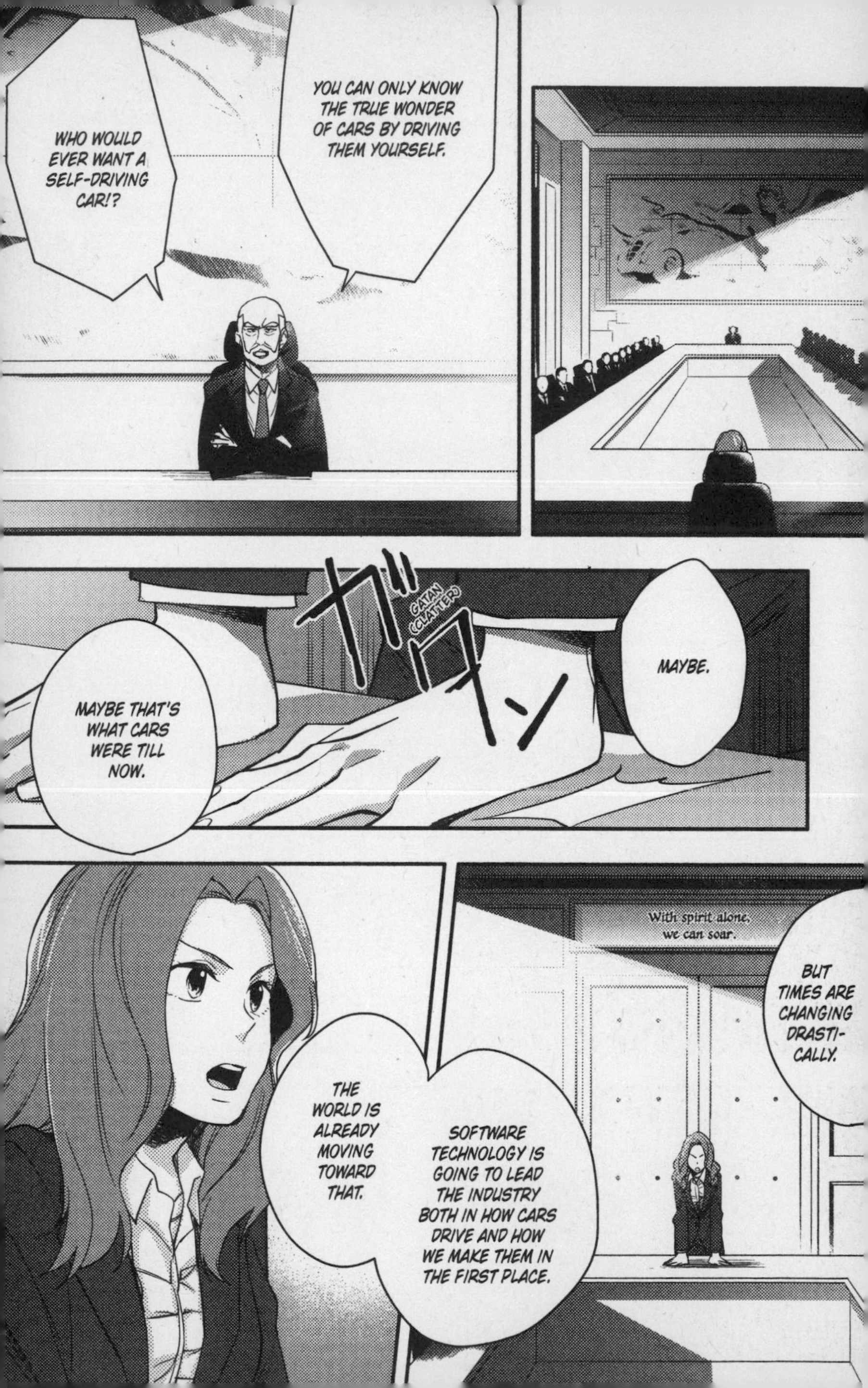
YOU CAN ONLY KNOW THE TRUE WONDER OF CARS BY DRIVING THEM YOURSELF.
WHO WOULD EVER WANT A SELF-DRIVING CAR!?
MAYBE.
GATAN (CLATTER)
MAYBE THAT'S WHAT CARS WERE TILL NOW.
With spirit alone, we can soar.
BUT TIMES ARE CHANGING DRASTI-CALLY.
SOFTWARE TECHNOLOGY IS GOING TO LEAD THE INDUSTRY BOTH IN HOW CARS DRIVE AND HOW WE MAKE THEM IN THE FIRST PLACE.
THE WORLD IS ALREADY MOVING TOWARD THAT.

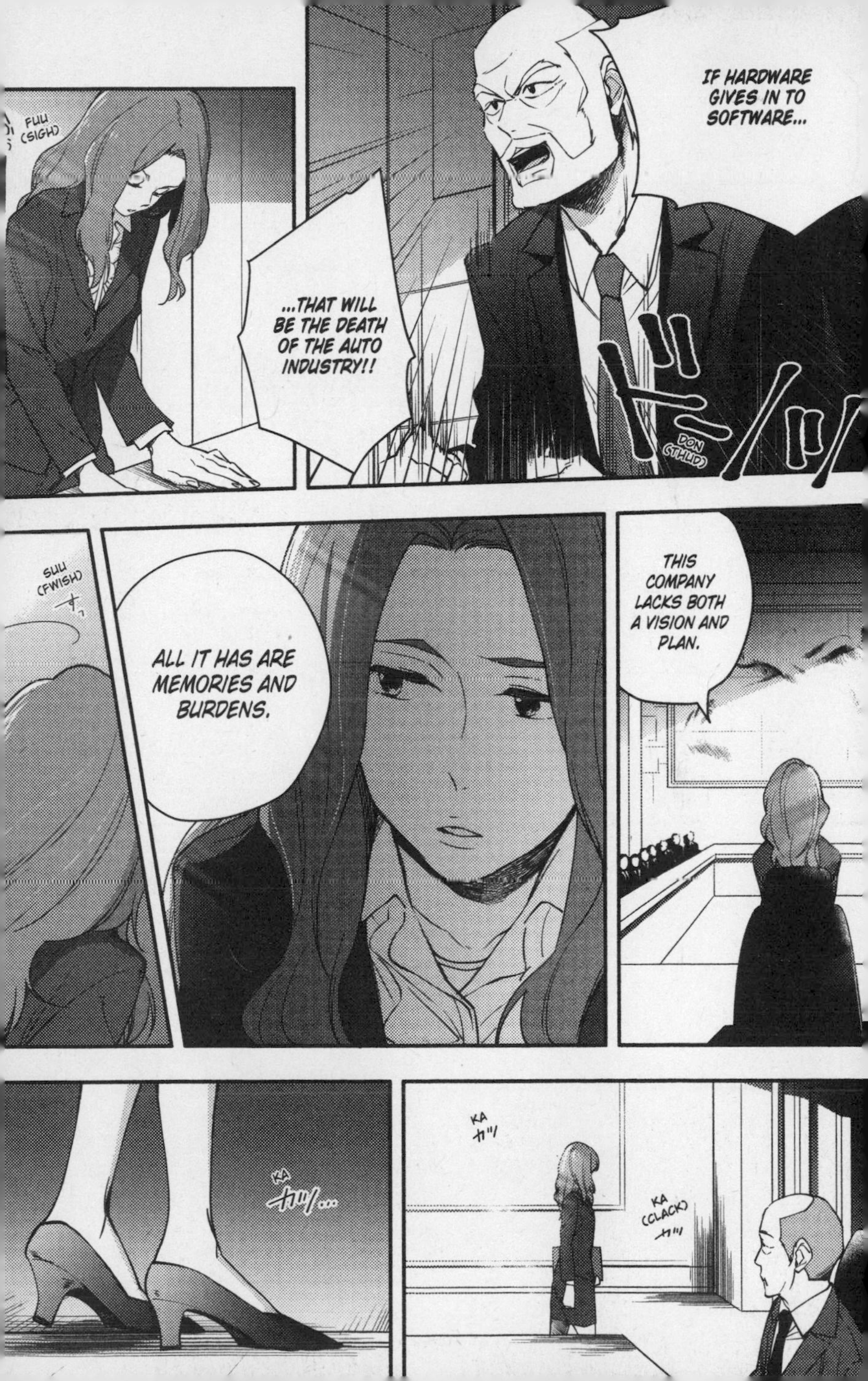
IF HARDWARE GIVES IN TO SOFTWARE...
...THAT WILL BE THE DEATH OF THE AUTO INDUSTRY!!
DON (THUD)
FUU (SIGH)
THIS COMPANY LACKS BOTH A VISION AND PLAN.
ALL IT HAS ARE MEMORIES AND BURDENS.
SUU (FWISH)
KA
KA (CLACK)
KA

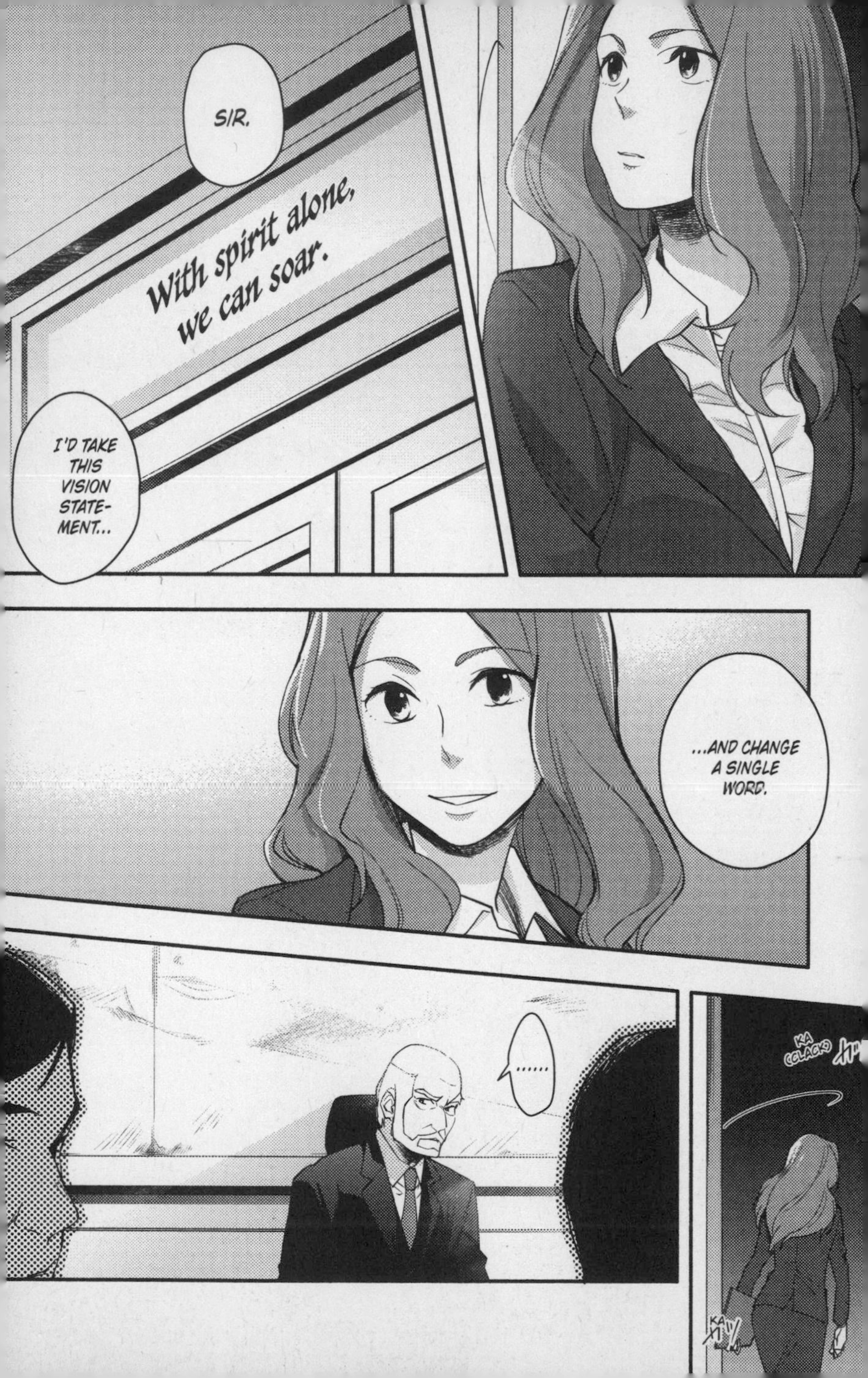
SIR.
With spirit alone, we can soar.
I'D TAKE THIS VISION STATEMENT...
...AND CHANGE A SINGLE WORD.
KA (CLACK)
......

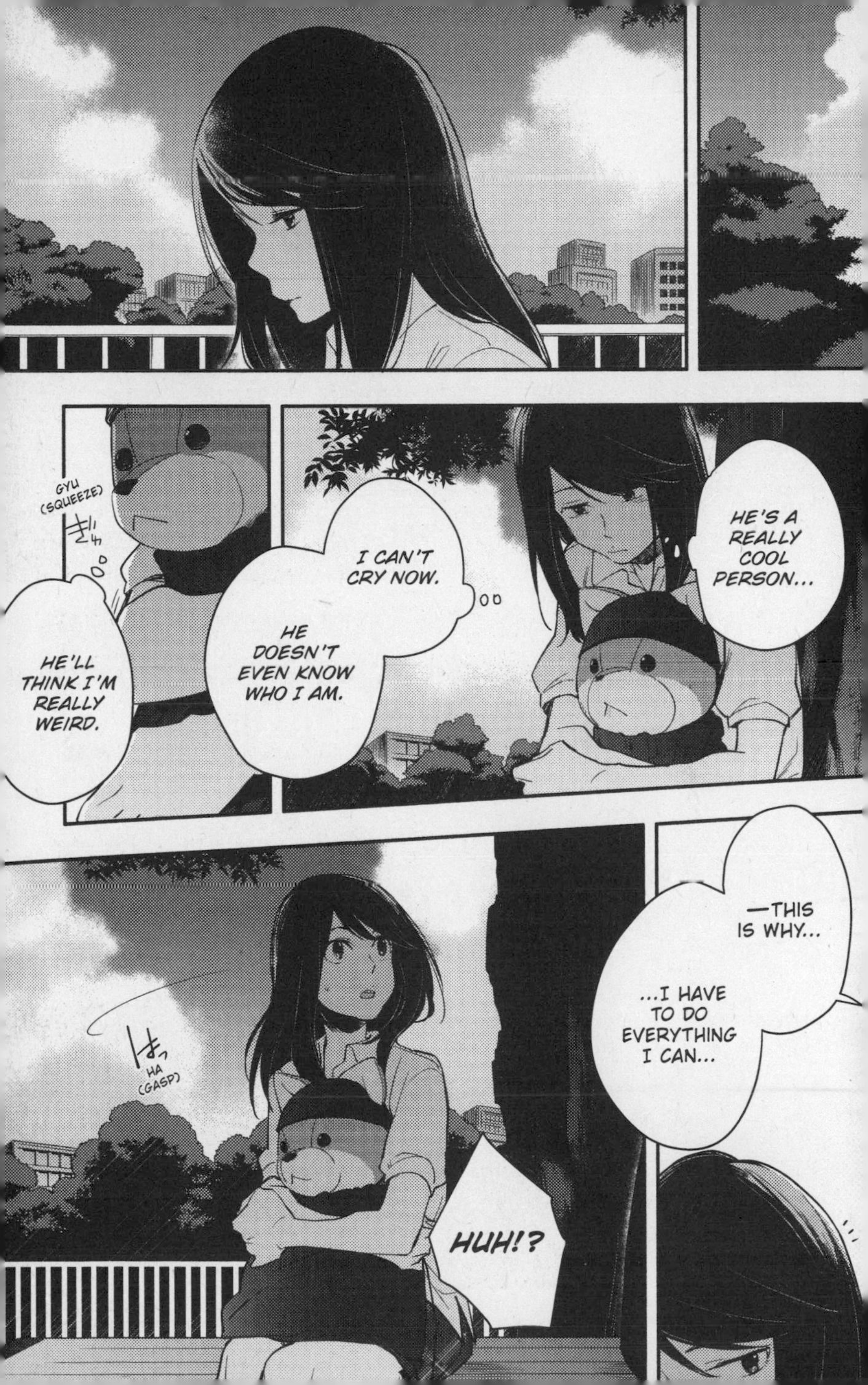
HE'S A REALLY COOL PERSON...
I CAN'T CRY NOW.
HE DOESN'T EVEN KNOW WHO I AM.
GYU (SQUEEZE)
HE'LL THINK I'M REALLY WEIRD.
—THIS IS WHY...
...I HAVE TO DO EVERYTHING I CAN...
HA (GASP)
HUH!?

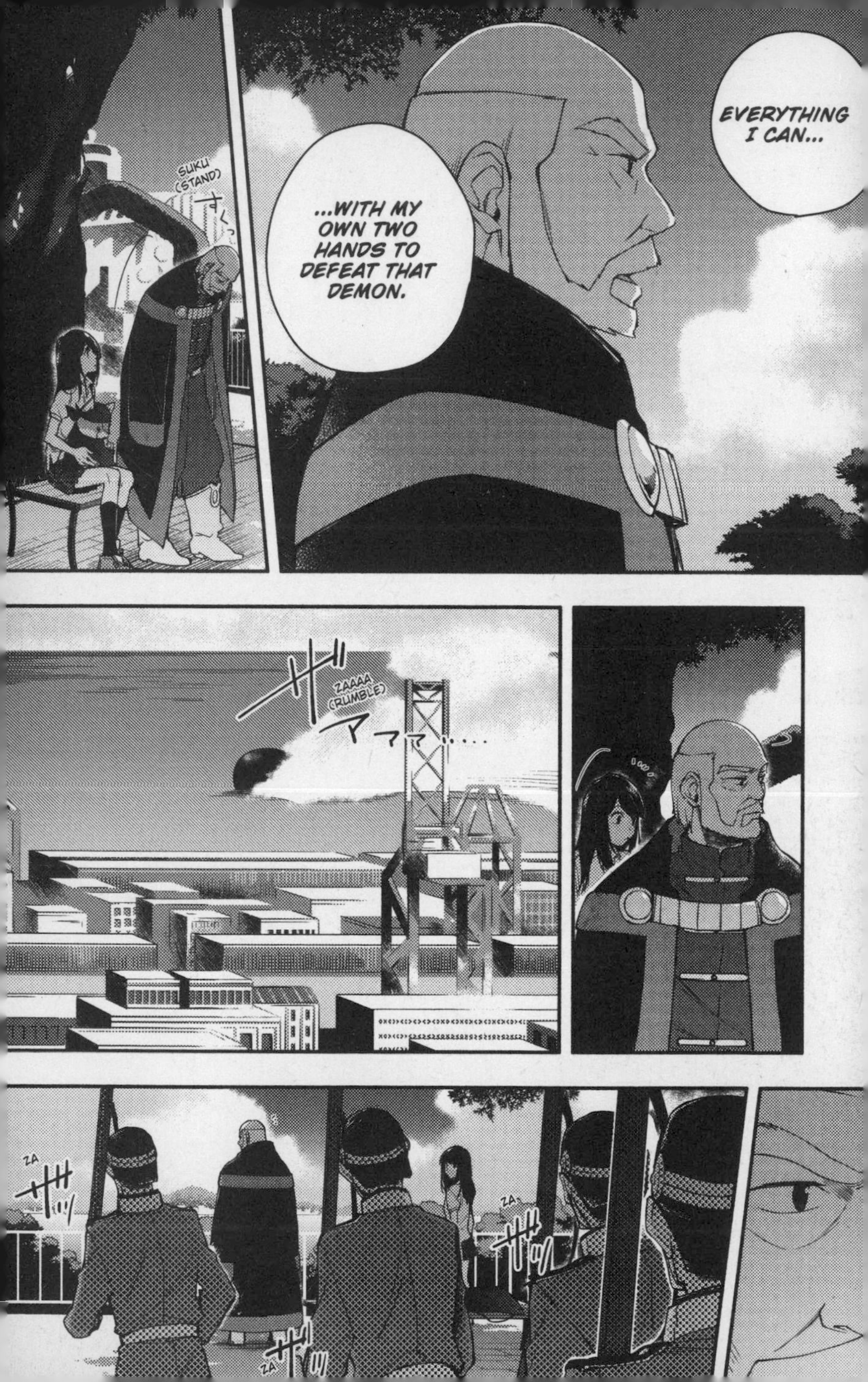
EVERYTHING I CAN...
...WITH MY OWN TWO HANDS TO DEFEAT THAT DEMON.
SUKU (STAND)
すくっ
ZAAAA (RUMBLE)
ザアアア……
ZA
ZA
ZA

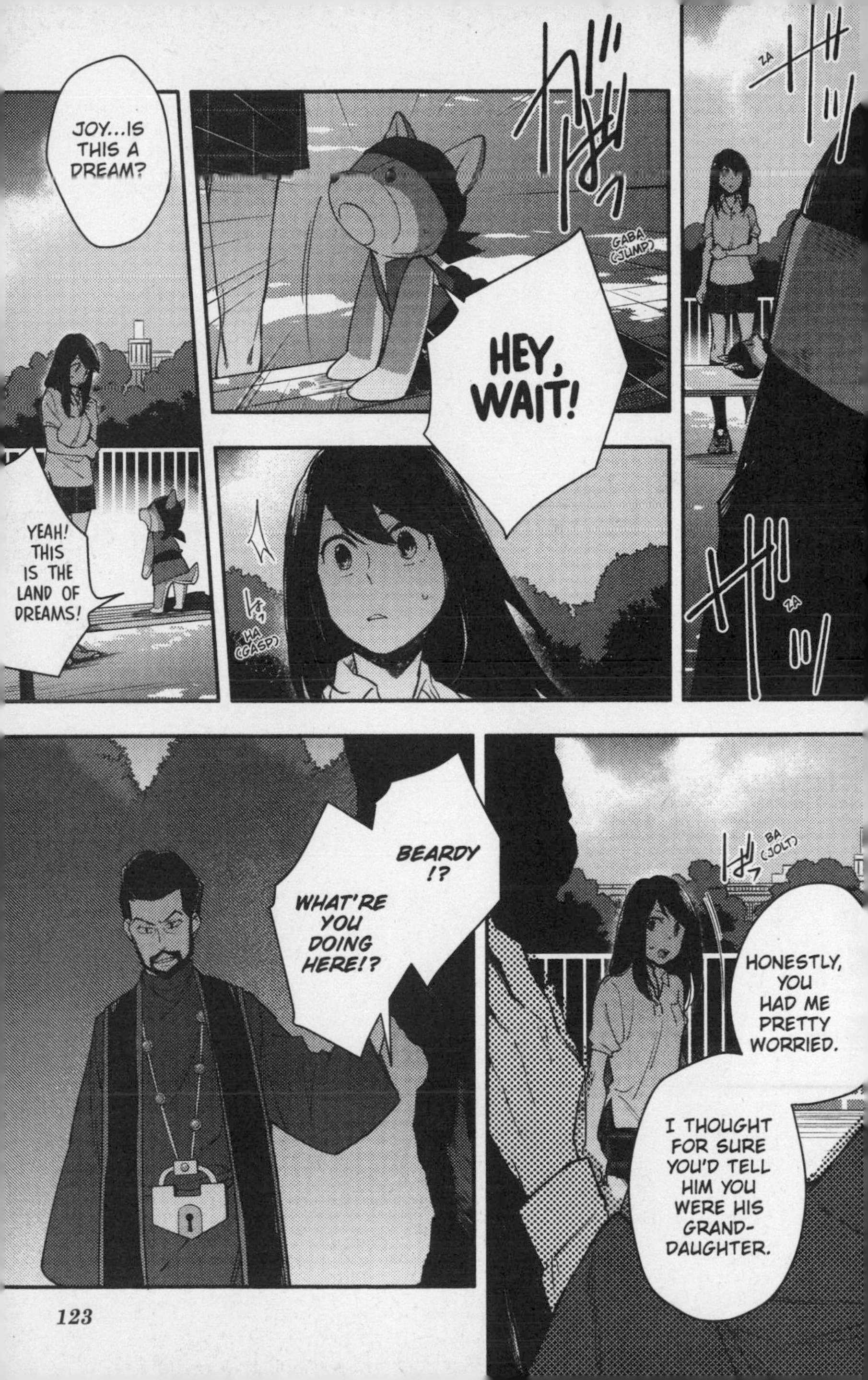

ZA
ZA
GABA (JUMP)
HEY, WAIT!
HA (GASP)
JOY...IS THIS A DREAM?
YEAH! THIS IS THE LAND OF DREAMS!
BA (JOLT)
HONESTLY, YOU HAD ME PRETTY WORRIED.
I THOUGHT FOR SURE YOU'D TELL HIM YOU WERE HIS GRAND-DAUGHTER.
BEARDY!?
WHAT'RE YOU DOING HERE!?

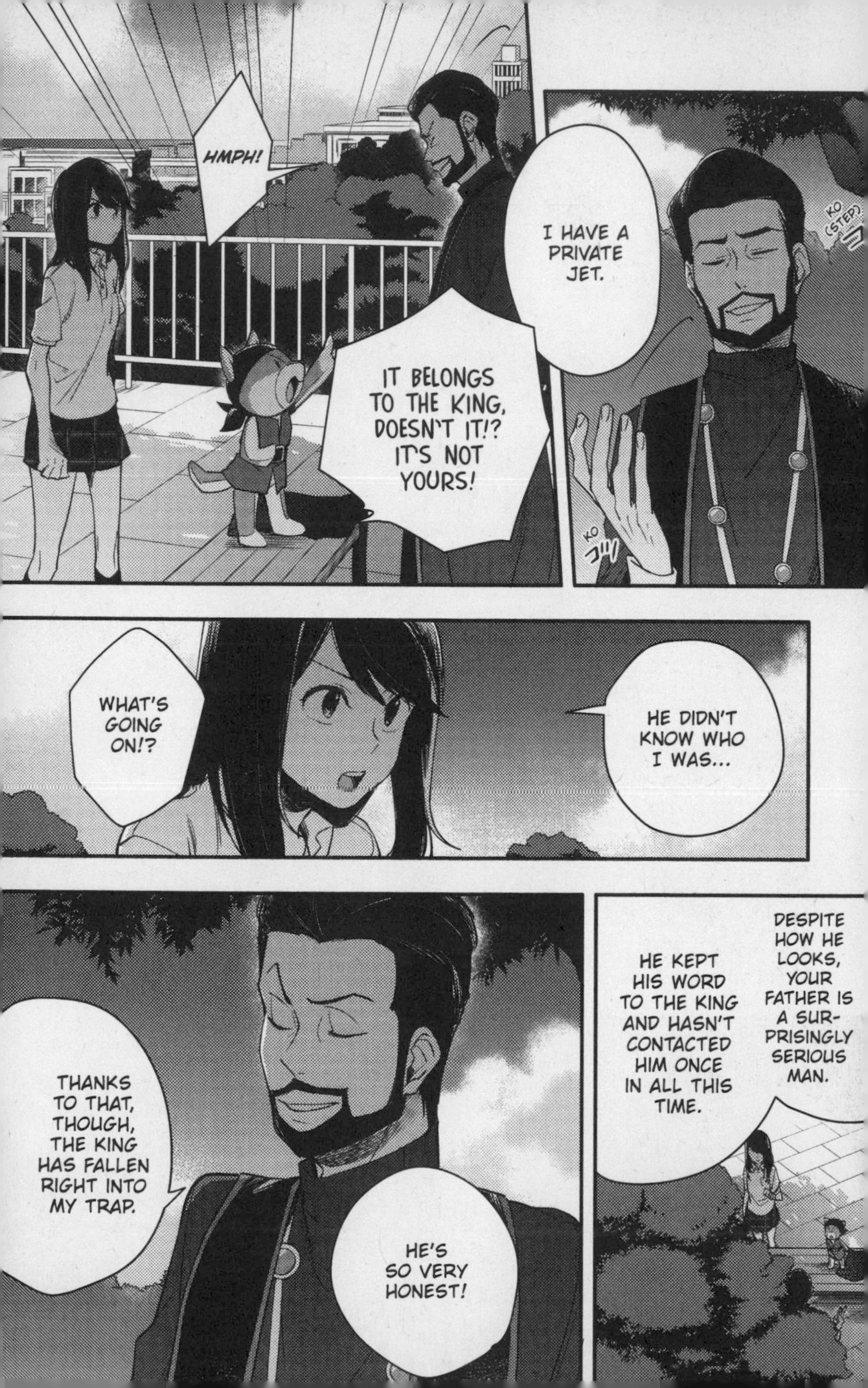
I HAVE A PRIVATE JET.
KO (STEP)
KO
HMPH!
IT BELONGS TO THE KING, DOESN'T IT!? IT'S NOT YOURS!
HE DIDN'T KNOW WHO I WAS...
WHAT'S GOING ON!?
DESPITE HOW HE LOOKS, YOUR FATHER IS A SUR-PRISINGLY SERIOUS MAN.
HE KEPT HIS WORD TO THE KING AND HASN'T CONTACTED HIM ONCE IN ALL THIS TIME.
THANKS TO THAT, THOUGH, THE KING HAS FALLEN RIGHT INTO MY TRAP.
HE'S SO VERY HONEST!

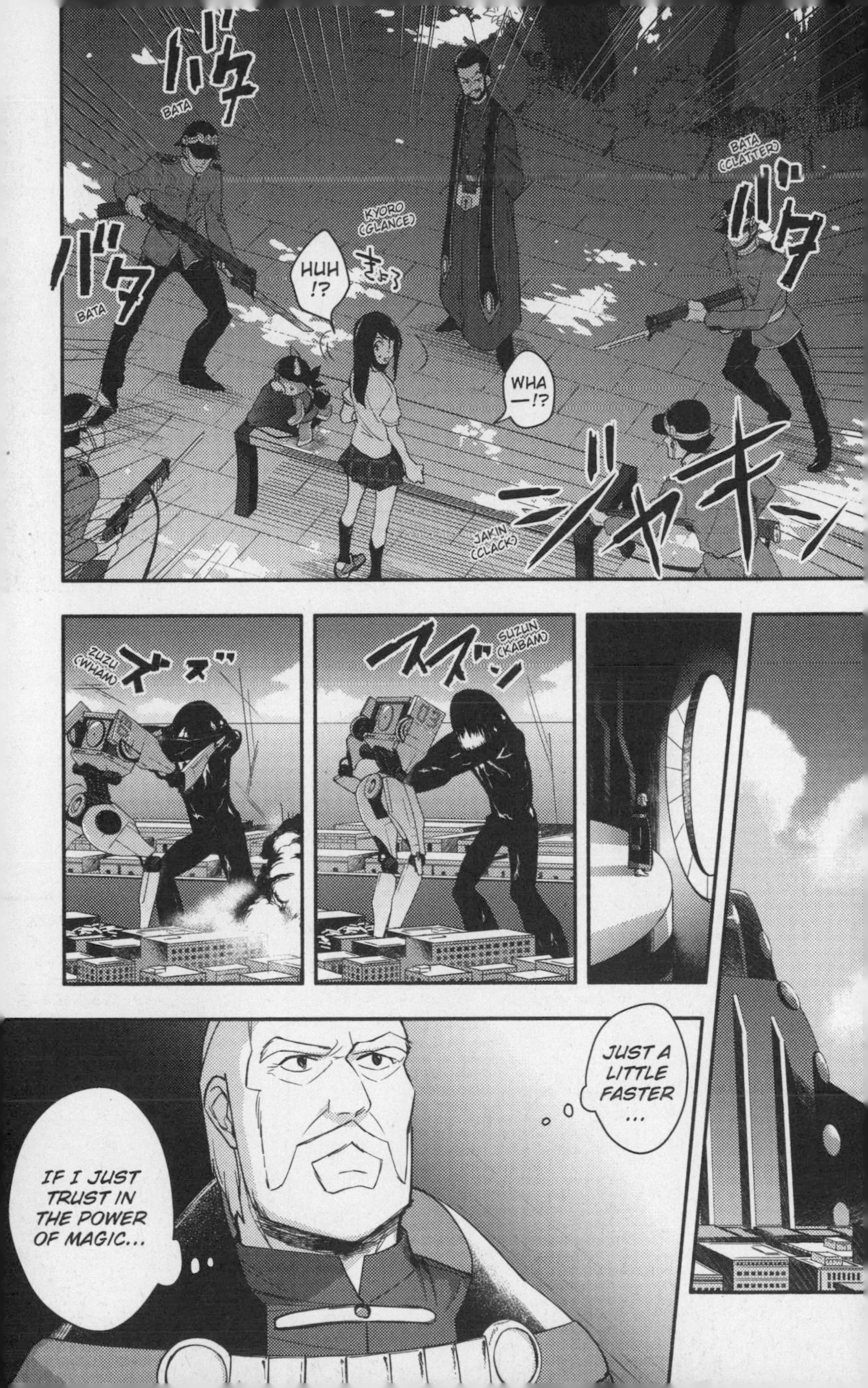
BATA (CLATTER)
バタ
KYORO (GLANCE)
きょろ
HUH !?
WHA —!?
ジャキーン
JAKIN (CLACK)
バタ
BATA
バタ
BATA
ズズーン
SUZUN (KABAM)
ズズ
ZUZU (WHAM)
JUST A LITTLE FASTER ...
IF I JUST TRUST IN THE POWER OF MAGIC...
...

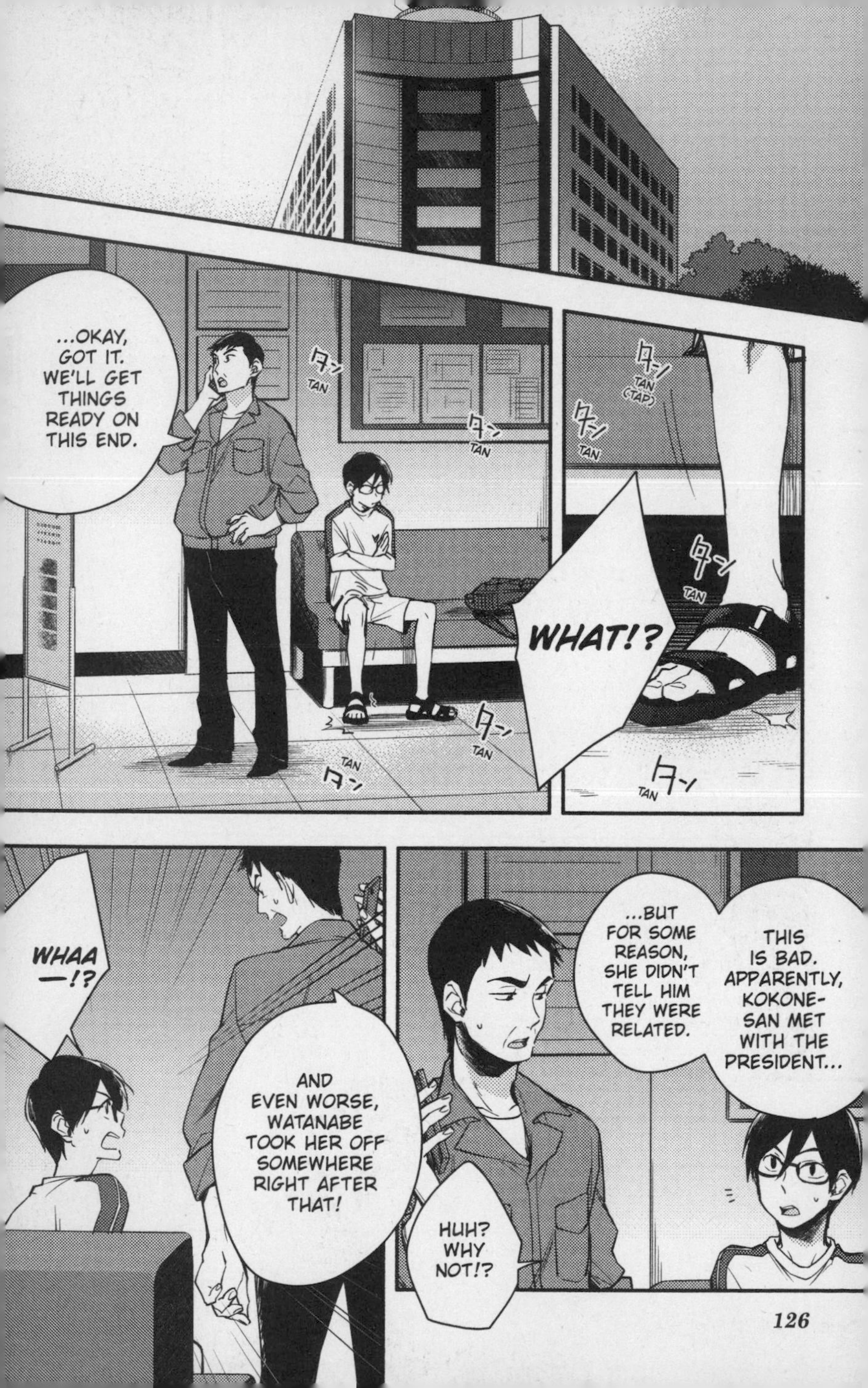
TAN (TAP)
TAN
TAN
TAN
WHAT!?
...OKAY, GOT IT. WE'LL GET THINGS READY ON THIS END.
TAN
TAN
TAN
TAN
THIS IS BAD. APPARENTLY, KOKONE-SAN MET WITH THE PRESIDENT...
...BUT FOR SOME REASON, SHE DIDN'T TELL HIM THEY WERE RELATED.
HUH? WHY NOT!?
AND EVEN WORSE, WATANABE TOOK HER OFF SOMEWHERE RIGHT AFTER THAT!
WHAA—!?

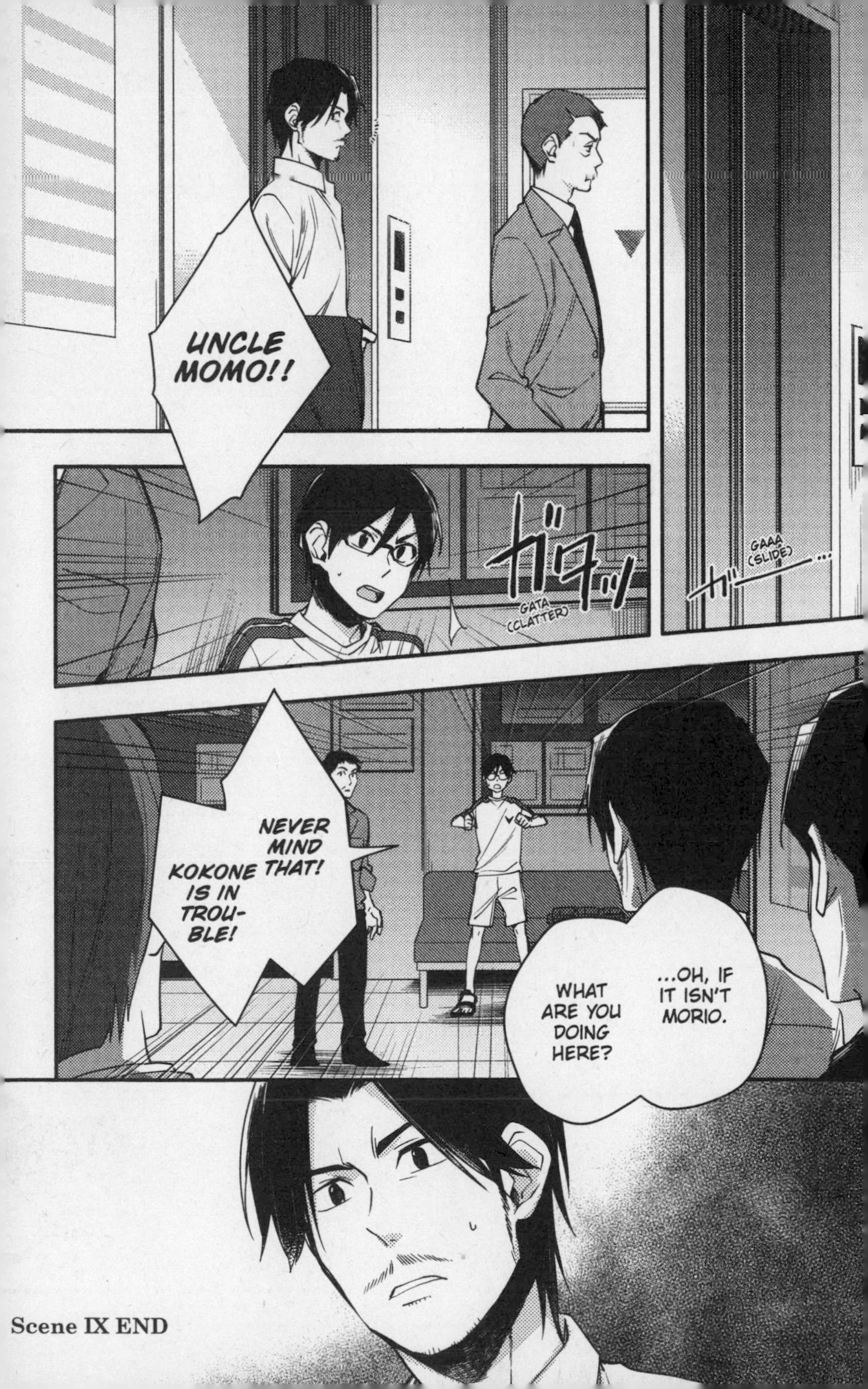
GAAA (SLIDE)...
UNCLE MOMO!!
GATA (CLATTER)
...OH, IF IT ISN'T MORIO.
WHAT ARE YOU DOING HERE?
NEVER MIND THAT!
KOKONE IS IN TROUBLE!

Scene IX END

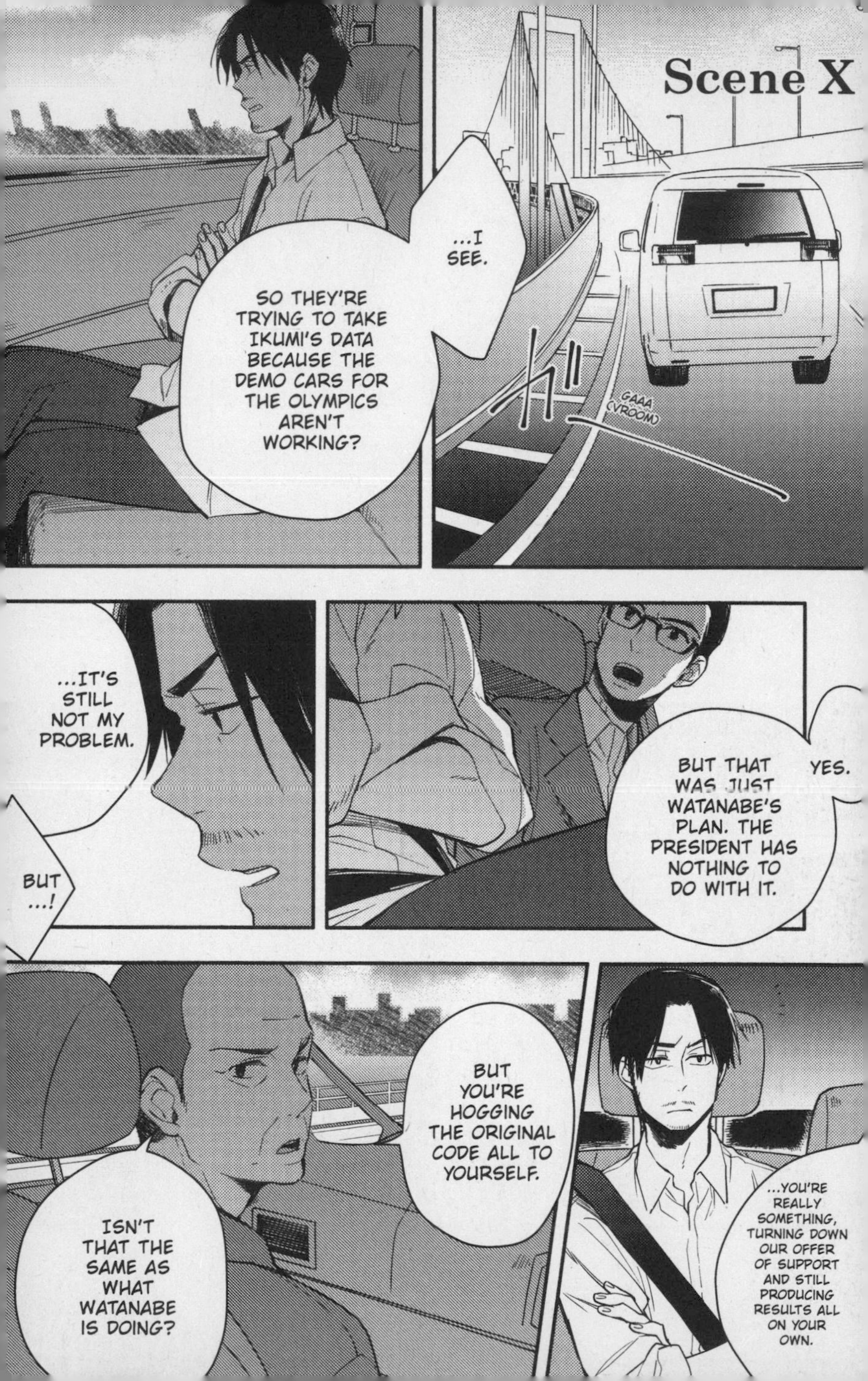
Scene X
...I SEE.
GAAA (VROOM)
SO THEY'RE TRYING TO TAKE IKUMI'S DATA BECAUSE THE DEMO CARS FOR THE OLYMPICS AREN'T WORKING?
YES.
BUT THAT WAS JUST WATANABE'S PLAN. THE PRESIDENT HAS NOTHING TO DO WITH IT.
...IT'S STILL NOT MY PROBLEM.
BUT ...!
...YOU'RE REALLY SOMETHING, TURNING DOWN OUR OFFER OF SUPPORT AND STILL PRODUCING RESULTS ALL ON YOUR OWN.
BUT YOU'RE HOGGING THE ORIGINAL CODE ALL TO YOURSELF.
ISN'T THAT THE SAME AS WHAT WATANABE IS DOING?

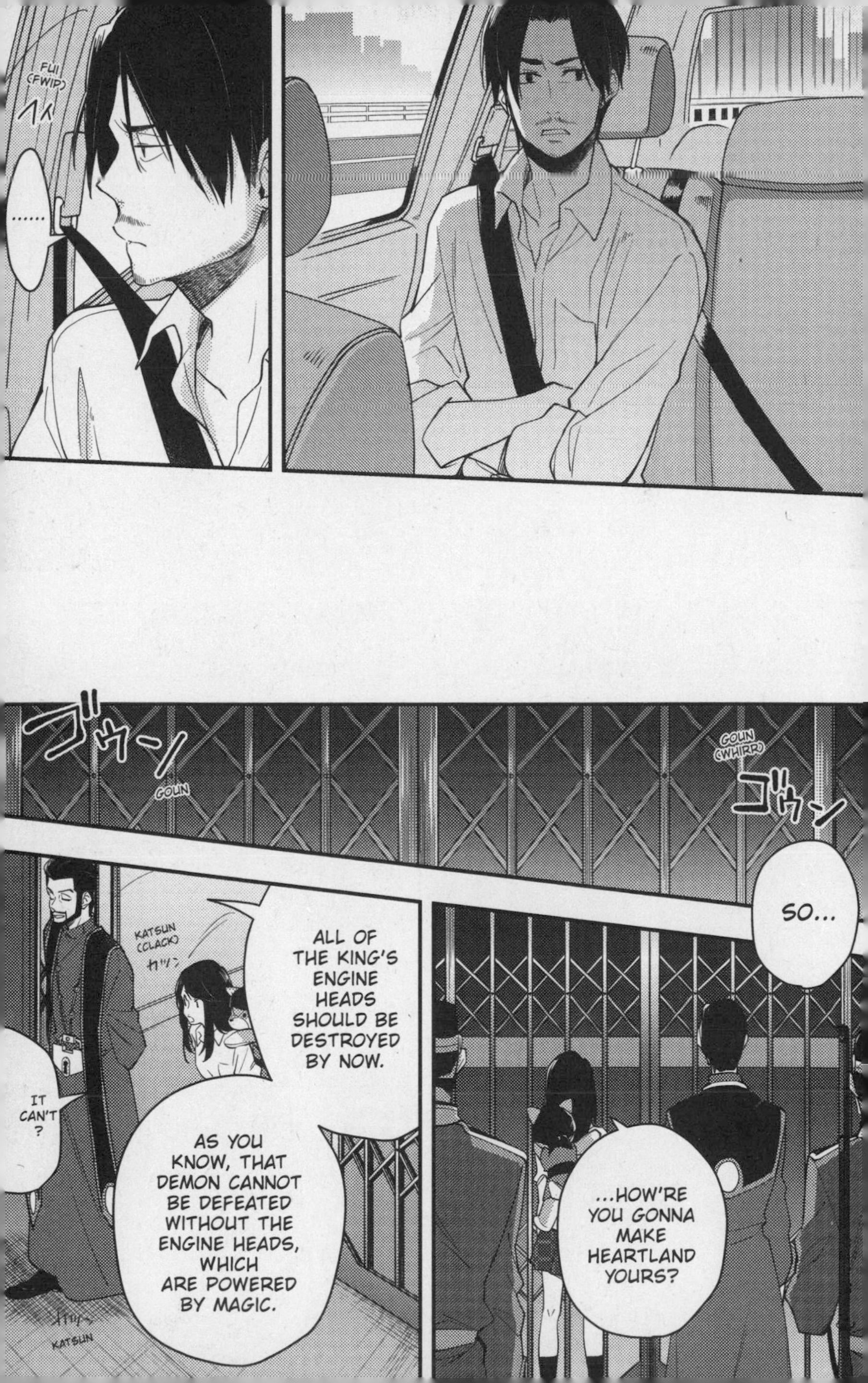
FUI (FWIP)
......
GOUN (WHIRR)
GOUN
SO...
...HOW'RE YOU GONNA MAKE HEARTLAND YOURS?
ALL OF THE KING'S ENGINE HEADS SHOULD BE DESTROYED BY NOW.
KATSUN (CLACK)
AS YOU KNOW, THAT DEMON CANNOT BE DEFEATED WITHOUT THE ENGINE HEADS, WHICH ARE POWERED BY MAGIC.
IT CAN'T?
KATSUN

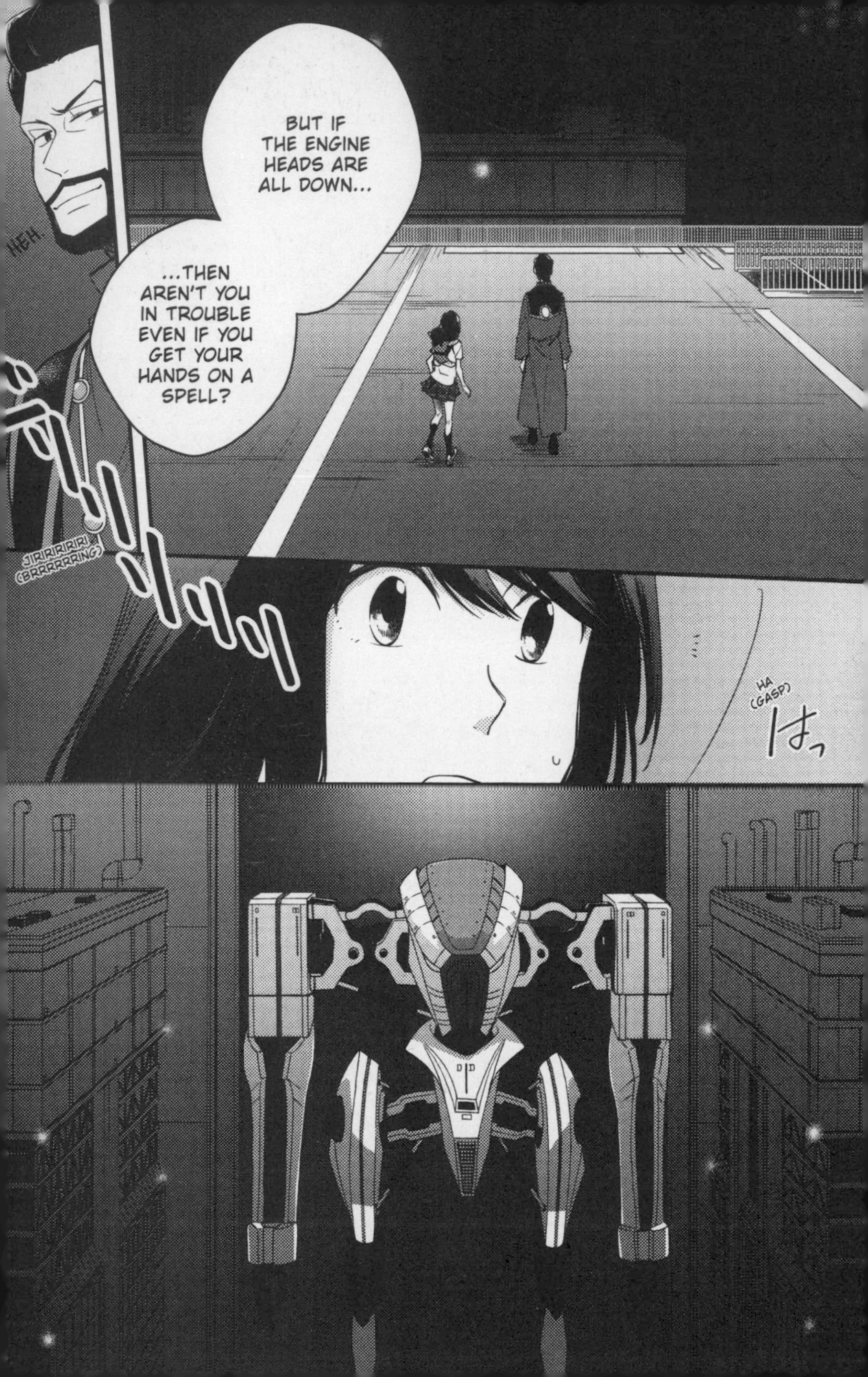
BUT IF THE ENGINE HEADS ARE ALL DOWN...
...THEN AREN'T YOU IN TROUBLE EVEN IF YOU GET YOUR HANDS ON A SPELL?
HEH.
JIRIRIRIRIRI (BRRRRRRRING)
HA (GASP)
はっ

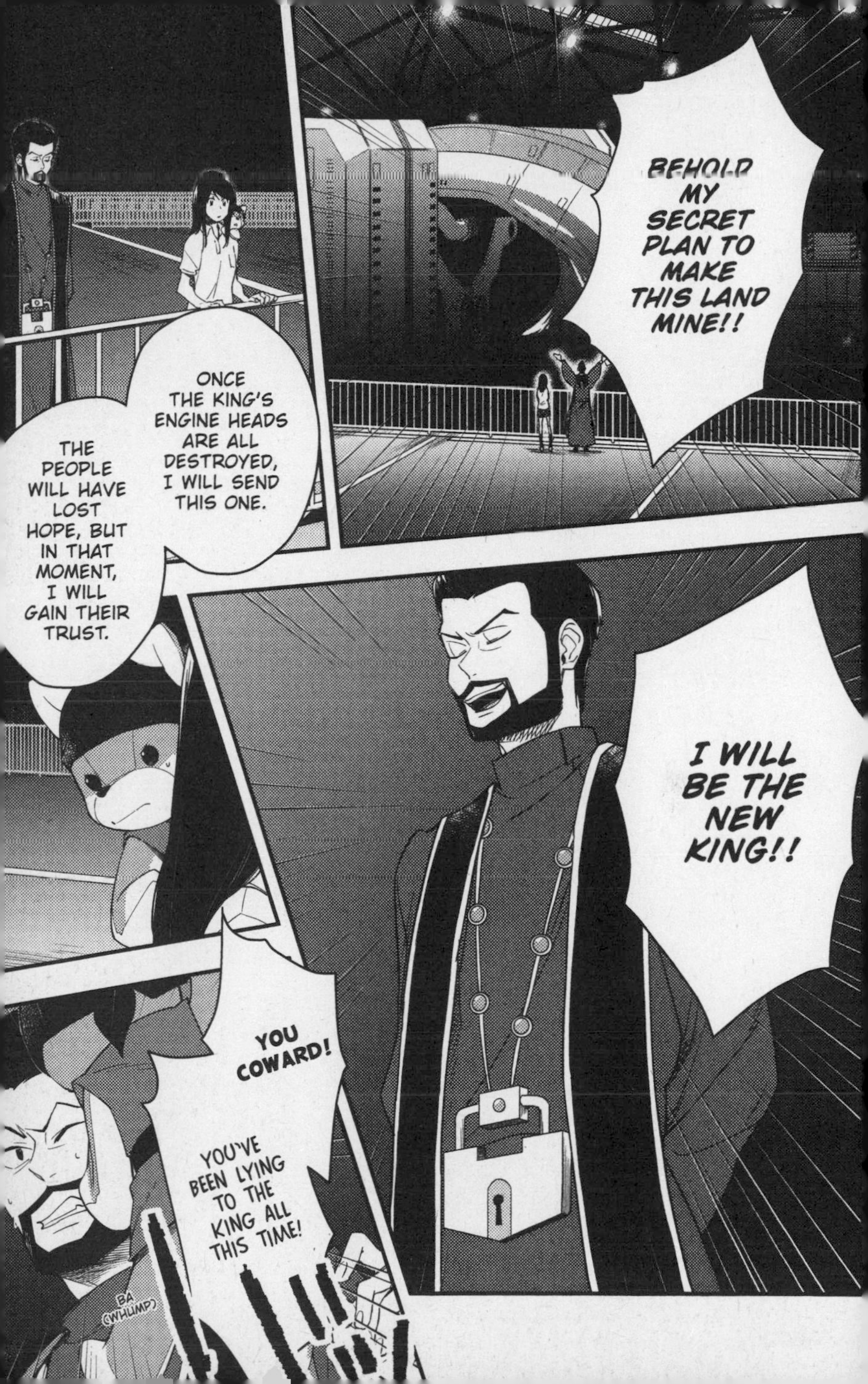
BEHOLD MY SECRET PLAN TO MAKE THIS LAND MINE!!
ONCE THE KING'S ENGINE HEADS ARE ALL DESTROYED, I WILL SEND THIS ONE.
THE PEOPLE WILL HAVE LOST HOPE, BUT IN THAT MOMENT, I WILL GAIN THEIR TRUST.
I WILL BE THE NEW KING!!
YOU COWARD!
YOU'VE BEEN LYING TO THE KING ALL THIS TIME!
BA (WHUMP)

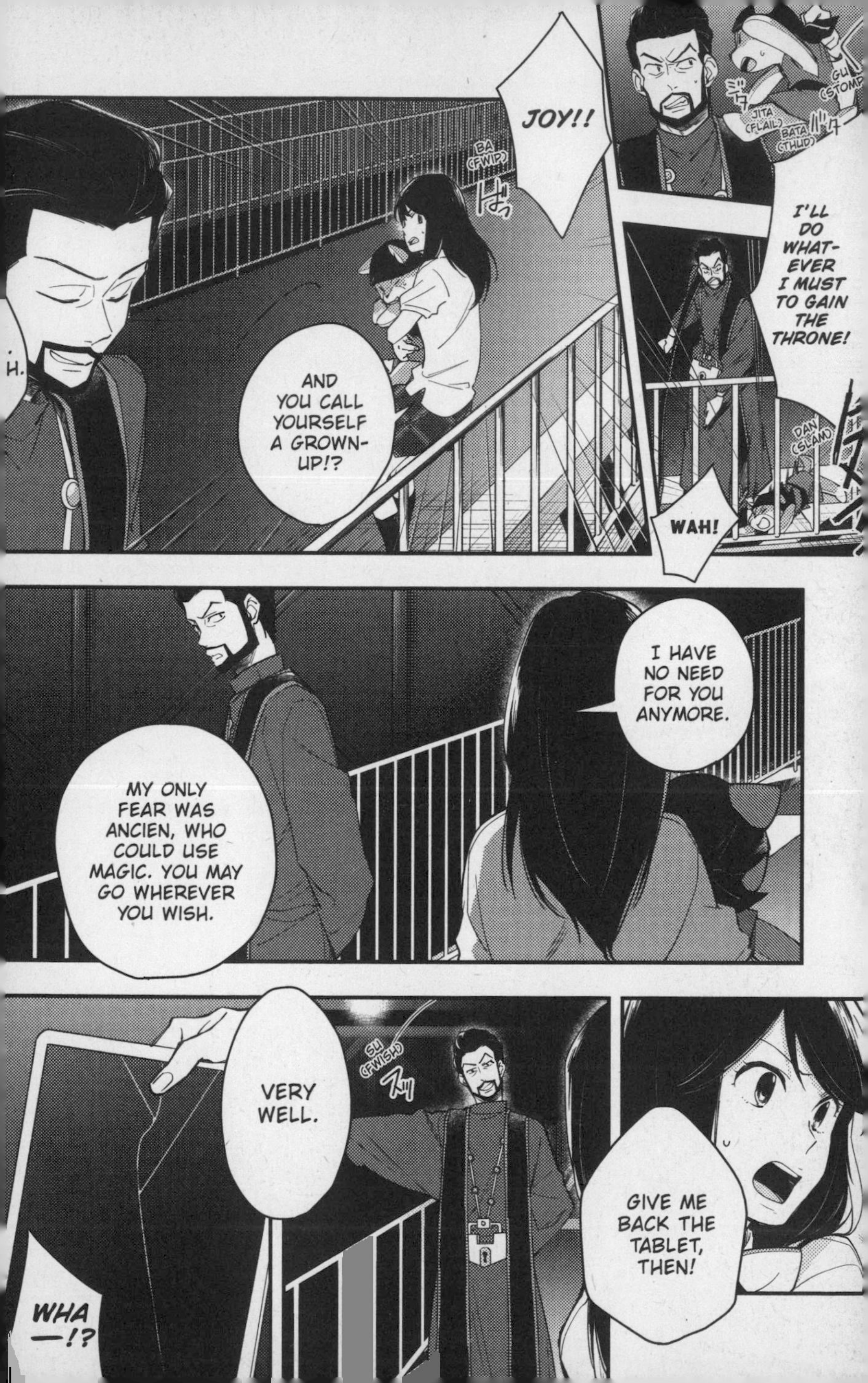
GU
(STOMP)
JITA
(FLAIL)
BATA
(THUD)
I'LL DO WHATEVER I MUST TO GAIN THE THRONE!
DAN
(SLAM)
WAH!
JOY!!
BA
(FWIP)
AND YOU CALL YOURSELF A GROWN-UP!?
I HAVE NO NEED FOR YOU ANYMORE.
MY ONLY FEAR WAS ANCIEN, WHO COULD USE MAGIC. YOU MAY GO WHEREVER YOU WISH.
GIVE ME BACK THE TABLET, THEN!
SU
(FWISH)
VERY WELL.
WHA—!?

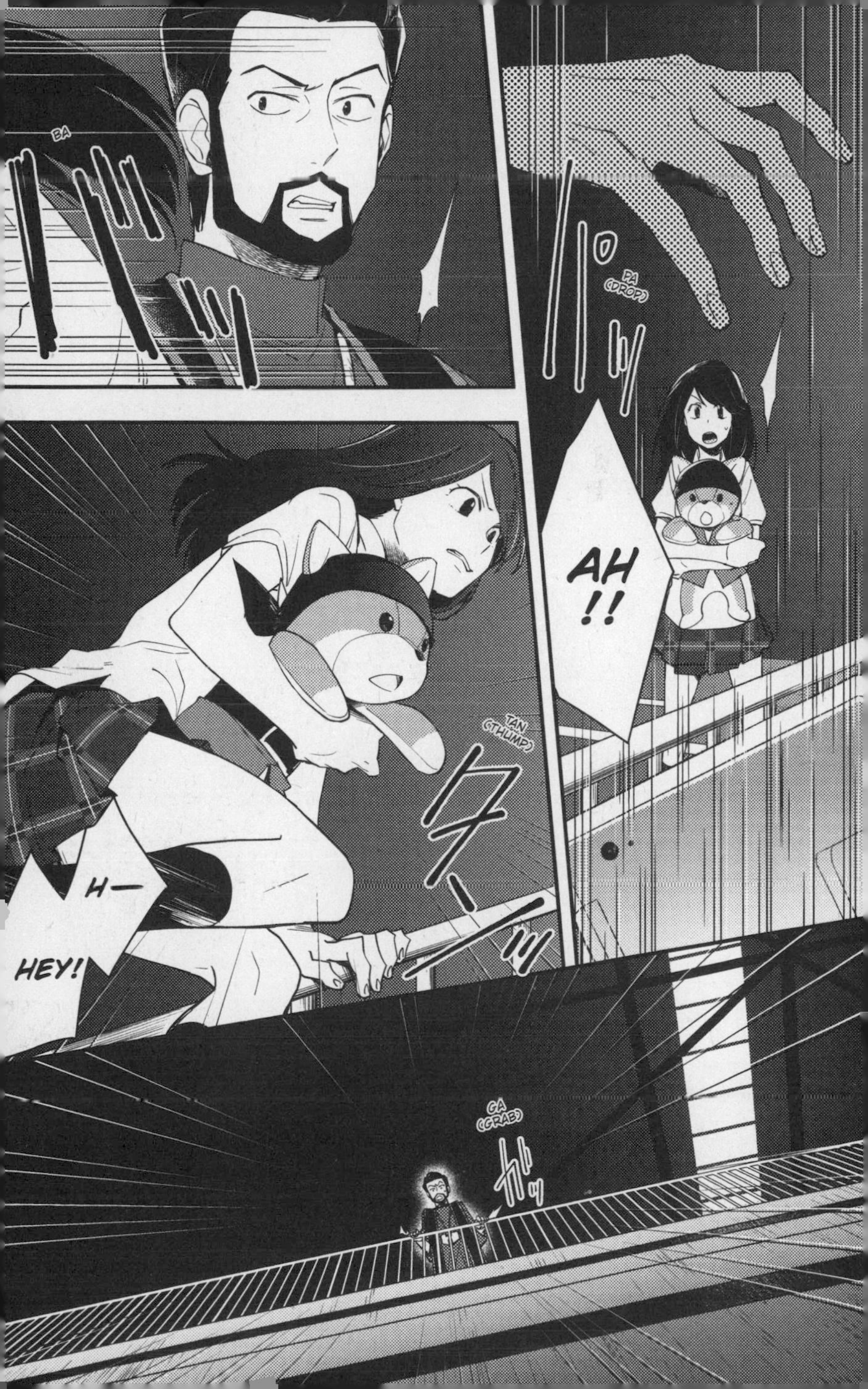
PA (DROP)
AH !!
BA
TAN (THUMP)
H—
HEY!
GA (GRAB)

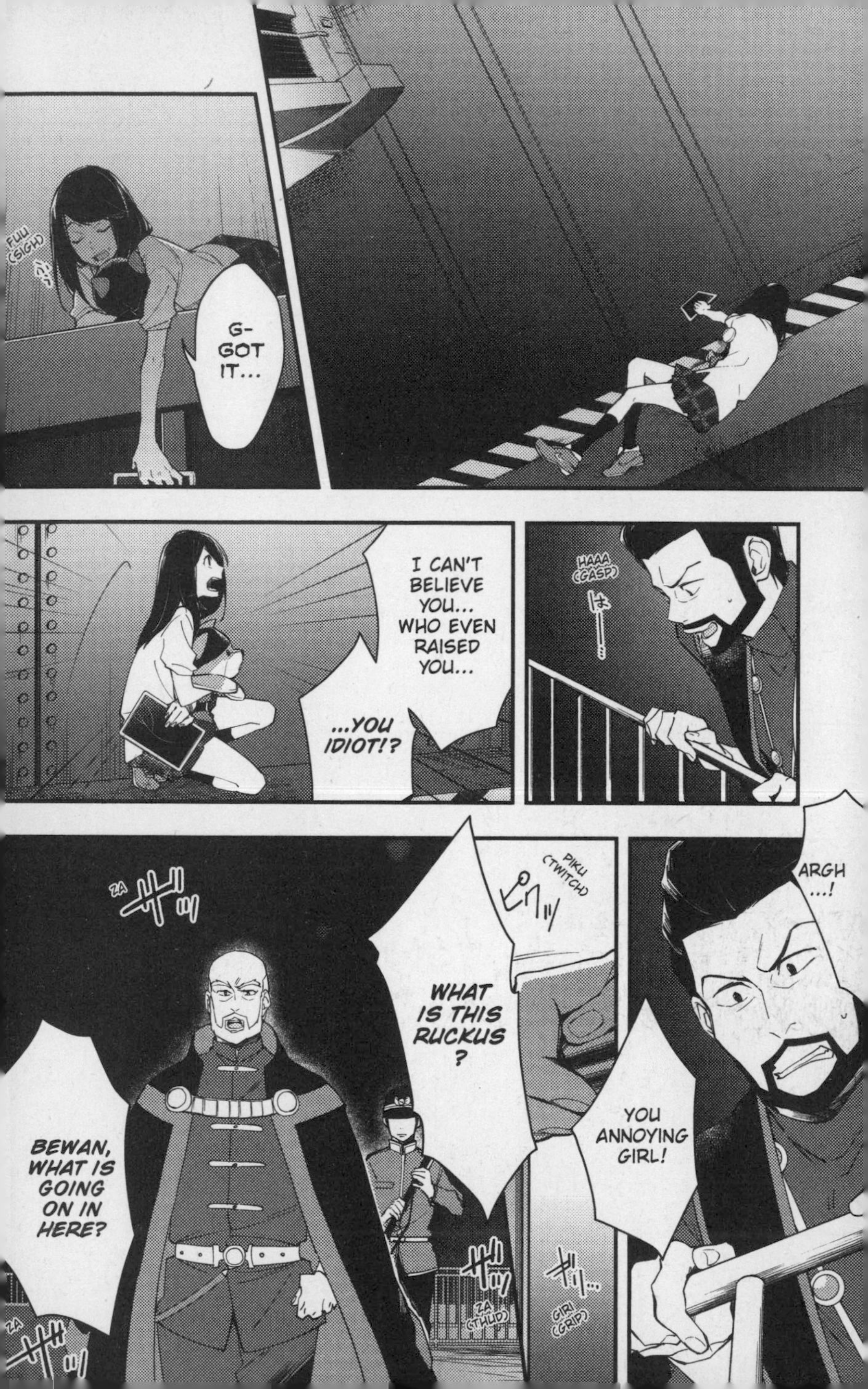
FUU (SIGH)
G-GOT IT...
HAAA (GASP)
I CAN'T BELIEVE YOU... WHO EVEN RAISED YOU...
...YOU IDIOT!?
ARGH ...!
YOU ANNOYING GIRL!
GIRI (GRIP)
PIKU (TWITCH)
WHAT IS THIS RUCKUS?
ZA
BEWAN, WHAT IS GOING ON IN HERE?
ZA (THUD)
ZA

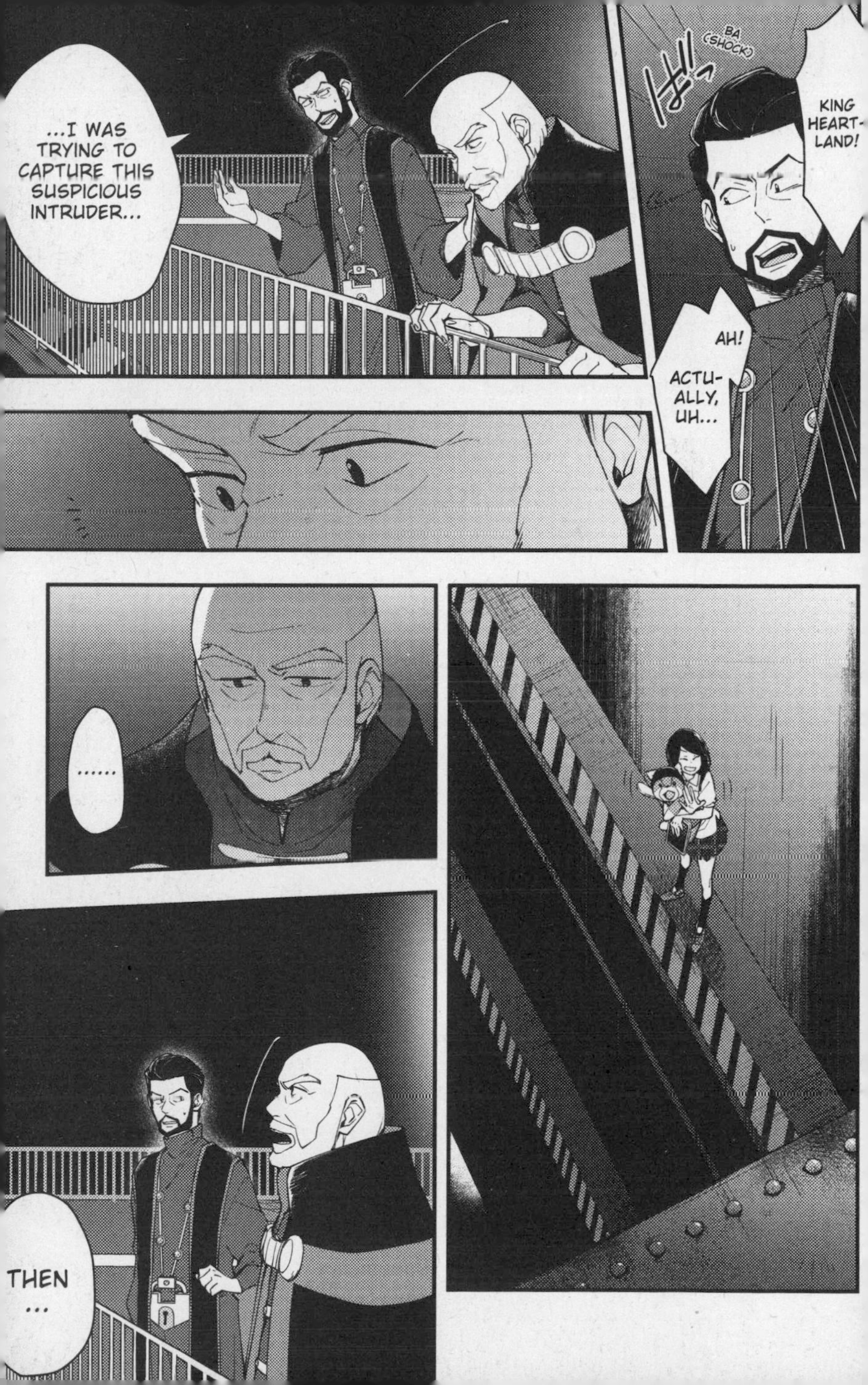
BA (SHOCK)
KING HEART-LAND!
AH!
ACTU-ALLY, UH...
...I WAS TRYING TO CAPTURE THIS SUSPICIOUS INTRUDER...
......
THEN...

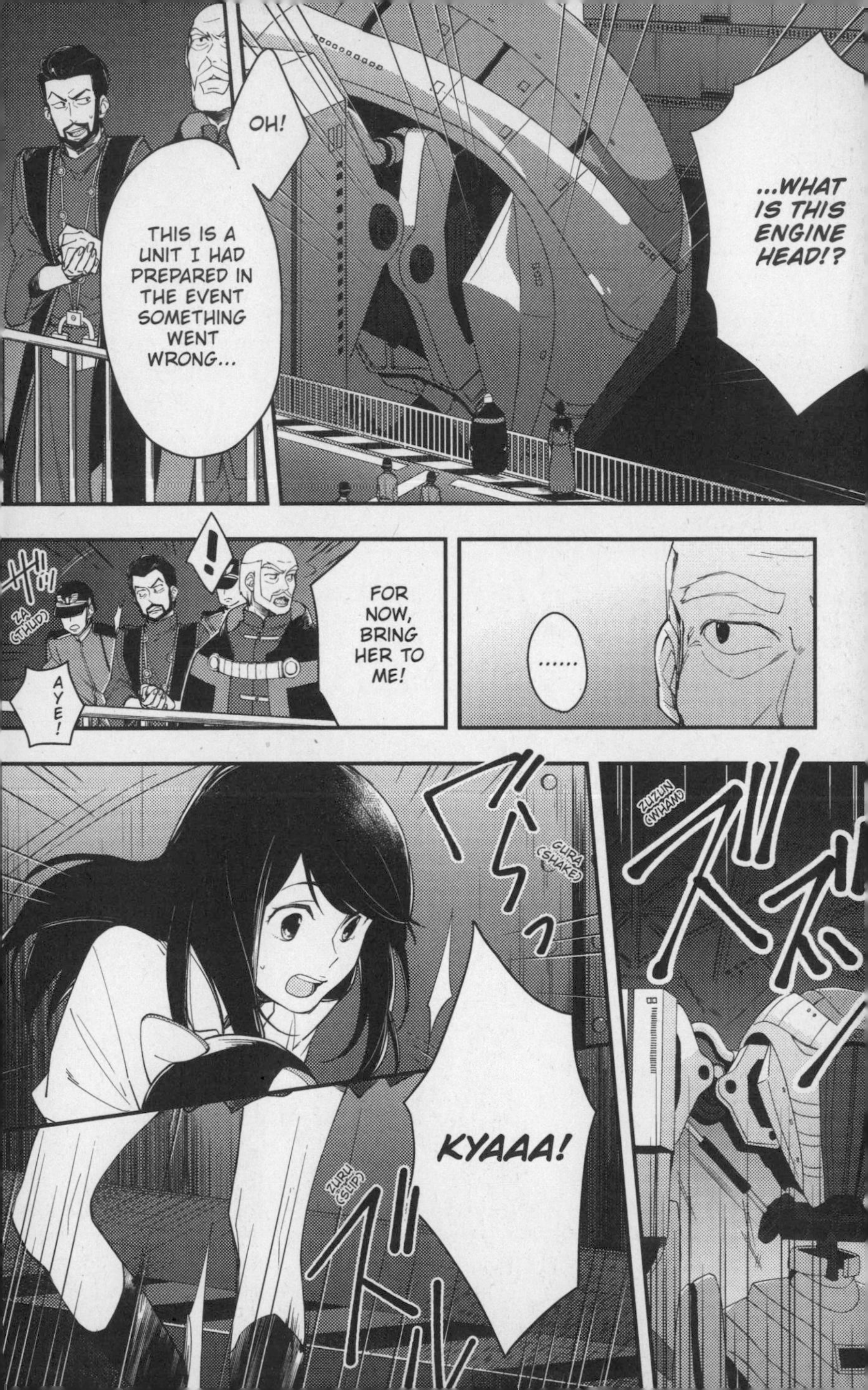
...WHAT IS THIS ENGINE HEAD!?
OH!
THIS IS A UNIT I HAD PREPARED IN THE EVENT SOMETHING WENT WRONG...
......
!
FOR NOW, BRING HER TO ME!
ZA (THUD)
AYE!
ZUZUN (WHAM)
GURA (SHAKE)
KYAAA!
ZURU (SLIP)

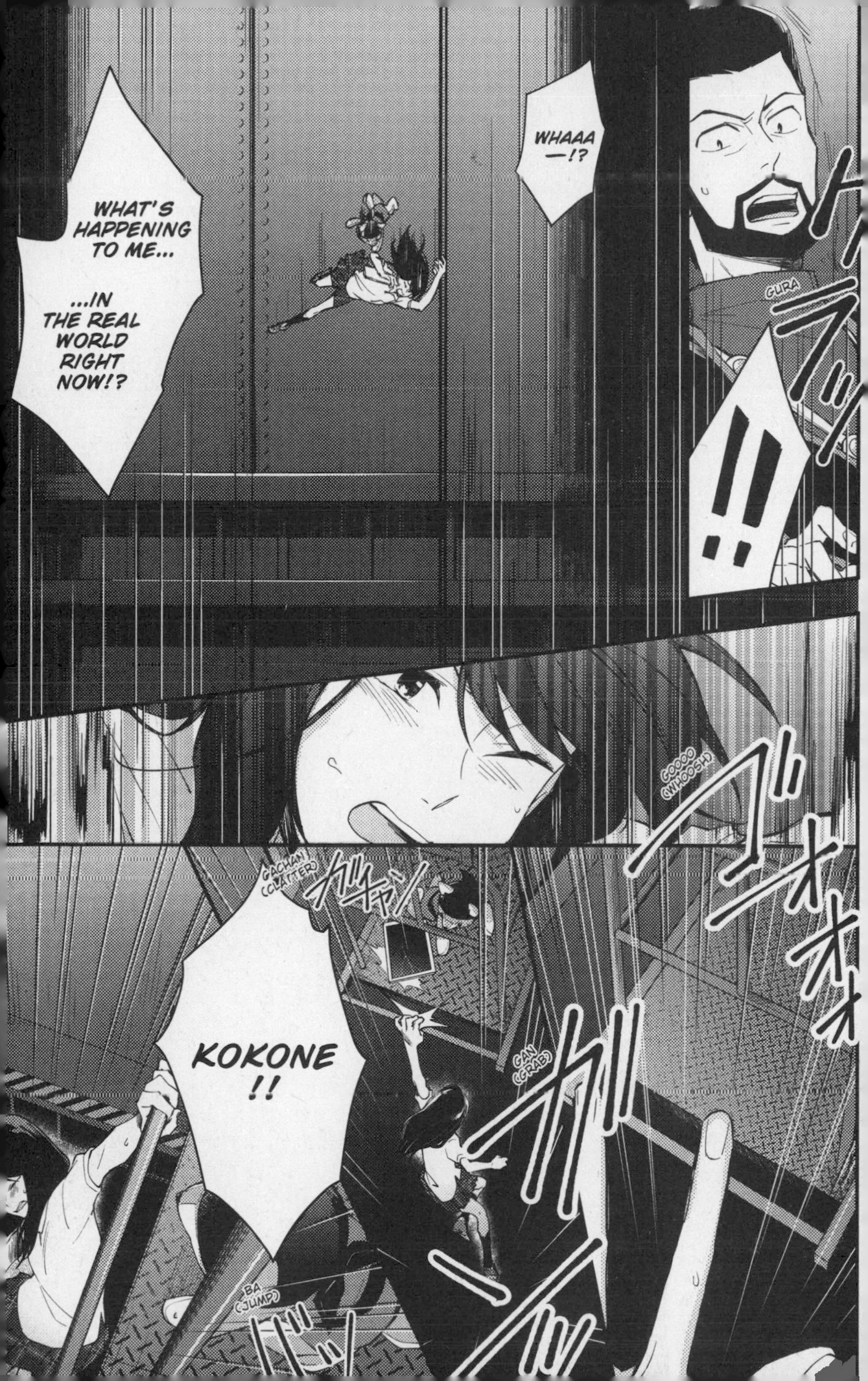
WHAAA—!?
GURA
!!
WHAT'S HAPPENING TO ME...
...IN THE REAL WORLD RIGHT NOW!?
GOOOO (WHOOSH)
GACHAN (CLATTER)
GAN (GRAB)
KOKONE!!
BA (JUMP)

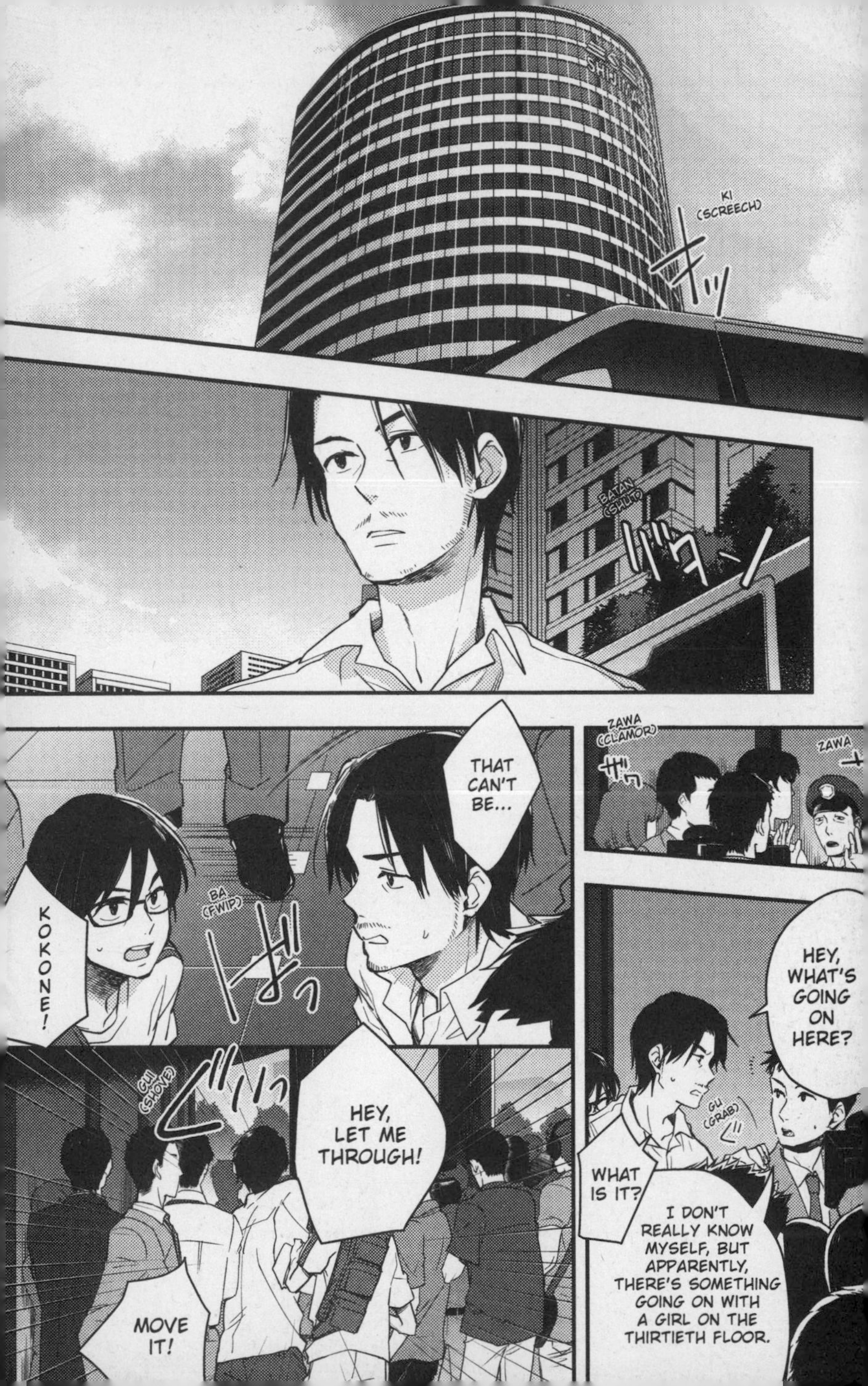
KI (SCREECH)
BATAN (SHUT)
ZAWA (CLAMOR)
ZAWA
HEY, WHAT'S GOING ON HERE?
GU (GRAB)
WHAT IS IT?
I DON'T REALLY KNOW MYSELF, BUT APPARENTLY, THERE'S SOMETHING GOING ON WITH A GIRL ON THE THIRTIETH FLOOR.
THAT CAN'T BE...
BA (FWIP)
KOKONE!
GUII (SHOVE)
HEY, LET ME THROUGH!
MOVE IT!

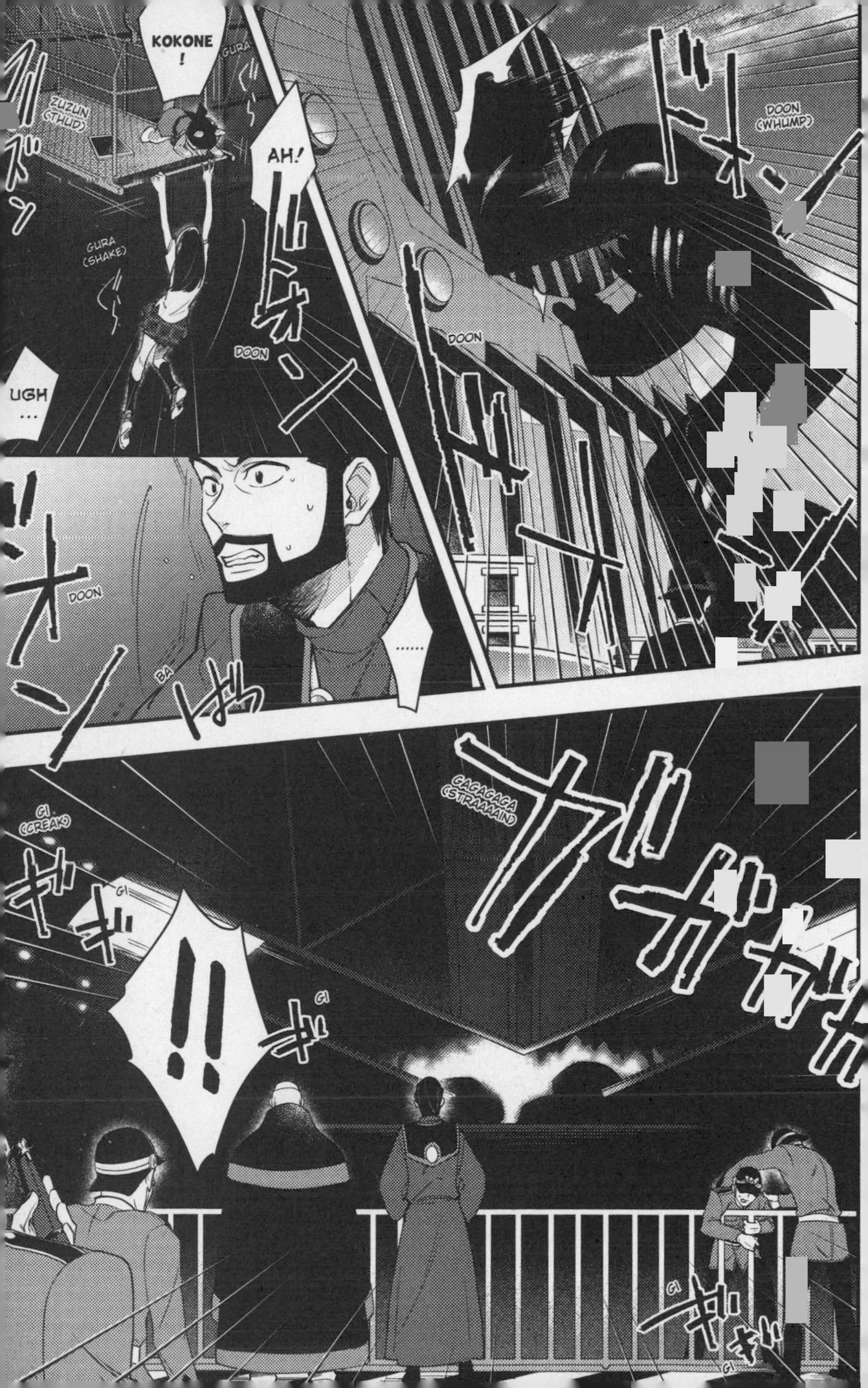
DOON (WHUMP)
DOON
KOKONE !
GURA
AH!
ZUZUN (THUD)
GURA (SHAKE)
DOON
UGH …
……
DOON
BA
GAGAGAGA (STRAAAAIN)
!!
GI
GI
GI (CREAK)
GI
GI
GI

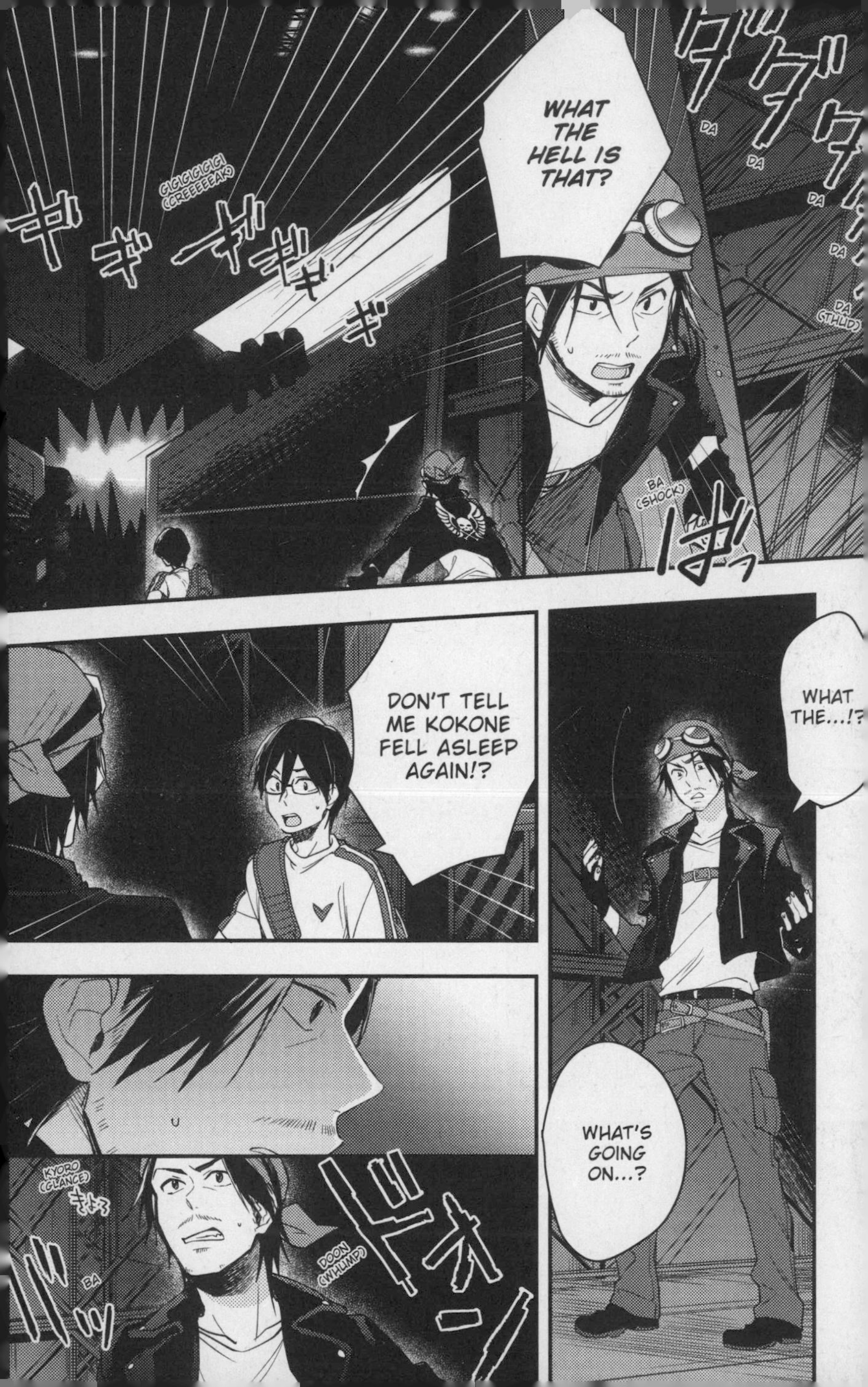
DA
DA
DA
DA
DA (THUD)
WHAT THE HELL IS THAT?
GIGIGIGIGI (CREEEEEAK)
BA (SHOCK)
WHAT THE...!?
WHAT'S GOING ON...?
DON'T TELL ME KOKONE FELL ASLEEP AGAIN!?
DOON (WHUMP)
KYORO (GLANCE)
BA

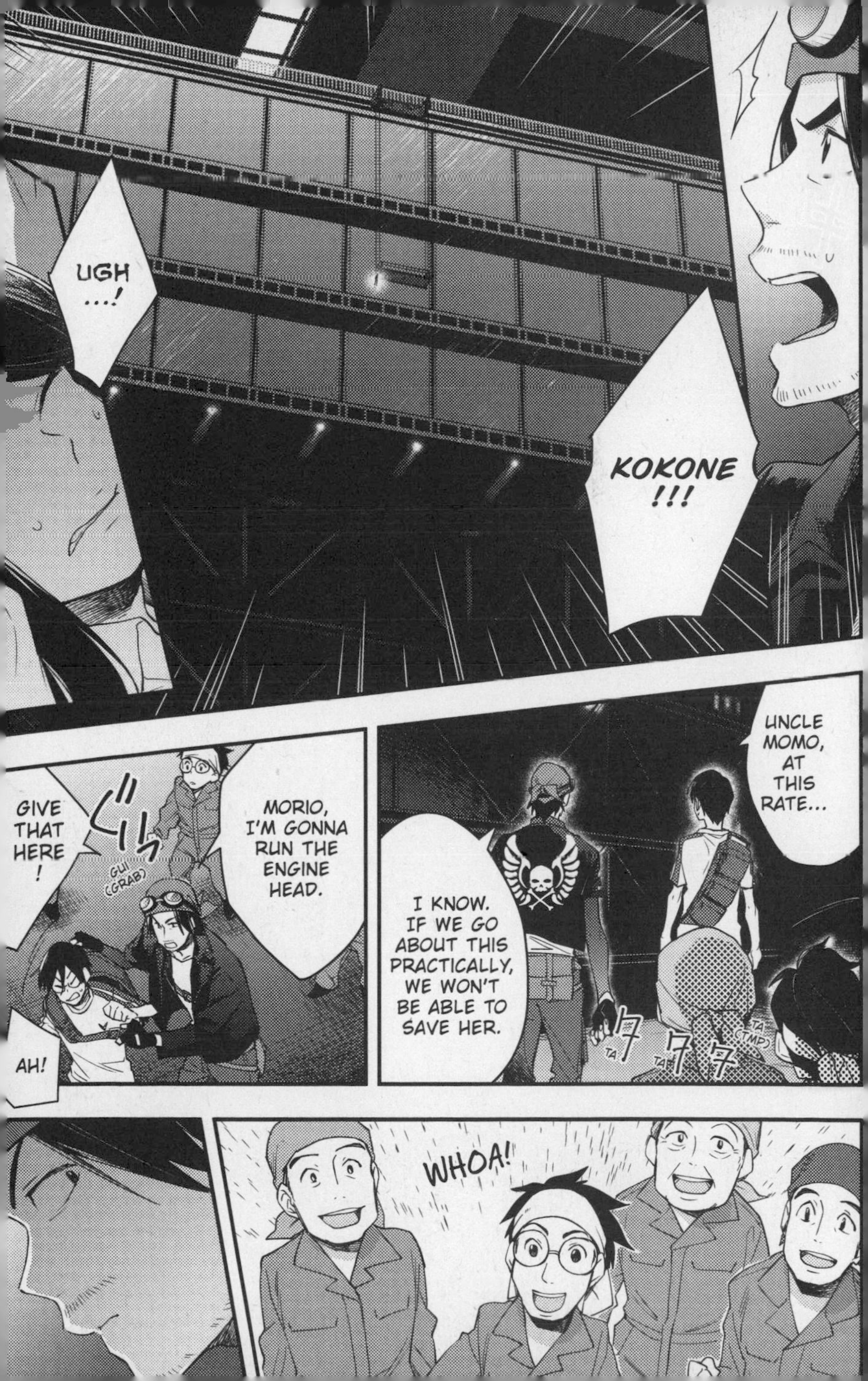
KOKONE!!!
UGH...!
UNCLE MOMO, AT THIS RATE...
I KNOW. IF WE GO ABOUT THIS PRACTICALLY, WE WON'T BE ABLE TO SAVE HER.
TA (TMP)
TA
TA
MORIO, I'M GONNA RUN THE ENGINE HEAD.
GIVE THAT HERE!
GUI (GRAB)
AH!
WHOA!

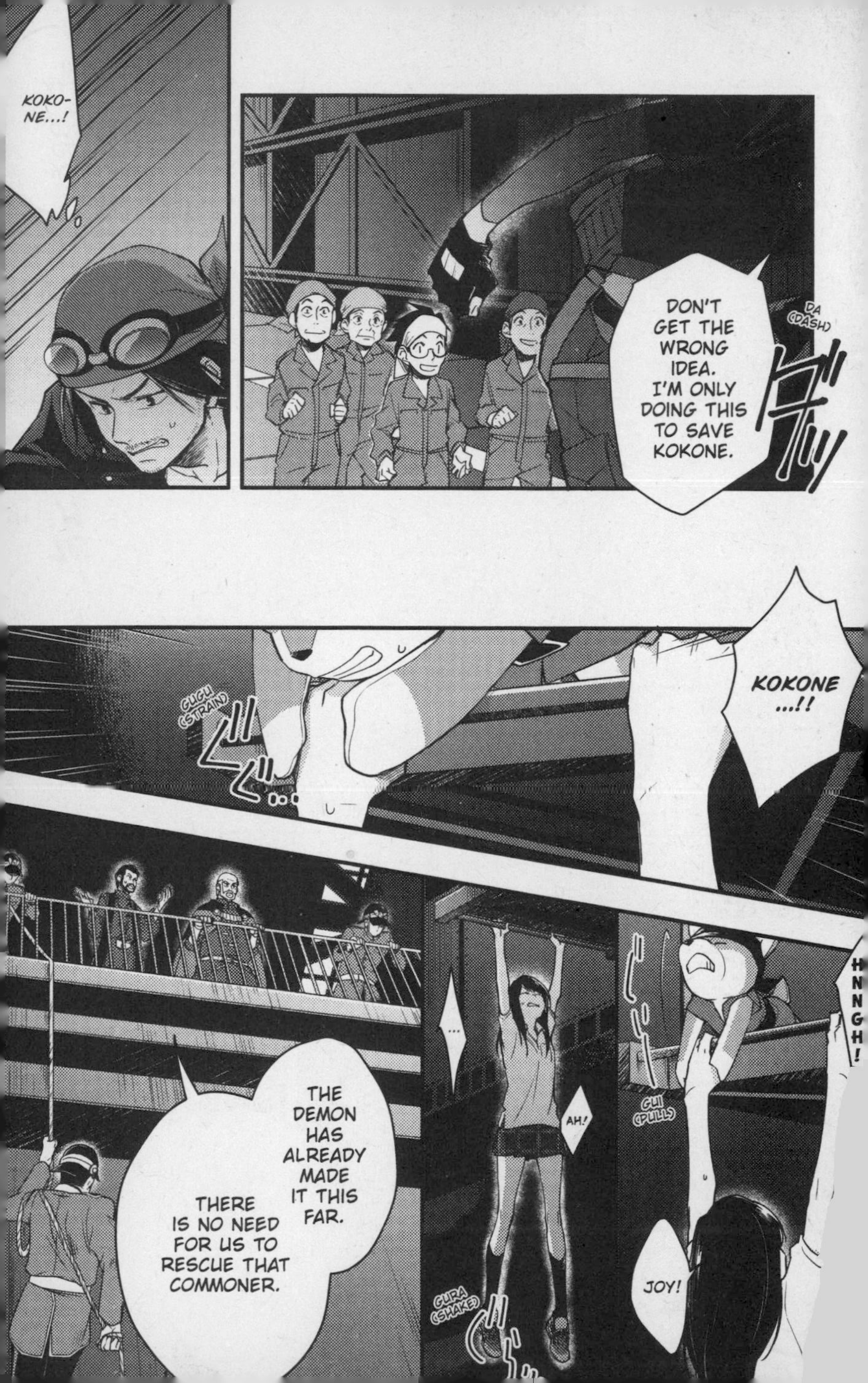
DON'T GET THE WRONG IDEA. I'M ONLY DOING THIS TO SAVE KOKONE.
DA (DASH)
KOKO-NE...!
KOKONE ...!!
GUGU (STRAIN)
HNNGH!
GUI (PULL)
JOY!
...
AH!
GURA (SHAKE)
THE DEMON HAS ALREADY MADE IT THIS FAR.
THERE IS NO NEED FOR US TO RESCUE THAT COMMONER.

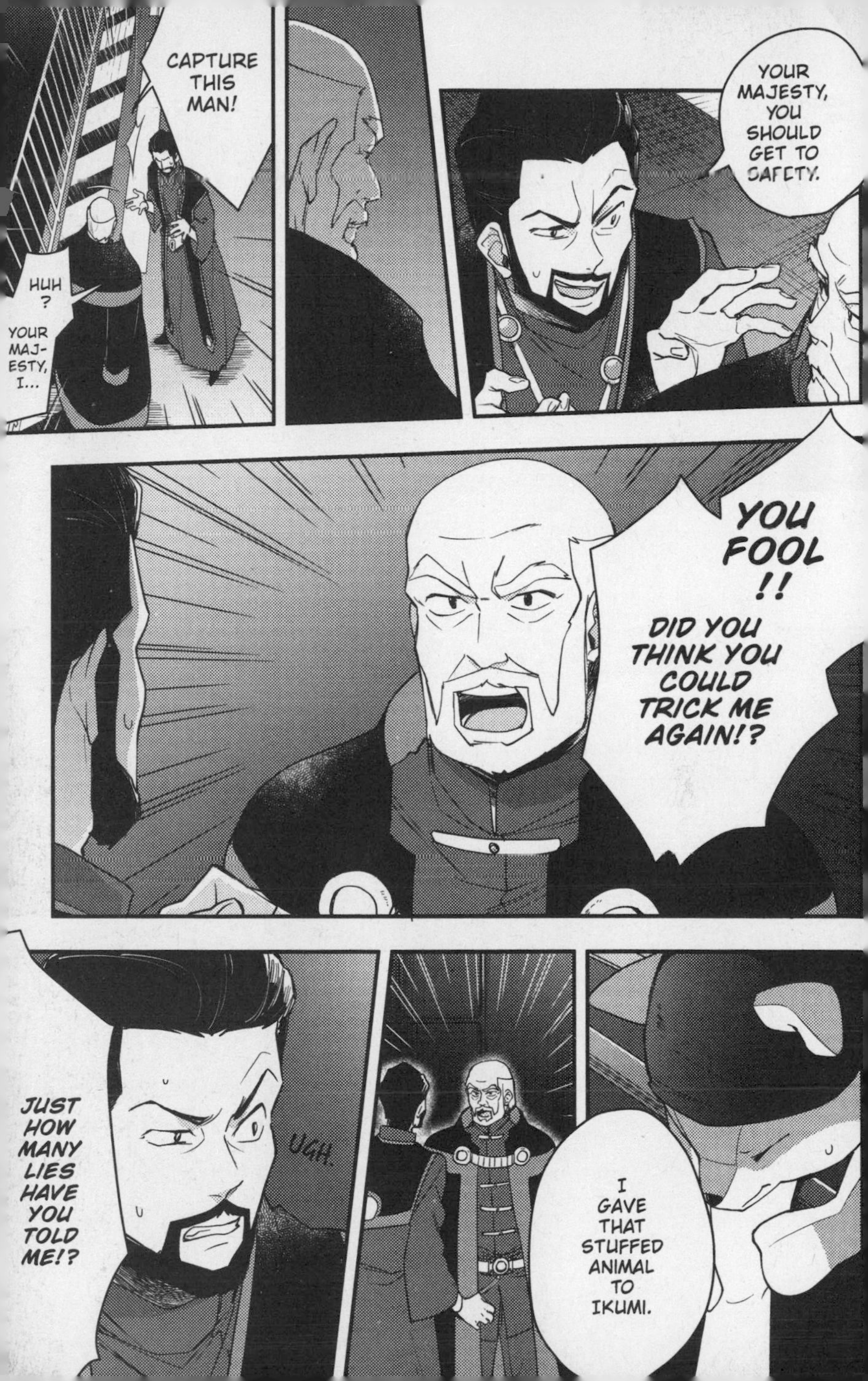
YOUR MAJESTY, YOU SHOULD GET TO SAFETY.
CAPTURE THIS MAN!
HUH?
YOUR MAJ-ESTY, I...
YOU FOOL!!
DID YOU THINK YOU COULD TRICK ME AGAIN!?
I GAVE THAT STUFFED ANIMAL TO IKUMI.
UGH.
JUST HOW MANY LIES HAVE YOU TOLD ME!?

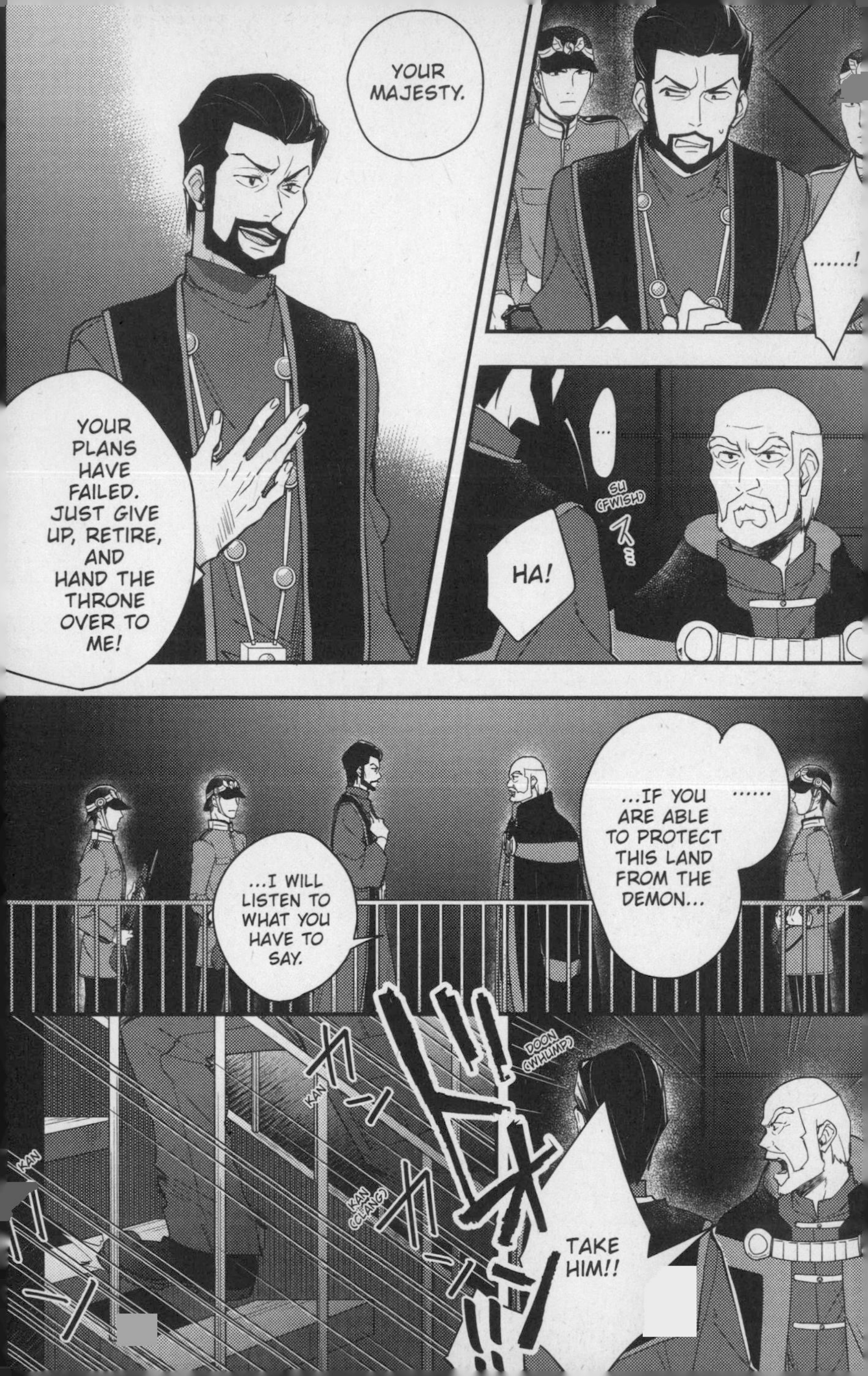
......!
...
SU (FWISH)
HA!
YOUR MAJESTY.
YOUR PLANS HAVE FAILED. JUST GIVE UP, RETIRE, AND HAND THE THRONE OVER TO ME!
......
...IF YOU ARE ABLE TO PROTECT THIS LAND FROM THE DEMON...
...I WILL LISTEN TO WHAT YOU HAVE TO SAY.
TAKE HIM!!
DOON (WHUMP)
KAN
KAN (CLANG)
KAN

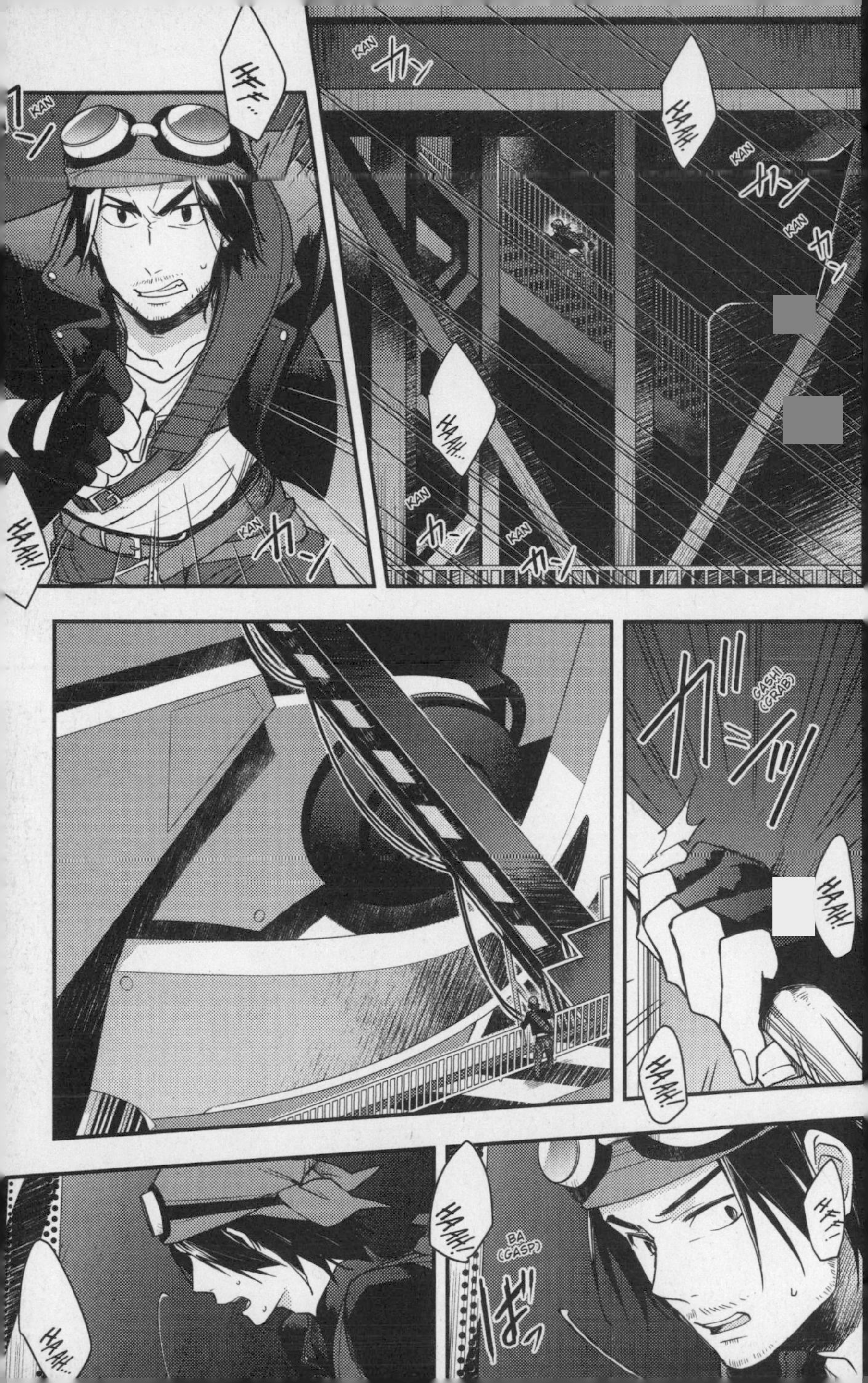
KAN
HAAH!
KAN
KAN
HAAH...
KAN
KAN
KAN
Hff...
HAAH!
KAN
GASH! (GRAB)
HAAH!
HAAH!
Hff!
HAAH!
BA (GASP)
HAAH...

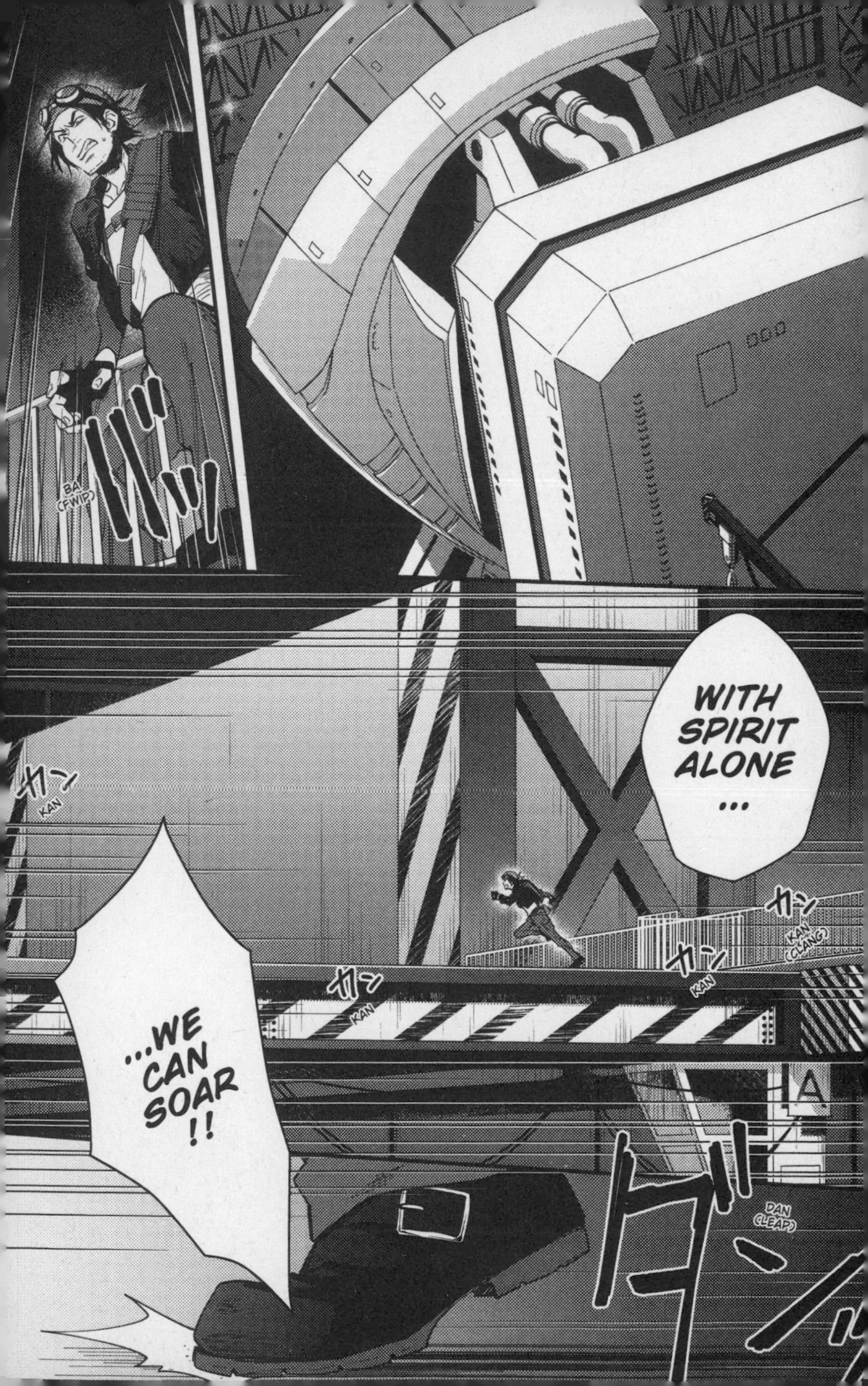
BA (FWIP)
WITH SPIRIT ALONE ...
KAN (CLANG)
KAN
KAN
KAN
...WE CAN SOAR !!
DAN (LEAP)

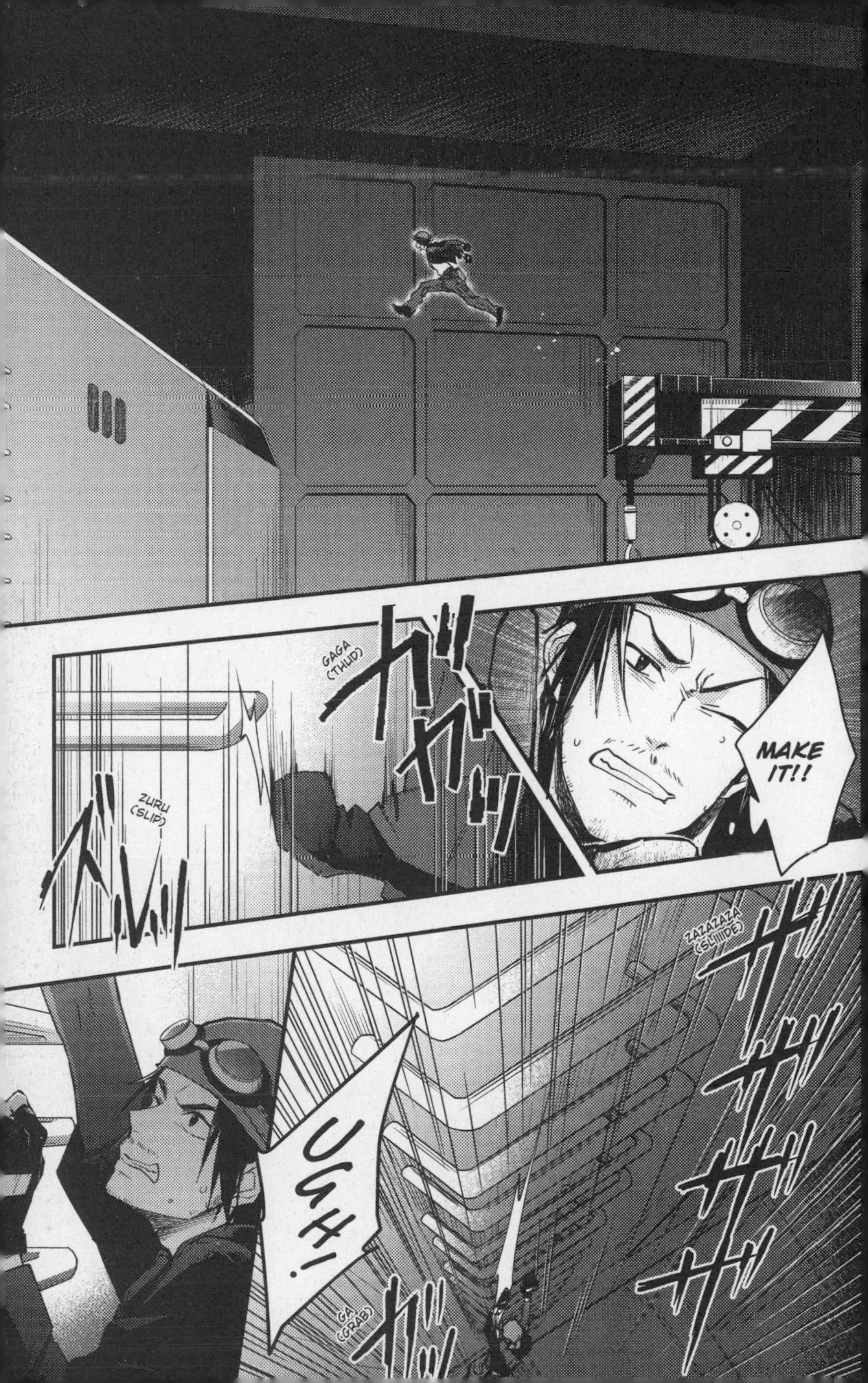
MAKE IT!!
GAGA (THUD)
ZURU (SLIP)
ZAZAZAZA (SLIIIIDE)
UGH!
GA (GRAB)

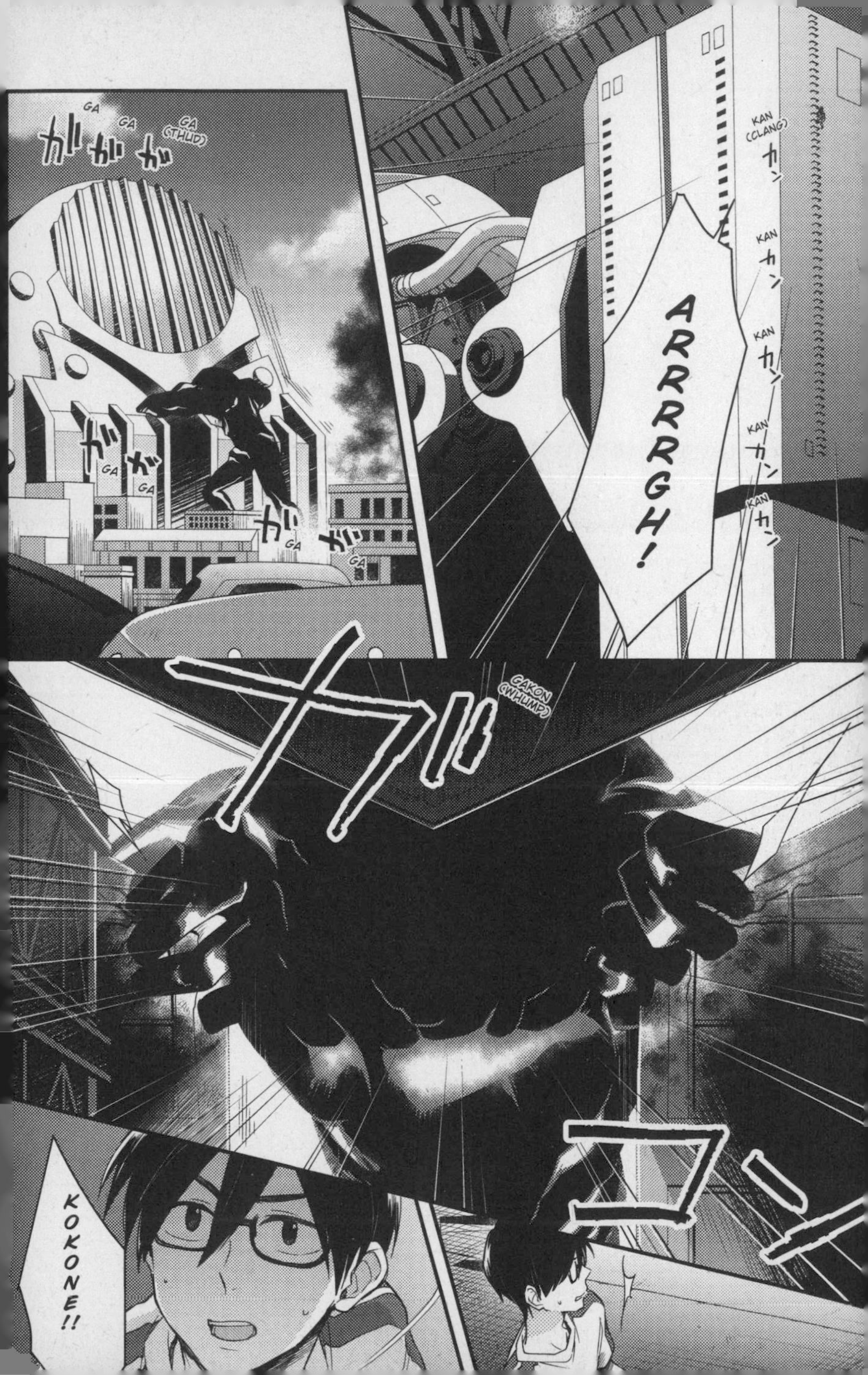
KAN (CLANG)
KAN
KAN
KAN
KAN
ARRRRGH!
GA GA GA (THUD)
GA GA
GA GA
GAKON (WHUMP)
KOKONE!!

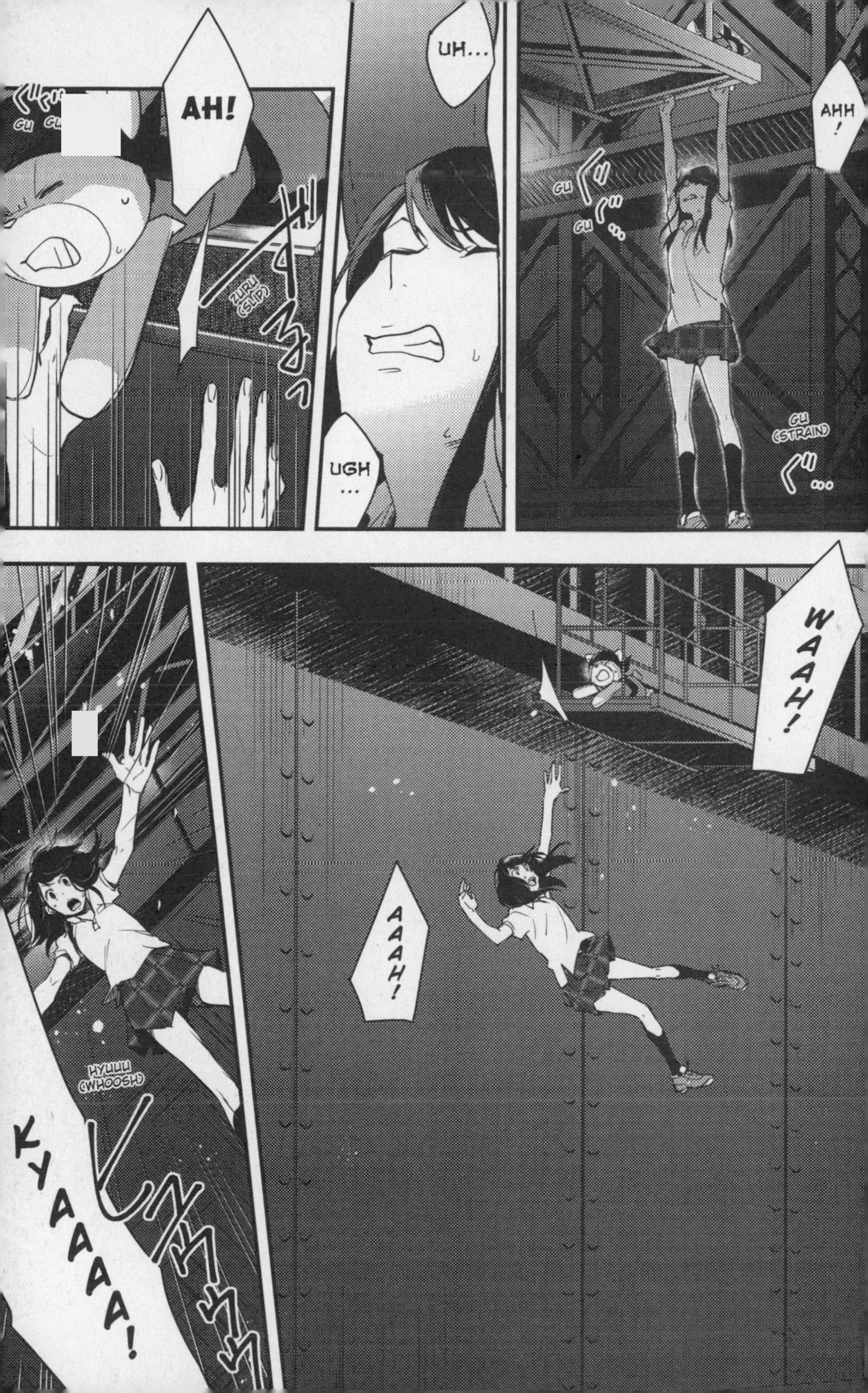
AHH!
GU
GU
GU (STRAIN)
UH...
UGH...
AH!
GU GU
ZURU (SLIP)
WAAAH!
AAAAH!
HYUUU (WHOOSH)
KYAAAAA!

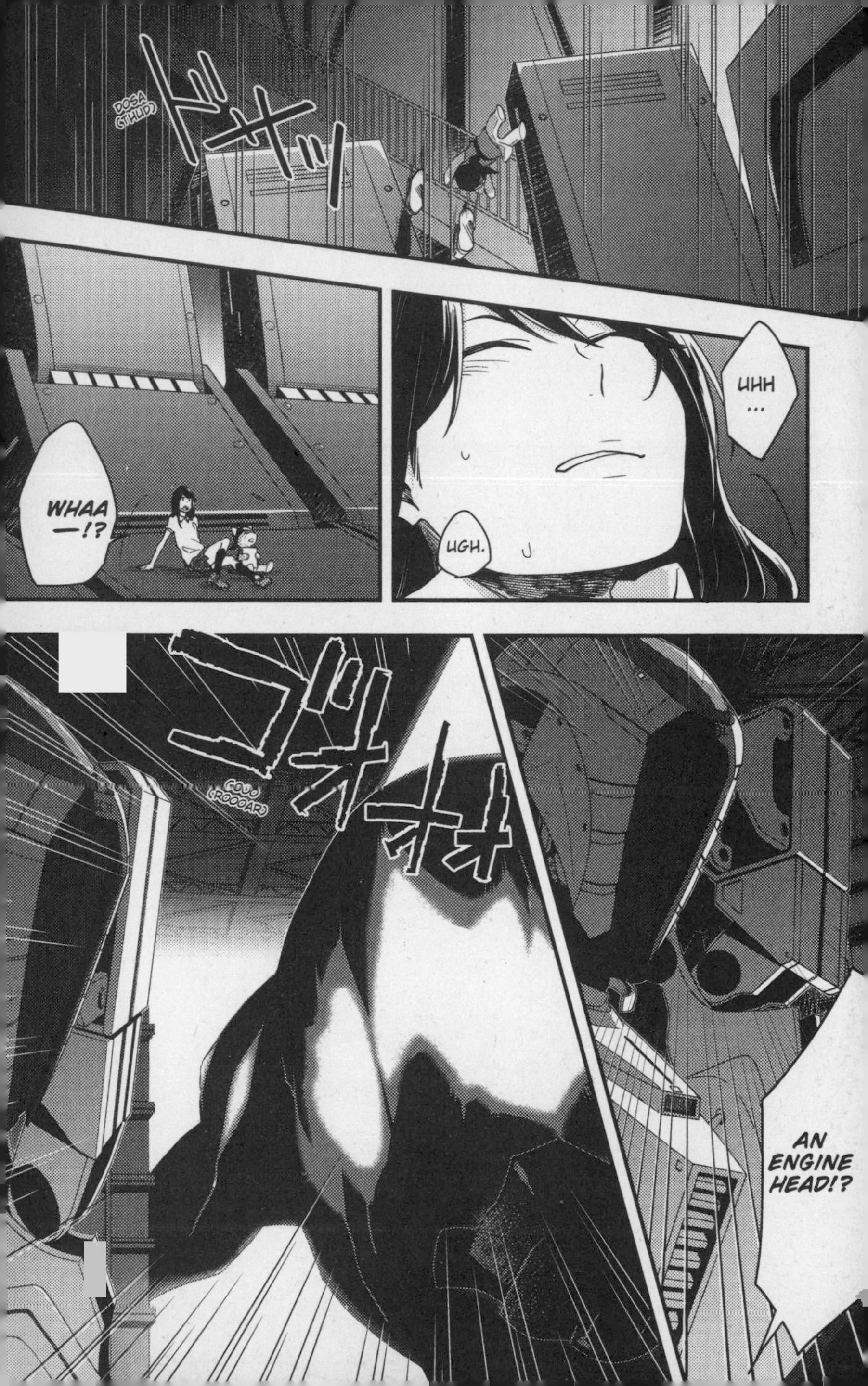
ドサッ
DOSA (THUD)
UHH ...
UGH.
WHAA —!?
ゴオォォ
GOJO (ROOOAR)
AN ENGINE HEAD!?

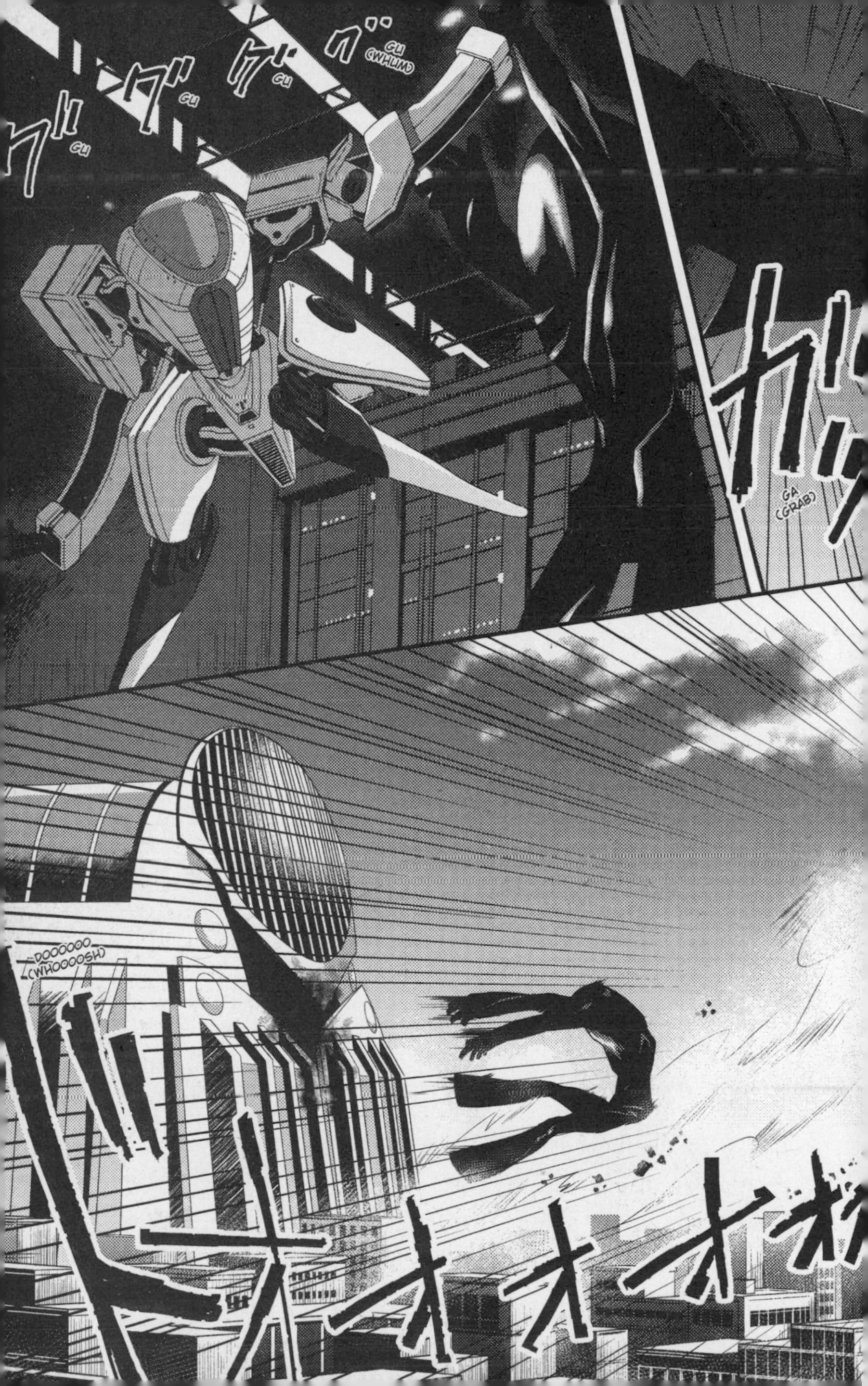
GU (WHUM)
GU
GU
GU
GA (GRAB)
DOOOOOO (WHOOOOOSH)

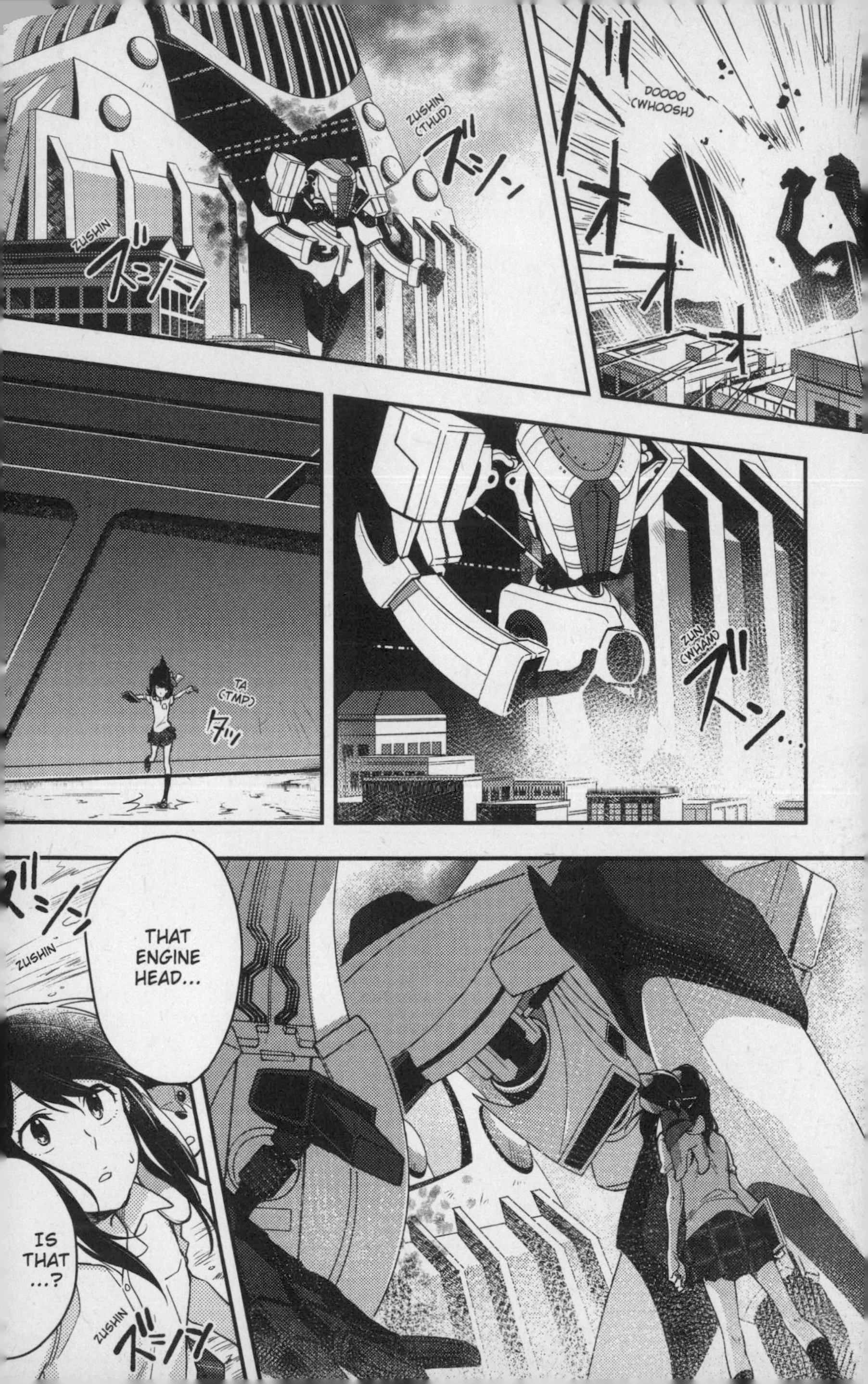
DOOOO
(WHOOSH)
ZUSHIN
(THUD)
ZUSHIN
ZUN
(WHAM)
TA
(TMP)
THAT ENGINE HEAD...
ZUSHIN
IS THAT ...?
ZUSHIN

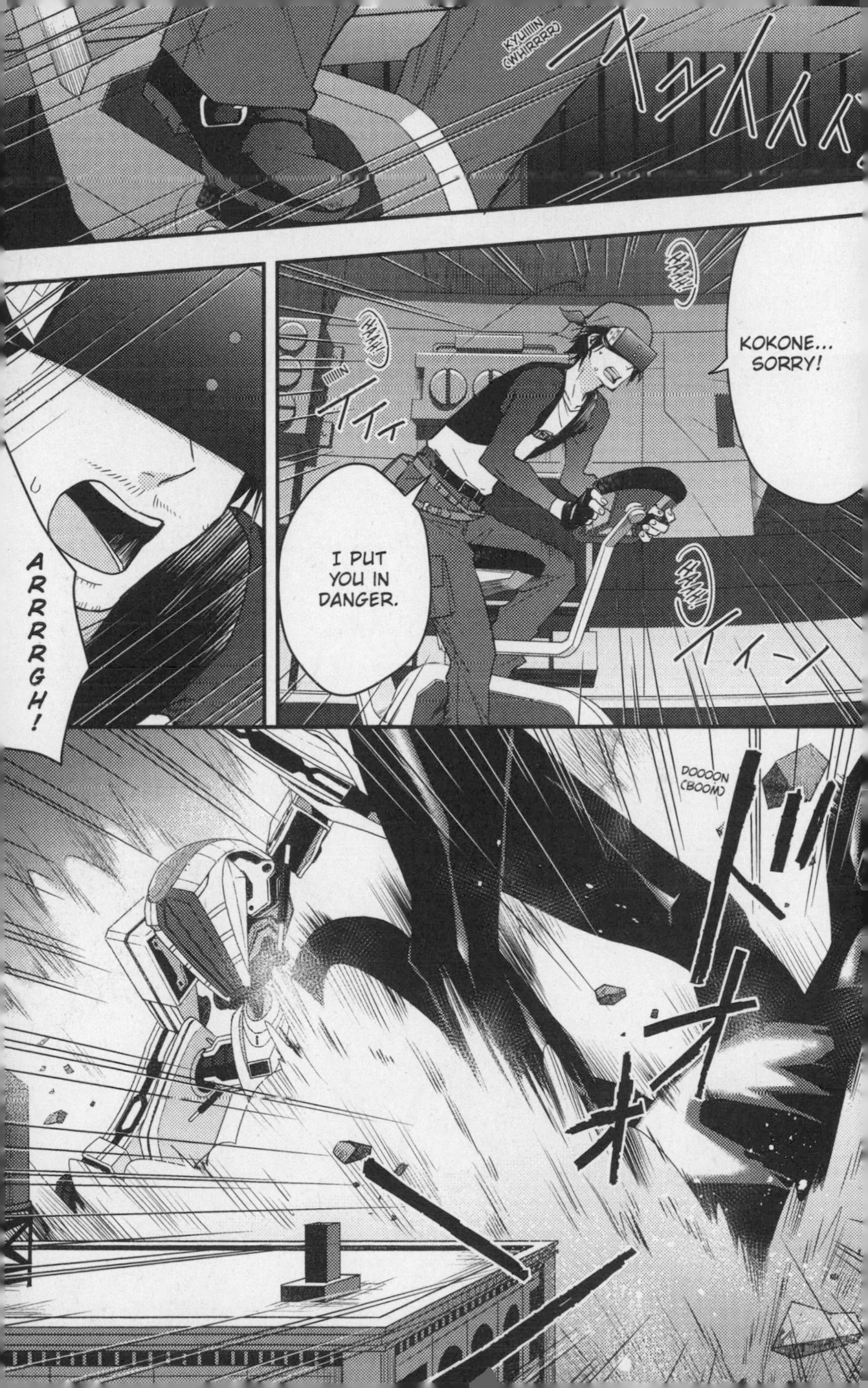
KYUIIIN (WHIRRRR)
HAAH!
KOKONE... SORRY!
HAAH!
I PUT YOU IN DANGER.
HAAAH!
ARRRRGH!
DOOOON (BOOM)

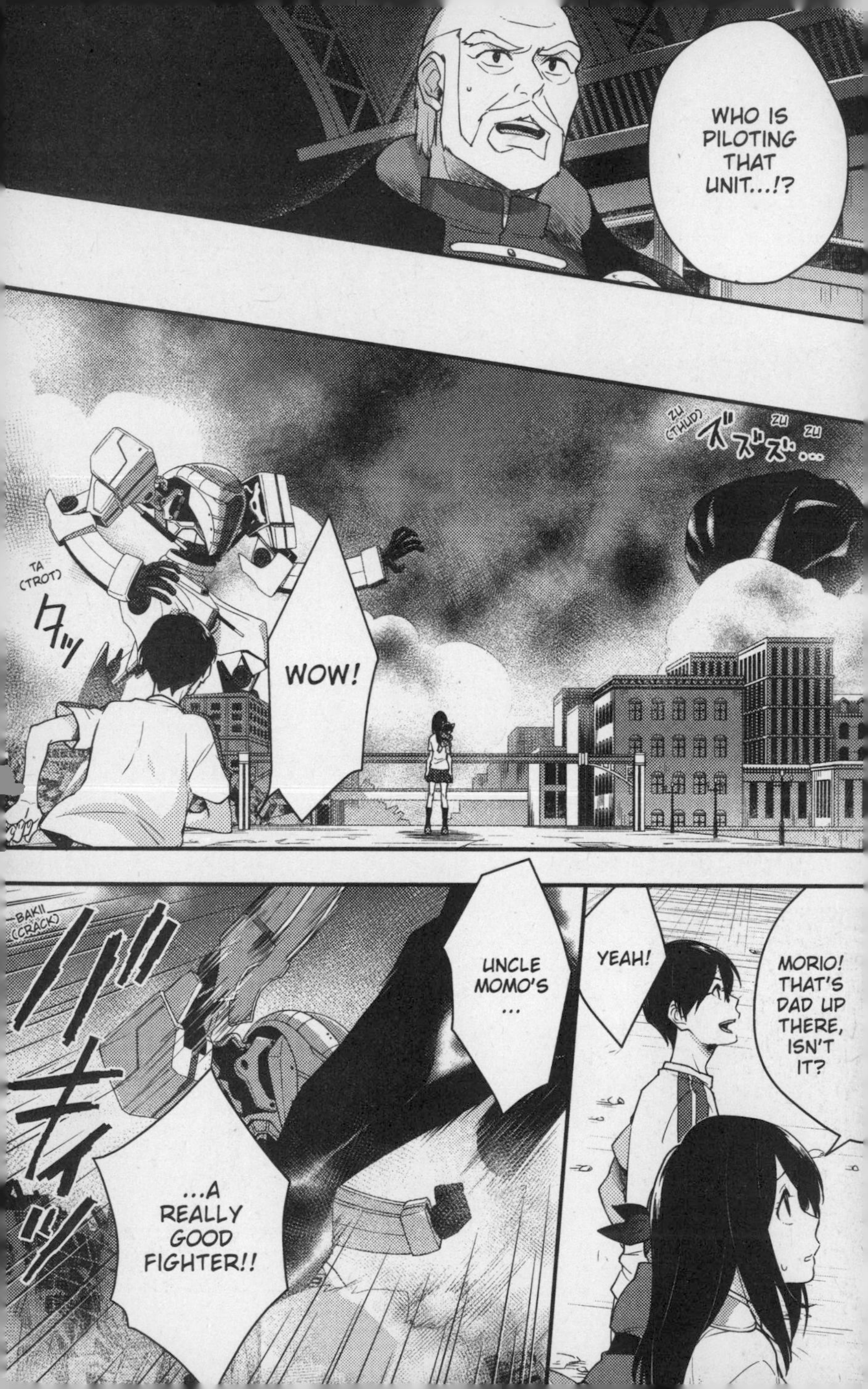
WHO IS PILOTING THAT UNIT...!?
ZU (THUD) ZU ZU
ズズズ...
WOW!
TA (TROT)
タッ
MORIO! THAT'S DAD UP THERE, ISN'T IT?
YEAH!
UNCLE MOMO'S ...
...A REALLY GOOD FIGHTER!!
BAKII (CRACK)

...THAT IS MY ENGINE HEAD.

IN OTHER WORDS, THIS LAND IS MINE.

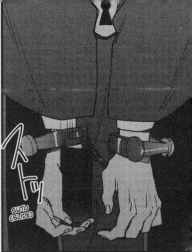

SUTO (SLIDE)

UGH!

PA (CLOMP)

AH!!

HE'S GOING TO CAST A CURSE!!!

HEY, YOU!

PI (BEEP)

SENDING

A | KA | SA

TA | NA | HA

MA | YA | RA

GU (STIR)

Shijima Motors did not complete their self-driving car for the Olympics.

SEND

A | KA | SA

TA | NA | HA

MA | YA | RA

SMALL | WA

GU

GU

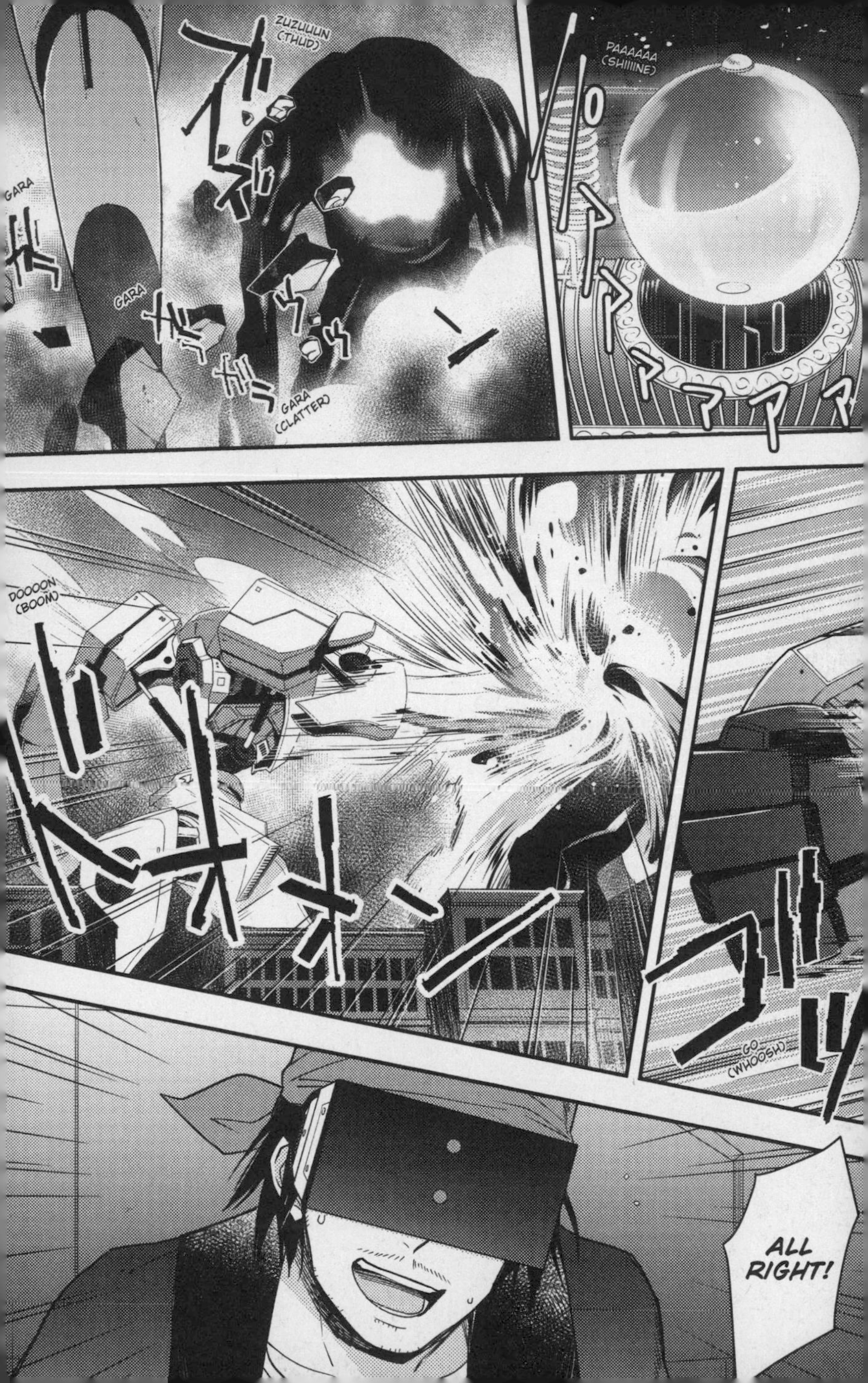
PAAAAAA (SHIIIINE)
ZUZUUUN (THUD)
GARA
GARA
GARA (CLATTER)
GO (WHOOSH)
DOOOON (BOOM)
ALL RIGHT!

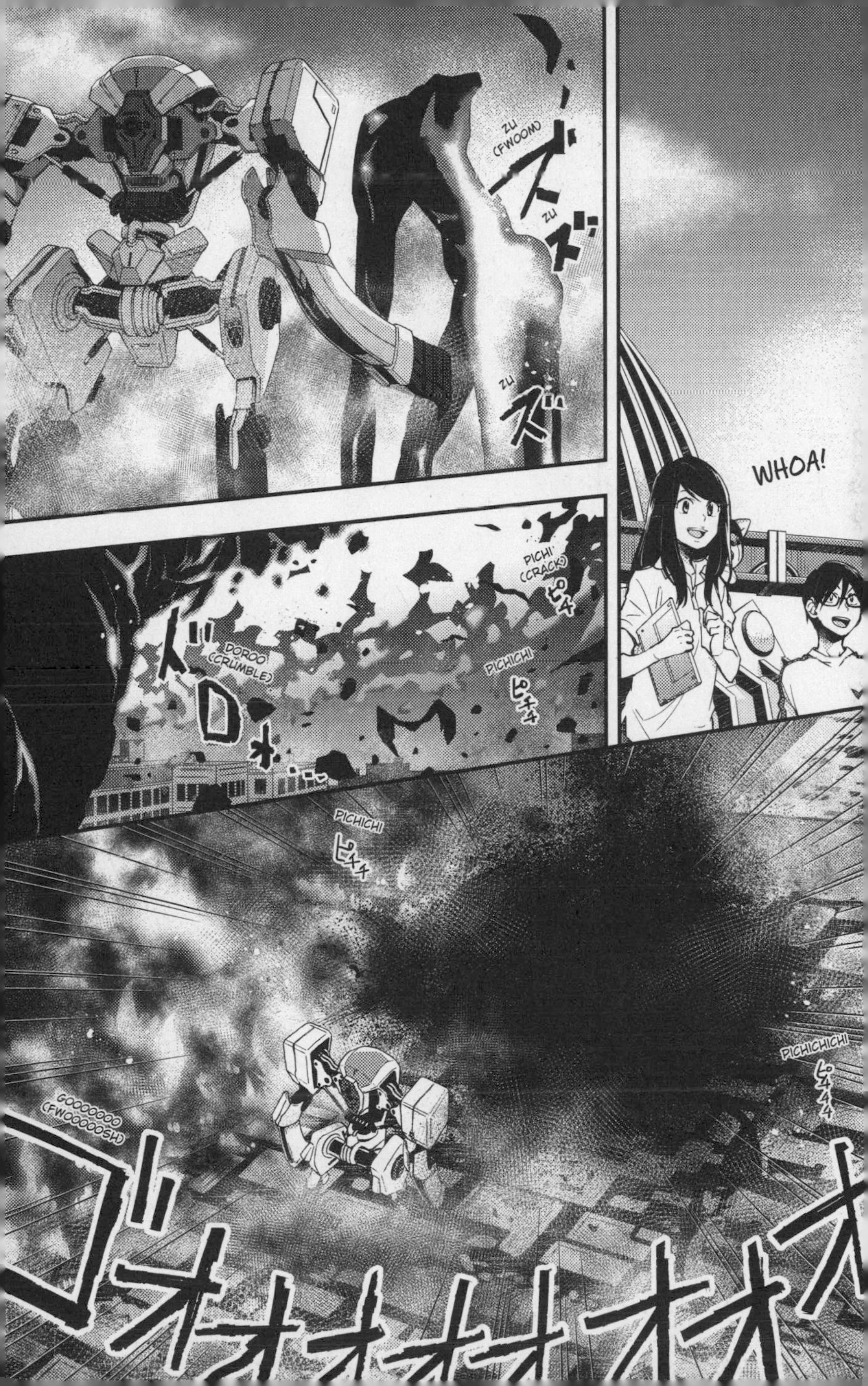
WHOA!
ZU (FWOOM)
ZU
ZU
PICHI (CRACK)
PICHICHI
DOROO (CRUMBLE)
PICHICHI
PICHICHICHI
GOOOOOOOO (FWOOOOOSH)

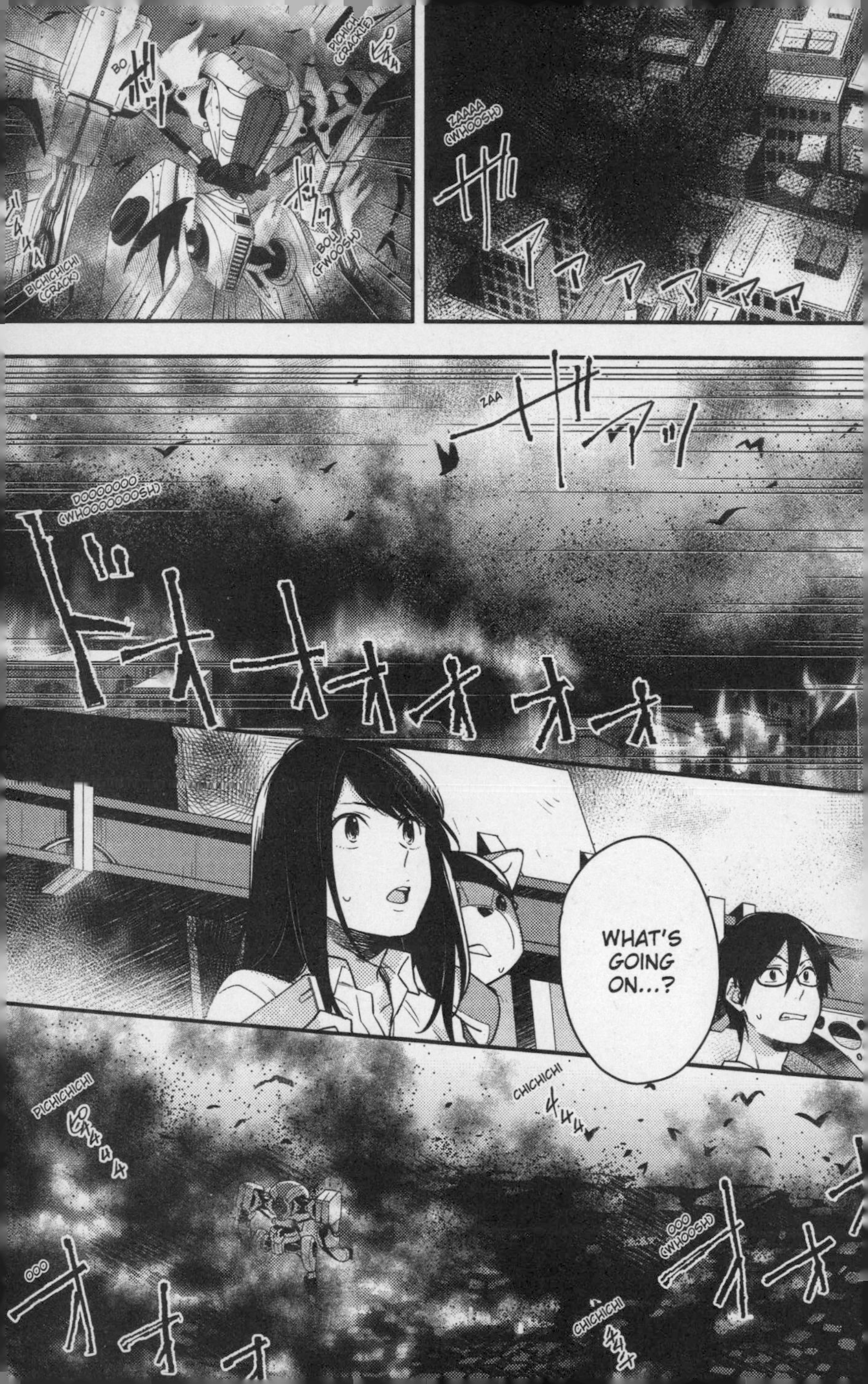
ZAAAA (WHOOSH)
BO
PICHICH (CRACKLE)
BOU (FWOOSH)
BICHICHICHI (CRACK)
ZAA
DOOOOOOO (WHOOOOOOOSH)
WHAT'S GOING ON...?
OOO (WHOOSH)
CHICHICHI
PICHICHICHI
OOO
CHICHICHI

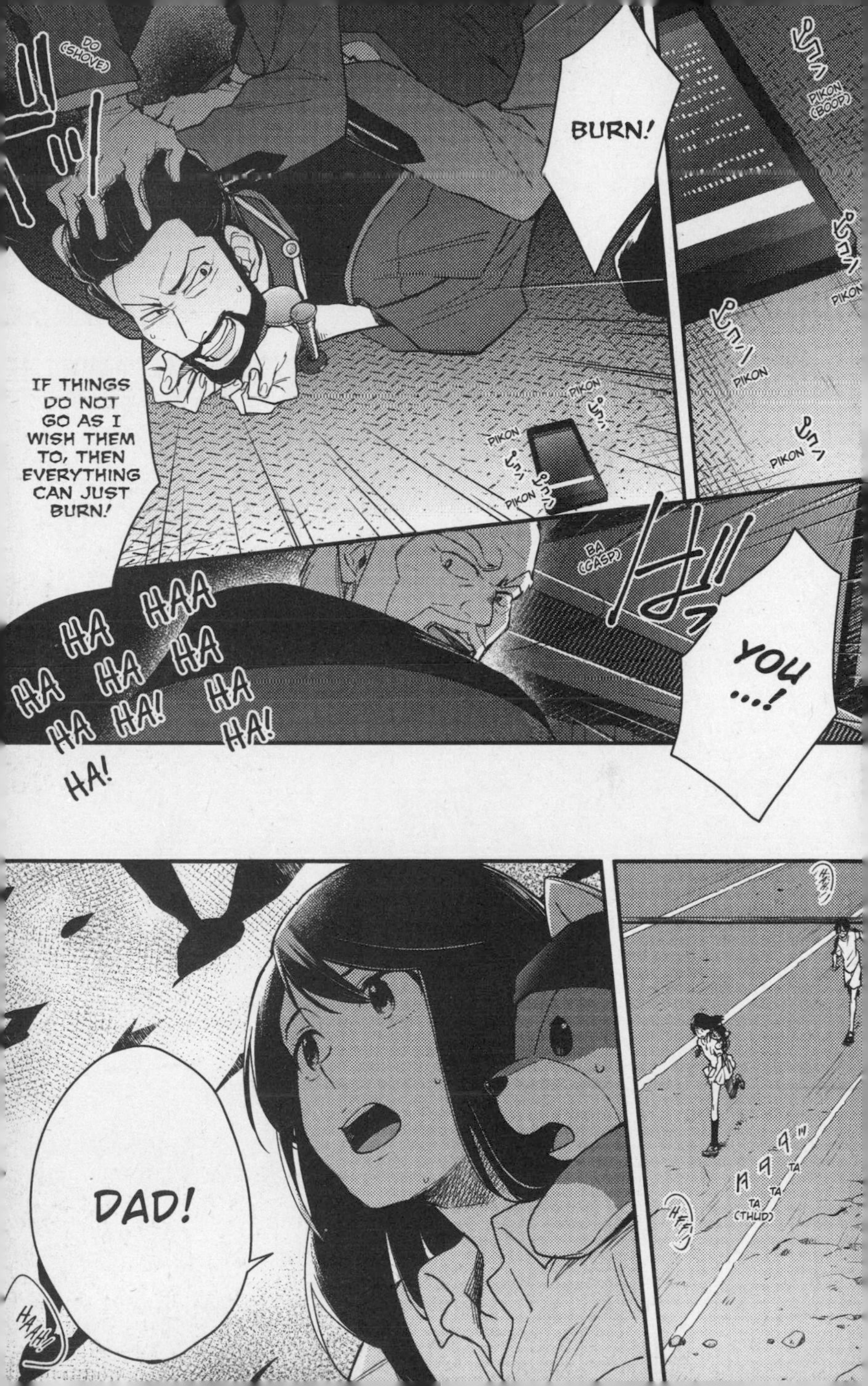
PIKON (BOOP)
BURN!
PIKON
PIKON
DO (SHOVE)
IF THINGS DO NOT GO AS I WISH THEM TO, THEN EVERYTHING CAN JUST BURN!
PIKON
PIKON
PIKON
PIKON
YOU ...!
BA (GASP)
HA HAA HA HA HA HA HA HA! HA HA! HA!
TA TA TA (THUD)
HFF
DAD!

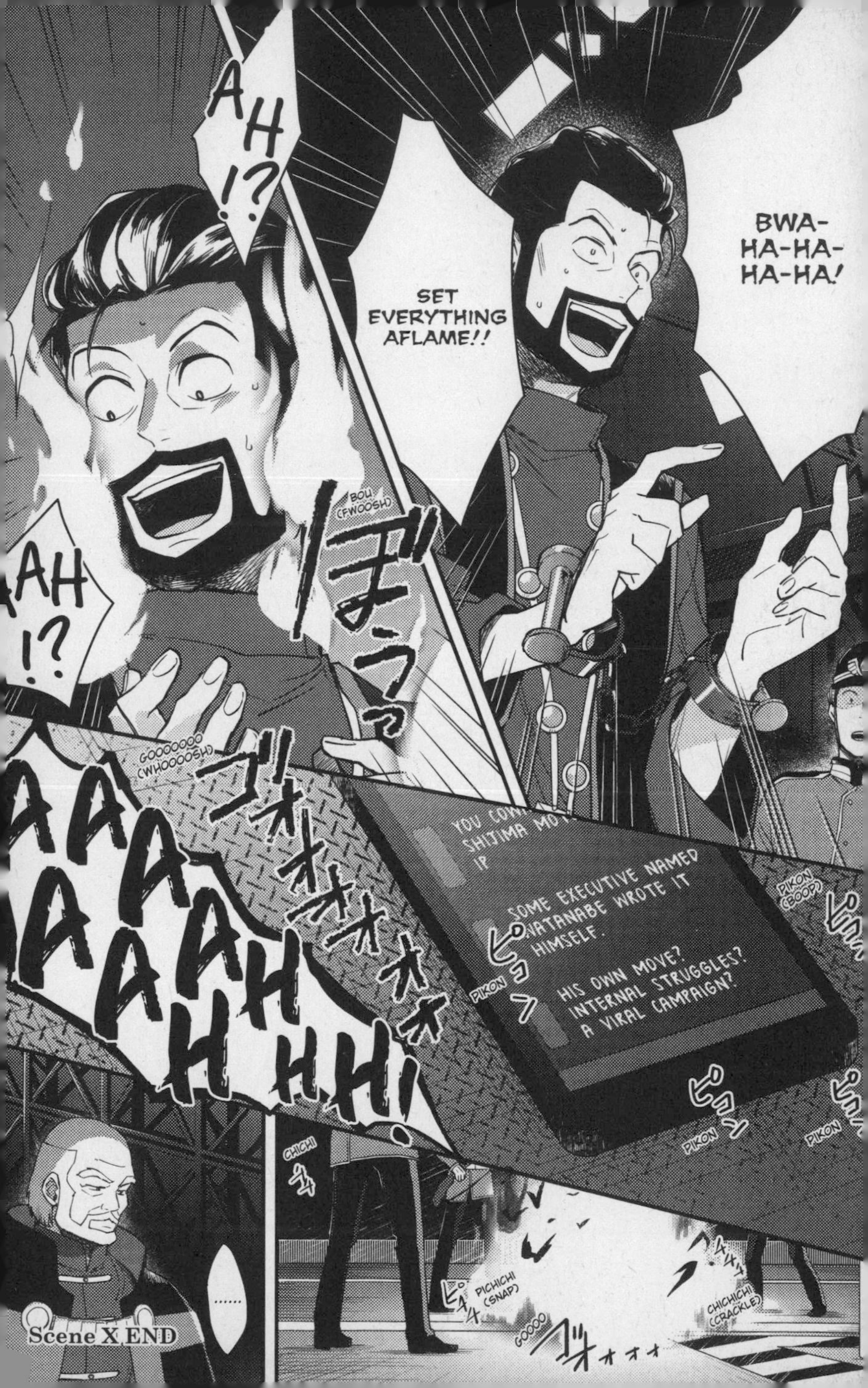
BWA-HA-HA-HA-HA!
SET EVERYTHING AFLAME!!
AH!?
AH!?
BOU (FWOOSH)
ぼっ
PIKON (BOOP)
PIKON
PIKON
PIKON
SOME EXECUTIVE NAMED WATANABE WROTE IT HIMSELF.
HIS OWN MOVE? INTERNAL STRUGGLES? A VIRAL CAMPAIGN?
GOOOOOOO (WHOOOOSH)
AAAAAAAAAAAHHH!
CHICHICHI (CRACKLE)
GOOOO
PICHICHI (SNAP)
CHICHI
......
Scene X END

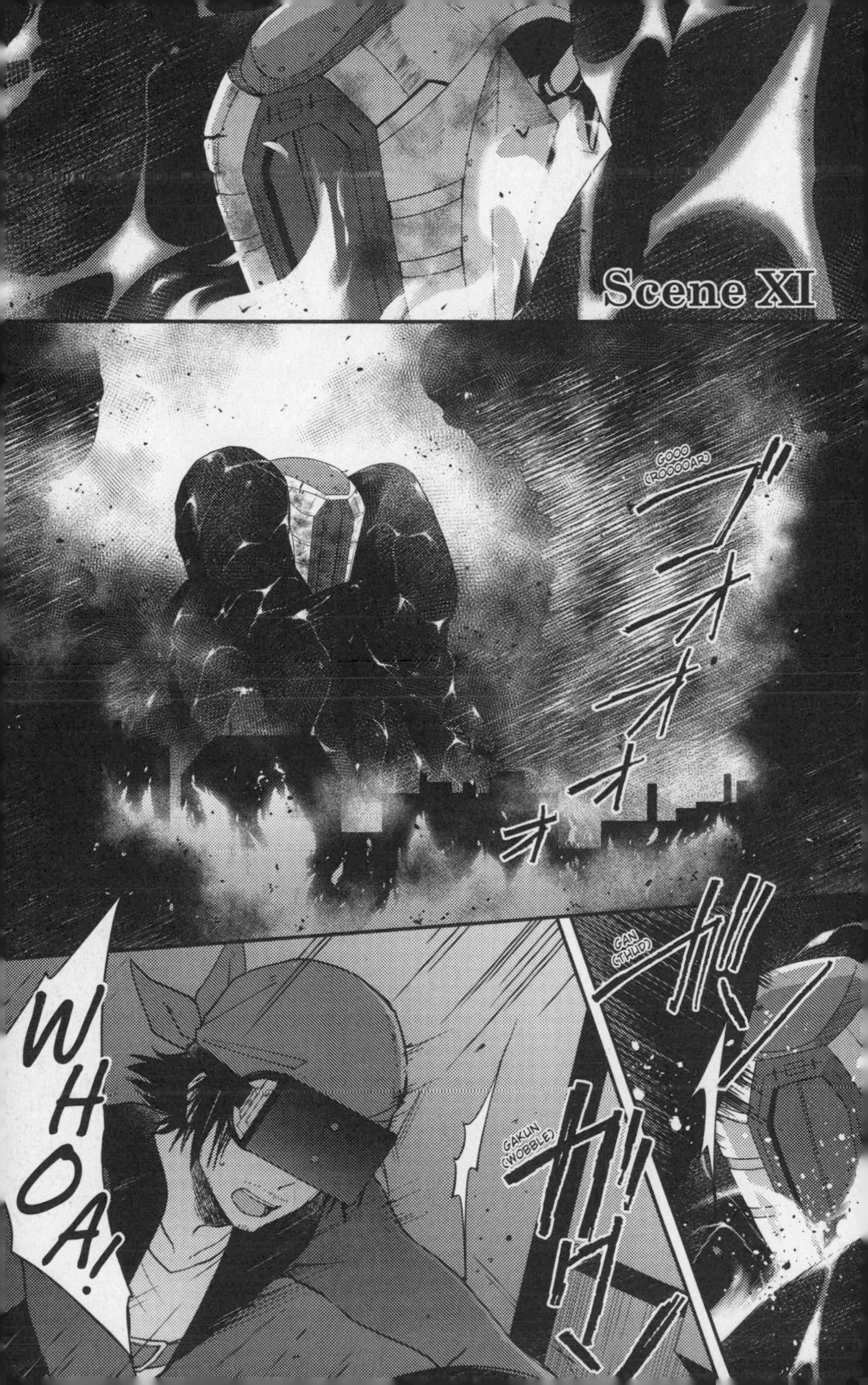
Scene XI
GOOO (ROOOOAR)
ゴオオオオオ
GAN (THUD)
ガン
GAKUN (WOBBLE)
ガクン
WHOA!

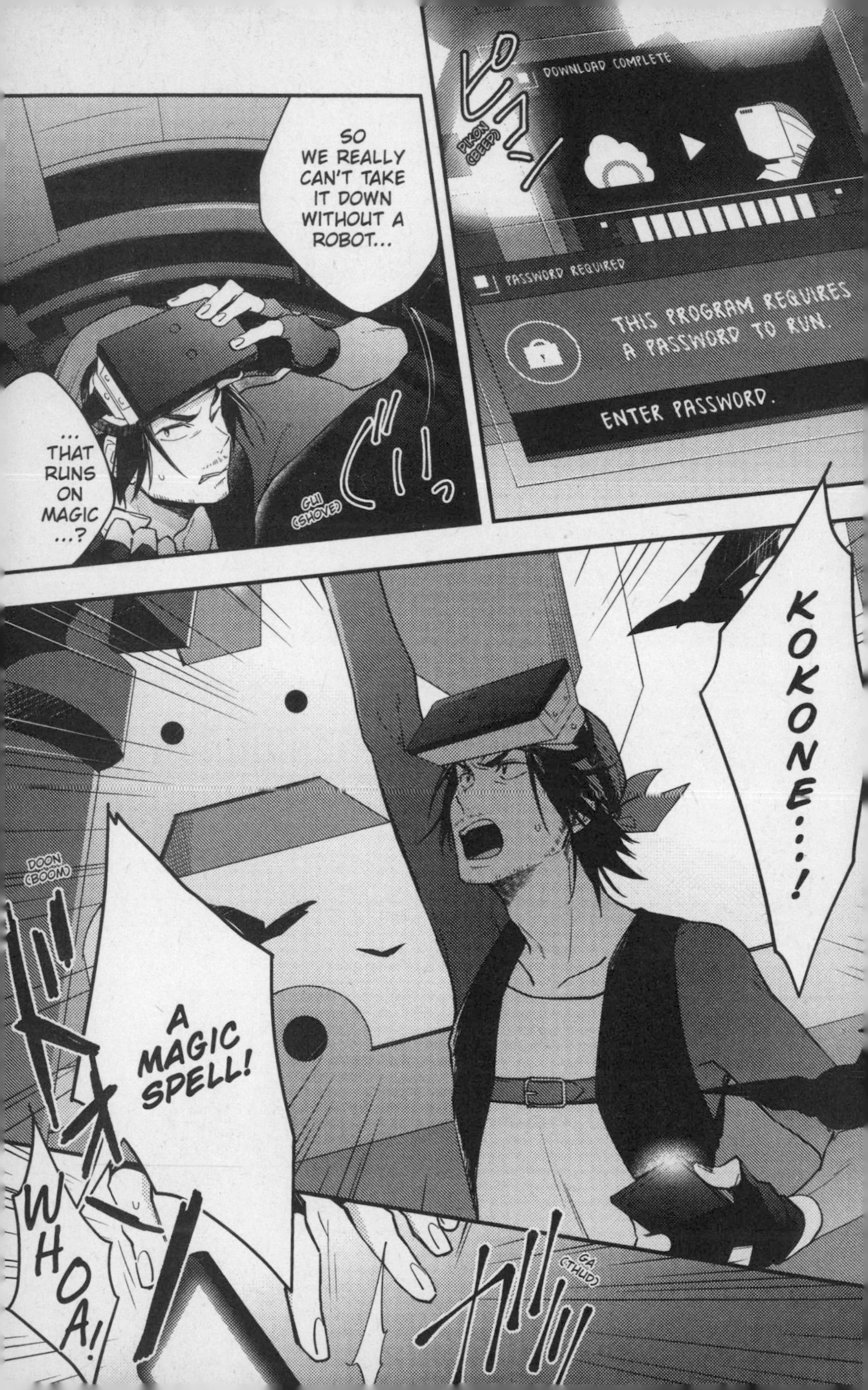
PIKON (BEEP)
DOWNLOAD COMPLETE
PASSWORD REQUIRED
THIS PROGRAM REQUIRES A PASSWORD TO RUN.
ENTER PASSWORD.
SO WE REALLY CAN'T TAKE IT DOWN WITHOUT A ROBOT...
...THAT RUNS ON MAGIC...?
GUI (SHOVE)
KOKONE...!
A MAGIC SPELL!
DOON (BOOM)
WHOA!
GA (THUD)

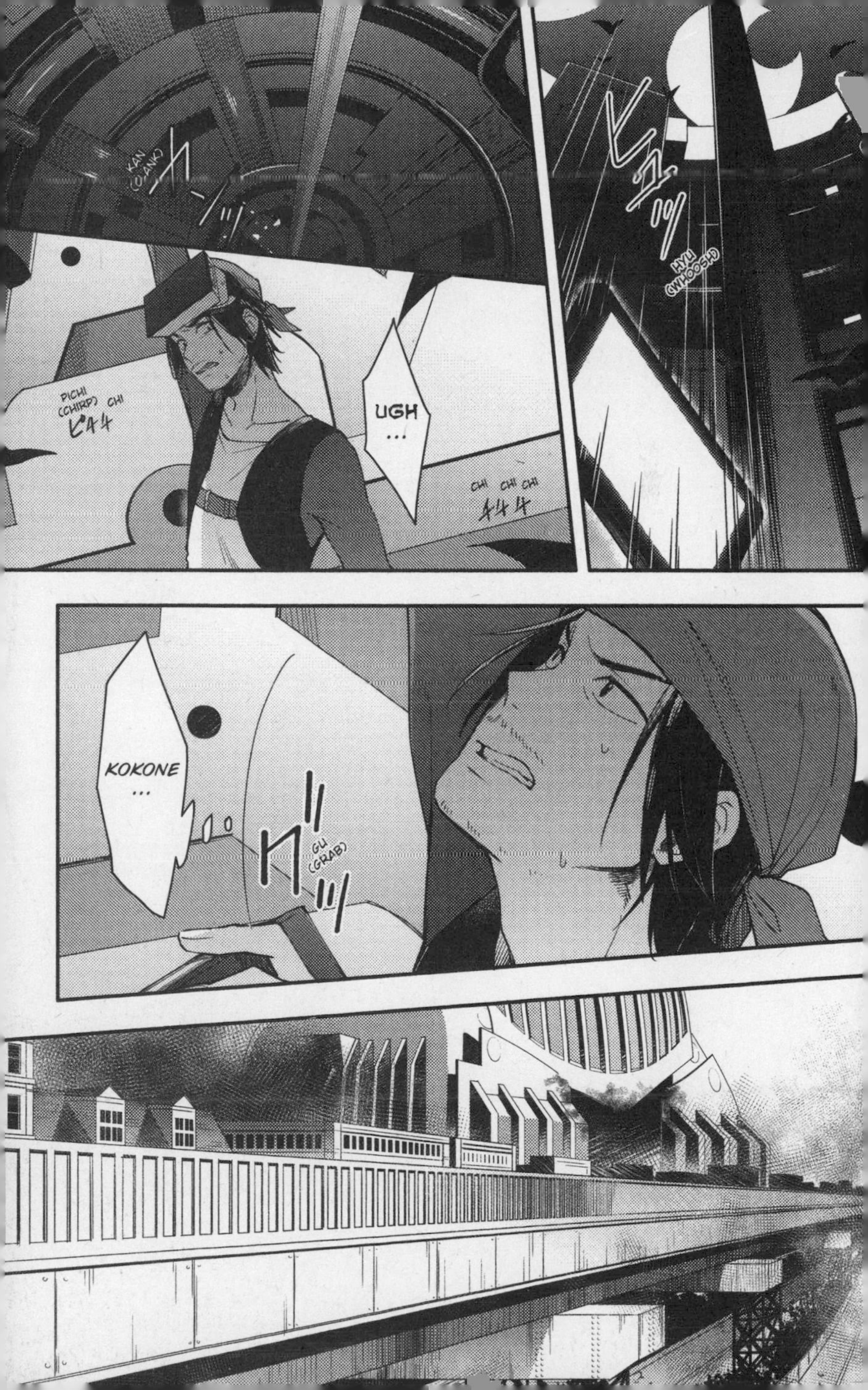
HYU (WHOOSH)
KAN (CLANK)
UGH ...
PICHI (CHIRP) CHI
CHI CHI CHI
KOKONE ...
GU (GRAB)

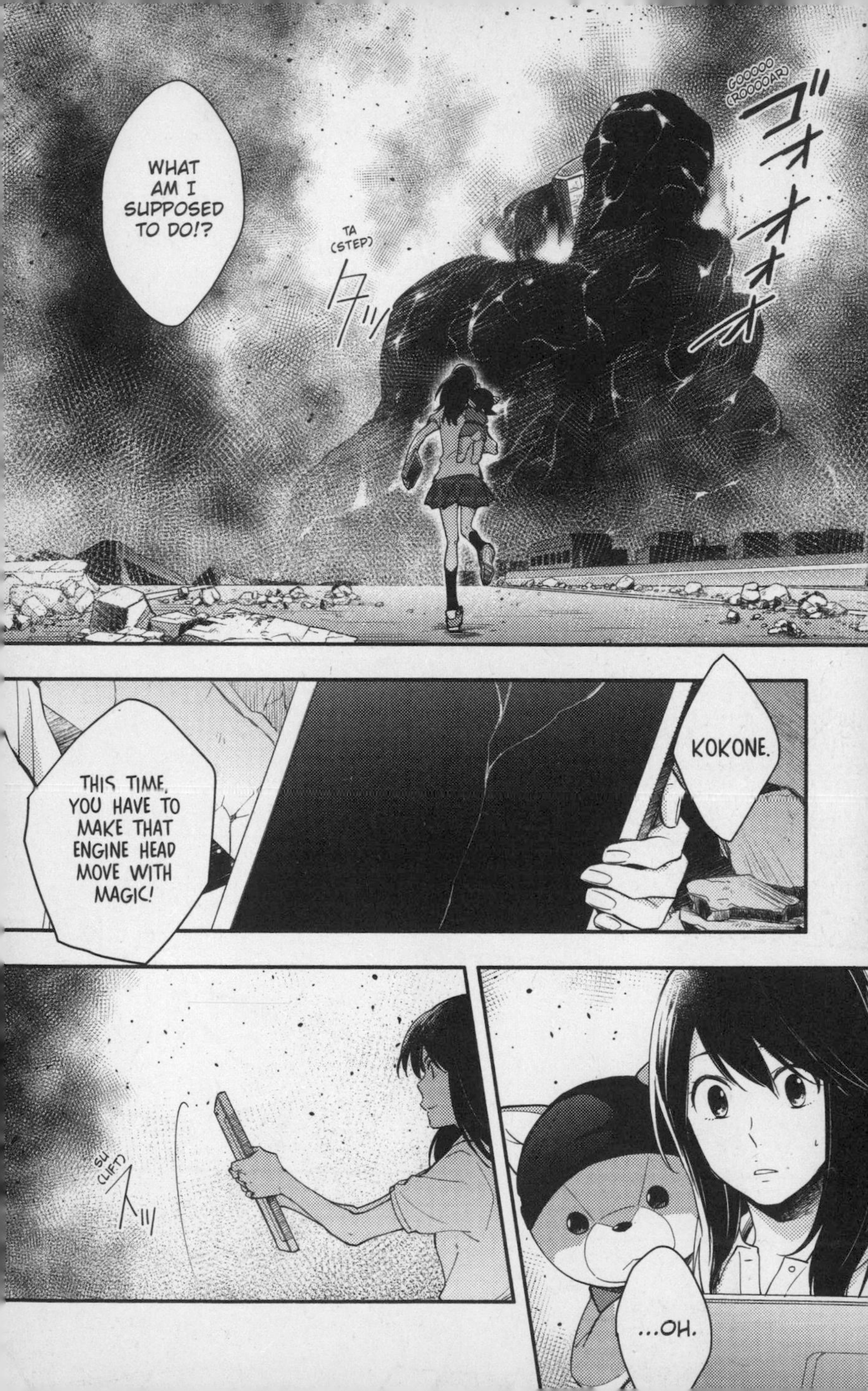
GOOOOO (ROOOOAR)
ゴォォォォ
TA (STEP)
タッ
WHAT AM I SUPPOSED TO DO!?
KOKONE.
THIS TIME, YOU HAVE TO MAKE THAT ENGINE HEAD MOVE WITH MAGIC!
...OH.
SU (LIFT)
スッ

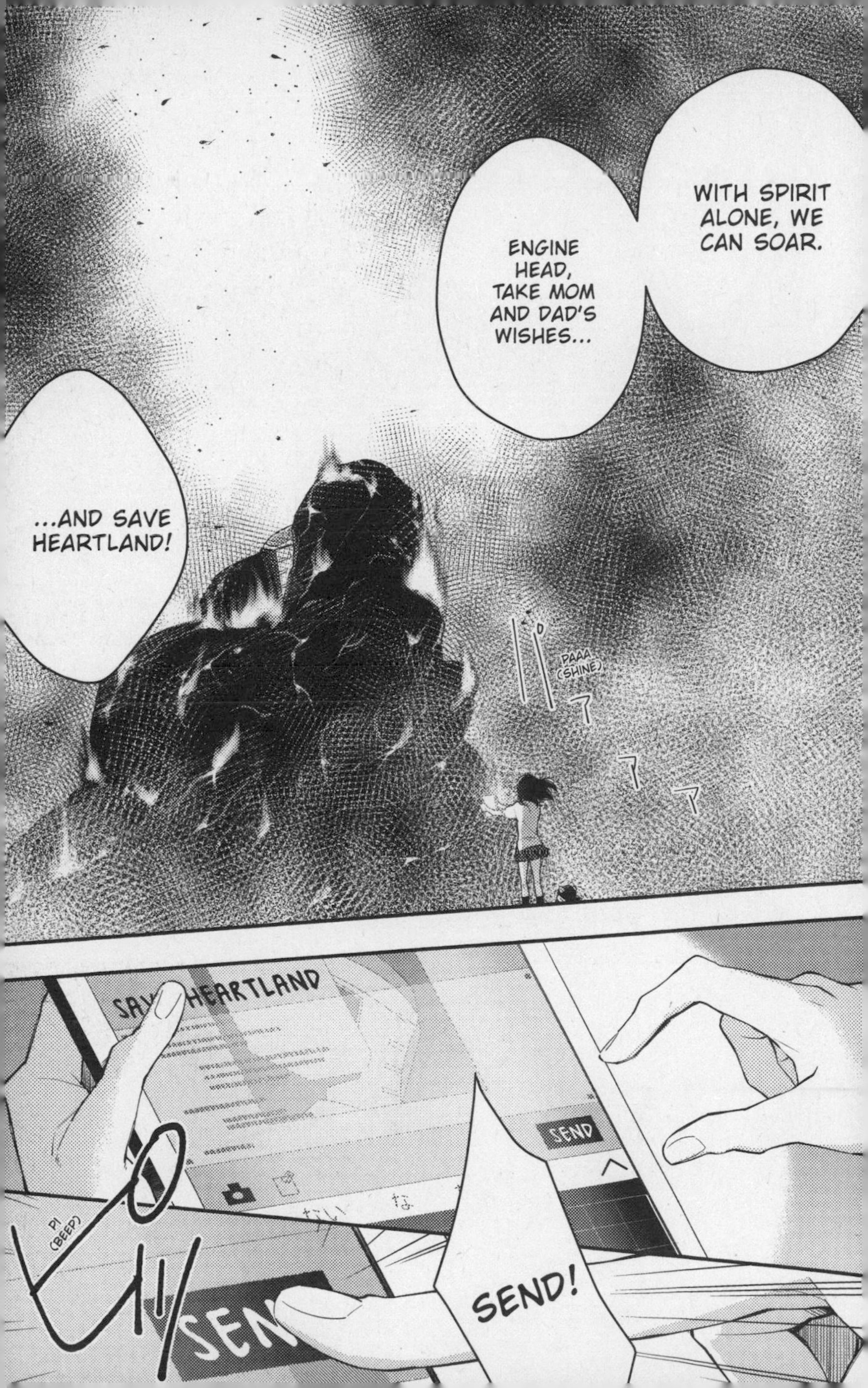
WITH SPIRIT ALONE, WE CAN SOAR.
ENGINE HEAD, TAKE MOM AND DAD'S WISHES...
...AND SAVE HEARTLAND!
PAAA (SHINE)
SAVE HEARTLAND
SEND
SEND!
PI (BEEP)

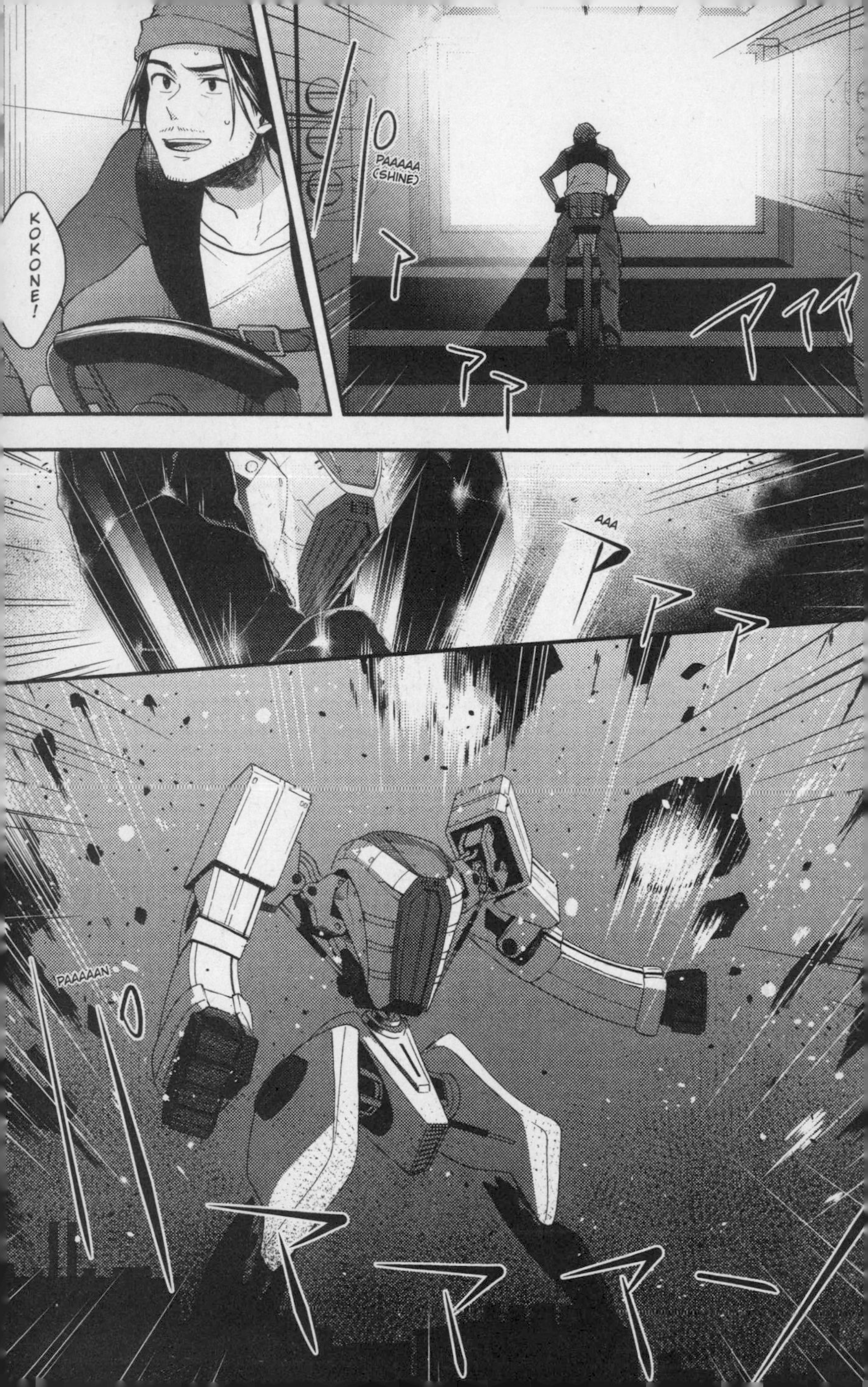
PAAAAA (SHINE)
KOKONE!
AAA
PAAAAAN

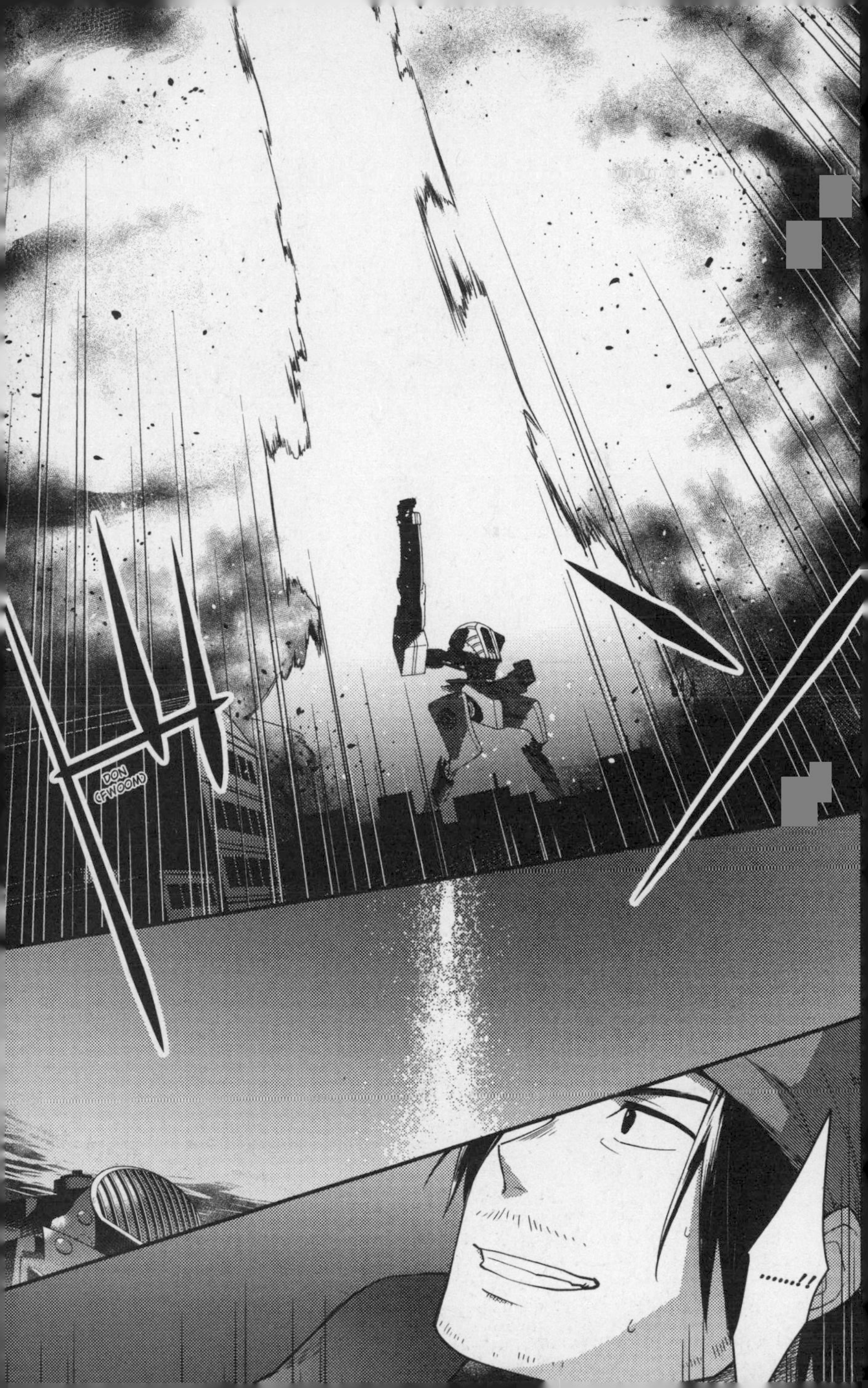
DON
(FWOOM)
......!!

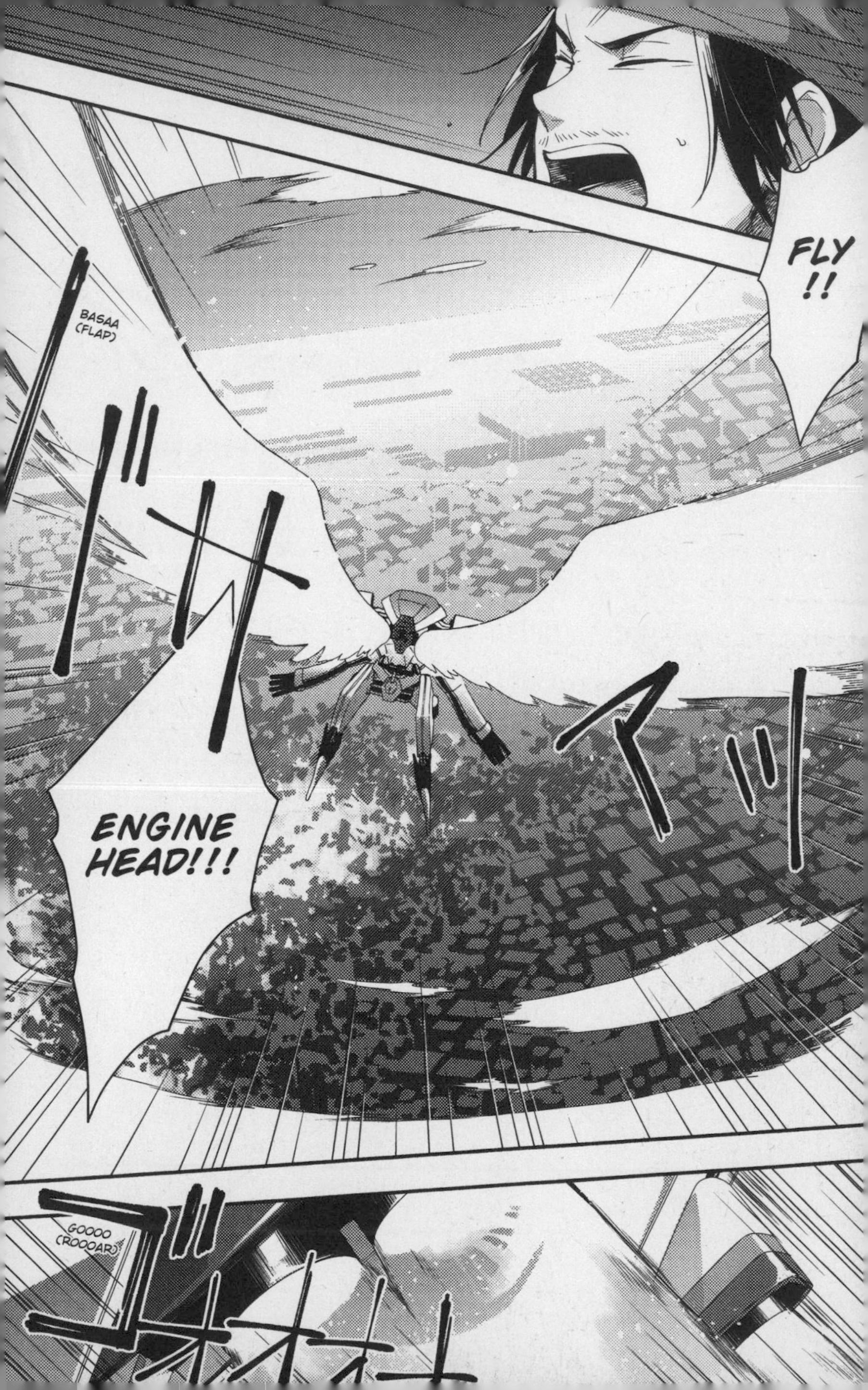
FLY !!
BASAA (FLAP)
ENGINE HEAD!!!
GOOOO (ROOOAR)

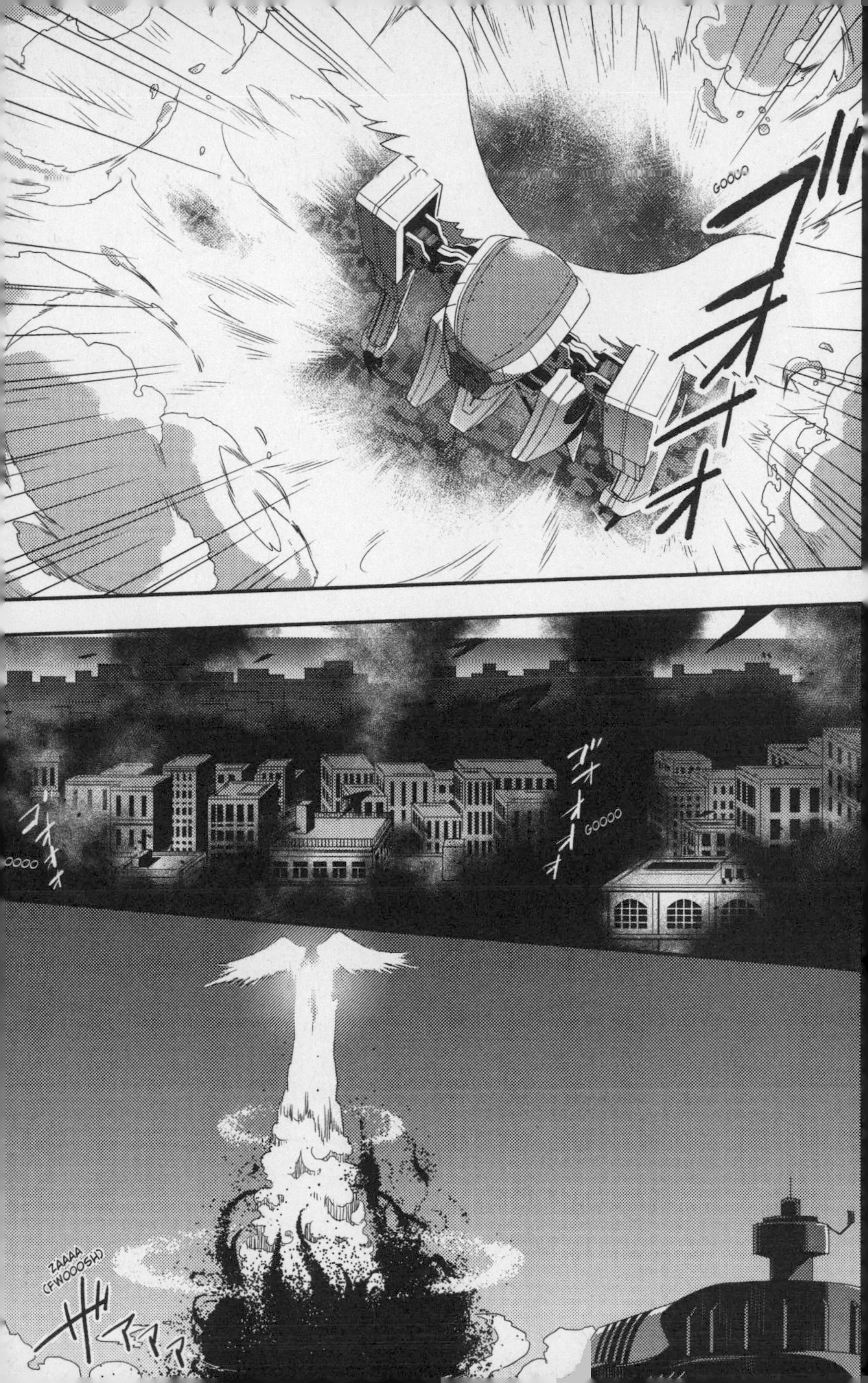

ゴォオオオ
GOO
ゴォオオオ
GOOOO
ゴォオオオ
OOOO
ザァァァ
ZAAAA (FWOOOSH)

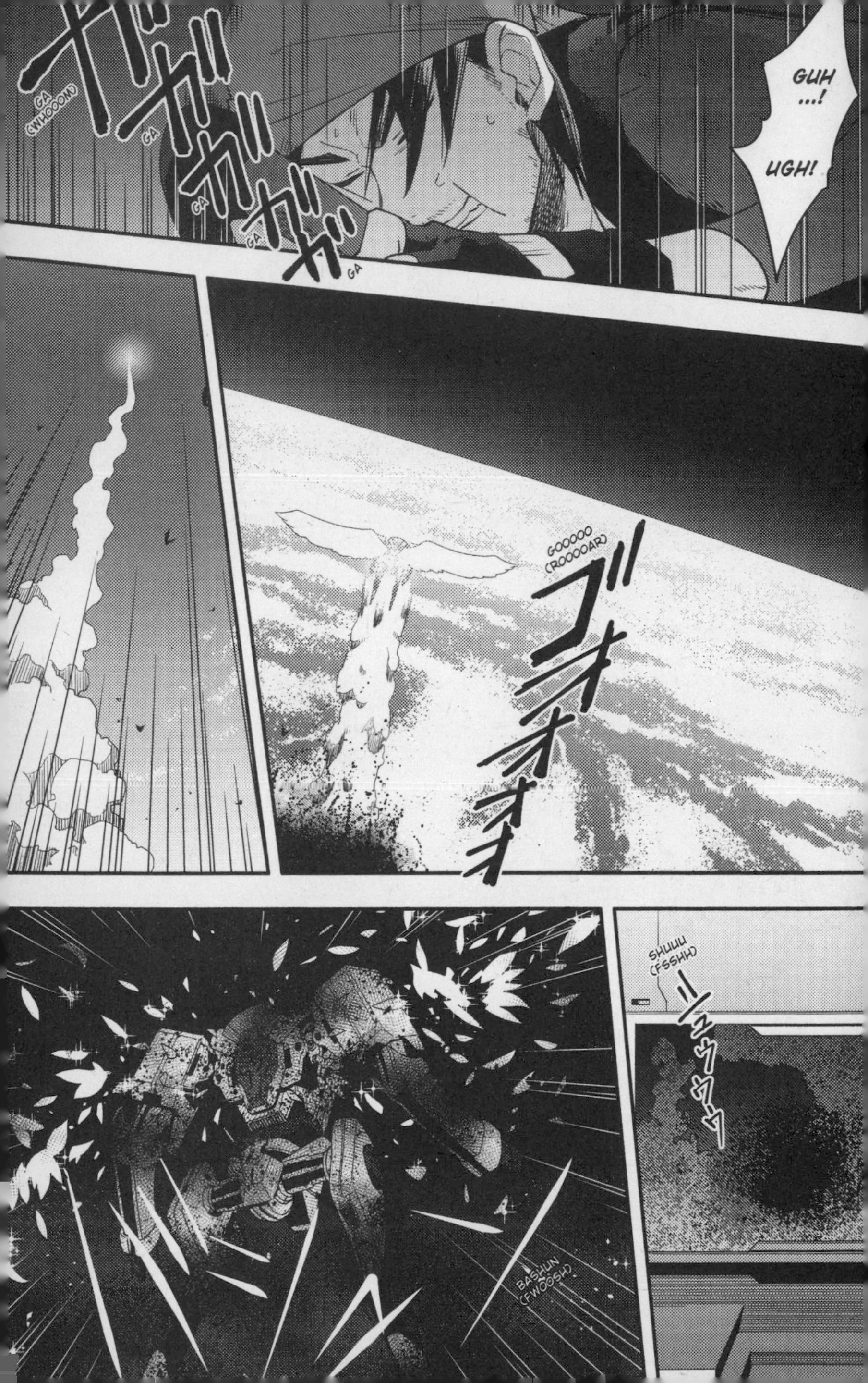
GUH ...!
UGH!
GA (WHOOOM)
GA
GA
GA
GA
GOOOOO (ROOOOAR)
SHUUU (FSSHH)
BASHUN (FWOOSH)

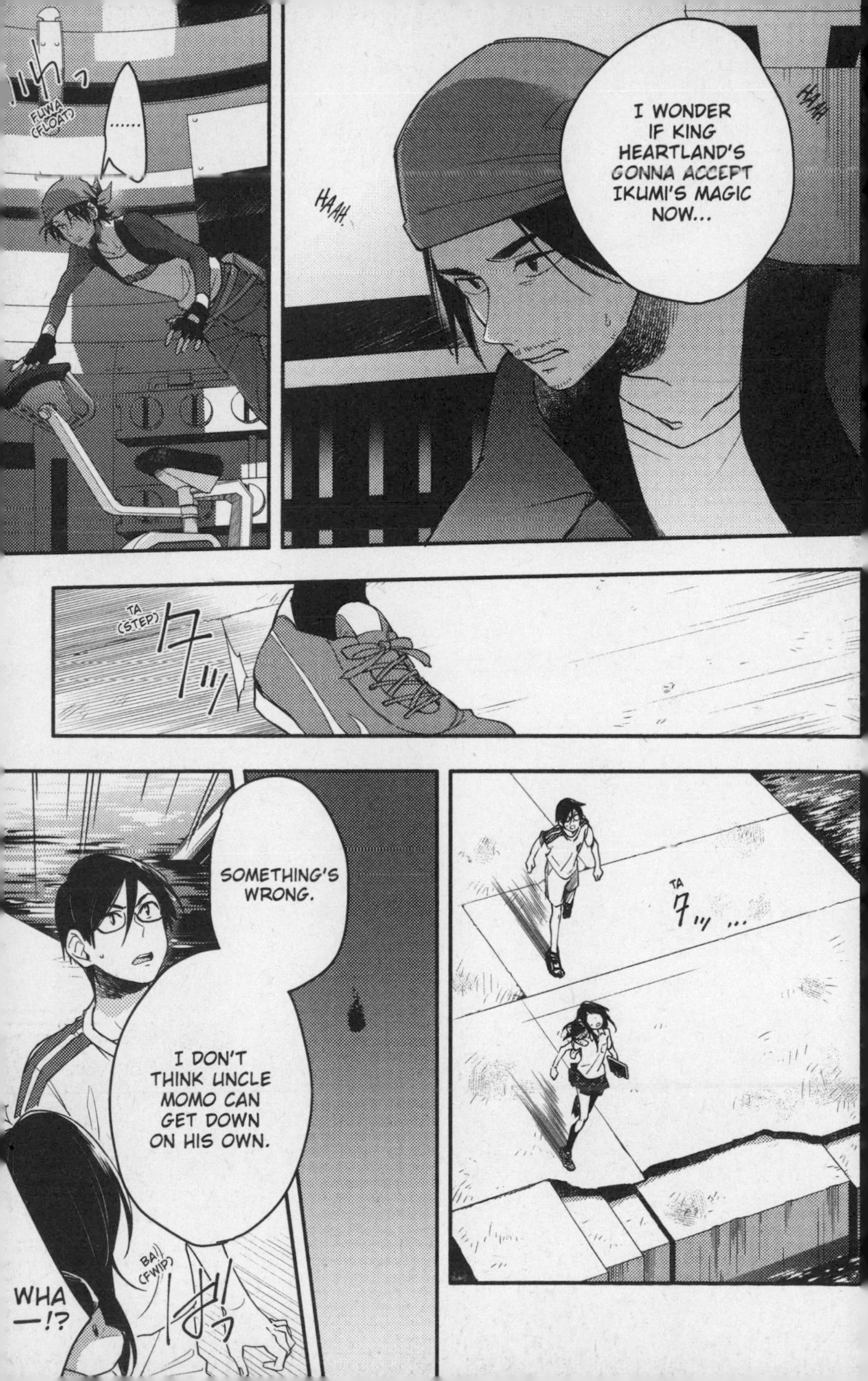
HAAH
I WONDER IF KING HEARTLAND'S GONNA ACCEPT IKUMI'S MAGIC NOW...
HAAH
......
FUWA (FLOAT)
TA (STEP)
TA
...
SOMETHING'S WRONG.
I DON'T THINK UNCLE MOMO CAN GET DOWN ON HIS OWN.
BA! (FWIP)
WHA—!?

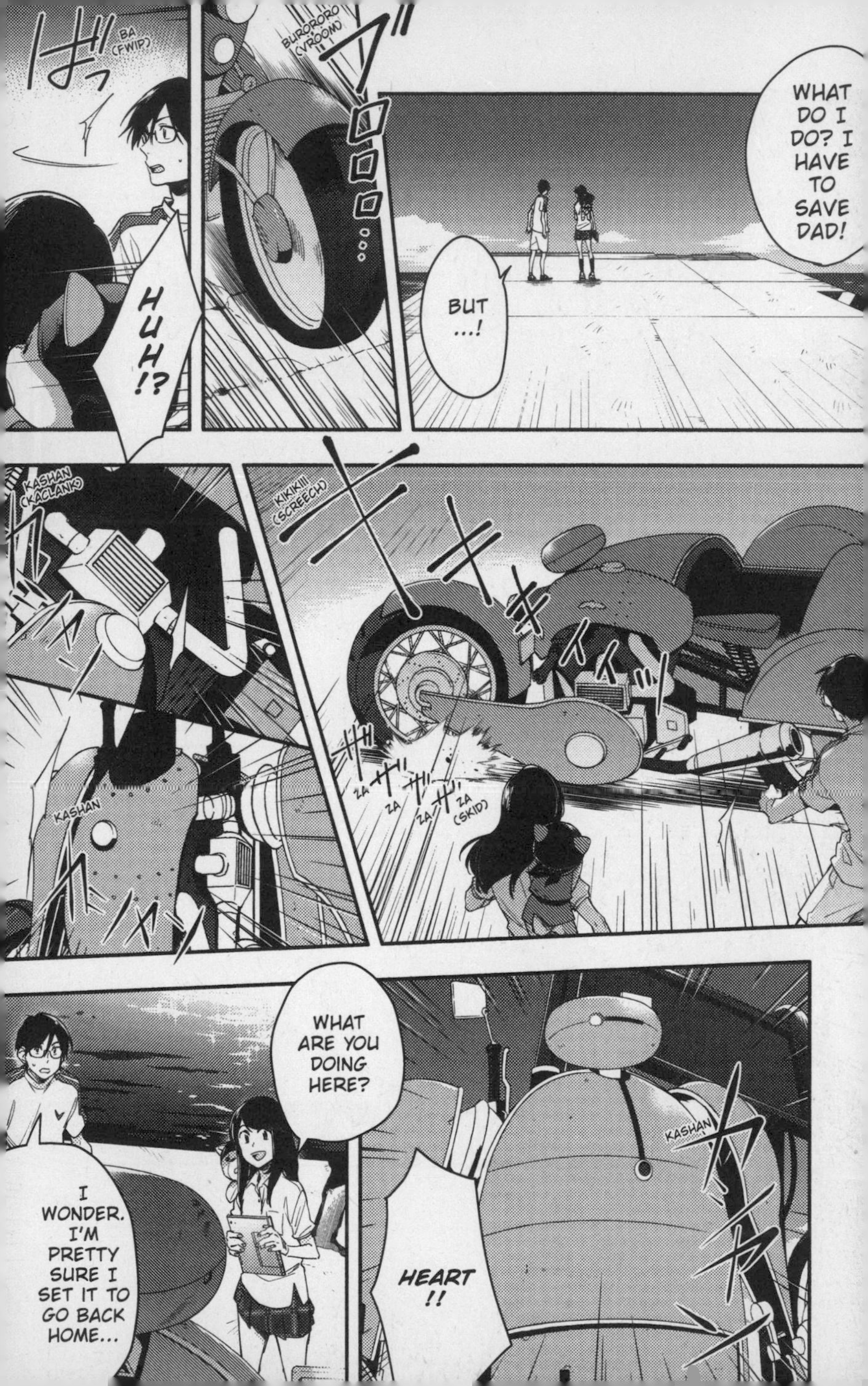
WHAT DO I DO? I HAVE TO SAVE DAD!
BUT ...!
BURORORO (VROOM)
BA (FWIP)
HUH!?
KIKIKII (SCREECH)
ZA ZA ZA ZA (SKID)
KASHAN (KACLANK)
KASHAN
KASHAN
HEART !!
WHAT ARE YOU DOING HERE?
I WONDER. I'M PRETTY SURE I SET IT TO GO BACK HOME...

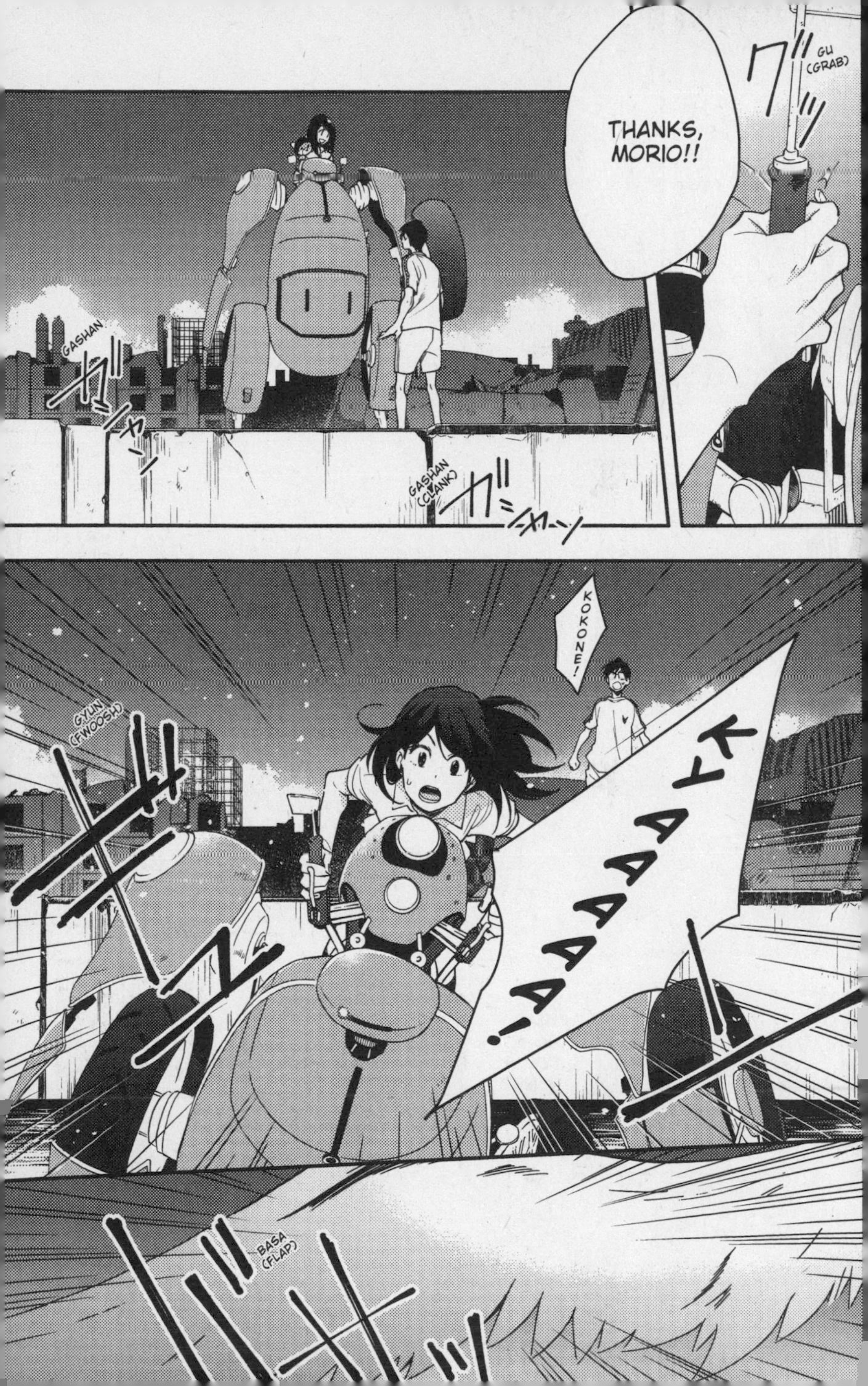
GU (GRAB)
THANKS, MORIO!!
GASHAN
GASHAN (CLANK)
KOKONE!
KYAAAAAA!
GYUN (FWOOSH)
BASA (FLAP)

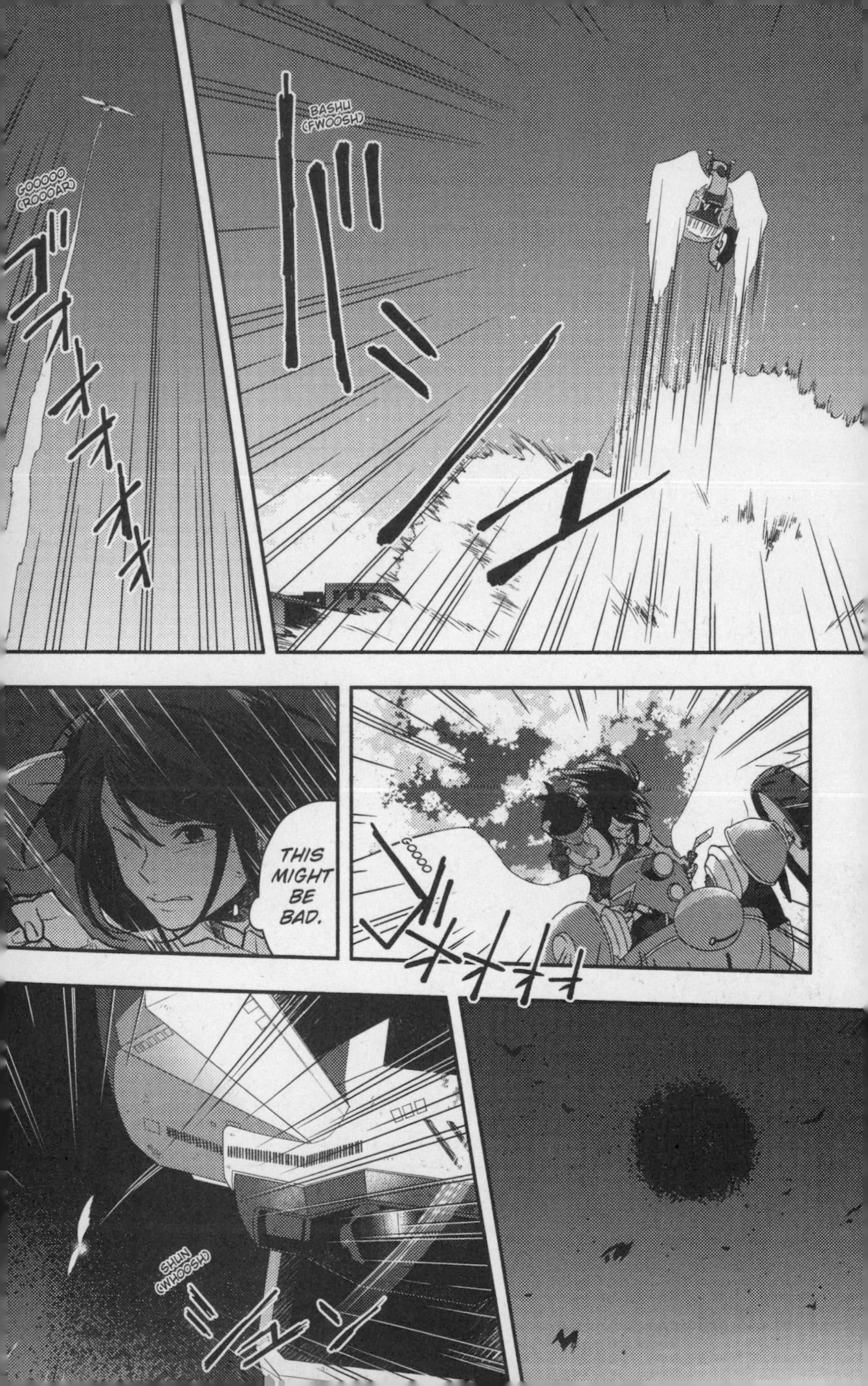
BASHU (FWOOSH)
GOOOOO (ROOOAR)
GOOOO
THIS MIGHT BE BAD.
SHUN (WHOOSH)

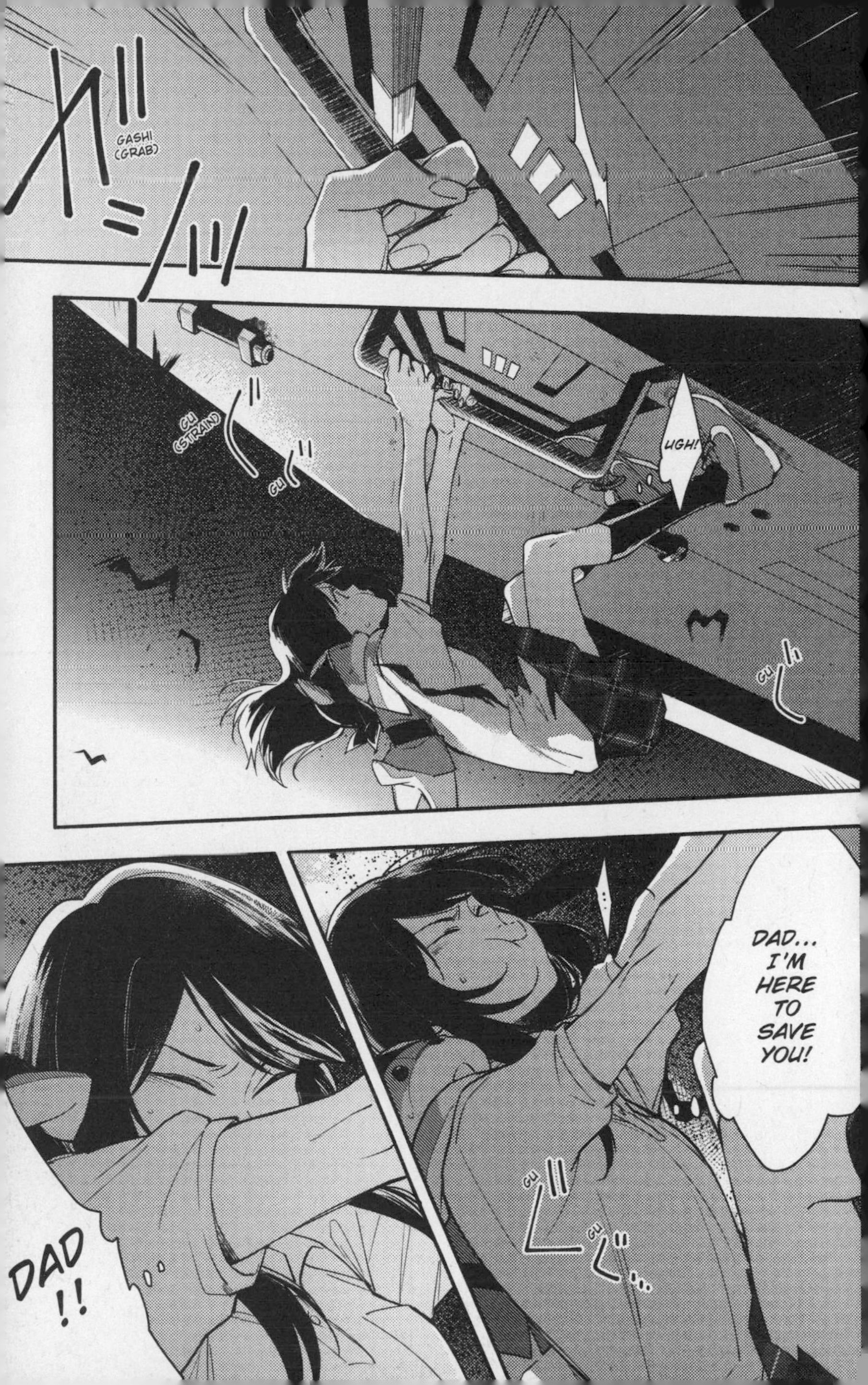
GASHI (GRAB)
GU (STRAIN)
GU
UGH!
GU
DAD... I'M HERE TO SAVE YOU!
GU
GU...
DAD!!

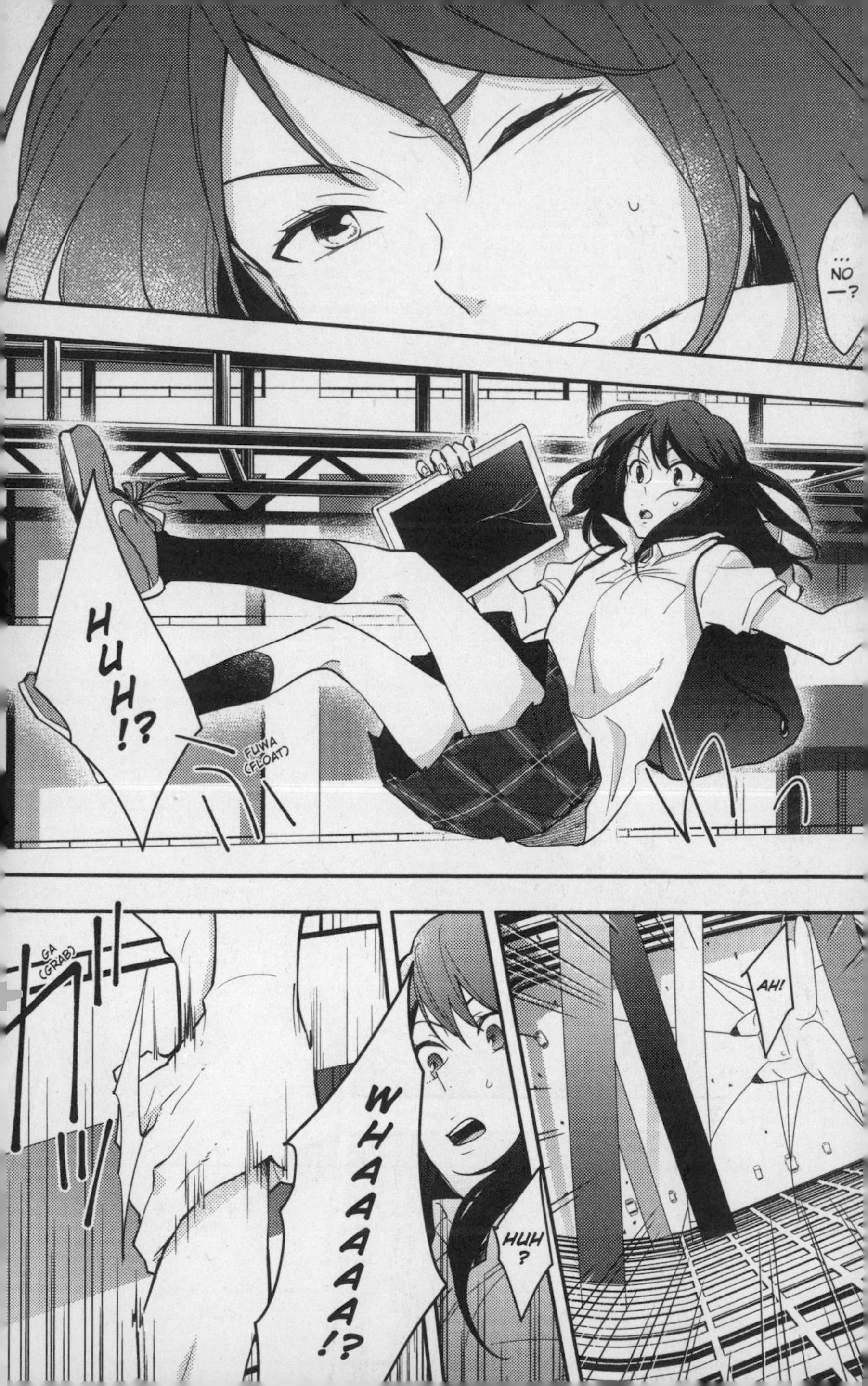
...NO—?
HUH!?
FUWA (FLOAT)
AH!
WHAAAAAAA!?
HUH?
GA (GRAB)

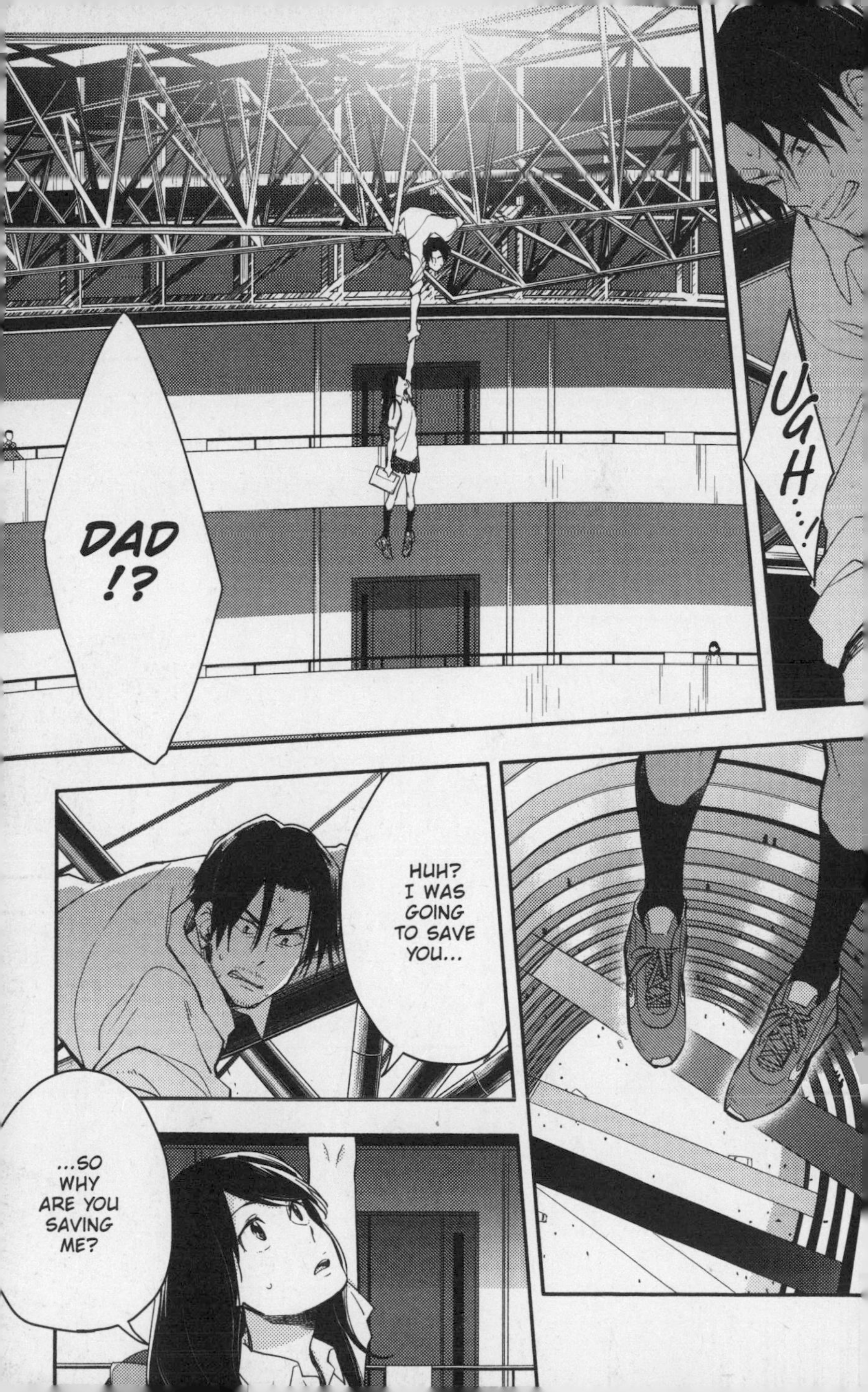
UGH...!
DAD !?
HUH? I WAS GOING TO SAVE YOU...
...SO WHY ARE YOU SAVING ME?

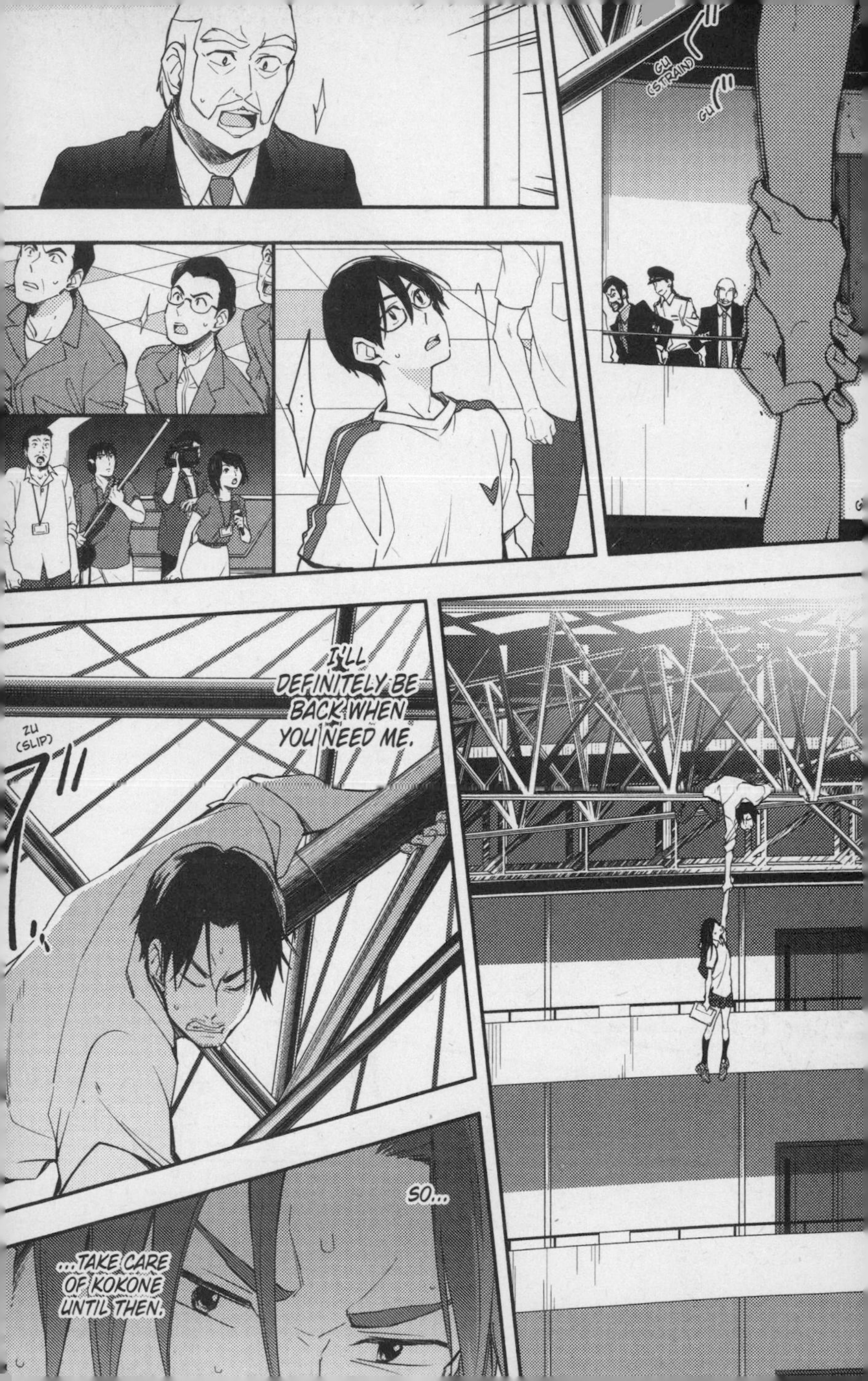
GU (STRAIN)
GU
I'LL DEFINITELY BE BACK WHEN YOU NEED ME.
ZU (SLIP)
SO...
...TAKE CARE OF KOKONE UNTIL THEN.

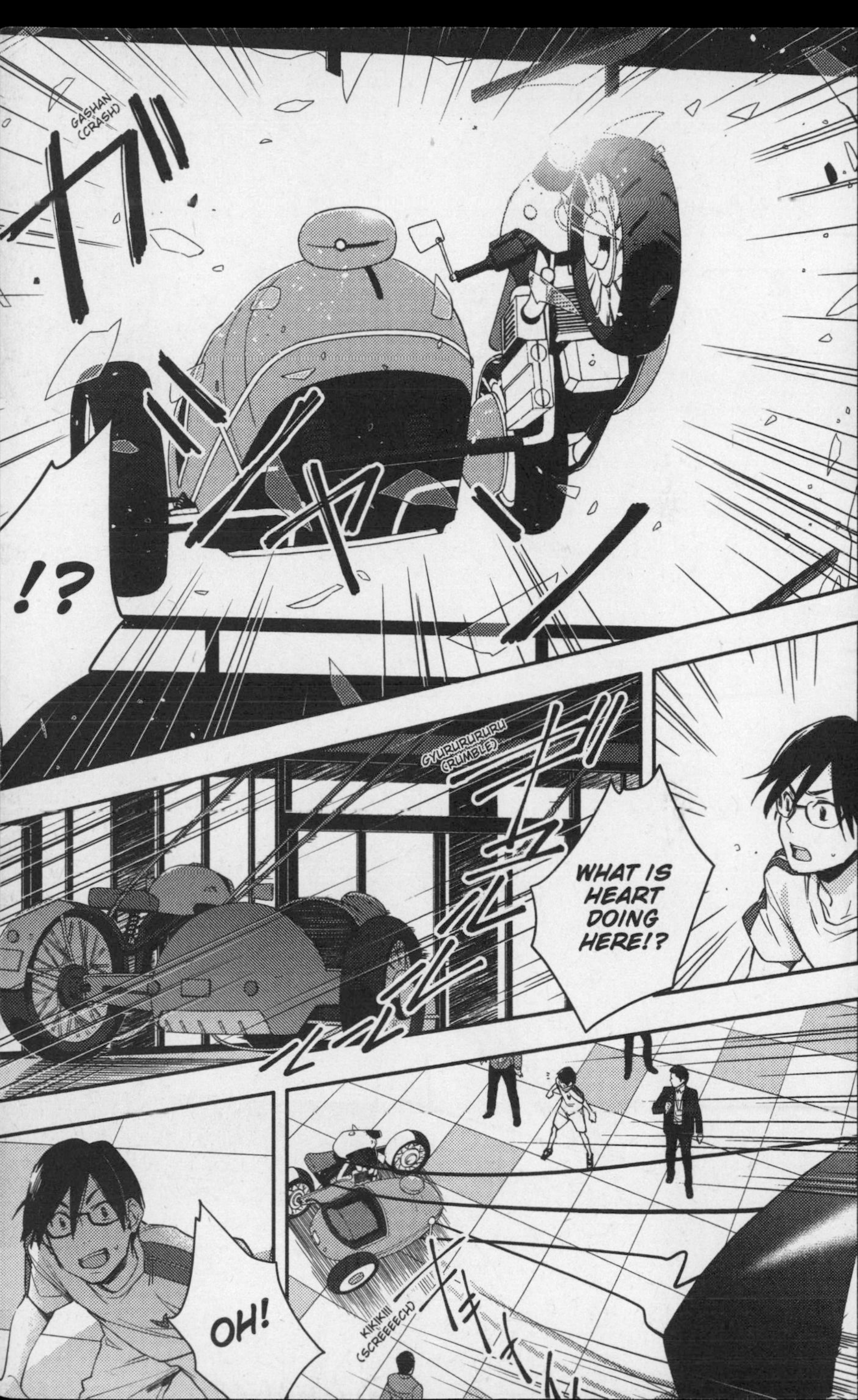
GASHAN (CRASH)
!?
GYURURURURU (RUMBLE)
WHAT IS HEART DOING HERE!?
KIKIKIII (SCREEEECH)
OH!

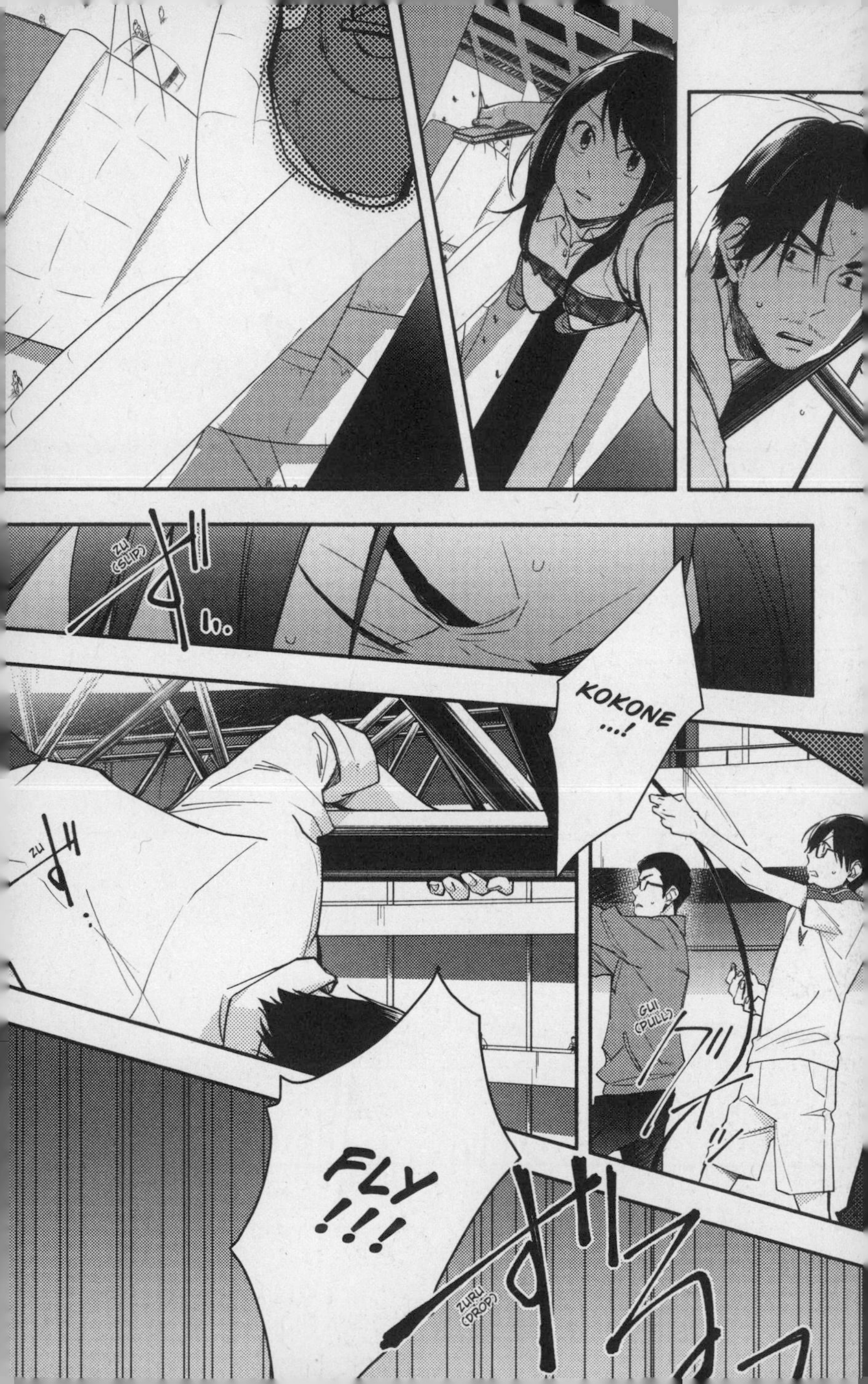
ZU (SLIP)
KOKONE ...!
GUI (PULL)
ZU
FLY!!!
ZURU (DROP)

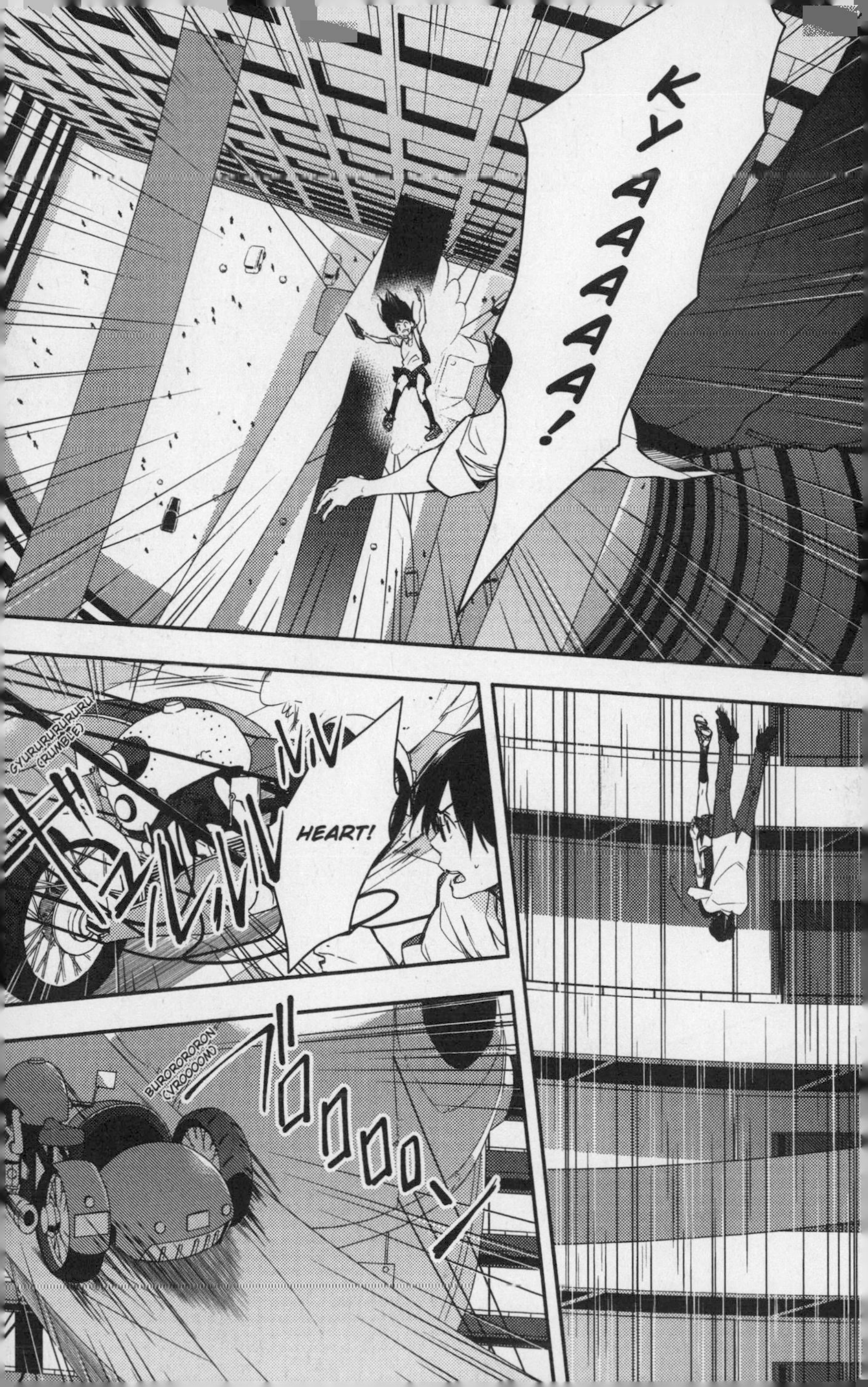
KYAAAAAAA!
HEART!
GYURURURURU (RUMBLE)
BURORORORON (VROOOOOM)

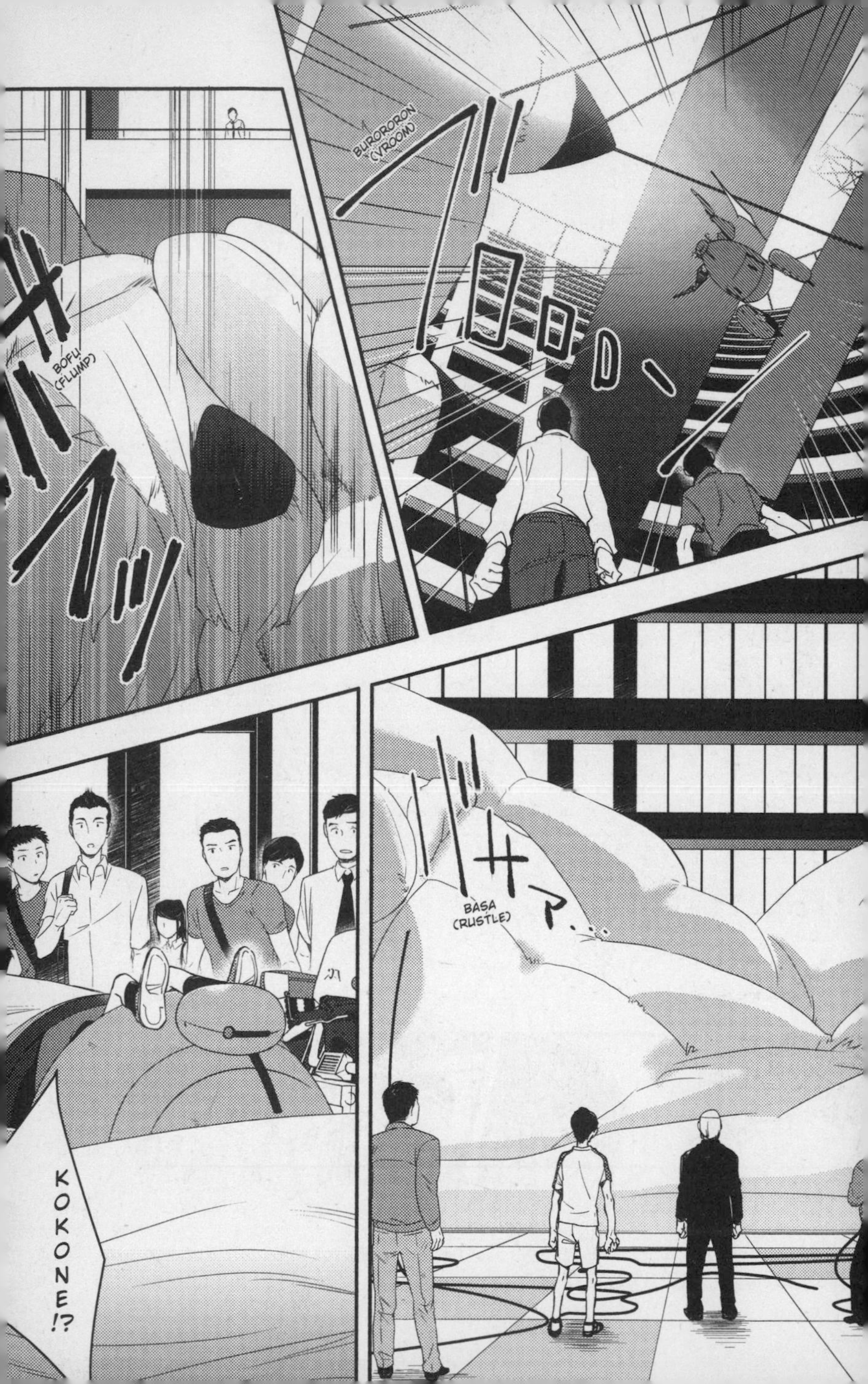
BUROROON (VROOM)
BOFU (FLUMP)
BASA (RUSTLE)
KOKONE!?

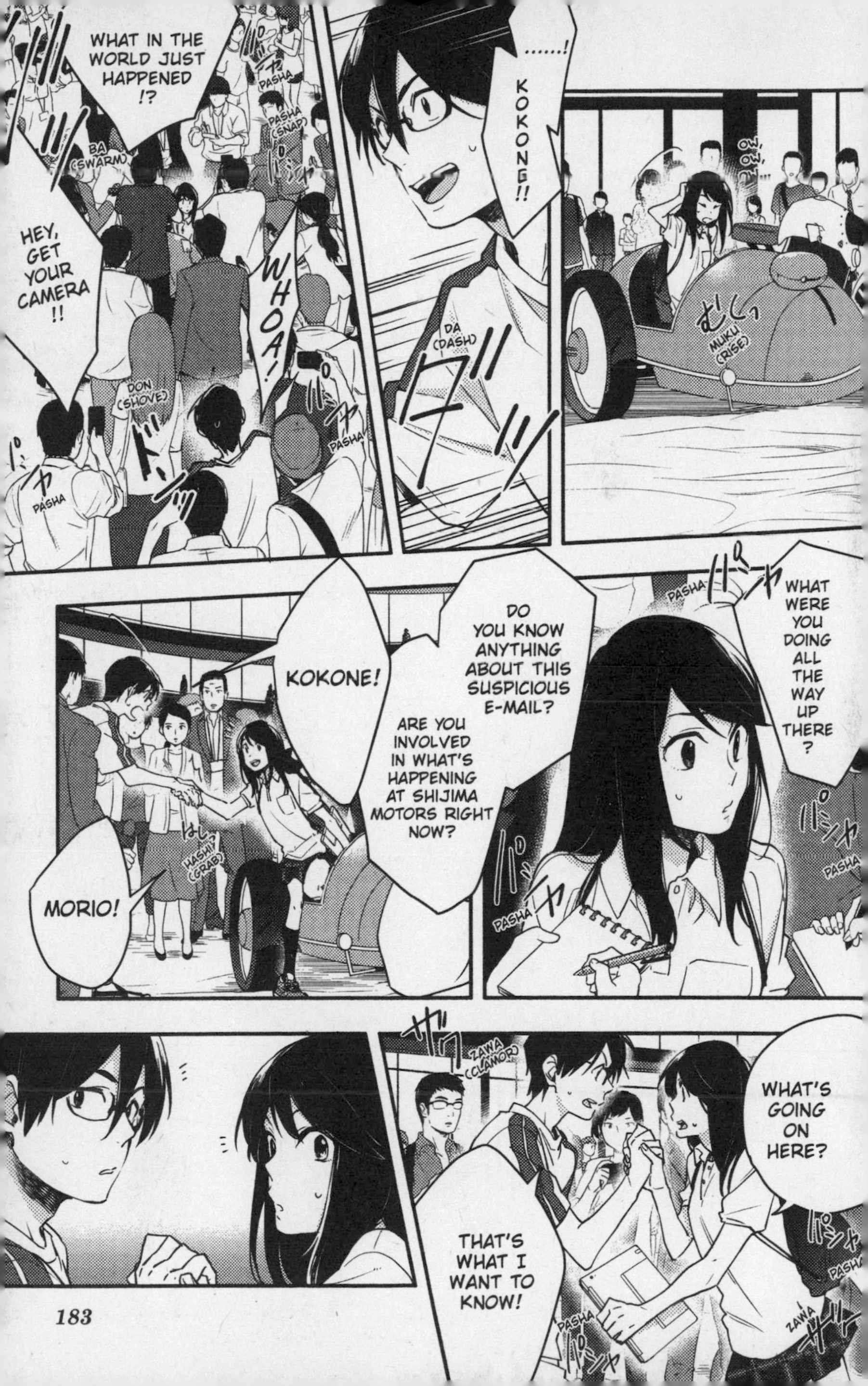
OW, OW, OW...
むくっ
MUKU (RISE)
......!
KOKONG!!
DA (DASH)
WHAT IN THE WORLD JUST HAPPENED!?
PASHA
PASHA (SNAP)
BA (SWARM)
HEY, GET YOUR CAMERA!!
WHOA!
DON (SHOVE)
PASHA
PASHA
PASHA
WHAT WERE YOU DOING ALL THE WAY UP THERE?
PASHA
DO YOU KNOW ANYTHING ABOUT THIS SUSPICIOUS E-MAIL?
ARE YOU INVOLVED IN WHAT'S HAPPENING AT SHIJIMA MOTORS RIGHT NOW?
PASHA
KOKONE!
HASHI (GRAB)
MORIO!
WHAT'S GOING ON HERE?
PASHA
ZAWA (CLAMOR)
THAT'S WHAT I WANT TO KNOW!
PASHA
ZAWA

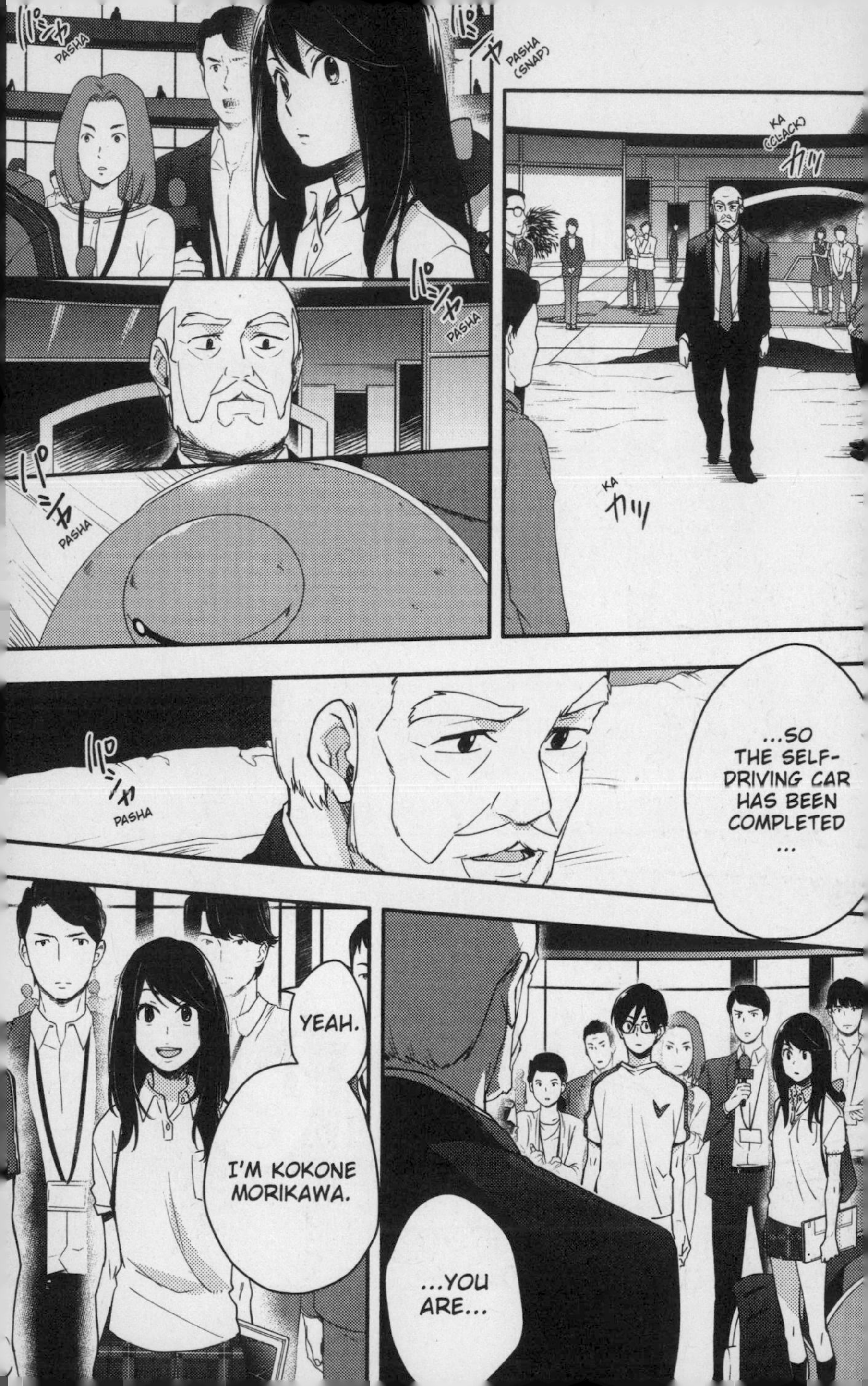

KA (CLACK)
KA
PASHA (SNAP)
PASHA
PASHA
PASHA
...SO THE SELF-DRIVING CAR HAS BEEN COMPLETED ...
PASHA
...YOU ARE...
YEAH.
I'M KOKONE MORIKAWA.

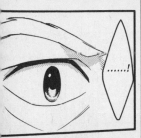

.......!

IT'S WRITTEN WITH THE CHARACTERS FOR "HEART" AND "WING"...

...AND PRONOUNCED KOKONE!

I SEE.

OH.

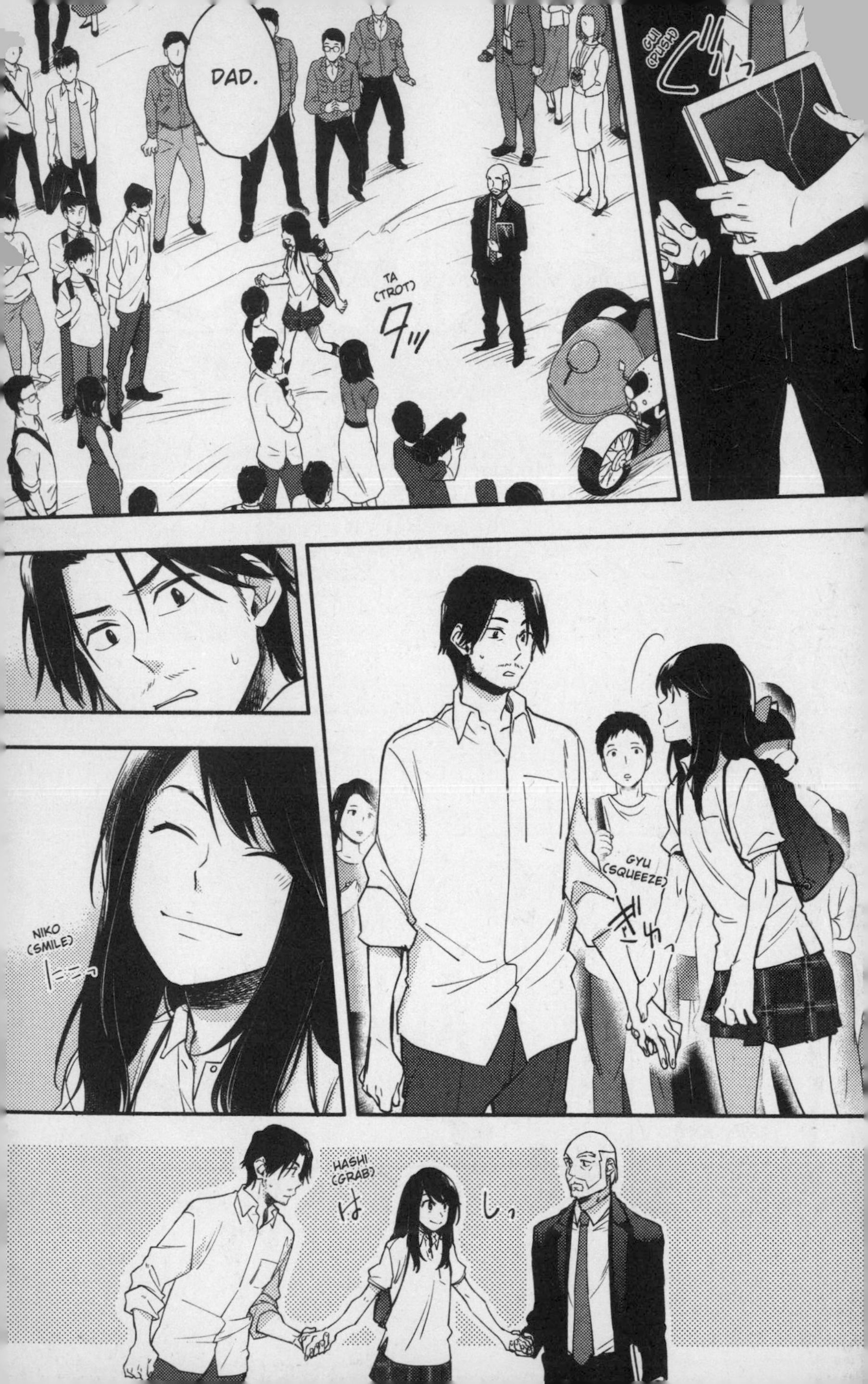
GUI (PUSH)
DAD.
TA (TROT)
GYU (SQUEEZE)
NIKO (SMILE)
HASHI (GRAB)

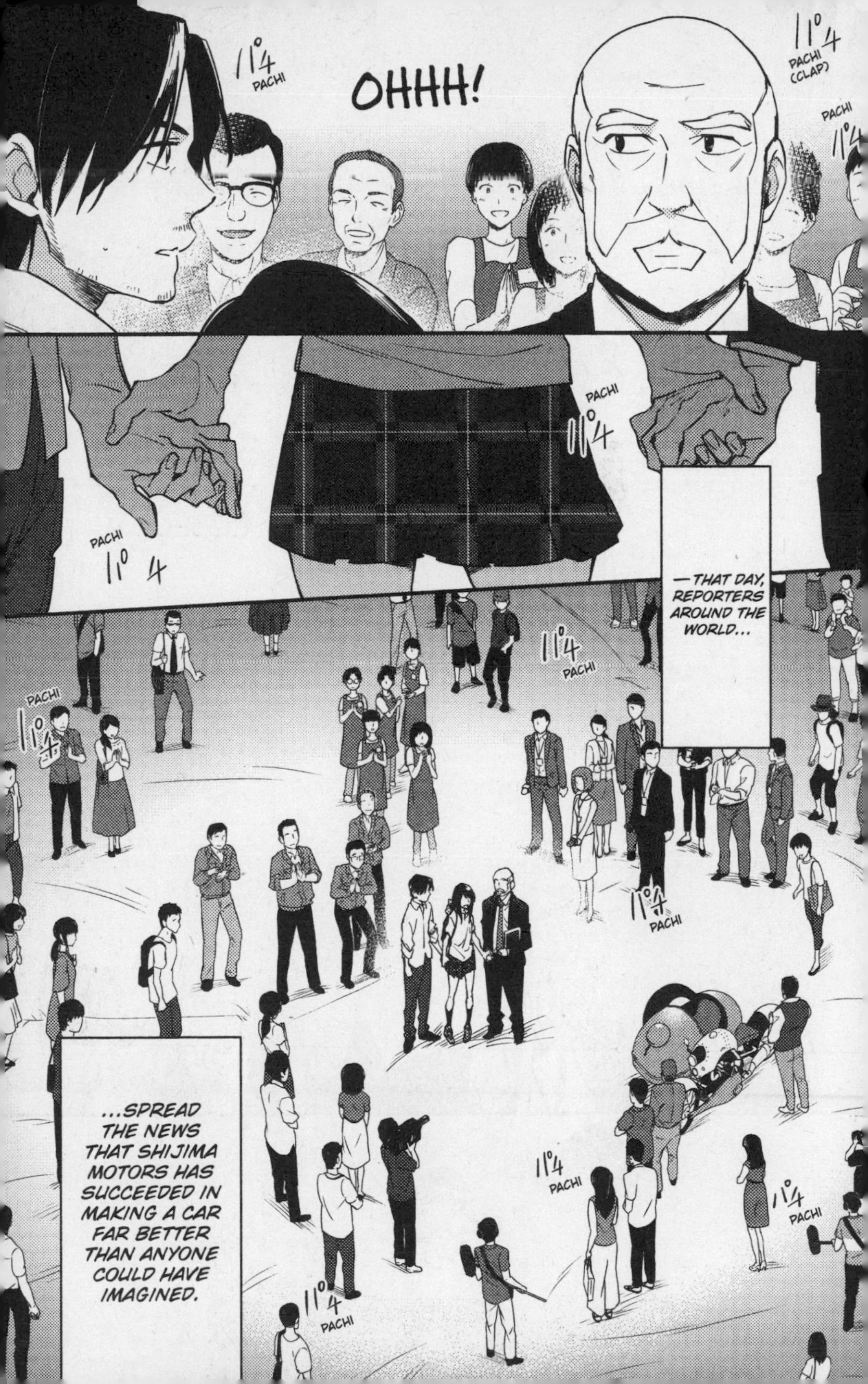
PACHI (CLAP)
PACHI
OHHH!
PACHI
PACHI
PACHI
—THAT DAY, REPORTERS AROUND THE WORLD...
PACHI
PACHI
PACHI
PACHI
PACHI
PACHI
...SPREAD THE NEWS THAT SHIJIMA MOTORS HAS SUCCEEDED IN MAKING A CAR FAR BETTER THAN ANYONE COULD HAVE IMAGINED.

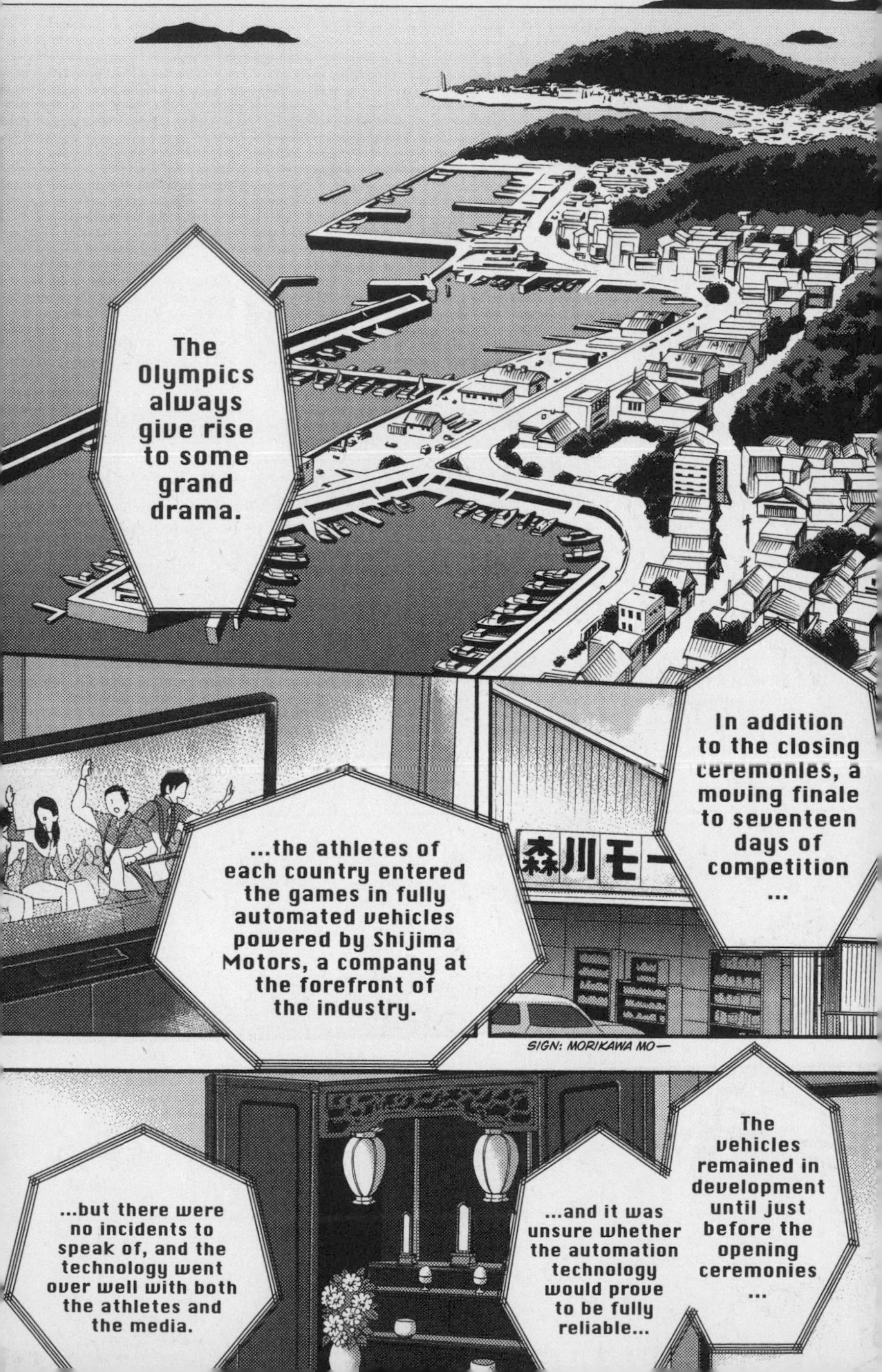
The Olympics always give rise to some grand drama.
In addition to the closing ceremonies, a moving finale to seventeen days of competition...
森川モー
SIGN: MORIKAWA MO—
...the athletes of each country entered the games in fully automated vehicles powered by Shijima Motors, a company at the forefront of the industry.
The vehicles remained in development until just before the opening ceremonies...
...and it was unsure whether the automation technology would prove to be fully reliable...
...but there were no incidents to speak of, and the technology went over well with both the athletes and the media.

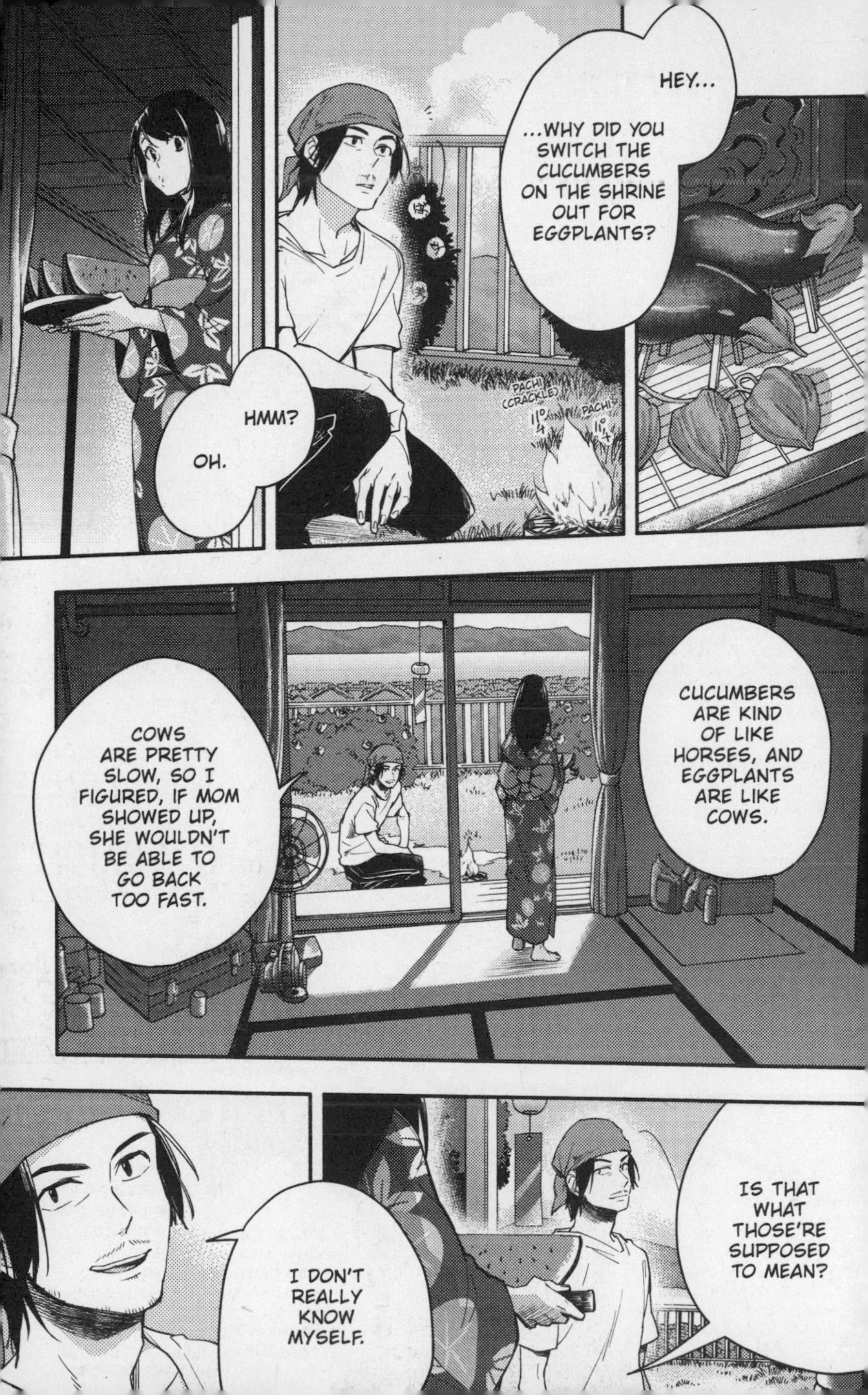
HEY... ...WHY DID YOU SWITCH THE CUCUMBERS ON THE SHRINE OUT FOR EGGPLANTS?
PACHI (CRACKLE)
PACHI
HMM?
OH.
CUCUMBERS ARE KIND OF LIKE HORSES, AND EGGPLANTS ARE LIKE COWS.
COWS ARE PRETTY SLOW, SO I FIGURED, IF MOM SHOWED UP, SHE WOULDN'T BE ABLE TO GO BACK TOO FAST.
IS THAT WHAT THOSE'RE SUPPOSED TO MEAN?
I DON'T REALLY KNOW MYSELF.

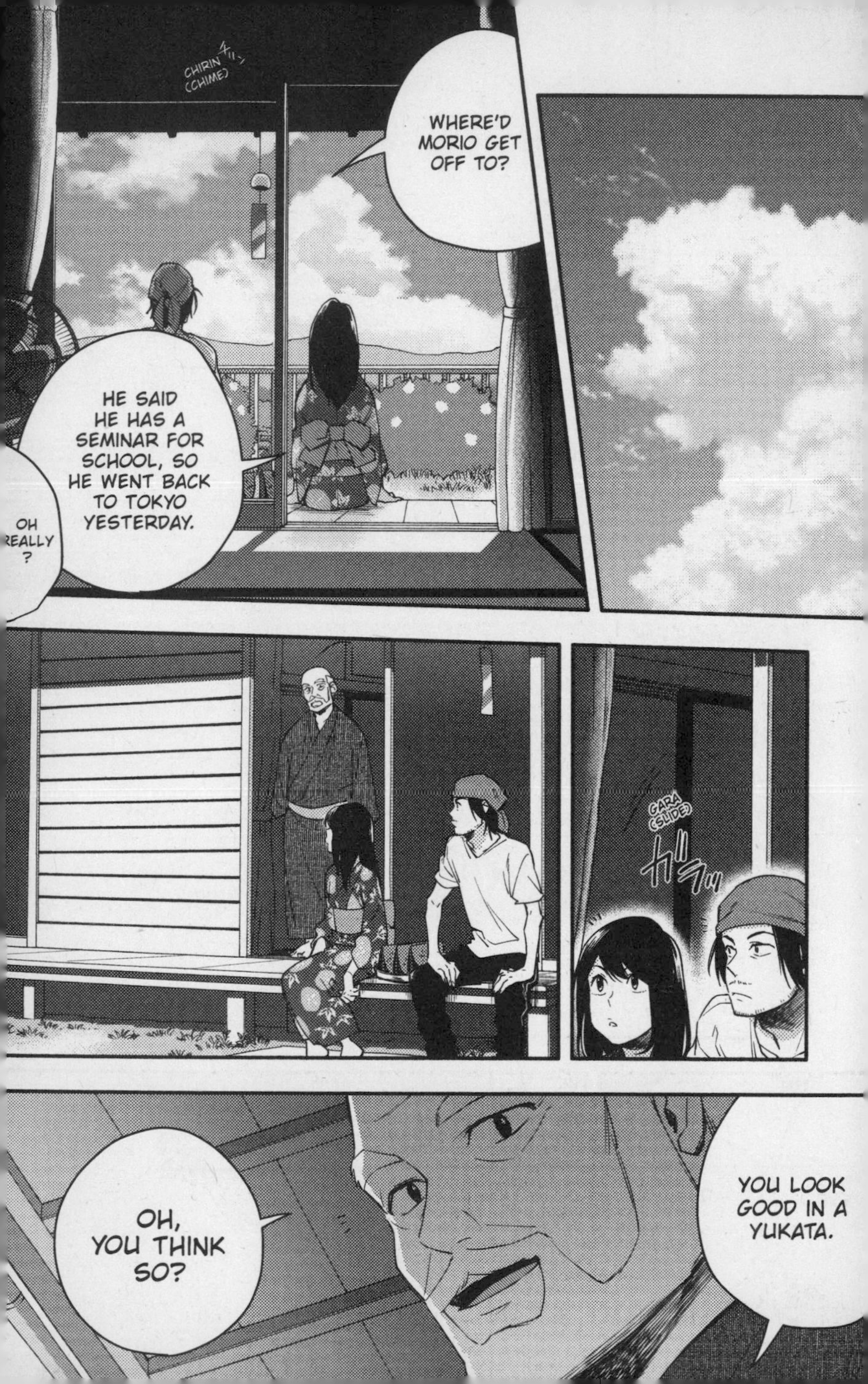
CHIRIN (CHIME)
WHERE'D MORIO GET OFF TO?
HE SAID HE HAS A SEMINAR FOR SCHOOL, SO HE WENT BACK TO TOKYO YESTERDAY.
OH REALLY?
GARA (SLIDE)
YOU LOOK GOOD IN A YUKATA.
OH, YOU THINK SO?

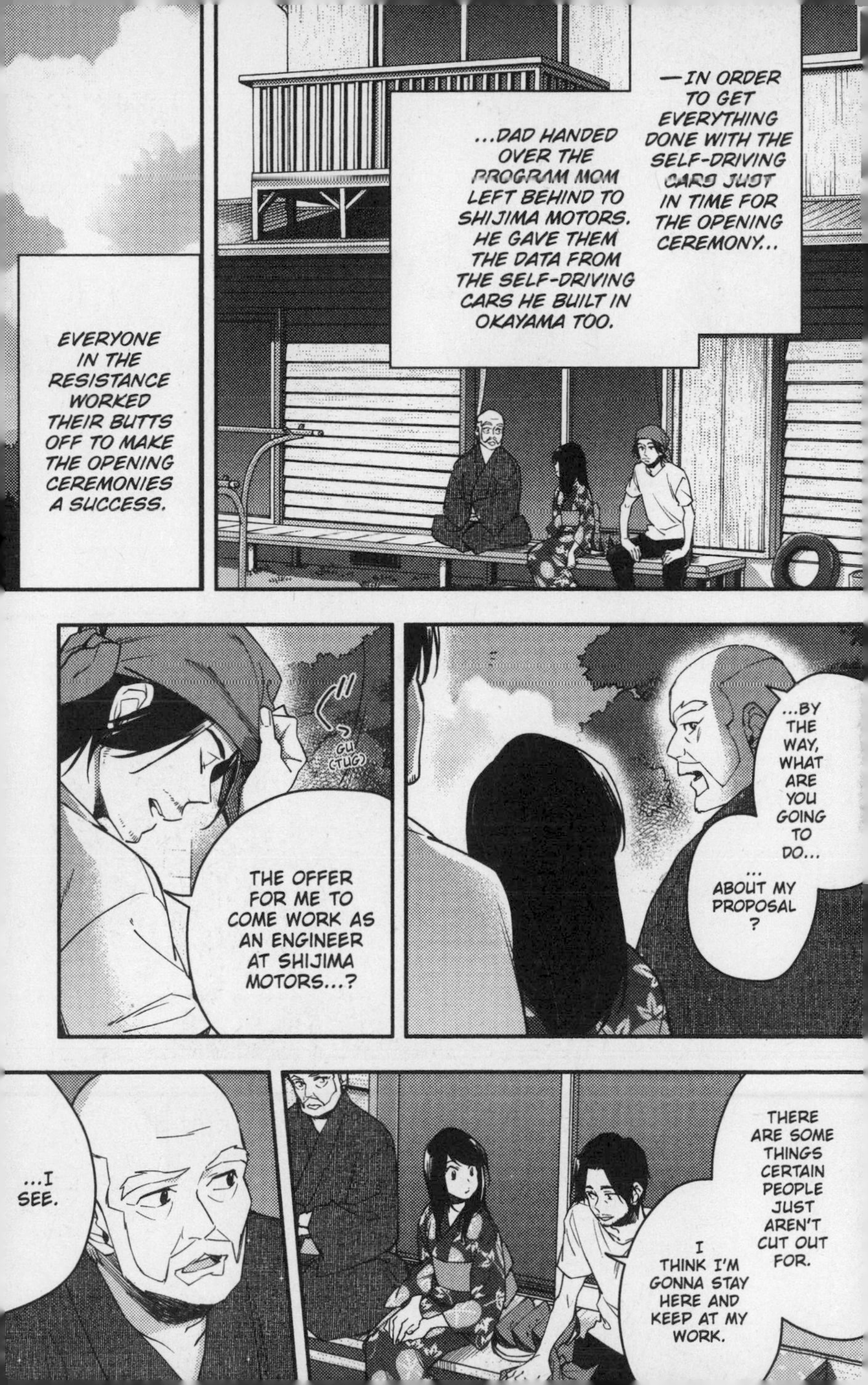
—IN ORDER TO GET EVERYTHING DONE WITH THE SELF-DRIVING CARS JUST IN TIME FOR THE OPENING CEREMONY...
...DAD HANDED OVER THE PROGRAM MOM LEFT BEHIND TO SHIJIMA MOTORS. HE GAVE THEM THE DATA FROM THE SELF-DRIVING CARS HE BUILT IN OKAYAMA TOO.
EVERYONE IN THE RESISTANCE WORKED THEIR BUTTS OFF TO MAKE THE OPENING CEREMONIES A SUCCESS.
...BY THE WAY, WHAT ARE YOU GOING TO DO...
...ABOUT MY PROPOSAL?
GU (TUG)
THE OFFER FOR ME TO COME WORK AS AN ENGINEER AT SHIJIMA MOTORS...?
THERE ARE SOME THINGS CERTAIN PEOPLE JUST AREN'T CUT OUT FOR.
I THINK I'M GONNA STAY HERE AND KEEP AT MY WORK.
...I SEE.

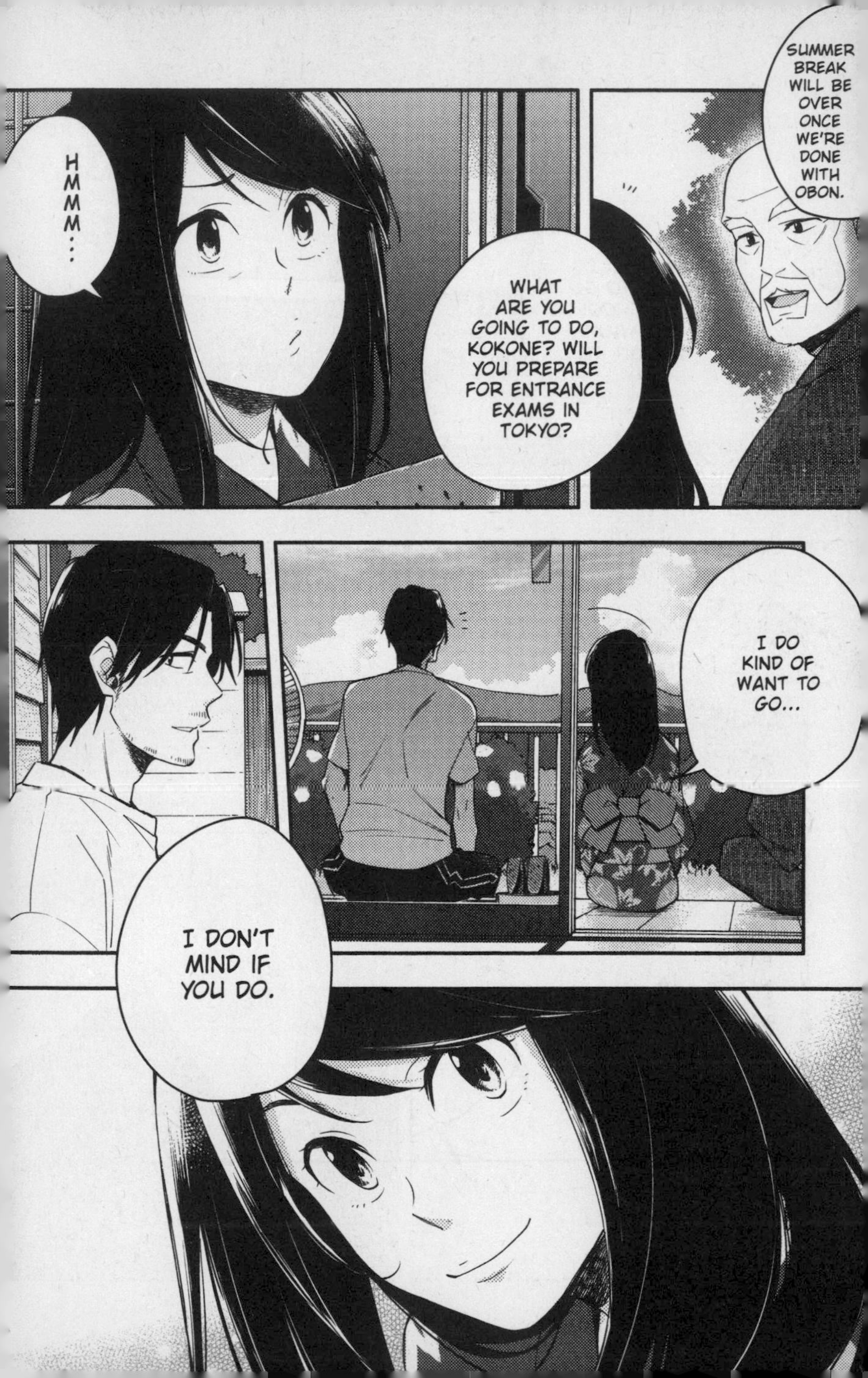
SUMMER BREAK WILL BE OVER ONCE WE'RE DONE WITH OBON.
WHAT ARE YOU GOING TO DO, KOKONE? WILL YOU PREPARE FOR ENTRANCE EXAMS IN TOKYO?
HMMM...
I DO KIND OF WANT TO GO...
I DON'T MIND IF YOU DO.

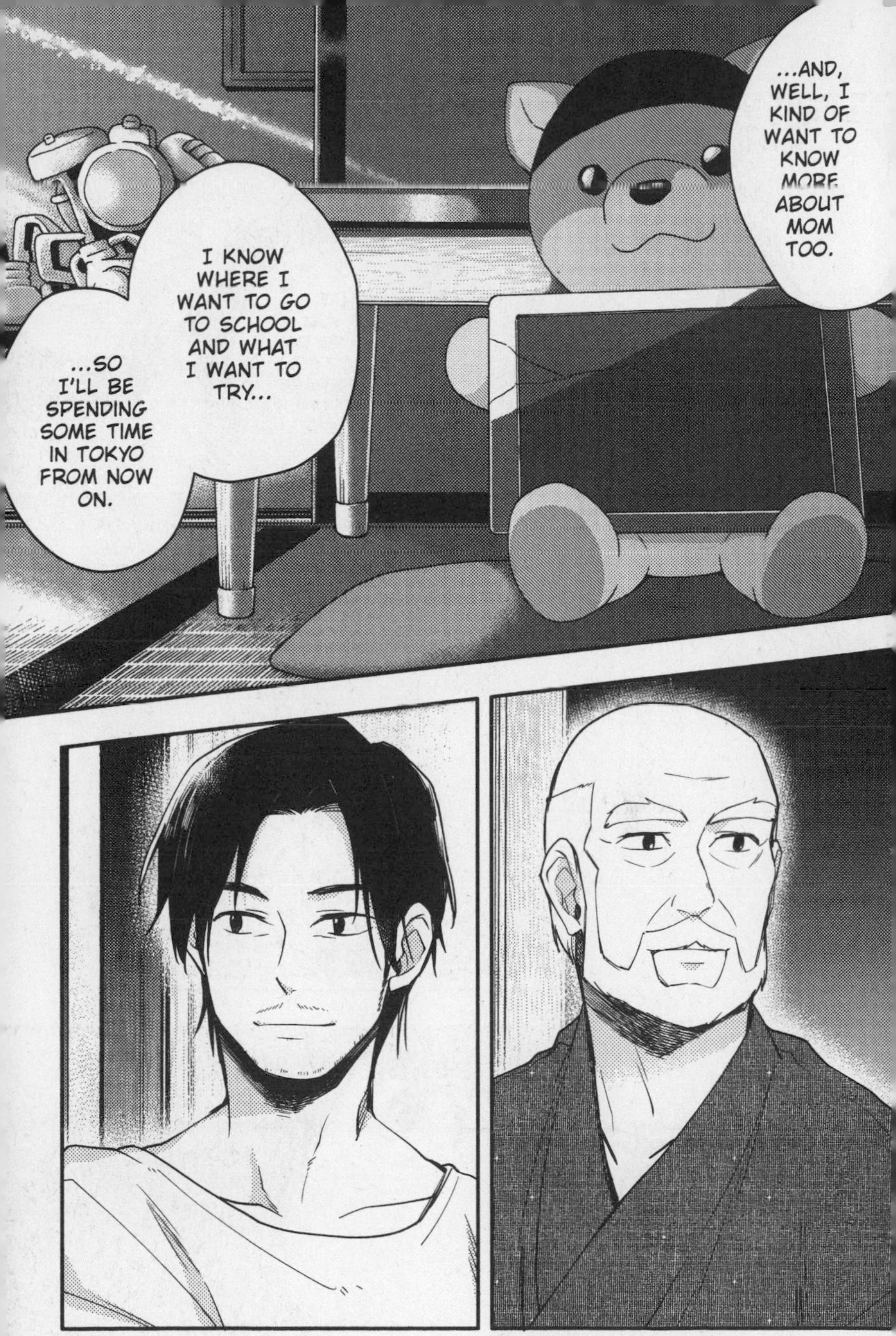
...AND, WELL, I KIND OF WANT TO KNOW MORE ABOUT MOM TOO.
I KNOW WHERE I WANT TO GO TO SCHOOL AND WHAT I WANT TO TRY...
...SO I'LL BE SPENDING SOME TIME IN TOKYO FROM NOW ON.

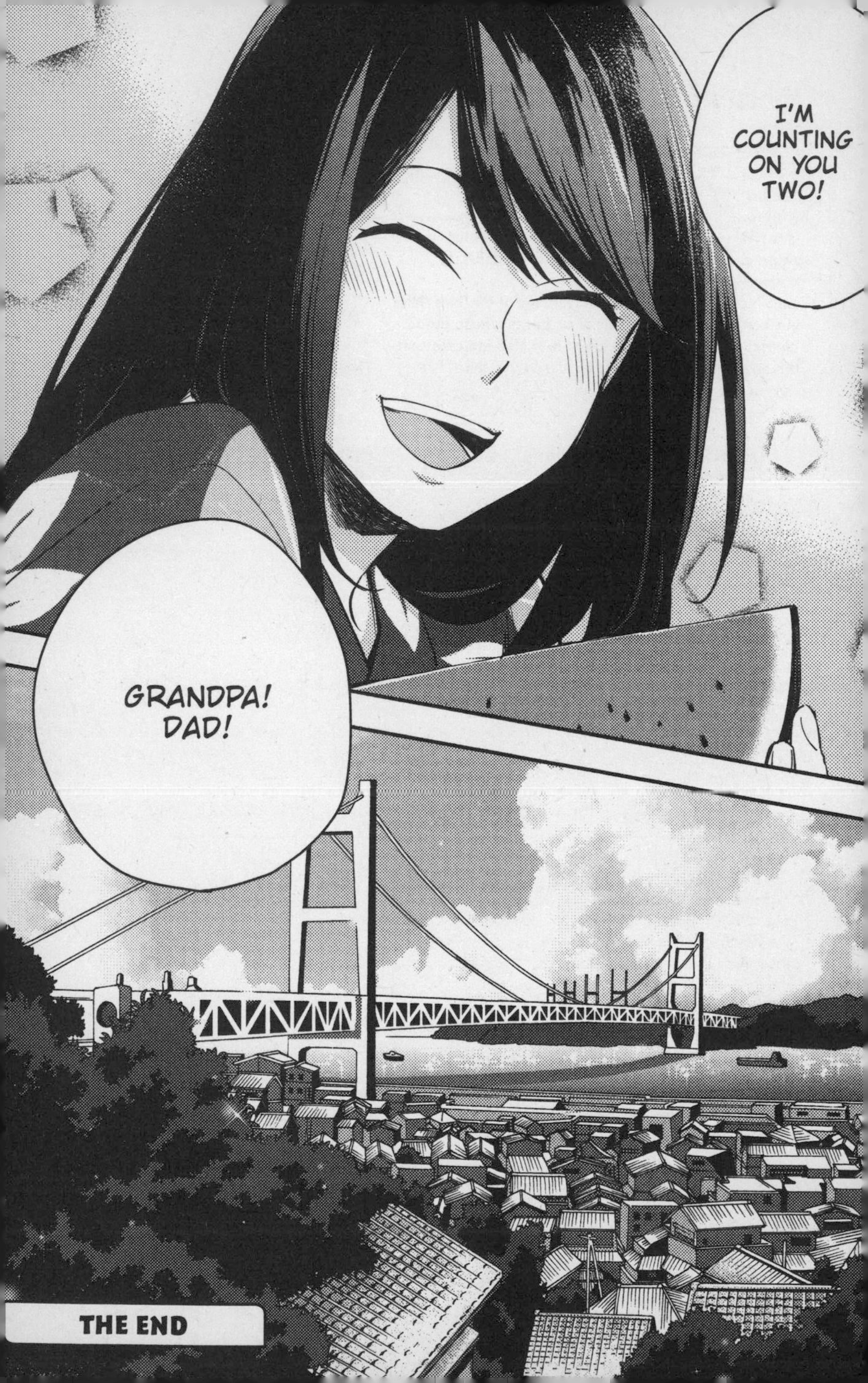
I'M COUNTING ON YOU TWO!
GRANDPA! DAD!
THE END

Translation Notes

COMMON HONORIFICS

no honorific: Indicates familiarity or closeness; if used without permission or reason, addressing someone in this manner would constitute an insult.
-san: The Japanese equivalent of Mr./Mrs./Miss. If a situation calls for politeness, this is the fail-safe honorific.
-shi: Not unlike -san; the equivament of Mr./Mrs./Miss but conveying a more official or bureaucratic mood.
-sama: Conveys great respect; may also indicate that the social status of the speaker is lower than that of the addressee.
-kun: Used most often when referring to boys, this indicates affection or familiarity. Occasionally used by older men among their peers, but it may also be used by anyone referring to a person of lower standing.
-chan: An affectionate honorific indicating familiarity used mostly in reference to girls; also used in reference to cute persons or animals of either gender.
-sensei: A respectful term for teachers, artists, or high-level professionals.

General Note
The exchange rate for the US dollar to the Japanese yen usually comes out as roughly $1 = ¥100. So two thousand yen is about twenty dollars.

Page 53
Ukki is the sound a monkey makes, whereas *kiji*, from the name **Takiji**, means "pheasant," thus the connection to a monkey and a pheasant.

Page 56
Morio is recognizing all the landmarks from Doutonbori, Osaka, except these all have slight quirks. The running man is Glico Man, a notable sign referenced here as "**Driko**." The building is Yukijirushi Metamiruku, a play on the large dairy company Yukijirushi Megumiruku.

Page 190
A **yukata** is a light, summer kimono made of cotton.

Page 192
Obon is a Buddhist custom where one honors their family's ancestral spirits, often by visiting and cleaning graves and household shrines.

Napping
Princess
The Story of the Unknown Me

AFTERWORD

THANK YOU SO MUCH FOR PICKING UP VOLUME 2 OF NAPPING PRINCESS: THE STORY OF THE UNKNOWN ME! I'M HANA ICHIKA. EVEN THOUGH THIS IS THE FINAL VOLUME, I'M REALLY GLAD IT ENDED WITH KOKONE SMILING ON THE VERY LAST PAGE. SMILES ARE GREAT, AND I LOVE BOTH DRAWING THEM AND SEEING THEM. I'M REALLY GRATEFUL TO HAVE BEEN INVOLVED WITH THIS STORY. I HOPE A LOT OF PEOPLE END UP LOVING IT. I HAD HELP FROM A LOT OF PEOPLE, AND I REALLY ENJOYED DRAWING IT. THANK YOU SO MUCH!

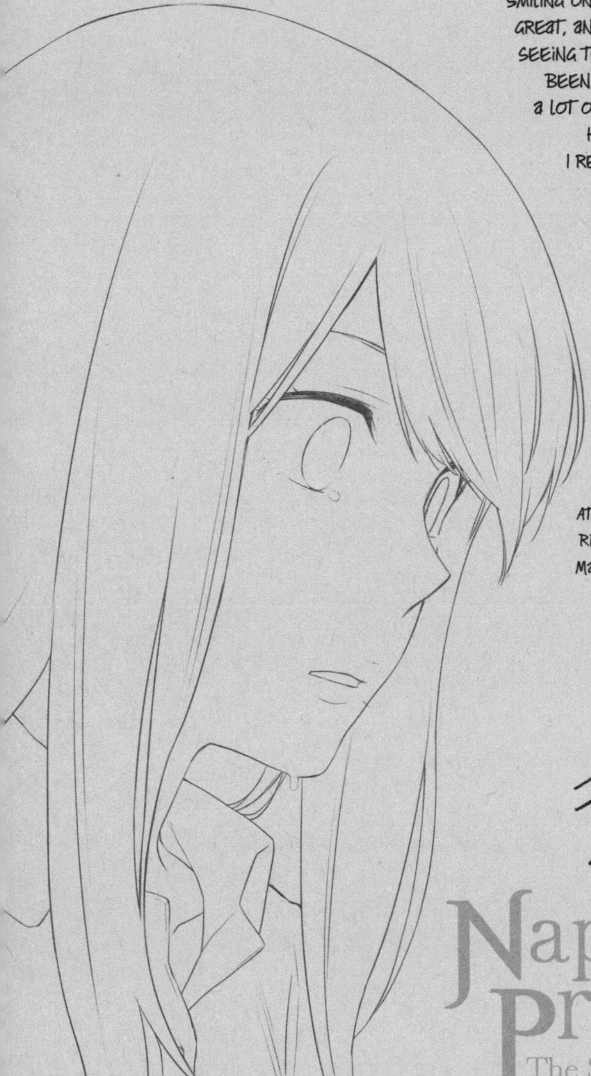

◊ SPECIAL THANKS ◊

ATSUYA ITOU-SAN • SATOMI HIKUMA-SAN

RINKO OONISHI-SAN • MIKI KAMITANI-SAN

MAYUMI IIDA-SAN • AYUMI OOTSUKA-SAN

ASUKA ENAMI-SAN • RIHO-CHAN

NANAFUSHI-SAN

MY EDITOR, KOUHEI ITOU-SAN

HANA ICHIKA

Napping Princess

The Story of the Unknown Me

Napping Princess
The Story of the Unknown Me
2

Original Story KENJI KAMIYAMA

Art HANA ICHIKA

Translation: Leighann Harvey · Lettering: Bianca Pistillo, Rachel Pierce

Napping Princess: The Story of the Unknown Me, Volume 2
©Hana ICHIKA 2017
©Kenji Kamiyama/2017 "ANCIEN AND THE MAGIC TABLET" Film Partners
First published in Japan in 2017 by KADOKAWA CORPORATION, Tokyo. English translation rights arranged with KADOKAWA CORPORATION, Tokyo, through TUTTLE-MORI AGENCY, INC., Tokyo.

English translation © 2018 by Yen Press, LLC

Yen Press
1290 Avenue of the Americas
New York, NY 10104

Visit us at yenpress.com
facebook.com/yenpress
twitter.com/yenpress
yenpress.tumblr.com
instagram.com/yenpress

First Yen Press Print Edition: October 2018
The chapters in this volume were originally published as eBooks by Yen Press.

Yen Press is an imprint of Yen Press, LLC.
The Yen Press name and logo are trademarks of Yen Press, LLC.

Library of Congress Control Number: 2018931542

ISBNs: 978-1-9753-8102-8 (paperback)
978-1-9753-0212-2 (ebook)

10 9 8 7 6 5 4 3 2 1

WOR

Printed in the United States of America